PENGUIN ENG

THREE RESTO

Gāmini Salgādo is Pr
University of Exeter. Pr   ecturer
in the School of Englis   merican Studies
at the University of Sussex. His publications
include a short study of *Sons and Lovers*, and he has
edited a collection of essays on the same novel, as
well as *Three Jacobean Tragedies* and *Cony Catchers
and Bawdy Baskets*, a collection of contemporary
accounts of the Elizabethan underworld, for the
Penguin English Library. His latest book is *The
Elizabethan Underworld* (1977).

Three
Restoration Comedies

EDITED WITH AN INTRODUCTION
BY GĀMINI SALGĀDO

ETHEREGE
THE MAN OF MODE

WYCHERLEY
THE COUNTRY WIFE

CONGREVE
LOVE FOR LOVE

Penguin Books

Penguin Books Ltd, Harmondsworth, Middlesex, England
Penguin Books, 625 Madison Avenue, New York, New York 10022, U.S.A.
Penguin Books Australia Ltd, Ringwood, Victoria, Australia
Penguin Books Canada Ltd, 2801 John Street, Markham, Ontario, Canada L3R 1B4
Penguin Books (N.Z.) Ltd, 182–190 Wairau Road, Auckland 10, New Zealand

—

Published in Penguin Books 1968
Reprinted 1973, 1976, 1978

—

Introduction and notes copyright © Gāmini Salgādo, 1968
All rights reserved

—

Made and printed in Great Britain
by Richard Clay (The Chaucer Press) Ltd,
Bungay, Suffolk
Set in Monotype Garamond

Contents

Acknowledgements

My grateful thanks to Tony Nuttall for reading through and commenting on the Introduction, and to Jane Snelling and Bea Mathews for helping with the proofs. My chief debt is recorded in the dedication.

G. S.

Introduction

I

1650 was a busy year for the Long Parliament. King Charles had been beheaded in the previous year and the theatres had been closed for eight years. In the intervals between passing laws ensuring the better packing of butter, the prohibition of trade with the Barbadoes, and the propagation and preaching of the Gospel in Wales, the triumphant Puritans found time for three Acts which are of special interest from the standpoint of Restoration comedy. The first was 'an Act for suppressing the detestable sins of incest, adultery and fornication'. The penalty for the first two crimes was death, without benefit of clergy. The third was also to be treated as a capital crime on the second offence. A month later, in June 1650, 'an Act for the better prevention of profane swearing and cursing' imposed fines ranging from three shillings to thirty shillings, depending on the social rank of the offender. Less than two months after this there followed the last and in some ways the most interesting of the three Acts. It was directed against 'several atheistical, blasphemous and execrable opinions, derogatory to the honour of God and destructive of human society'. In copious and comprehensive detail it enumerates all those whose opinions are deemed to fall within this category (including those who identify God with his creation and those who identify Him with themselves), swooping down finally on all who profess 'that the acts of adultery, drunkenness, swearing and the like open wickedness, are in their own nature as holy and righteous as the duties of prayer, preaching and giving thanks to God . . . that whatsoever is acted by them (whether whoredom, adultery, drunkenness, or the like open wickedness) may be committed without sin . . . that heaven and all happiness consists in the acting of those things which are sin and wickedness; or that such men and women are most perfect, or like to God or eternity, which do commit the greatest sins with the least remorse or sense . . .' All those against whom these charges could be proved were liable to six months' imprisonment for the first offence, and, if they persisted in their opinions, to banishment from the realm.

Less than fifteen years later, in 1664, the first Restoration comedy was played before a wildly enthusiastic audience, including many who had returned to the realm from their 'banishment', the most distinguished of whom was the new king himself. *The Comical Revenge* or *Love in a Tub* set the pattern for comic drama till the early years of the new century. And almost without exception these comedies, while on the whole eschewing incest, were distinguished by having adultery and fornication for their subject-matter, a liberal use of 'profane swearing and cursing' as a prominent part of their idiom, and as heroes and heroines young men and women who made no secret of their 'atheistical, blasphemous and execrable opinions' and specifically of their view 'that heaven and all happiness consists in the acting of those things which are sin and wickedness'. So much so that when, two years before the end of the century, the Rev. Jeremy Collier blew his shattering trumpet blast against 'the profaneness and immorality of the stage' (entitled, with misleading modesty, *A Short View* . . .) the language he uses to condemn these plays could almost have been taken from the Acts of Parliament I have just mentioned.

So it is easy, tempting and in a general way justifiable to see Restoration comedy as a Royalist reaction to Puritan rigour. Its outlook on life appears to be that of the bivouac – pitch camp for the night and let joy be unconfined, for who knows what the morrow will bring? – and its strategy that of the hunt applied to the pursuit of women. Behind it lies what is indisputably the golden age of English drama, the age of Shakespeare and Jonson, of Webster, Middleton and Ford; after it comes what is equally indisputably the dullest drama England has produced – the 'sentimental comedy' of Steele and Lillo and Cumberland, as colourless as it is blameless. And we usually account for the tedium of the latter by attributing it to the success of the Puritan counter-attack which was originally inspired by the uninhibited gaiety of the Restoration stage. (Though Collier himself was a High Church parson, not a Puritan.)

But the situation is not quite so neat and simple as this (it seldom is). The first bit of over-simplification has to do with the word 'restoration' itself, as applied to the drama. It is a convenient enough label as long as we do not expect from it the precision it has when used to describe the historical event of Charles II's return to the throne. The first Restoration comedy came four years after this, but comedies on this general pattern were being written and performed well into the reign of Queen Anne. Furthermore, while Restoration comedy is, as we shall see, new in interesting and important ways, it did not spring fully armed from the comic Muse's head, nor was it, as Thackeray and Macaulay among others stoutly maintained, a noxious foreign importation utterly unrelated to the solid and wholesome English dramatic tradition. To take only one point, the English reader or spectator need go no farther afield than Shakespeare's Princess of France (*Love's Labour's Lost*) or Rosalind or Viola or Beatrice to discover the stage ancestry of Angelica in *Love for Love* or Harriet in *The Man of Mode*. The Restoration dramatists occasionally filched their plots from Molière and certainly owed some of their dash and elegance to the French plays they had seen, but the spirit of their comedy is English to the core.

Indeed, the more one looks into it, the clearer it becomes that the closing of the theatres by the Puritans in 1642 does not mark any decisive break in the continuity of the English drama. It is true that the Restoration audience, especially at the beginning, was the most cliquish ever to have patronized the English stage. It consisted of courtiers and their ladies and those who came to gawp at the fine ladies or drum up custom among the young gallants. But the narrowing of the audience to an upper-class *élite* had already gone a long way in the reign of the first King Charles. The only important theatres left to be closed in 1642 were all 'private' theatres catering to those who could afford a shilling or more for admission. The Elizabethan hey-day when the theatre was a truly national pastime had long passed.

Again, though the theatres were closed, dramatic performances continued to take place. Wealthy patrons put on private performances and even, particularly in the provinces, clandestine public entertainments, while the poorer people had one-act farces and other such 'drolls' for their diversion.

Finally, there is the difference in theatrical presentation and technique. Here the changes are more significant, though the threads of continuity are not completely broken. The most obvious change is in the physical appearance of the theatre. Just as the action of an Elizabethan or Jacobean play does not reveal its full significance except when performed on the sort of stage for which it was intended – basically an 'apron' jutting out on three sides into the auditorium, no curtains or painted scenery, a balcony and an inner stage at the back – so Restoration comedy is obviously intended for the kind of stage with which we today are most familiar – the 'picture frame' stage with a proscenium arch cutting off the area of darkness in which the audience sits from the brightly lit stage action and 'perspective' scenery. But this kind of stage was often used for the performance of masques in the 'private' theatres, and there is evidence to suggest that the reason why the public theatres did not use painted scenery in the early years of the seventeenth century was that they could not afford it. And as for the most celebrated (or notorious) innovation of the Restoration stage, the introduction of women as performers, this was also common in masques, as well as in the public practice of visiting French theatrical groups. It was ten years before the closing of the theatres (to go no further back), that Henrietta Maria, Charles I's queen, appeared in a masque and so outraged the Puritan William Prynne that he published an attack on theatrical entertainment (*Histriomastix*) which cost him his ears. All in all it is true to say that the theatre of Charles II shows us in a heightened form the characteristics which are already apparent in that of Charles I. And as if to provide final confirmation of this, we may note that the most popular plays in the early years of the Restoration were just those Jacobean and Caroline dramas which held the stage immediately before the theatres were closed.

But if the line of English comic drama continued unbroken

into the Restoration it did not do so unchanged. Indeed, the change initiated by Etherege's first play, *Love in a Tub*, is so great that one critic has called it 'rather a revolution than a development'.[1] This may be true, but it is still worth insisting that it is a revolution which has its roots in the conventions it overthrows. Etherege's contemporaries certainly sensed that something new had appeared on the stage, for almost overnight the dramatist rose from obscurity to the height of fame. That he himself was aware of his innovation is indicated by the prologue in which, disclaiming comparison with 'Fletcher's nature or the art of Ben (Jonson)',

> Our author therefore begs you would forget,
> Most reverend judges, the records of wit;
> And only think upon the modern way
> Of writing, while you're censuring his play.

But exactly what is 'this modern way of writing' which the audience is invited to respond to? In the first place it was the presentation of a new world, gay, bright and brittle, a world where grace and style are all-important, where elegance of dress and deportment is matched by polished epigram and lively repartee. The new comedy was distinguished, in Dryden's words, by 'the improvement of our wit, language and conversation', the older writers being unfortunate because 'they wanted the benefit of converse'. In an age when conversation was the distinguishing mark of the gentleman, the stage provided the wittiest conversation to be heard. In comedy polite society saw a glittering image of itself, an image it was delighted to recognize and applaud. The point is vividly if somewhat rhapsodically made by Hazlitt:

We are admitted behind the scenes like spectators at court, on a levee or birthday; but it is the court, the gala day of wit and pleasure, of gallantry and Charles II! What an air breathes from the name! what a rustling of silks and waving of plumes! what a sparkling of diamond ear-rings and shoe-buckles! What bright eyes, (ah, those were Waller's Sacharissa's as she passed!) what killing looks and graceful motions! How the faces of the whole ring are dressed in smiles! how the repartee goes round! how wit

1. John Palmer, *The Comedy of Manners*, Bell, 1913.

and folly, elegance and awkward imitation of it, set one another
off! Happy, thoughtless age, when kings and nobles led purely
ornamental lives; when the utmost stretch of a morning's study
went no farther than the choice of a sword-knot, or the adjustment
of a side-curl; when the soul spoke out in all the pleasing eloquence
of dress; and beaux and belles, enamoured of themselves in one
another's follies, fluttered like gilded butterflies, in giddy mazes,
through the walks of St James' Park![1]

Dowries and legacies were at least as important to the gallants
of Restoration comedy and their ladies as sword-knots and
side-curls, but there is no doubt that part of its attraction, as
well as its novelty, lies in this revelation of a world which at
least on the surface is gay, brilliant and charming.

Comedy had traditionally dealt, according to one version
of Aristotle's dictum, with low life. (Even Shakespeare – certainly no Aristotelian – is only a partial exception; the rude
mechanicals are never very far from the central action in his
romantic comedies.) In elevating comedy socially, the Restoration dramatists created a new kind of comedy where, to quote
Dryden again, 'Gentlemen will now be entertained with the
follies of each other', and Aristotle was reinterpreted to mean
by low characters not those of humble birth or fortune, but
those deficient in the manners and accomplishments of a gentleman, whose efforts to make up for this deficiency made them
ridiculous. Thus was born a character who becomes a staple
type in Restoration comedy, the would-be gallant or fop. When
Ben Jonson asserted that the true object of comedy was 'to
sport with human follies, not with crimes', he showed by his
practice that the follies he had in mind were basic human
weaknesses, lust, avarice, vanity and so on, and he scourged
them with all the fury of his satiric wit. But the follies which
the Restoration dramatists laugh at are, generally speaking,
those which concern manners rather than morals, which is
why Charles Lamb's phrase 'comedy of manners', in spite of
the criticism it has recently received, is still a fairly apt description of one aspect of this comedy. Sir Fopling Flutter in
Etherege's *Man of Mode*, for example, is only a slightly dis-
torted mirror-image of the hero, Dorimant, and Sparkish and

1. William Hazlitt, *Lectures on the English Comic Writers*, IV.

Tattle have almost the same relation to the heroes of the two other plays. The fop is laughed at not because he is trying to be something in itself contemptible, but rather because he is trying unsuccessfully to be something which, if he succeeded, would make him the play's hero. The laughter which he invites is therefore a long way from the harsh mockery which underlies Jonson's attitude to Volpone. It is far more genial and self-indulgent. (It is significant that a contemporary believed that the character of Sir Fopling was based on the dramatist himself; Etherege was a great dandy in an age of dandies.) There is satire in Restoration comedy, as we can see in *The Country Wife*, but it is rarely directed towards the fop. The dramatist's attitude to the fop is usually about as satirical as Mr P. G. Wodehouse's attitude to Bertie Wooster:

> . . . satire scarce dares grin, 'tis grown so mild
> Or only shows its teeth as if it smiled.

And as Bertie's principal function is to highlight Jeeves' brain-power (a faculty which, without this emphasis of contrast, might well escape notice), so the fop often serves to make the gallant's wit seem brighter than it is. (Though occasionally the fop can be almost as witty as the gallant, when he stands in the same relation to a minor character as the gallant does to the heroine; see for instance, Tattle's lines in the scene where he makes love to Miss Prue in *Love for Love*.)

Thus, while the older comedy of 'humours' set out to correct human vices by laughing them to scorn, the new comedy proposed to itself the more modest aim of showing manners both exemplified and travestied. Affectation became the chief butt of comedy, but the didactic intent is hardly present, since the dramatist is preaching to an audience of the converted. The spectator presumably saw in the gallant a satisfactorily idealized portrait of himself and in the fop a portrait of his neighbour. Some such assumption is certainly needed to account for the enthusiastic reaction to even the most forthright criticism of the audience, such as that found in the prologue to *The Man of Mode*:

> So among you, there starts up every day,
> Some new unheard-of fool for us to play.

Then for your own sakes, be not too severe,
Nor what you all admire at home, damn here.
Since each is fond of his own ugly face,
Why should you, when we hold it, break the glass?

Affectation is one form of disguise; it is disguise which is imperfectly aware of its own nature and objectives, and as such it comes half-way between conscious dissimulation and the candid presentation of the 'real' personality. All comedy makes use of disguise in one form or another and nearly all literature is concerned with the difference between the outward appearance and the inner reality. What makes Restoration comedy distinctive is first, the frequency with which disguise is used and the major part it plays in the action, and secondly, the new view which these dramatists take of the relationship between outward form and inner nature. The first point is self-evident. There is hardly any Restoration comedy in which disguise does not figure prominently; certainly it is a prime element in the three plays included here. And the masked ball which forms a dramatic climax in two of them may serve as a metaphor for the social necessity of disguise. In this comedy was certainly a mirror of the age, for disguise and masquerade were a part not only of the festive celebrations of high society but of its day-to-day dealings. The exploits of Charles II in his numerous varieties of fancy dress are well known, and some of them are well documented. The Earl of Rochester, the Restoration gallant *par excellence* (he is said to have been the model for Dorimant), disguised himself first as a city merchant and later as an Italian quack. The Duchess of Cleveland used to visit Wycherley disguised as a country lass. Pepys was hardly exaggerating when he exclaimed: 'But good God! what an age is this, and what a world is this! that a man cannot live without playing the knave and dissimulation!'

But more significant than the ubiquitousness of disguise is the relationship it points to between appearance and reality. Up to this time, it had been taken for granted that if the outer form did not correspond to the inner nature, this was something out of the ordinary which had to be specially accounted for, a cause for pleased surprise or outrage. When Claudio,

the young gallant in Shakespeare's *Much Ado About Nothing*,
disowns his bride-to-be because of her alleged infidelity, he
cries out to the assembled congregation:

> Would you not swear,
> All you that see her, that she were a maid
> By these exterior shows? But she is none:
> She knows the heat of a luxurious bed;
> Her blush is guiltiness, not modesty.

The assumption is clearly that there is something monstrous
about Hero looking like a modest and innocent virgin ('Be-
hold how like a maid she blushes here!'), when (according to
Claudio's mistaken notion) she is neither innocent nor modest.
But in the later seventeenth century, and specifically in Restoration drama, we encounter for the first time the idea that
the discrepancy between form and nature is not only not surprising but necessary and even desirable. Norman Holland,
in the best general study of Restoration comedy which I have
read, states the matter succinctly:

> The crucial change is that formerly men had felt that what shows
> either was or *should be* a true reflection of what is; now, at the end of
> the seventeenth century, men came increasingly to feel that what
> shows not only was not but often *ought not to be* a true reflection of
> what is.[1]

The exigencies of social intercourse oblige men and women to
dress up their real thoughts and feelings in polite trifling and
elegant gesture, to hide the true expression on their faces behind a delicately wrought fan. The hero is the man who accepts this necessity and performs it with grace and dexterity,
the fop the man who makes a hash of it because he doesn't
really understand what he is doing or why he is doing it.

In this new conception of the relationship between appearance and 'nature' we can see clearly one of the ways in which
new developments in scientific thought and activity were
shaping the imaginative vision of the age. It is no accident
that the Restoration period sees the founding of the Royal
Society, or that many of the leading literary figures of the day

1. Norman Holland, *The First Modern Comedies*, Harvard, 1959. Italics
in the original.

were keenly interested in its activities. For all its irresponsible gaiety the court of Charles II was very much alive to new ways of thinking in science and philosophy. There is an evident connexion, for instance, between the way the dramatists take for granted the existence of a discrepancy between inner and outer nature, and the visual revelation of such a gap through microscopic and ordinary observation; nor is it difficult to see a parallel between the Cartesian stress on mathematically measurable qualities (mass and volume) and distrust of sensory appearances and the sceptical temper of the dramatists' inquiry into the way in which the 'accidentals' of dress, discourse and gesture were connected with the 'substance' of true character. The key figure here is Thomas Hobbes, a personal favourite of Charles II (though not of the Royal Society) and a man who was both Freud and Marx in the intellectual life of his day. The values and outlook of Restoration comedy as well as its tone and temper bear constant witness to the pervasive influence of Hobbes.

Thus the new drama, taking its cue from the larger world of society and ideas, produces a new kind of hero – elegant in dress and deportment, lively and quick-witted in conversation, sceptical, even cynical in his attitude to himself and his fellows (though the cynicism is often no more than part of his carefully assumed disguise). But in literature, as in life, nothing is ever completely new, and the Restoration hero, as Dale Underwood points out in his study of *Etherege and the Seventeenth-Century Comedy of Manners* is clearly related to the 'Machiavel' of Elizabethan and Jacobean drama, to figures such as Edmund, Iago and Richard III. But there is one important difference. The Machiavel is aware of an absolute standard of morality which he rejects and is eventually judged by (though in the figure of the young Prince Hal as he grows to be King Henry V Shakespeare shows us another kind of Machiavel, one who accepts as a tragic necessity the gap between ends and means, between public welfare and private morality). The society against which the earlier Machiavel pits himself is, for all its imperfections, a divinely sanctioned one and the sanctions of divinity inevitably destroy the evil-doer. The society of the Restoration on the other hand was, and was universally felt to be, human, all too human. The last king who believed in his own divinity had been beheaded and to believe in the divinity of the Merry Monarch required more faith than the whole age possessed, monarch and all included. The scepticism of the age made belief in absolute values difficult if not impossible, and much of the satire against the older generation is directed at their belief in the old order of things, oblivious of the inroads made in that order by the new ways of thinking. Reacting against the rigid standards of Puritan morality, the Restoration gallant found a perilous freedom. He is free to act as he sees fit, but the image of himself which such action offers him is invariably a reductivist one, of man reduced to his appetites, sexual and alimentary. 'What is man?' mused Hamlet, 'if the chief good and market of his time, Be but to sleep and feed?' Restoration comedy tries, with a gaiety often desperate, to find an answer.

This is something we need to remember as we read Hazlitt's ecstatic outpourings or Lamb's celebrated apologia for 'the Utopia of gallantry, where pleasure is duty, and the manners perfect freedom'. And indeed we are not likely to forget it in reading the plays included in this volume, for in all of them the principal figure is isolated, thrown back upon himself, imprisoned in his own reduced image of himself as a creature of mere appetite. For all the obvious gaiety and high spirits in these comedies, there is an undercurrent of loneliness against which the heroes are obscurely struggling. Horner, indeed, has given up the struggle when *The Country Wife* begins, and is determined to submit himself completely to the experiment of living entirely in the world of appetite without feeling, of fact without value. But it is Harcourt rather than Horner who is the isolated gallant in this play. Similarly, Dorimant in *The Man of Mode* has just discarded his former mistress, and there is a kind of despairing doggedness in the way he braces himself up for the pursuit of the next; we sense his relief when, with the conquest of Harriet, the chase is ended. And in Valentine, the hero of *Love for Love*, we see both the hero's isolation and his desire for a more satisfying release from it than is afforded by the incessant pursuit of complaisant women.

Without this sense of the hero's struggle to escape from the implications of his own 'freedom', Restoration comedy would certainly be open to the charge which has often been levelled against it, of intellectual and moral dishonesty, that is, of taking up four acts to show how marriage is a fate worse than death, to be avoided at all costs, and in the fifth pretending that it is the most desirable of conditions and a fitting climax to the amours of the hero and heroine. And there is no point in denying that in most Restoration comedies, marriage is little more than a conventional conclusion, something to end the comedy with because all comedies have to end in marriage. But in the three comedies with which we are here concerned, there is an intellectually consistent and dramatically satisfying connexion between the love intrigue and the marriage. In the first place we may note that what is ridiculed in these comedies is not so much the institution of marriage itself as marriage attempted or undertaken for the wrong reasons. The distinction is an important one which is firmly rooted in the social conditions of the time. In the years following the Restoration, political power came to depend less and less upon royal favour and more and more on the ownership of land. It has been suggested that this accounts for the widespread prevalence of *arranged* marriages during this period, such marriages being one of the quickest and handiest means of acquiring landed property.[1] When the Restoration dramatists mock at marriage, therefore, they have in mind marriage whose sole basis has been a mercenary one, and a good part of the action of the comedy consists of a determined effort on the part of the hero and heroine to achieve a real marriage, one based on spontaneous affection and a recognition of affinity, without shutting their eyes to the economic realities of life. Valentine's attempt to prevent his father from thwarting him of his inheritance is significant precisely because it shows that his affection for Angelica is not prompted by her large fortune:

I never valued fortune but as it was subservient to my pleasure, and my only pleasure was to please this lady. I have made many

1. See P. F. Vernon, 'Marriage of Convenience and the Moral Code of Restoration Comedy', *Essays in Criticism*, October 1962.

vain attempts, and find at last that nothing but my ruin can effect it, which for that reason I will sign to.

The objects of contempt are Sir Sampson, who tries to bribe Angelica into marriage, and Mrs Frail, who makes no secret of her predatory intentions towards sailor Ben. The punitive marriage suffered by herself and Tattle is a judgement on their debasement of marriage rather than a criticism of marriage itself. In *The Country Wife*, the situation is even clearer, for here we have a carefully contrived counterpointing of a series of sexual relationships, the central one providing the norm and the others deviations from it. Harcourt and Alithea are the pair whose union springs from mutual understanding and affection. In spite of the fact that Horner and his doings are much better known, it is this pair whose growing affection for each other occupies the bulk of the play. Ranged on either side of them are Sir Jasper and Lady Fidget, he distinguished for minding his business more than his wife, she for the resolute hypocrisy with which she seeks to satisfy her sexual desires while denying their existence. Pinchwife, the ex-whore-monger, regards his wife exactly like a piece of property, while Sparkish's main reason for wanting Alithea, apart from her fortune, seems to be so that she may add further lustre to his image of himself. And opposed to all this calculation, possessiveness and self-esteem is the artless spontaneity of the country wife Margery herself (though the merely naïve side of this artlessness is sufficiently 'placed' by the whole action). Even Dorimant is willing to make the supreme sacrifice – a married life spent buried in the country – for the sake of a relationship which begins as injured vanity but ends in mutual recognition. The comic dramatists' view of marriage is neatly summed up in a couplet from another play by Wycherley, *Love in a Wood*:

> The end of Marriage, now is liberty,
> And two are bound – to set each other free.

It is important to note that the heroine in each of the three plays – Angelica, Harriet and Alithea – has a fortune of her own. One reason for this is to enable the hero to 'prove' that he loves her for herself alone and not her yellow gold. A more important reason is that an independent income is a condition of a woman's social and intellectual independence in this man's world. The romantic heroines of Shakespeare's comedies do not have to worry about money – their fathers are dukes or kings and in any case their young men invariably turn out to have fortunes of their own. Money never becomes an issue in the comedy (or when it does, as in *The Merchant of Venice*, the comedy has a distinctly different flavour). But in the new world of Restoration comedy money, by a familiar paradox, is the only guarantee against a life dominated by mercenary considerations. The alternative is to be an open fortune-hunter like Mrs Frail or one by proxy like Miss Prue, who in a moment of sharp clarity sees the consequences of her failure:

What, and must not I have e'er a husband then? What, must I go to bed to nurse again, and be a child as long as she's an old woman?

But the independence which money secured for the heroine was not a total gain. If the Restoration gallant did not make precisely contradictory demands on the young lady who would finally gain his heart – that she should have all the *savoir-faire* and expertise of a seasoned mistress without having actually been one – he came very close to doing so. (In this he is a direct ancestor of those contemporary males who make a sharp distinction between the girls whom they have 'fun' with and those whom they would consider marrying, the former category automatically excluding the latter.) The result was that not only quick-wittedness, sexual tact and caution but certain less desirable attributes came to have a definite survival-value for the heroine. There is an undeniable hardness in Angelica's final censure of Sir Sampson:

You have not more faults than he has virtues, and 'tis hardly more pleasure to me that I can make him and myself happy than that I can punish you.

– a hardness even more pronounced in Harriet's parting words to the rejected Mrs Loveit:

Mr Dorimant has been your God almighty long enough, 'tis time to think of another –

It is the inevitable dark side of their spontaneity and live-liness.

Restoration comedy is both realistic and escapist. It is realis-tic in its vivid sense of contemporary life – albeit a very small segment of it, the streets, ordinaries and pleasure gardens of fashionable London. It is realistic too in its consistently secular temper and its constant concern with the attempts of its heroes to find some sort of satisfactory and durable per-sonal fulfilment in the face of almost permanent financial em-barrassment. And most of all it is realistic in portraying more sharply than anywhere else the social conflict between the Royalist aristocracy and the increasingly prosperous Puritan citizenry which is one of the facts of English economic life in the late seventeenth century. But it is also escapist, not only in its idealization of the gallant and his lady, but in the fact that the resolution it proposes to the problem of money ver-sus free choice represents a fantasy of wish-fulfilment. Spon-taneity always wins in the end, money problems are always satisfactorily solved, the young always overcome the old. The lost paradise where freedom and service are in perfect har-mony is always regained in the last act. But perhaps in this sense all comedy is 'escapist', for it presents us with a world where the shows of things are joyously submitted to the de-sires of the mind.

*

Since Jeremy Collier threw down the gauntlet in 1698, the battle about Restoration comedy has raged with a din loud, long and still unabated. The dramatists themselves were not slow to take up the challenge. Collier had accused them of cor-rupting the age by their lewdness and blasphemy. They re-torted that they took the age as their model, not vice versa. There followed a steady stream of attacks and counter-attacks which have come to be known as the Collier controversy, the impact of which the interested reader may learn about from J. W. Krutch's *Comedy and Conscience after the Restoration*. Mil-ton, the author of a Restoration 'comedy' of a very different kind, wrote with majestic contempt of

> the bought smile
> Of harlots, loveless, joyless, unindear'd,
> Casual fruition . . .
> Court amours,
> Mixt dance, or wanton mask, or midnight ball

censuring at once the age and the mirror which the stage held up to it. In the nineteenth century Hazlitt, Lamb and Leigh Hunt came to the defence of the dramatists, while Macaulay restated Collier's case against their morals with memorable partiality, using for his occasion a review of Leigh Hunt's edition of four Restoration dramatists. 'Wycherley's indecency,' he protested, 'is protected against the critics as a skunk is protected against the hunters. It is safe, because it is too filthy to handle, and too noisome even to approach.' His words were echoed by William Archer in the nineteen-twenties when he said, 'A stench is a stench even if it is wafted across two hundred years.' On the whole, those modern critics who have attacked Restoration comedy have been more impressive, both in number and quality, than its defenders. Harley Granville-Barker found it not only offensive but lacking in stagecraft and declared roundly that 'this talk about the moral purpose of Restoration comedy is all stuff and nonsense, and the present claims made for the "art" of it are not much better'.[1] With equal forthrightness Professor L. C. Knights concluded a celebrated essay with the words: 'The criticism that defenders of Restoration comedy need to answer is not that the comedies are "immoral", but that they are trivial, gross and dull.'[2]

There are many ways in which Restoration comedy may be defended against the charges that have been levelled against it, not all of them compatible with one another. We may argue, with Lamb, that the charge of immorality is irrelevant because this comedy leads us into a dream-world and was never meant to apply to everyday life. Or, slightly varying this view, as John Palmer does in his pioneering study,

1. H. Granville-Barker, *On Dramatic Method*, Sidgwick and Jackson, 1931.

2. L. C. Knights, 'Restoration Comedy, the Reality and the Myth', *Explorations*, Chatto & Windus, 1932.

The Comedy of Manners, we may say that art makes its own rules and should be judged by aesthetic rather than moral standards. The trouble with this line of argument is that it tends to make the comedies seem trivial exercises in stagecraft, without any particular human relevance, and our admiration not different in kind from that which we give to, say, the man who makes a model of Hampton Court out of used matchsticks or writes out the Magna Carta on a golf ball.

Alternatively, we could make the defence which the dramatists themselves made, and in which they were followed by Hazlitt and fitfully by Palmer, that the stage gives us the most vivid picture of the life of the age. Collier anticipates this defence, for he asks what the point is of giving us a picture of a way of life which is so uniformly abominable. To which Granville-Barker adds that the picture of the age which the comedy gives us is by no means representative, as we may see by reading the Verney papers or the letters of Dorothy Osborne. In any case, this sort of defence would again downgrade the comedies to the level of *mere* social documentary, and we surely expect more than this from great drama. Who reads Molière *only* to find out about life in seventeenth-century France?

A more ingenious line of defence is to argue that what we have in Restoration comedy is not just a mirror-image of the times, but a *satirical* portrait of society and its mores. Now, while it is reasonably easy to show that this or that character or situation is satirically depicted (chiefly by contrasting him with characters and situations which are not so depicted) it seems impossible to prove or disprove that an entire body of drama is satirically intended, quite apart from the colossal improbability of the assumption.

Finally, we can accept the view that all great imaginative writing must in some sense, however elusive of definition, have to do with morality, and go on to suggest that the morality of Restoration comedy is a finer and subtler thing than Collier, with his crudely didactic view of art and his instinctive abhorrence of the theatre (*all* theatre, not just that of the Restoration), could comprehend. It is a morality, for instance, which cries out against the treatment of human beings as

goods and chattels and the debasement of marriage to a com-
mercial contract. It is a morality which has an open and proper
regard for the body's needs and desires. It is a morality where
indecency of expression (apart from being often very funny)
is nearly always a sign of high spirits rather than of calculated
wickedness.

We could say all this, and the reader will have seen that
by and large this is what I have said. But it is more than time
to make the necessary qualifications without which the defence would be too goody-goody to be true. Let me say here,
then, that I do not think any convincing justification of
Restoration comedy as a whole is possible. Most of it is plainly
dull, dreary and deservedly forgotten (so, proportionately, is
most Elizabethan and Jacobean comedy). Much Restoration
comedy is 'high' not only in the sense of being about high
society but also in the sense of being gamey; a good deal is
distinctly off. The flesh wearies on one's bones at the mechani-
cal peddling of pointless obscenities and the tortuous con-
volutions of plot of which Granville-Barker justly remarked:
'How could an audience both be clever enough to understand
the story and stupid enough to be interested by it when they
did?' Fortunately I do not need to defend all Restoration
comedy. In what follows I shall try to show why I believe the
three plays included here are great comedies by any standard
and to relate each very briefly to its author's life and his other
works.

II

The Man of Mode or *Sir Fopling Flutter* was Sir George Etherege's third and last play and comes second in chronological
order of the three plays included here. But Etherege is the
obvious dramatist in our group to begin with, not only because he is the acknowledged pioneer of the new comedy but
also because in himself he typified so much that is characteris-
tic of the Restoration ethos. No less a figure than Dryden re-
garded him as the leading prose stylist of his day, and certainly, coming to Etherege from reading the prose writers of
the earlier seventeenth century we are at once aware of a more

elegant and orderly rhythm as well as of an idiom which is harder and less resonant. In his private life, both in England and in Germany (where as English envoy he scandalized the good burghers of Ratisbon by openly carrying on with a visiting actress), he seems to have tried very hard to put into practice the way of life which we associate with the Restoration gallant.

The date of Etherege's birth is not certainly known, but is probably 1634 or 1635. His intimate knowledge of French language and literature suggests that he spent some part of his early life in France. (His father died there in 1649.) He was something of an amateur musician and, apart from the three comedies on which his fame rests, wrote some accomplished light verse, and his published correspondence shows him to have had a keen eye for scene and character, qualities which are everywhere evident in his plays.

The first of these, *The Comical Revenge* or *Love in a Tub*, was produced in 1664 and was a sensational success. It earned the company the splendid sum of one thousand pounds in a month. It is made up of three plots, though the incident which gives it its title really belongs to none of them. The 'high' plot, dealing with the loves of Lord Beaufort and Colonel Bruce for Graciana, is in rhyming couplets and reminds one of the absurdities of the so-called heroic tragedy, while the 'low' plot, concerned with the doings of two rogues, Wheadle and Palmer, is still very close to Jacobean comedy. It was the 'middle' plot, devoted to Sir Frederick Frolick's pursuit of the Widow Rich, which laid the basis for the later comedy.

The success of his first play brought Etherege into close contact with the wits of Charles II's court, and for the next three years he drank and revelled with the best of them. His second play, *She Would If She Could*, appeared in 1668, and in spite of an apparently indifferent production, was a great success. As may be expected, this is much more recognizably a Restoration comedy than Etherege's first. Instead of the double or treble plot inherited from the older drama, there are two pairs of lovers counter-pointed. Lady Cockwood is the prototype not only of Loveit but of Lady Fidget and a host of other figures whose concern for their honour is matched only by the lengths to which they will go to lose it. And in this play we have the vivid sense of London as a glittering pleasure ground and of the country as the region of outer darkness.

Etherege is typical of the Restoration wit not only in being a dashing man about town but in his devotion to the idea of the gentleman-amateur (we may recall Congreve's insistence, when Voltaire came to visit him, that he be judged as an English gentleman rather than a writer) and the cultivation of that 'noble laziness of mind' of which the king was the most distinguished exemplar. Accordingly it was nearly ten years before his third and last play appeared, in 1676. This was not only a great stage success but also seems to have prompted contemporaries to play the game of identifying the real-life counterparts of the stage characters portrayed. In 1679 Etherege married 'a rich old widow' and in 1685 was sent as British envoy to the Diet of the Empire at Ratisbon (Regensburg) and his letters are full of nostalgia for the gay life of London. At the Revolution of 1688 he remained faithful to James II and fled to Paris where he died four years later.

All Etherege's plays are good but *The Man of Mode* is undoubtedly his masterpiece. Its chief merit consists in the uncompromising realism with which it investigates the implications of Restoration libertinism. When we first meet the hero, Dorimant, he has just cast off one mistress and is about to take on another. He has no scruples about faking a jealous rage in order to get rid of Mrs Loveit, nor has his new lady love Belinda any about aiding and abetting him. There is no reason why this process of changing mistresses should not go on for ever, in which case the play would deserve Professor Knights' condemnation for demonstrating nothing 'except the physical stamina of Dorimant'. In fact it demonstrates a great deal more, for it deals with the education of Dorimant from what Mr John Wain has aptly called 'the fighter-pilot's mentality' (he must get them before they get him) to a genuine regard for another person (Harriet) which must overcome a great deal of vanity and ill-will before he can acknowledge it even to himself.

The plot is neat without being over-ingenious. Basically, it has two interlocking triangles, each consisting of a young man and two women. Harriet, Young Bellair and Emilia in one, Mrs Loveit, Dorimant and Belinda on the other. In each case the woman whom the young man wants is not the one who wants him.

But while formally these two groups parallel each other, they are also contrasted in the values which guide them. The second group represents the standard Restoration sexual intrigue with no holds barred and women considered as well equipped as men for the contest. The other embodies the struggle of genuine affection to overcome mercenary pressures, for Young Bellair and Harriet both resist the attempts made by their families to unite them against their will; Harriet even pretends to be in love with him long enough for him to fool his father and marry Emilia whom he loves and who loves him.

It is significant that Dorimant starts at the very bottom of the scale, where sexual love is equated with sheer animal appetite. The appropriate note is struck at the very beginning by the two 'low-life' characters, Foggy (bloated) Nan and Swearing Tom (who are also perhaps emblematic, as Mr Holland suggests, of 'two scales along which the other characters are ranged' – Nan's business being fruit, symbolizing 'natural' desires, and Tom dealing with shoes, standing for clothing and external appearance generally). Much of the imagery associated with Dorimant's earlier intrigues has to do with eating, disease or hunting and it is only when his relationship with Harriet has developed into something more serious than an intrigue that the imagery begins to present love as a religion – a metaphor which goes back at least as far as the medieval courtly love tradition, though here used with a genial irony that was one of the many things which aroused the pious Collier's ire. Harriet speaks of 'men who have been long hardened in sin' and 'the first signs of repentance', while Dorimant is full of 'renunciation' and 'the prospect of such a heaven'. His final exile to the country is to be understood as a strictly temporary penitence, much like the year of visiting the sick in hospital to which Rosaline sentences the young nobleman of Navarre in *Love's Labour's Lost*. London has already been established in the play as the only possible centre of civilized existence.

The 'man of mode' of the play's title is of course the would-be gallant, Sir Fopling Flutter, but while Etherege has a great deal of fun at the expense of this fop who has no real notion of manners, it is clear that 'manners' in the context of this play have to do with matters a great deal more important than Hazlitt's sword-knots and side-curls. Indeed, the point about Sir Fopling is that he is in fact presumably an expert on sword-knots and side-curls – and only that. He is totally pre-occupied with outward appearance and imparts a fresh insignificance to the idea that the proper study of mankind is man; 'in a glass a man may entertain himself'. The tension between outward form and inner nature which is a central concern in Restoration comedy leaves Sir Fopling unscathed, for he has no inner nature. His affectation hides nothing, for there is nothing to him but affectation.

But Sir Fopling is not, as he is sometimes considered to be, merely a brilliant but isolated comic creation with no necessary relationship to the play as a whole. Affectation, in one form or another, is the besetting vice of all the young men in the play, Bellair, Medley, even, most insidiously, Dorimant himself. When Harriet says 'the man indeed wears his clothes fashionably, and has a pretty negligent way with him, very courtly and much affected; he bows and talks and smiles so agreeably, as he thinks . . . Varnished over with good breeding, many a blockhead makes a tolerable show', she is speaking not of Sir Fopling but of Young Bellair. Medley, in addition to having a rather precious mode of speech and the 'filthy trick' of kissing his men friends, is affected in so far as he has more or less withdrawn to the side-lines and is content to live up to his stereotype as 'a living libel, a breathing lampoon'. Dorimant's affectation is his image of himself as a Don Juan, an image which is first undermined and finally demolished by Harriet, whose chief weapon is affectation of affectation, that is, the mocking imitation of Dorimant's manner: 'I do not go begging the men's as you do the ladies' good liking, with a sly softness in your looks and a gentle slowness in your bows as you pass by 'em – as thus, sir (*acts him*). Is not this like you?'

But affectation has two sides to it. On the one hand, it signifies hypocrisy, dissimulation and mere vanity but on the other it stands for the necessary and desirable social forms through which the 'natural man' must find expression. In the three older people we find examples of both kinds. Young Bellair's aunt, Lady Townley, is a model of social decorum, while Harriet's mother and Old Bellair embody in their courtship a ridiculous and out-of-date gallantry which is only faintly parodied by Dorimant as 'Courtage'. Again, in Belinda and even more strikingly in Mrs Loveit we see the result of insufficient 'affectation' (in the good sense), of wearing one's heart always on one's sleeve. (Paradoxically, it forces them to constant deception and subterfuge, while the deception which Harriet, Emilia and Young Bellair engage in has a strictly limited objective.) Only Harriet has the resource and tact to strike a balance between desire and decorum. And when, in the best comic tradition, the hero has learnt the lessons which the heroine knew all along, the comedy is over.

III

Like Etherege, William Wycherley did not become a public figure until the performance in 1671 of his first play *Love in a Wood* (one of a rash of plays which modelled their titles on Etherege's *Love in a Tub*). He was born in 1640, the son of a Shropshire gentleman. He had his early education in France, where he became a Roman Catholic (though in later life he went back to his original Protestantism). He also went to Queen's College, Oxford, but apparently left without taking a degree and studied at one of the Inns of Court, though he does not seem to have practised as a lawyer. Apart from *Love in a Wood* and *The Country Wife* he also wrote *The Gentleman Dancing-Master* (1672) and *The Plain Dealer* (1676) after whose principal character the dramatist came to be called 'Manly' Wycherley by his contemporaries. He also wrote several poems, but even the young Pope could not do much to

improve them, and they were the occasion of a quarrel between the two men in Wycherley's old age.

After the success of his first play, Wycherley found favour
with the Duchess of Cleveland, the king's second best-known
mistress, and through her with the monarch himself. His
popularity in the court circle continued until his secret marriage to the Countess of Drogheda in 1679 which greatly dis-
pleased the king. The Countess died shortly after and Wycherley, having lost all her fortune to relatives, spent seven years
in the Fleet prison for debt. He remarried a few days before
his death in 1715.

If *The Man of Mode* is the realistic triumph of Restoration
drama, *The Country Wife* is its satirical masterpiece. His contemporaries recognized Wycherley's pre-eminence as a satirical dramatist. Evelyn's lines are typical:

> As long as men are false and women vain,
> Whilst gold continues to be virtue's bane,
> In pointed satire Wycherley shall reign.

Thus, while most of the Restoration dramatists have a super-
ficial resemblance to Molière, there is a real affinity between
Wycherley and both Molière and Jonson, for he has something
of the urbanity of the one and the comic fury of the other.
The Country Wife is very far from being merely a dirty joke, to
be defiant or apologetic about. Nor do I agree with Mr John
Wain that Wycherley 'never achieved clarity on any basic
moral issue'.[1] To argue, as Mr Wain does, that the play is
morally confused because we are asked to admire Harcourt
for his attempt to achieve honourable matrimony while our
admiration for Horner is invited for just the opposite reason,
is to overlook two things. The first is that Horner cannot,
properly speaking, be said to be a character at all. He begins
and continues as the tool of the dramatist's satiric intention,
and in the end, as Mr Bateson has said, is reduced to a mere
grotesque. His actions are not governed by any consistent
notion of character but vary according to the needs of the
satiric theme; he is equally capable of exposing the essential

1. John Wain, 'Restoration Comedy and its Modern Critics', *Pre-
liminary Essays*, Macmillan, 1957.

baseness of Pinchwife's attitude to Margery and of attempting to seduce Margery himself. Thus, as the dramatist makes no moral inquiry into Horner, so he invites no moral judgement on him from us.

The second point is that there is all the difference in the world, as I have already suggested, between the marriage which Harcourt succeeds in achieving with Alithea, based as it is on mutual knowledge and affection, and the relationships in which Horner contrives to make a third. Once again, the difference is suggested in the language of the play. The Harcourt–Alithea relationship is presented in terms of the love-as-a-religion metaphor ('Alithea' is the Greek for 'truth'), a metaphor which is saved from cliché only by being persistently contrasted with those of food and money which are used for the other relationships in the play. The dramatist who holds up to ridicule marriages based on mere acquisitiveness and the most hypocritical conception of 'honour' and offers a touchstone by which such marriages are judged and found wanting can hardly be guilty of moral confusion.

The particular aspect of the gap between appearances and the realities of things which *The Country Wife* examines is that concerned with true and false sexual honour. On one side are the town ladies, the Fidgets and the Squeamishes, to whom the outward form is all. 'A pox on 'em,' cries Horner, 'and all that force nature, and would be still what she forbids 'em! Affectation is her greatest monster.' On the other is the simple and forthright country wife who has no use at all for forms and ceremonies. The celebrated 'China scene' brings to a brilliant climax all the comic ironies involved in the town ladies' regard for their 'dear honour', the crowning irony being that the exposer of their 'affectations' is himself the greatest monster of affectation of them all. Wycherley probably found the trick which he gives to Horner in Terence's play *Eunuchus*, but his use of it is not only very funny but bitingly satirical. Of the many resonances which the image of 'china' has, probably the two most relevant and powerful are those of china as a vessel for food (sex as appetite) and as something highly artificial and smooth-surfaced.

But this scene is only the most outstanding example of

verbal *double-entendre* in a play which is shot through not only with doubleness of language but a kind of doubleness in the action itself. In many of the key scenes, the action is not what it appears to be, as when both Sir Jasper and Pinchwife literally push their wives into Horner's arms, or when Harcourt, disguised as a priest, earnestly attempts to 'marry' Alithea in one sense even as he only pretends to do so in another. Appearance and reality are related to each other in many puzzling ways.

But the need for 'appearance' is never seriously questioned. That is why, for all her *ingénue* charm, the country wife Margery remains throughout the play a victim rather than an agent. She does not have the experience of society which would enable her natural vitality to find its true fulfilment. Only in Harcourt and Alithea do we find the harmonious union of 'social' wisdom and spontaneous affection. Alithea shows her genuine 'honour' in the steadfastness with which she devotes herself to Sparkish, but has yet to learn to recognize outward form by itself (Sparkish) for what it is. Harcourt is a more idealized portrait of the Restoration gallant than Dorimant and (perhaps for that reason) somewhat insipid. *The Country Wife* is probably open to the same charge as is Jonson's *Volpone* – that the 'good' characters are dull and colourless compared to the grotesque energy of the 'bad' ones. But Harcourt and Alithea have far more life in them than Celia and Bonario and it would be easy to see the central position they occupy in the play's pattern of relationships, especially in a good production.

IV

Congreve was only ten years old at the Restoration. By the time his first play, *The Old Bachelor*, appeared in 1693, Etherege had already been dead two years and Wycherley had retired from the stage for twelve – which is one more reminder of the scope of the period loosely labelled 'Restoration'.

William Congreve was born at Bardsley in Yorkshire. His family was Royalist and aristocratic, and Congreve spent his early youth in Ireland, where his father served as a military officer. He was educated at Kilkenny and Trinity College, Dublin, and at both places was a contemporary of Jonathan Swift. Coming to England, he entered the Middle Temple but, like Wycherley, does not appear to have practised law.

As an undergraduate Congreve wrote a novel, *Incognita* (1692), of which Dr Johnson wrote that he would rather praise it than read it. His ambition to be a playwright is already evident in the preface to this work. His first play was a great success and was followed by *The Double Dealer* (1693), *Love for Love* (1695) and *The Way of the World* (1700) which was coolly received by his contemporaries, though many consider it to be the great masterpiece of Restoration comedy. He also wrote a tragedy, *The Mourning Bride*, in which Dr Johnson claimed he had found 'the most poetical paragraph' in the whole of English poetry, and some verse. Like Wycherley, he retired from the stage after *The Way of the World*, having obtained government sinecures from his patron Charles Montague, later Lord Halifax. All his plays were written before he was thirty. He died in 1729 and is buried in Westminster Abbey.

From his own time down to ours, *Love for Love* has remained the most popular of Congreve's plays. Even in the nineteenth century, when Restoration comedy was virtually banished from the stage, two (bowdlerized) versions were produced. Sir John Gielgud's 1942 production ran for 471 performances, a record for a classic revival on the London stage, while the current National Theatre production is an outstanding popular success.

Nor are the reasons for this popularity difficult to see. The dialogue is witty without being over-clever and not only the professed wits, but minor figures such as the Nurse, Jeremy Fetch and Ben sparkle in their own way. Tattle is almost as hilarious a fool as Sir Fopling Flutter, and the mockery of the superstitious Foresight is genial enough for general enjoyment. Finally the plot, while it has the usual complications of disguise and counterpointing of contrasted pairs, has not the numbing complexity of much Restoration comedy. On the stage, as the National Theatre production shows, *Love for*

Love is a glittering, witty and continuously interesting comic action.

But it is more than this. We may begin by noting that the picture of the witty gallant, while by no means satirical, is not quite so flattering as in the other two plays, nor is the hero's libertinism of quite such central importance. Congreve, at the very end of the century, is writing for a rather wider audience than either Etherege or Wycherley, an audience whose wits are of the coffee-house rather than the Court, which, in any case, had long ceased to be the 'mob of gentlemen who wrote with ease' associated with Charles II. Significantly, the play was first performed not at the Drury Lane theatre, the centre of former royal patronage, but at a new theatre near Lincoln's Inn.

Once again, we find the familiar series of parallels and contrasts, love versus money, spontaneity versus calculation, young versus old, and the rest. As far as the plot is concerned, there are two basic ironies. The first is that it is those whose intrigues are deepest – Mrs Frail, Sir Sampson, Tattle – who find themselves most closely enmeshed in it at the end. The second and contrasting irony is that, in the end, it is not intrigue and calculation which enables the hero to capture the heroine but a simple and direct confession of his love. In the course of the action, Valentine assumes many disguises, literal and figurative; he assumes the roles of poet, madman, buffoon and martyr. In all of them he is thwarted, principally by the heroine herself. Only when he drops all pretence and declares his true feelings is he able to succeed in his quest.

But though directness and forthrightness succeed where stratagem fails, they succeed only for those who are themselves skilled in strategem, for such skill is the mark of that social wisdom which is a necessary requirement of civilized existence. Opposed to Valentine and Angelica on either side are Tattle, Mrs Frail and Foresight, for whom calculation is all, and sailor Ben and Prue, for whom it is nothing. Ben's nautical language, besides being comic in itself and yielding the occasional *double-entendre*, also sets him apart from the others, a 'sea-beast' among 'land monsters'. To the end he keeps his comic dignity and innocence, which is more than we can say for Miss Prue, who has neither the courage of her rural convictions nor the resolution to adopt whole-heartedly the 'affections' of the town.

Foresight's superstition, besides being a superbly theatrical comic target (rapt in the heavens, he can't see what's happening in his own bed), is the outstanding instance of judging merely by appearances – stars and omens – for here the appearances are only conjecturally related to the things they are supposed to signify. The gap between inner and outer reality could hardly go farther. At the other end of the scale is Tattle, who teaches Miss Prue (what he himself sincerely believes) that only the 'inner' reality, that is, actions alone, matter. Somewhere in between fall both Mrs Foresight, who would deny if she could the reality of her domestic situation ('I have told you, you must not call me mother,' she tells Prue), and Sir Sampson, who affects to believe in a 'natural' right of fatherhood which his action in trying to dispossess his firstborn does nothing to uphold. Scandal, like Medley in *The Man of Mode*, remains a spectator until the end (except for a routine affair with Mrs Foresight), when he is almost reclaimed by the heroine's shining example – 'I was an infidel to your sex, and you have converted me.'

Of the three plays here collected, *Love for Love* is the one in which money occupies the most important position. The wrangle about inheritance between father and son is of course a fairly common theme in comedy, but it is here used in the first place to define the hero's character (it is only by having his own money that he can prove he is not a fortune-hunter; furthermore, his poverty is due to his devotion to Angelica) and secondly, to show up by contrast the mercenary motives of Mrs Frail and Mrs Foresight. Implicit in the title *Love for Love* are the various forms of 'love (in exchange) for money' which are displayed throughout the action.

*

Restoration comedy has, as we have seen, been defended as being, among other things, realistic, satirical or escapist. As long as it is clearly understood that we are dealing with questions of emphasis and not with watertight categories, I think it is true to say that Etherege's play is best described by the first epithet, Wycherley's by the second and Congreve's by the third. The reader may feel that in writing about them, I have made unduly heavy weather of their 'moral outlook', 'theme' and so on, and not said enough about the fact that these plays are often brilliantly witty and magnificent in the theatre. This I have done deliberately. The wit is almost invariably apparent, and where it is not, no amount of introductory propaganda will make it so. Similarly, anyone who has ever seen one of these plays performed does not need to be told how splendidly effective they are on the stage. I have been trying instead, to show that, like all great comedy, these plays deal with matters of serious and contemporary relevance. The mirror which Restoration comedy holds up to life may be a small, even a broken one, but the image it reflects is bright, sharp and pertinent, undimmed with the breath of years.

GĀMINI SALGĀDO

University of Sussex
1 January 1967

A Note on Texts

The Man of Mode or, Sir Fopling Flutter was first published, in a quarto edition, in 1676. There was one more quarto edition in Etherege's lifetime, published in 1684, while a third appeared in 1693, two years after his death. I have used as my text the original 1676 quarto, which is generally acknowledged to be the only one with any real authority, though I have profited immensely from H. F. B. Brett-Smith's edition (1927), and have consulted that of A. W. Verity (1888).

The Country Wife first appeared in 1675 in a quarto edition, and though four more quartos and an octavo edition appeared in Wycherley's lifetime – in 1683, 1688, 1695 (twice), and 1713 respectively – once again the original quarto of 1675 is the soundest text, and I have used a facsimile of it in preparing this edition. Where a reading from another edition has been adopted, this has been indicated in the footnotes. I have also consulted the editions of Montague Summers (1924) and Thomas Fujimura (1965).

Love for Love was first published in 1695, was reprinted in the same year and went into two more editions before the collected *Works* in 1710 (1695 and 1697). Congreve himself described the 1710 edition of the *Works* as 'the least faulty impression which has yet been printed', but the fact is that many errors and alterations (some of them due to Collier's celebrated attack on the theatre) found their way into all editions after the first, including a new system of scene division inappropriate for Congreve's plays. I have therefore used a facsimile of the first (1695) quarto as my copy-text, and occasionally referred to readings from other quartos and the *Works*. I have also consulted the editions of Summers (1924) and F. W. Bateson (1930).

In *The Man of Mode*, I have discarded the irritating practice of the quarto of printing Etherege's sturdy, flowing prose as a kind of bastard blank verse.

In all three plays, the punctuation and spelling have been modernized, though I have occasionally retained an older form of spelling (or the deliberate misspelling of a foreign word) if it seemed to point to a definite variation in pronunciation. All editorial interpolations (mainly stage directions) are in *round* brackets.

I am grateful to the Universities of Cincinnati and Chicago for providing fascimiles of the first editions of the three plays.

G. S.

Title-page of the first edition, 1676

THE
Man of Mode,
OR,
Sʳ Fopling Flutter.
A
COMEDY.

Acted at the *Duke's Theatre.*

By *George Etherege* Esq;.

LICENSED,

June 3.
1676.

Roger L'Estrange.

LONDON,

Printed by *J. Macock*, for *Henry Herringman*, at the Sign of
the *Blew Anchor* in the Lower Walk of the
New Exchange, 1676.

Dramatis Personae

MR DORIMANT
MR MEDLEY
OLD BELLAIR } *Gentlemen*
YOUNG BELLAIR
SIR FOPLING FLUTTER

LADY TOWNLEY
EMILIA
MRS LOVEIT } *Gentlewomen*
BELINDA
LADY WOODVILL AND
   HARRIET HER DAUGHTER

PERT
AND } *Waiting Women*
BUSY

A SHOEMAKER
AN ORANGE-WOMAN
THREE SLOVENLY BULLIES
TWO CHAIR-MEN
MR SMIRK, A PARSON
HANDY, A VALET DE CHAMBRE
PAGES, FOOTMAN, ETC.

Prologue

BY SIR CAR SCROOPE, BARONET

Like dancers on the ropes poor poets fare,
Most perish young, the rest in danger are.
This, one would think, should make our authors wary,
But, gamester-like, the giddy fools miscarry.
A lucky hand or two so tempts 'em on,
They cannot leave off play till they're undone.
With modest fears a Muse does first begin,
Like a young wench newly enticed to sin;
But tickled once with praise by her good Will,
The wanton fool would never more lie still.
'Tis an old mistress you'll meet here tonight,
Whose charms you once have looked on with delight.
But now of late such dirty drabs have known you,
A Muse o'th' better sort's ashamed to own you.
Nature well drawn, and wit, must now give place
To gaudy nonsense and to dull grimace.
Nor is it strange that you should like so much
That kind of wit, for most of yours is such.
But I'm afraid that while to France we go,
To bring you home fine dresses, dance and show,
The stage, like you, will but more foppish grow.
Of foreign wares why should we fetch the scum,
When we can be so richly served at home?
For Heav'n be thanked, 'tis not so wise an age,
But your own follies may supply the stage.
Tho' often ploughed, there's no great fear the soil
Should barren grow by the too frequent toil,
While at your doors are to be daily found
Such loads of dunghill to manure the ground.
'Tis by your follies that we players thrive,
As the physicians by diseases live.
And as each year some new distemper reigns,
Whose friendly poison helps to increase their gains,

So among you, there starts up every day,
Some new unheard-of fool for us to play.
Then for your own sakes, be not too severe,
Nor what you all admire at home, damn here.
Since each is fond of his own ugly face,
Why should you, when we hold it, break the glass?

Act One

SCENE ONE

A dressing-room, a table covered with a toilet, clothes laid ready.

Enter DORIMANT *in his gown and slippers, with a note in his hand made up, repeating verses.*

DORIMANT: *Now for some ages had the pride of Spain,*
      Made the sun shine on half the world in vain.[1]
    Then looking on the note.

For Mrs Loveit. What a dull insipid thing is a billet doux written in cold blood, after the heat of the business is over! It is a tax upon good nature which I have here been labouring to pay, and have done it, but with as much regret as ever fanatic paid the Royal Aid or Church Duties. 'Twill have the same fate, I know, that all my notes to her have had of late; 'twill not be thought kind enough. Faith, women are i'the right when they jealously examine our letters, for in them we always first discover our decay of passion. – Hey! – Who waits!

    Enter HANDY.

HANDY: Sir?

DORIMANT: Call a footman.

HANDY: None of 'em are come yet.

DORIMANT: Dogs! Will they ever lie snoring a-bed till noon?

HANDY: 'Tis all one, sir: if they're up, you indulge 'em so, they're ever poaching after whores all the morning.

DORIMANT: Take notice henceforward who's wanting in his duty; the next clap he gets, he shall rot for an example. What vermin are those chattering without?

HANDY: Foggy[2] Nan the orange-woman, and swearing Tom the shoemaker.

---

1. *Now for . . . in vain*: the opening couplet of Waller's poem *Upon a War with Spain*. John Wilmot, earl of Rochester, on whom the character of Dorimant is founded, is said to have been very fond of quoting from Waller.   2. *Foggy*: bloated.

DORIMANT: Go, call in that overgrown jade with the flasket of guts before her; fruit is refreshing in a morning.

> *It is not that I love you less*
> *Than when before your feet I lay.*[1]

Exit HANDY.

Enter ORANGE-WOMAN.

How now double tripe, what news do you bring?

ORANGE-WOMAN: News! Here's the best fruit has come to town t'year. Gad, I was up before four o'clock this morning, and bought all the choice i'the market.

DORIMANT: The nasty refuse of your shop.

ORANGE-WOMAN: You need not make mouths at it, I assure you 'tis all culled[2] ware.

DORIMANT: The citizens buy better on a holiday in their walk to Totnam.

ORANGE-WOMAN: Good or bad, 'tis all one; I never knew you commend anything. Lord, would the ladies had heard you talk of 'em as I have done! Here, bid your man give me an angel. [*Sets down the fruit.*]

DORIMANT: Give the bawd her fruit again.

ORANGE-WOMAN: Well, on my conscience, there never was the like of you. God's my life, I had almost forgot to tell you; there is a young gentlewoman lately come to town with her mother, that is so taken with you.

DORIMANT: Is she handsome?

ORANGE-WOMAN: Nay, gad, there are few finer women, I tell you but so, and a hugeous fortune they say. Here, eat this peach, it comes from the stone, 'tis better than any Newington y'have tasted.

DORIMANT [*taking the peach*]: This fine woman, I'll lay my life, is some awkward ill-fashioned country toad, who, not having above four dozen of black hairs on her head, has adorned her baldness with a large white fruz,[3] that she may look sparkishly in the forefront of the king's box at an old play.

ORANGE-WOMAN: Gad, you'd change your note quickly if you did but see her.

1. *It is . . . I lay*: opening lines of Waller's poem *The Self-banished*.
2. *Culled*: selected.
3. *Fruz*: wig.

DORIMANT: How came she to know me?

ORANGE-WOMAN: She saw you yesterday at the Change.[1] She told me you came and fooled with the woman at the next shop.

DORIMANT: I remember there was a mask[2] observed me indeed. Fooled, did she say?

ORANGE-WOMAN: Ay, I vow she told me twenty things you said too, and acted with head and with her body so like you –

Enter MEDLEY.

MEDLEY: Dorimant my life, my joy, my darling-sin; how dost thou?

ORANGE-WOMAN: Lord what a filthy trick these men have got of kissing one another! [*She spits.*]

MEDLEY: Why do you suffer this cartload of scandal to come near you, and make your neighbours think you so improvident to need a bawd?

ORANGE-WOMAN: Good now, we shall have it, you did but want him to help you; come, pay me for my fruit.

MEDLEY: Make us thankful for it, huswife, bawds are as much out of fashion as gentlemen ushers; none but old formal ladies use the one, and none but foppish old stagers employ the other; go, you are an insignificant brandy bottle.

DORIMANT: Nay, there you wrong her; three quarts of canary[3] is her business.

ORANGE-WOMAN: What you please, gentlemen.

DORIMANT: To him, give him as good as he brings.

ORANGE-WOMAN: Hang him, there is not such another heathen in the town again, except it be the shoemaker without.

MEDLEY: I shall see you hold up your hand at the bar next sessions for murder, huswife; that shoemaker can take his oath you are in fee with the doctors to sell green fruit to the gentry, that the crudities may breed diseases.

ORANGE-WOMAN: Pray give me my money.

1. *Change*: Exchange, a fashionable arcade.
2. *Mask*: euphemism for whore.
3. *Canary*: wine. Also a slang term for a whore.

DORIMANT: Not a penny. When you bring the gentlewoman hither you spoke of, you shall be paid.

ORANGE-WOMAN: The gentlewoman! The gentlewoman may be as honest as your sisters for ought as I know. Pray pay me, Mr Dorimant, and do not abuse me so; I have an honester way of living, you know it.

MEDLEY: Was there ever such a resty[1] bawd?

DORIMANT: Some jade's tricks she has, but she makes amends when she's on good humour. Come, tell me the lady's name, and Handy shall pay you.

ORANGE-WOMAN: I must not, she forbid me.

DORIMANT: That's a sure sign she would have you.

MEDLEY: Where does she live?

ORANGE-WOMAN: They lodge at my house.

MEDLEY: Nay, then she's in a hopeful way.

ORANGE-WOMAN: Good Mr Medley, say your pleasure of me, but take heed how you affront my house. God's my life, in a hopeful way!

DORIMANT: Prithee peace. What kind of woman's the mother?

ORANGE-WOMAN: A goodly grave gentlewoman. Lord, how she talks against the wild young men o'the town; as for your part, she thinks you an arrant devil. Should she see you, on my conscience she would look if you had not a cloven foot.

DORIMANT: Does she know me?

ORANGE-WOMAN: Only by hearsay. A thousand horrid stories have been told her of you, and she believes 'em all.

MEDLEY: By the character, this should be the famous Lady Woodvill, and her daughter Harriet.

ORANGE-WOMAN: The devil's in him for guessing, I think.

DORIMANT: Do you know 'em?

MEDLEY: Both very well; the mother's a great admirer of the forms and civility of the last age.

DORIMANT: An antiquated beauty may be allowed to be out of humour at the freedoms of the present. This is a good account of the mother. Pray, what is the daughter?

MEDLEY: Why, first she's an heiress, vastly rich.

1. *Resty*: lazy.

DORIMANT: And handsome?

MEDLEY: What alteration a twelve-month may have bred in her I know not, but a year ago she was the beautifullest creature I ever saw. A fine, easy, clean shape, light brown hair in abundance; her features regular, her complexion clear and lively, large wanton eyes, but above all, a mouth that has made me kiss it a thousand times in imagination, teeth white and even, and pretty pouting lips, with a little moisture ever hanging on them, that look like the Provence rose fresh on the bush, 'ere the morning sun has quite drawn up the dew.

DORIMANT: Rapture,[1] mere rapture!

ORANGE-WOMAN: Nay, gad, he tells you true, she's a delicate creature.

DORIMANT: Has she wit?

MEDLEY: More than is usual in her sex, and as much malice. Then she's as wild as you would wish her, and has a demureness in her looks that makes it so surprising.

DORIMANT: Flesh and blood cannot hear this and not long to know her.

MEDLEY: I wonder what makes her mother bring her up to town? An old doting keeper cannot be more jealous of his mistress.

ORANGE-WOMAN: She made me laugh yesterday. There was a judge came to visit 'em, and the old man she told me did so stare upon her, and when he saluted her smacked so heartily. Who would think it of 'em?

MEDLEY: God a-mercy judge![2]

DORIMANT: Do 'em right, the gentlemen of the long robe have not been wanting by their good examples to countenance the crying sin o'the nation.

MEDLEY: Come, on with your trappings; 'tis later than you imagine.

DORIMANT: Call in the shoemaker, Handy.

ORANGE-WOMAN: Good Mr Dorimant, pay me. Gad, I had rather give you my fruit than stay to be abused by that foul-mouthed rogue; what you gentlemen say it matters

---

1. *Rapture*: a fit of madness.
2. *God a-mercy judge!*: thank you, judge!

not much, but such a dirty fellow does one more disgrace.

DORIMANT: Give her ten shillings – and be sure you tell the young gentlewoman I must be acquainted with her.

ORANGE-WOMAN: Now do you long to be tempting this pretty creature. Well, heavens mend you.

MEDLEY: Farewell, bog –

Exit ORANGE-WOMAN *and* HANDY.

Dorimant, when did you see your pis aller[1] as you call her, Mrs Loveit?

DORIMANT: Not these two days.

MEDLEY: And how stand affairs between you?

DORIMANT: There has been great patching of late, much ado; we make a shift to hang together.

MEDLEY: I wonder how her mighty spirit bears it.

DORIMANT: Ill enough on all conscience; I never knew so violent a creature.

MEDLEY: She's the most passionate in her love, and the most extravagant in her jealousy of any woman I ever heard of. What note is that?

DORIMANT: An excuse I am going to send her for the neglect I am guilty of.

MEDLEY: Prithee, read it.

DORIMANT: No, but if you will take the pains you may.

MEDLEY *reads*.

MEDLEY: *I never was a lover of business, but now I have a just reason to hate it, since it has kept me these two days from seeing you. I intend to wait upon you in the afternoon, and in the pleasure of your conversation forget all I have suffered during this tedious absence.* This business of yours, Dorimant, has been with a vizard[2] at the playhouse; I have had an eye on you. If some malicious body should betray you, this kind note would hardly make your peace with her.

DORIMANT: I desire no better.

MEDLEY: Why, would her knowledge of it oblige you?

DORIMANT: Most infinitely. Next to the coming to a good

---

1. *Pis aller*: choice made for lack of a better.
2. *Vizard*: a mask; here, a masked woman. The word commonly signified a prostitute.

understanding with a new mistress, I love a quarrel with an old one. But the devil's in't; there has been such a calm in my affairs of late, I have not had the pleasure of making a woman so much as break her fan, to be sullen, or forswear herself these three days.

MEDLEY: A very great misfortune. Let me see, I love mischief well enough to forward this business myself. I'll about it presently; and though I know the truth of what y'ave done, will set her a-raving. I'll heighten it a little with invention, leave her in a fit o'the mother,[1] and be here again before y'are ready.

DORIMANT: Pray stay, you may spare yourself the labour: the business is undertaken already by one who will manage it with as much address, and I think with a little more malice than you can.

MEDLEY: Who i'the devil's name can this be!

DORIMANT: Why the vizard, that very vizard you saw me with.

MEDLEY: Does she love mischief so well as to betray herself to spite another?

DORIMANT: Not so neither, Medley. I will make you comprehend the mystery; this mask, for a farther confirmation of what I have been these two days swearing to her, made me yesterday at the playhouse make her a promise, before her face, utterly to break off with Loveit; and because she tenders[2] my reputation, and would not have me do a barbarous thing, has contrived a way to give me a handsome occasion.

MEDLEY: Very good.

DORIMANT: She intends, about an hour before me this afternoon, to make Loveit a visit, and, having the privilege by reason of a professed friendship between 'em, to talk of her concerns.

MEDLEY: Is she a friend?

DORIMANT: Oh, an intimate friend!

MEDLEY: Better and better; pray proceed.

DORIMANT: She means insensibly to insinuate a discourse of

1. *Mother*: hysteria.
2. *Tenders*: regards tenderly.

me, and artificially raise her jealousy to such a height, that, transported with the first motions of her passion, she shall fly upon me with all the fury imaginable, as soon as ever I enter. The quarrel being thus happily begun, I am to play my part, confess and justify all my roguery, swear her impertinence and ill humour makes her intolerable, tax her with the next fop that comes into my head, and in a huff march away, slight her and leave her to be taken by whosoever thinks it worth his time to lie down before her.

MEDLEY: This vizard is a spark, and has a genius that makes her worthy of yourself, Dorimant.

Enter HANDY, SHOEMAKER, *and* FOOTMAN.

DORIMANT: You rogue there, who sneak like a dog that has flung down a dish, if you do not mend your waiting I'll uncase you and turn you loose to the wheel of fortune. Handy, seal this and let him run with it presently.[1]

Exit HANDY *and* FOOTMAN.

MEDLEY: Since y'are resolved on a quarrel, why do you send her this kind note?

DORIMANT: To keep her at home in order to the business. [*To the* SHOEMAKER] How now, you drunken sot?

SHOEMAKER: 'Zbud, you have no reason to talk, I have not had a bottle of sack of yours in my belly this fortnight.

MEDLEY: The orange-woman says your neighbours take notice what a heathen you are, and design to inform the bishop and have you burned for an atheist.

SHOEMAKER: Damn her, dunghill! If her husband does not remove her, she stinks so, the parish intend to indite him for a nuisance.

MEDLEY: I advise you like a friend, reform your life. You have brought the envy of the world upon you by living above yourself. Whoring and swearing are vices too genteel for a shoemaker.

SHOEMAKER: 'Zbud, I think you men of quality will grow as unreasonable as the women. You would ingross[2] the sins o'the nation. Poor folks can no sooner be wicked, but th'are railed at by their betters.

1. *Presently*: at once.
2. *Ingross*: monopolize

DORIMANT: Sirrah, I'll have you stand i'the pillory for this libel.

SHOEMAKER: Some of you deserve it, I'm sure. There are so many of 'em that our journeymen nowadays instead of harmless ballads sing nothing but your damned lampoons.

DORIMANT: Our lampoons, you rogue?

SHOEMAKER: Nay, good master, why should not you write your own commentaries as well as Caesar?

MEDLEY: The rascal's read, I perceive.

SHOEMAKER: You know the old proverb, ale and history.[1]

DORIMANT: Draw on my shoes, sirrah.

SHOEMAKER: Here's a shoe!

DORIMANT: Sits with more wrinkles than there are in an angry bull's forehead.

SHOEMAKER: 'Zbud, as smooth as your mistress's skin does upon her; so, strike your foot in home. 'Zbud, if e'er a monsieur of 'em all make more fashionable ware, I'll be content to have my ears whipped off with my own paring knife.

MEDLEY: And served up in a ragout, instead of coxcombs, to a company of French shoemakers for a collation.

SHOEMAKER: Hold, hold. Damn 'em, caterpillars, let 'em feed upon cabbage. Come master, your health this morning! Next my heart now.

DORIMANT: Go, get you home and govern your family better. Do not let your wife follow you to the alehouse, beat your whore, and lead you home in triumph.

SHOEMAKER: 'Zbud, there's never a man i'the town lives more like a gentleman with his wife than I do. I never mind her motions, she never inquires into mine; we speak to one another civilly, hate one another heartily, and because 'tis vulgar to lie and soak together, we have each of us our several[2] settle-bed.

DORIMANT: Give him half a crown.

MEDLEY: Not without he will promise to be bloody drunk.

SHOEMAKER: Tope's[3] the word i'the eye of the world. For

---

1. *Ale and history*: 'Truth is in ale as in history.'
2. *Several*: own.
3. *Tope's the word . . .*: i.e. a more gentlemanly word than 'drunk'.

my master's honour, Robin.

DORIMANT: Do not debauch my servants, sirrah.

SHOEMAKER: I only tip him the wink, he knows an alehouse from a hovel.

Exit SHOEMAKER.

DORIMANT: My clothes, quickly.

MEDLEY: Where shall we dine today?

Enter YOUNG BELLAIR.

DORIMANT: Where you will; here comes a good third man.

YOUNG BELLAIR: Your servant, gentlemen.

MEDLEY: Gentle sir. – How will you answer this visit to your honourable mistress? 'Tis not her interest you should keep company with men of sense who will be talking reason.

YOUNG BELLAIR: I do not fear her pardon; do you but grant me yours for my neglect of late.

MEDLEY: Though y'ave made us miserable by the want of your good company, to show you I am free from all resentment, may the beautiful cause of our misfortune give you all the joys happy lovers have shared ever since the world began.

YOUNG BELLAIR: You wish me in Heaven, but you believe me on my journey to hell.

MEDLEY: You have a good strong faith, and that may contribute much towards your salvation. I confess I am but of an untoward constitution, apt to have doubts and scruples, and in love they are no less distracting than in religion. Were I so near marriage, I should cry out by fits as I ride in my coach, 'Cuckold, Cuckold!' with no less fury than the mad fanatic[1] does 'Glory!' in Bethlem.[2]

YOUNG BELLAIR: Because religion makes some run mad, must I live an atheist?

MEDLEY: Is it not great indiscretion for a man of credit, who may have money enough on his word, to go and deal with Jews, who for little sums make men enter into bonds and give judgements?[3]

---

1. *Mad fanatic*: Oliver Cromwell's porter, to whom there are frequent references in contemporary plays and poems.

2. *Bethlem*: Bethlehem hospital, a lunatic asylum (commonly 'Bedlam').

3. *Judgement*: assignment of property by legal decree.

YOUNG BELLAIR: Preach no more on this text; I am determined, and there is no hope of my conversion.

DORIMANT [*to* HANDY, *who is fiddling about him*]: Leave your unnecessary fiddling; a wasp that's buzzing about a man's nose at dinner is not more troublesome than thou art.

HANDY: You love to have your clothes hang just, sir.

DORIMANT: I love to be well dressed, sir, and think it no scandal to my understanding.

HANDY: Will you use the essence, or orange-flower water?

DORIMANT: I will smell as I do today, no offence to the ladies' noses.

HANDY: Your pleasure, sir.

DORIMANT: That a man's excellency should lie in neatly tying of a ribbon or a cravat! How careful's nature in furnishing the world with necessary coxcombs!

YOUNG BELLAIR: That's a mighty pretty suit of yours, Dorimant.

DORIMANT: I am glad 't has your approbation.

YOUNG BELLAIR: No man in town has a better fancy in his clothes than you have.

DORIMANT: You will make me have an opinion of my genius.

MEDLEY: There is a great critic, I hear, in these matters, lately arrived piping hot from Paris.

YOUNG BELLAIR: Sir Fopling Flutter, you mean.

MEDLEY: The same.

YOUNG BELLAIR: He thinks himself the pattern of modern gallantry.

DORIMANT: He is indeed the pattern of modern foppery.

MEDLEY: He was yesterday at the play, with a pair of gloves up to his elbows, and a periwig more exactly curled than a lady's head newly dressed for a ball.

YOUNG BELLAIR: What a pretty lisp he has!

DORIMANT: Ho, that he affects in imitation of the people of quality of France.

MEDLEY: His head stands for the most part on one side, and his looks are more languishing than a lady's when she lolls at stretch in her coach, or leans her head carelessly against the side of a box i'the playhouse.

DORIMANT: He is a person, indeed, of great acquired follies.

MEDLEY: He is like many others, beholding to his education for making him so eminent a coxcomb. Many a fool had been lost to the world had their indulgent parents wisely bestowed neither learning nor good breeding on 'em.

YOUNG BELLAIR: He has been, as the sparkish word is, brisk upon the ladies already. He was yesterday at my aunt Townley's, and gave Mrs Loveit a catalogue of his good qualities under the character of a complete gentleman, who, according to Sir Fopling, ought to dress well, dance well, fence well, have a genius for love letters, an agreeable voice for a chamber, be very amorous, something discreet, but not over-constant.

MEDLEY: Pretty ingredients to make an accomplished person.

DORIMANT: I am glad he pitched upon Loveit.

YOUNG BELLAIR: How so?

DORIMANT: I wanted a fop to lay to her charge, and this is as pat as may be.

YOUNG BELLAIR: I am confident she loves no man but you.

DORIMANT: The good fortune were enough to make me vain, but that I am in my nature modest.

YOUNG BELLAIR: Hark you, Dorimant, with your leave, Mr Medley, 'tis only a secret concerning a fair lady. (*Whispers.*)

MEDLEY: Your good breeding, sir, gives you too much trouble; you might have whispered without all this ceremony.

YOUNG BELLAIR [*to* DORIMANT]: How stand your affairs with Belinda of late?

DORIMANT: She's a little jilting baggage.

YOUNG BELLAIR: Nay, I believe her false enough, but she's ne'er the worse for your purpose; she was with you yesterday in a disguise at the play.

DORIMANT: There we fell out, and resolved never to speak to one another more.

YOUNG BELLAIR: The occasion?

DORIMANT: Want of courage to meet me at the place appointed. These young women apprehend[1] loving as much as the young men do fighting at first; but once entered, like them too, they all turn bullies straight.

1. *Apprehend*: fear.

Enter HANDY *to* YOUNG BELLAIR.

HANDY: Sir, your man without desires to speak with you.

YOUNG BELLAIR: Gentlemen, I'll return immediately.

Exit YOUNG BELLAIR.

MEDLEY: A very pretty fellow this.

DORIMANT: He's handsome, well-bred, and by much the most tolerable of all the young men that do not abound in wit.

MEDLEY: Ever well dressed, always complaisant, and seldom impertinent. You and he are grown very intimate, I see.

DORIMANT: It is our mutual interest to be so. It makes the women think the better of his understanding, and judge more favourably of my reputation. It makes him pass upon some for a man of very good sense, and I upon others for a very civil person.

MEDLEY: What was that whisper?

DORIMANT: A thing which he would fain have known but I did not think it fit to tell him; it might have frighted him from his honourable intentions of marrying.

MEDLEY: Emilia, give her her due, has the best reputation of any young woman about the town who has beauty enough to provoke detraction; her carriage is unaffected, her discourse modest, not at all censorious, nor pretending, like the counterfeits of the age.

DORIMANT: She's a discreet maid, and I believe nothing can corrupt her but a husband.

MEDLEY: A husband?

DORIMANT: Yes, a husband; I have known many women make a difficulty of losing a maidenhead, who have afterwards made none of making a cuckold.

MEDLEY: This prudent consideration, I am apt to think, has made you confirm poor Bellair in the desperate resolution he has taken.

DORIMANT: Indeed, the little hope I found there was of her, in the state she was in, has made me by my advice, contribute something towards the changing of her condition.

Enter YOUNG BELLAIR.

Dear Bellair, by heavens I thought we had lost thee. Men in love are never to be reckoned on when we would form a company.

YOUNG BELLAIR: Dorimant, I am undone. My man has brought the most surprising news i'the world.

DORIMANT: Some strange misfortune is befal'n your love.

YOUNG BELLAIR: My father came to town last night, and lodges i'the very house where Emilia lies.

MEDLEY: Does he know it is with her you are in love?

YOUNG BELLAIR: He knows I love, but knows not whom, without some officious sot has betrayed me.

DORIMANT: Your aunt Townley is your confidante, and favours the business.

YOUNG BELLAIR: I do not apprehend any ill office from her. I have received a letter in which I am commanded by my father to meet him at my aunt's this afternoon. He tells me farther he has made a match for me, and bids me resolve to be obedient to his will, or expect to be disinherited.

MEDLEY: Now's your time, Bellair. Never had lover such an opportunity of giving a generous proof of his passion.

YOUNG BELLAIR: As how, I pray?

MEDLEY: Why, hang an estate, marry Emilia out of hand, and provoke your father to do what he threatens. 'Tis but despising a coach, humbling yourself to a pair of goloshoes, being out of countenance when you meet your friends, pointed at and pitied wherever you go by all the amorous fops that know you, and your fame will be immortal.

YOUNG BELLAIR: I could find in my heart to resolve not to marry at all.

DORIMANT: Fie, fie! That would spoil a good jest and disappoint the well-natured town of an occasion of laughing at you.

YOUNG BELLAIR: The storm I have so long expected hangs o'er my head, and begins to pour down upon me. I am on the rack, and can have no rest till I'm satisfied in what I fear. Where do you dine?

DORIMANT: At Long's, or Locket's.[1]

MEDLEY: At Long's let it be.

YOUNG BELLAIR: I'll run and see Emilia, and inform myself how matters stand. If my misfortunes are not so great as to make me unfit for company, I'll be with you.

1. *Long's, or Locket's*: two famous taverns.

Exit YOUNG BELLAIR.

Enter a FOOTMAN *with a letter.*

FOOTMAN: Here's a letter, sir. [*To* DORIMANT.]

DORIMANT: The superscription's right: for Mr Dorimant.

MEDLEY: Let's see, the very scrawl and spelling of a true-bred whore.

DORIMANT: I know the hand, the style is admirable I assure you.

MEDLEY: Prithee, read it.

DORIMANT [*reads*]: *I told a you you dud not love me, if you dud, you would have seen me again e're now; I have no money and am very mallicolly; pray send me a guynie to see the operies. Your Servant to Command, Molly.*

MEDLEY: Pray let the whore have a favourable answer, that she may spark it in a box and do honour to her profession.

DORIMANT: She shall; and perk up i'the face of quality. Is the coach at door?

HANDY: You did not bid me send for it.

DORIMANT: Eternal blockhead!

    HANDY *offers to go out.*

Hey sot –

HANDY: Did you call me, sir?

DORIMANT: I hope you have no just exception to the name, sir?

HANDY: I have sense, sir.

DORIMANT: Not so much as a fly in winter. – How did you come, Medley?

MEDLEY: In a chair.

FOOTMAN: You may have a hackney coach if you please, sir.

DORIMANT: I may ride the elephant if I please, sir; call another chair, and let my coach follow to Long's.

            Be calm ye great parents, etc.

    Exit singing.

Act Two

Enter MY LADY TOWNLEY *and* EMILIA.

LADY TOWNLEY: I was afraid, Emilia, all had been discovered.

EMILIA: I tremble with the apprehension still.

LADY TOWNLEY: That my brother should take lodgings i'the very house where you lie!

EMILIA: 'Twas lucky we had timely notice to warn the people to be secret. He seems to be a mighty good-humoured old man.

LADY TOWNLEY: He ever had a notable smirking[1] way with him.

EMILIA: He calls me rogue, tells me he can't abide me, and does so bepat me.

LADY TOWNLEY: On my word, you are much in his favour then.

EMILIA: He has been very inquisitive, I am told, about my family, my reputation and my fortune.

LADY TOWNLEY: I am confident he does not i'the least suspect you are the woman his son's in love with.

EMILIA: What should make him then inform himself so particularly of me?

LADY TOWNLEY: He was always of a very loving temper himself. It may be he had a doting fit upon him, who knows?

EMILIA: It cannot be.

Enter YOUNG BELLAIR.

LADY TOWNLEY: Here comes my nephew. Where did you leave your father?

YOUNG BELLAIR: Writing a note within. Emilia, this early visit looks as if some kind jealousy would not let you rest at home.

EMILIA: The knowledge I have of my rival gives me a little cause to fear your constancy.

1. *Smirking*: pleasant.

YOUNG BELLAIR: My constancy! I vow —

EMILIA: Do not vow. Our love is frail as is our life, and full as little in our power. And are you sure you shall outlive this day?

YOUNG BELLAIR: I am not; but when we are in perfect health, 'twere an idle thing to fright ourselves with the thoughts of sudden death.

LADY TOWNLEY: Pray, what has passed between you and your father i'the garden?

YOUNG BELLAIR: He's firm in his resolution, tells me I must marry Mrs Harriet, or swears he'll marry himself, and disinherit me. When I saw I could not prevail with him to be more indulgent, I dissembled an obedience to his will, which has composed his passion, and will give us time, and I hope opportunity to deceive him.

Enter OLD BELLAIR, *with a note in his hand.*

LADY TOWNLEY: Peace, here he comes.

OLD BELLAIR: Harry, take this, and let your man carry it for me to Mr Forbes' chamber, my lawyer i'the Temple.

Exit YOUNG BELLAIR.

[*To* EMILIA] Neighbour, a-dod I am glad to see thee here, make much of her, sister, she's one of the best of your acquaintance. I like her countenance and her behaviour well; she has a modesty that is not common i'this age, a-dod she has.

LADY TOWNLEY: I know her value, brother, and esteem her accordingly.

OLD BELLAIR: Advise her to wear a little more mirth in her face, a-dod she's too serious.

LADY TOWNLEY: The fault is very excusable in a young woman.

OLD BELLAIR: Nay, a-dod, I like her ne'er the worse, a melancholy beauty has her charms. I love a pretty sadness in a face which varies now and then, like changeable colours, into a smile.

LADY TOWNLEY: Methinks you speak very feelingly, brother.

OLD BELLAIR: I am but five and fifty, sister, you know, an age not altogether unsensible! [*To* EMILIA] Cheer up, sweetheart; I have a secret to tell thee may chance to make thee merry; we three will make collation together anon, i'the meantime. – Mum, I can't abide you, go, I can't abide you.

Enter YOUNG BELLAIR.

Harry, come, you must along with me to my Lady Woodvill's.

I am going to slip the boy at a mistress.

YOUNG BELLAIR: At a wife, sir, you would say.

OLD BELLAIR: You need not look so glum, sir. A wife is no curse when she brings the blessing of a good estate with her. But an idle town flirt with a painted face, a rotten reputation, and a crazy[1] fortune, a-dod is the devil and all; and such a one I hear you are in league with.

YOUNG BELLAIR: I cannot help detraction, sir.

OLD BELLAIR: Out a pise o'their breeches, there are keeping fools enough for such flaunting baggages, and they are e'en too good for 'em. Remember night; go, y'are a rogue, y'are a rogue. [*To* EMILIA] Fare you well, fare you well. Come, come, come along, sir.

Exit OLD *and* YOUNG BELLAIR.

LADY TOWNLEY: On my word, the old man comes on apace; I'll lay my life he's smitten.

EMILIA: This is nothing but the pleasantness of his humour.

LADY TOWNLEY: I know him better than you. Let it work, it may prove lucky.

Enter a PAGE.

PAGE: Madam, Mr Medley has sent to know whether a visit will not be troublesome this afternoon?

LADY TOWNLEY: Send him word his visits never are so.

(*Exit* PAGE.)

EMILIA: He's a very pleasant man.

LADY TOWNLEY: He's a very necessary man among us women. He's not scandalous i'the least, perpetually contriving to bring good company together, and always ready to stop up a gap at ombre;[2] then, he knows all the little news o'the town.

EMILIA: I love to hear him talk o'the intrigues; let 'em be

1. *Crazy*: shaky, frail.   2. *Ombre*: popular card game.

never so dull in themselves, he'll make 'em pleasant i'the relation.

LADY TOWNLEY: But he improves things so much one can take no measure of the truth from him. Mr Dorimant swears a flea or a maggot is not made more monstrous by a magnifying glass than a story is by his telling it.

Enter MEDLEY.

EMILIA: Hold, here he comes.

LADY TOWNLEY: Mr Medley.

MEDLEY: Your servant, madam.

LADY TOWNLEY: You have made yourself a stranger of late.

EMILIA: I believe you took a surfeit of ombre last time you were here.

MEDLEY: Indeed, I had my bellyful of that termagant Lady Dealer. There never was so unsatiable a carder; an old gleeker[1] never loved to sit to't like her. I have played with her now at least a dozen times, till she 'as worn out all her fine complexion, and her tour[2] would keep in curl no longer.

LADY TOWNLEY: Blame her not, poor woman, she loves nothing so well as a black ace.[3]

MEDLEY: The pleasure I have seen her in when she has had hope in drawing for a matadore.[4]

EMILIA: 'Tis as pretty sport to her as persuading masks off is to you to make discoveries.

LADY TOWNLEY: Pray, where's your friend, Mr Dorimant?

MEDLEY: Soliciting his affairs: he's a man of great employment, has more mistresses now depending than the most eminent lawyer in England has causes.

EMILIA: Here has been Mrs Loveit, so uneasy and out of humour these two days.

LADY TOWNLEY: How strangely love and jealousy rage in that poor woman!

MEDLEY: She could not have picked out a devil upon earth so proper to torment her, has made her break a dozen or two of fans already, tear half a score points[5] in pieces, and destroy hoods and knots[6] without number.

1. *Gleeker*: from 'gleek', an old card game for three players.
2. *Tour*: front of false hair.   3. *Black ace*: sexual innuendo.
4. *Matadore*: principal cards in ombre.
5. *Points*: needle-lacework.   6. *Knots*: hair-knots, tight curls.

LADY TOWNLEY: We heard of a pleasant serenade he gave her t'other night.

MEDLEY: A Danish serenade, with kettle drums and trumpets.

EMILIA: O barbarous!

MEDLEY: What, you are of the number of the ladies whose ears are grown so delicate since our operas,[1] you can be charmed with nothing but flute doux,[2] and French oboes?

EMILIA: Leave your raillery and tell us, is there any new wit come forth, songs or novels?

MEDLEY: A very pretty piece of gallantry, by an eminent author, called *The Diversions of Bruxelles*, very necessary to be read by all old ladies who are desirous to improve themselves at questions and commands, blind man's buff, and the like fashionable recreations.

EMILIA: O ridiculous!

MEDLEY: Then there is the *Art of Affectation*, written by a late beauty of quality, teaching you how to draw up your breasts, stretch up your neck, to thrust out your breech, to play with your head, to toss up your nose, to bite your lips, to turn up your eyes, to speak in a silly soft tone of a voice, and use all the foolish French words that will infallibly make your person and conversation charming, with a short apology at the latter end, in the behalf of young ladies, who notoriously wash, and paint, though they have naturally good complexions.

EMILIA: What a deal of stuff you tell us!

MEDLEY: Such as the town affords, madam. The Russians, hearing the great respect we have for foreign dancing, have lately sent over some of their best balladins, who are now practising a famous ballet which will be suddenly[3] danced at the Bear-Garden.

LADY TOWNLEY: Pray forbear your idle stories, and give us an account of the state of love as it now stands.

MEDLEY: Truly there has been some revolutions in those affairs, great chopping and changing among the old, and

---

1. *Operas*: Italian operas were just coming into fashion in London.
2. *Flute doux*: a narrow-bore flute, popular in France at the time.
3. *Suddenly*: very soon.

some new lovers whom malice, indiscretion, and misfortune
have luckily brought into play.

LADY TOWNLEY: What think you of walking into the next
room and sitting down before you engage in this business?

MEDLEY: I wait upon you, and I hope, though women are
commonly unreasonable, by the plenty of scandal I shall
discover, to give you very good content, ladies.

Exeunt.

SCENE TWO

Enter MRS LOVEIT *and* PERT.

MRS LOVEIT *putting up a letter, then pulling out her pocket
glass and looking in it.*

MRS LOVEIT: Pert.

PERT: Madam?

MRS LOVEIT: I hate myself, I look so ill today.

PERT: Hate the wicked cause on't, that base man Mr Dorimant, who makes you torment and vex yourself contin-
ually.

MRS LOVEIT: He is to blame indeed.

PERT: To blame! To be two days without sending, writing,
or coming near you, contrary to his oath and covenant?
'Twas to much purpose to make him swear. I'll lay my life
there's not an article but he has broken; talked to the vizards
i'the pit, waited upon the ladies from the boxes to their
coaches; gone behind the scenes and fawned upon those
little insignificant creatures, the players. 'Tis impossible
for a man of his inconstant temper to forbear, I'm sure.

MRS LOVEIT: I know he is a devil, but he has something of
the angel yet undefaced in him, which makes him so charming and agreeable that I must love him, be he never so
wicked.

PERT: I little thought, madam, to see your spirit tamed to this
degree, who banished poor Mr Lackwit but for taking up
another lady's fan in your presence.

MRS LOVEIT: My knowing of such odious fools contributes
to the making of me love Dorimant the better.

PERT: Your knowing of Mr Dorimant, in my mind, should rather make you hate all mankind.

MRS LOVEIT: So it does, besides himself.

PERT: Pray, what excuse does he make in his letter?

MRS LOVEIT: He has had business.

PERT: Business in general terms would not have been a current excuse for another. A modish man is always very busy when he is in pursuit of a new mistress.

MRS LOVEIT: Some fop has bribed you to rail at him. He had business, I will believe it, and will forgive him.

PERT: You may forgive him anything, but I shall never forgive him his turning me into ridicule, as I hear he does.

MRS LOVEIT: I perceive you are of the number of those fools his wit had made his enemies.

PERT: I am of the number of those he's pleased to rally, madam; and if we may believe Mr Wagfan and Mr Caperwell, he sometimes makes merry with yourself too, among his laughing companions.

MRS LOVEIT: Blockheads are as malicious to witty men as ugly women are to the handsome; 'tis their interest, and they make it their business to defame 'em.

PERT: I wish Mr Dorimant would not make it his business to defame you.

MRS LOVEIT: Should he, I had rather be made infamous by him than owe my reputation to the dull discretion of those fops you talk of. [*Enter* BELINDA.]
Belinda! [*Running to her.*]

BELINDA: My dear!

MRS LOVEIT: You have been unkind of late.

BELINDA: Do not say unkind, say unhappy.

MRS LOVEIT: I could chide you. Where have you been these two days?

BELINDA: Pity me rather, my dear, where I have been so tired with two or three country gentlewomen whose conversation has been more unsufferable than a country fiddle.

MRS LOVEIT: Are they relations?

BELINDA: No, Welsh acquaintance I made when I was last year at St Winefreds. They have asked me a thousand questions of the modes and intrigues of the town, and I have told 'em almost as many things for news that hardly were so when their gowns were in fashion.

MRS LOVEIT: Provoking creatures! How could you endure 'em?

BELINDA [aside]: Now to carry on my plot. Nothing but love could make me capable of so much falsehood; 'tis time to begin, lest Dorimant should come before her jealousy has stung her. [Laughs and then speaks on.] I was yesterday at a play with 'em, where I was fain to shew 'em the living, as the man at Westminster[1] does the dead. That is Mrs such-a-one admired for her beauty, this is Mr such-a-one cried up for a wit, that is sparkish Mr such-a-one who keeps reverend Mrs such-a-one, and there sits fine Mrs such-a-one who was lately cast off by my Lord such-a-one.

MRS LOVEIT: Did you see Dorimant there?

BELINDA: I did, and imagine you were there with him and have no mind to own it.

MRS LOVEIT: What should make you think so?

BELINDA: A lady masked in a pretty dishabillie whom Dorimant entertained with more respect than the gallants do a common vizard.

MRS LOVEIT [aside]: Dorimant at the play entertaining a mask – O heavens!

BELINDA [aside]: Good.

MRS LOVEIT: Did he stay all the while?

BELINDA: 'Till the play was done, and then led her out, which confirms me it was you.

MRS LOVEIT: Traitor!

PERT: Now you may believe he had business, and you may forgive him too.

MRS LOVEIT: Ingrateful perjured man!

BELINDA: You seem so much concerned, my dear, I fear I have told you unawares what I had better have concealed for your quiet.

MRS LOVEIT: What manner of shape had she?

BELINDA: Tall and slender, her motions were very genteel; certainly she must be some person of condition.

1. *Man at Westminster*: official guide who conducted visitors round the Abbey.

MRS LOVEIT: Shame and confusion be ever in her face when she shows it!

BELINDA: I should blame your discretion for loving that wild man, my dear, but they say he has a way so bewitching that few can defend their hearts who know him.

MRS LOVEIT: I will tear him from mine, or die i'the attempt.

BELINDA: Be more moderate.

MRS LOVEIT: Would I had daggers, darts, or poisoned arrows in my breast, so I could but remove the thoughts of him from thence.

BELINDA: Fie, fie, your transports are too violent, my dear. This may be but an accidental gallantry, and 'tis likely ended at her coach.

PERT: Should it proceed farther, let your comfort be, the conduct Mr Dorimant affects will quickly make you know your rival, ten to one let you see her ruined, her reputation exposed to the town – a happiness none will envy her but yourself, madam.

MRS LOVEIT: Whoe'er she be, all the harm I wish her is, may she love him as well as I do, and may he give her as much cause to hate him.

PERT: Never doubt the latter end of your curse, madam.

MRS LOVEIT: May all the passions that are raised by neglected love, jealousy, indignation, spite and thirst of revenge eternally rage in her soul, as they do now in mine. [*Walks up and down with a distracted air.*]

 Enter a PAGE.

PAGE: Madam, Mr Dorimant –

MRS LOVEIT: I will not see him.

PAGE: I told him you were within, madam.

MRS LOVEIT: Say you lied, say I'm busy, shut the door. Say anything.

 Enter DORIMANT.

PAGE: He's here, madam.

DORIMANT:
> *They taste of death who do at Heaven arrive,*
> *But we this paradise approach alive.*[1]

[*To* MRS LOVEIT] What, dancing the galloping nag without

1. *They taste . . . alive*: opening couplet of Waller's *Of Her Chamber*.

a fiddle? [*Offers to catch her by the hand; she flings away and walks on.*] I fear this restlessness of the body, madam, proceeds from an unquietness of the mind. [*Pursuing her.*] What unlucky accident puts you out of humour? A point illwashed, knots spoiled i'the making up, hair shaded awry, or some other little mistake in setting you in order?

PERT: A trifle in my opinion, sir, more inconsiderable than any you mention.

DORIMANT: Oh Mrs Pert, I never knew you sullen enough to be silent; come, let me know the business.

PERT: The business, sir, is the business that has taken you up these two days. How have I seen you laugh at men of business, and now to become a man of business yourself!

DORIMANT: We are not masters of our own affections; our inclinations daily alter. Now we love pleasure, and anon we shall dote on business; human frailty will have it so, and who can help it?

MRS LOVEIT: Faithless, inhumane, barbarous man –

DORIMANT: Good, now the alarm strikes –

MRS LOVEIT: Without sense of love, of honour, or of gratitude. Tell me, for I will know, what devil masked she was you were with at the play yesterday?

DORIMANT: Faith, I resolved as much as you, but the devil was obstinate, and would not tell me.

MRS LOVEIT: False in this as in your vows to me. You do know.

DORIMANT: The truth is I did all I could to know.

MRS LOVEIT: And dare you own it to my face? Hell and furies! [*Tears her fan in pieces.*]

DORIMANT: Spare your fan, madam, you are growing hot, and will want it to cool you.

MRS LOVEIT: Horror and distraction seize you, sorrow and remorse gnaw your soul, and punish all your perjuries to me – [*Weeps.*]

DORIMANT

> *So thunder breaks the cloud in twain,*
> *And makes a passage for the rain.*

[*Turning to* BELINDA]: Belinda, you are the devil that have raised this storm. You were at the play yesterday, and have been making discoveries to your dear.

BELINDA: Y'are the most mistaken man i'the world.

DORIMANT: It must be so. And here I vow revenge, resolve to pursue and persecute you more impertinently than ever any loving fop did his mistress, hunt you i'the Park, trace you i'the Mall,[1] dog you in every visit you make, haunt you at the plays and i'the drawing room, hang my nose in your neck, and talk to you whether you will or no, and ever look upon you with such dying eyes, till your friends grow jealous of me, send you out of town, and the world suspect your reputation. [*In a lower voice*] At my Lady Townley's when we go from hence. [*He looks kindly on* BELINDA.]

BELINDA: I'll meet you there.

DORIMANT: Enough.

MRS LOVEIT: Stand off, you sha' not stare upon her so. [*Pushing* DORIMANT *away*.]

DORIMANT: Good! There's one made jealous already.

MRS LOVEIT: Is this the constancy you vowed?

DORIMANT: Constancy at my years! 'Tis not a virtue in season; you might as well expect the fruit the autumn ripens i'the spring.

MRS LOVEIT: Monstrous principle!

DORIMANT: Youth has a long journey to go, madam. Should I have set up my rest at the first inn I lodged at, I should never have arrived at the happiness I now enjoy.

MRS LOVEIT: Dissembler, damned dissembler!

DORIMANT: I am so, I confess; good nature and good manners corrupt me. I am honest in my inclinations, and would not, wer't not to avoid offence, make a lady a little in years believe I think her young, wilfully mistake art for nature, and seem as fond of a thing I am weary of, as when I doted on't in earnest.

MRS LOVEIT: False man!

DORIMANT: True woman.

MRS LOVEIT: Now you begin to show yourself!

DORIMANT: Love gilds us over, and makes us show fine

1. *Mall*: a fashionable walk in St James Park, constructed by Charles II for playing the game of pall mall.

things to one another for a time, but soon the gold wears off and then again the native brass appears.

MRS LOVEIT: Think on your oaths, your vows and protestations, perjured man!

DORIMANT: I made 'em when I was in love.

MRS LOVEIT: And therefore ought they not to bind? Oh impious!

DORIMANT: What we swear at such a time may be a certain proof of a present passion, but to say truth, in love there is no security to be given for the future.

MRS LOVEIT: Horrid and ingrateful, begone, and never see me more!

DORIMANT: I am not one of those troublesome coxcombs who, because they were once well received, take the privilege to plague a woman with their love ever after. I shall obey you, madam, though I do myself some violence. [*He offers to go, and* LOVEIT *pulls him back.*]

MRS LOVEIT: Come back, you sha' not go. Could you have the ill nature to offer it?

DORIMANT: When love grows diseased, the best thing we can do is to put it to a violent death. I cannot endure the torture of a lingering and consumptive passion.

MRS LOVEIT: Can you think mine sickly?

DORIMANT: Oh, 'tis desperately ill! What worse symptoms are there than your being always uneasy when I visit you, your picking quarrels with me on slight occasions, and in my absence kindly listening to the impertinences of every fashionable fool that talks to you?

MRS LOVEIT: What fashionable fool can you lay to my charge?

DORIMANT: Why the very cock-fool of all those fools, Sir Fopling Flutter.

MRS LOVEIT: I never saw him in my life but once.

DORIMANT: The worse woman you, at first sight to put on all your charms, to entertain him with that softness in your voice, and all that wanton kindness in your eyes you so notoriously affect when you design a conquest.

MRS LOVEIT: So damned a lie did never malice yet invent. Who told you this?

DORIMANT: No matter. That ever I should love a woman that can dote on a senseless caper, a tawdry French riband and a formal cravat.

MRS LOVEIT: You make me mad.

DORIMANT: A guilty conscience may do much. Go on, be the game-mistress o'the town, and enter all our young fops as fast as they come from travail.

MRS LOVEIT: Base and scurrilous!

DORIMANT: A fine mortifying reputation 't will be for a woman of your pride, wit and quality!

MRS LOVEIT: This jealousy's a mere pretence, a cursed trick of your own devising; I know you.

DORIMANT: Believe it, and all the ill of me you can. I would not have a woman have the least good thought of me that can think well of Fopling. Farewell, fall to, and much good may do[1] you with your coxcomb.

MRS LOVEIT: Stay, oh stay, and I will tell you all.

DORIMANT: I have been told too much already. [*Exit* DORIMANT.]

MRS LOVEIT: Call him again.

PERT: E'en let him go. A fair riddance!

MRS LOVEIT: Run I say, call him again. I will have him called.

PERT: The devil should carry him away first, were it my concern. [*Exit* PERT.]

BELINDA: H'as frightened me from the very thoughts of loving men. For Heaven's sake, my dear, do not discover what I told you. I dread his tongue as much as you ought to have done his friendship.

Enter PERT.

PERT: He's gone madam.

MRS LOVEIT: Lightning blast him!

PERT: When I told him you desired him to come back, he smiled, made a mouth at me, flung into his coach, and said –

MRS LOVEIT: What did he say?

PERT: 'Drive away', and then repeated verses.

MRS LOVEIT: Would I had made a contract to be a witch

1. *May do*: a frequent Restoration form of 'may it do'.

when first I entertained this greater devil, monster, barbarian. I could tear myself in pieces. Revenge, nothing but revenge can ease me. Plague, war, famine, fire, all that can bring universal ruin and misery on mankind, with joy I'd perish to have you in my power but this moment. [*Exit* LOVEIT.]

PERT: Follow madam, leave her not in this outrageous passion. [PERT *gathers up the things.*]

BELINDA: H'as given me the proof which I desired of his love but 'tis a proof of his ill nature too; I wish I had not seen him use her so.

> I sigh to think that Dorimant may be
> One day as faithless and unkind to me.

Exeunt.

Act Three

LADY WOODVILL'S *lodgings.*
Enter HARRIET, *and* BUSY, *her woman.*

BUSY: Dear madam, let me set that curl in order.

HARRIET: Let me alone, I will shake 'em all out of order.

BUSY: Will you never leave this wildness?

HARRIET: Torment me not.

BUSY: Look, there's a knot falling off.

HARRIET: Let it drop.

BUSY: But one pin, dear madam.

HARRIET: How do I daily suffer under thy officious fingers!

BUSY: Ah, the difference that is between you and my Lady Dapper! How uneasy she is if the least thing be amiss about her!

HARRIET: She is indeed most exact. Nothing is ever wanting to make her ugliness remarkable.

BUSY: Jeering people say so.

HARRIET: Her powdering, painting, and her patching never fail in public to draw the tongues and eyes of all the men upon her.

BUSY: She is indeed a little too pretending.

HARRIET: That women should set up for beauty as much in spite of nature, as some men have done for wit!

BUSY: I hope without offence one may endeavour to make oneself agreeable?

HARRIET: Not when 'tis impossible. Women then ought to be no more fond of dressing than fools should be of talking. Hoods and modesty, masks and silence, things that shadow and conceal; they should think of nothing else.

BUSY: Jesu! Madam, what will your mother think is become of you? For Heaven's sake go in again.

HARRIET: I won't!

BUSY: This is the extravagant'st thing that ever you did in your life, to leave her and a gentleman who is to be your husband.

HARRIET: My husband! Hast thou so little wit to think I spoke what I meant when I over-joyed her in the country, with a low curtsy, and *What you please, madam, I shall ever be obedient?*

BUSY: Nay, I know not, you have so many fetches.

HARRIET: And this was one, to get her up to London. Nothing else, I assure thee.

BUSY: Well, the man, in my mind, is a fine man.

HARRIET: The man, indeed, wears his clothes fashionably, and has a pretty negligent way with him, very courtly, and much affected; he bows, and talks, and smiles so agreeably, as he thinks.

BUSY: I never saw anything so genteel.

HARRIET: Varnished over with good breeding, many a blockhead makes a tolerable show.

BUSY: I wonder you do not like him.

HARRIET: I think I might be brought to endure him, and that is all a reasonable woman should expect in a husband but there is duty i'the case . . . and like the haughty Merab,[1] *I find much aversion in my stubborn mind,* which *is bred by being promised and designed.*

BUSY: I wish you do not design your own ruin. I partly guess your inclinations, madam – that Mr Dorimant –

HARRIET: Leave your prating, and sing some foolish song or other.

BUSY: I will, the song you love so well ever since you saw Mr Dorimant.

SONG

When first Amintas charmed my heart,
    My heedless sheep began to stray;
The wolves soon stole the greatest part,
    And all will now be made a prey.

Ah, let not love your thoughts possess,
    'Tis fatal to a shepherdess;
The dang'rous passion you must shun,
    Or else like me be quite undone.

---

1. *Merab*: see I Samuel 14. 49 and 18. 17–19.

HARRIET: Shall I be paid down by a covetous parent for a purchase? I need no land; no, I'll lay myself out all in love. It is decreed –

Enter YOUNG BELLAIR.

YOUNG BELLAIR: What generous resolution are you making, madam?

HARRIET: Only to be disobedient, sir.

YOUNG BELLAIR: Let me join hands with you in that.

HARRIET: With all my heart. I never thought I should have given you mine so willingly. Here I Harriet –

YOUNG BELLAIR: And I Harry –

HARRIET: Do solemnly protest –

YOUNG BELLAIR: And vow –

HARRIET: That I with you –

YOUNG BELLAIR: And I with you –

BOTH: Will never marry –

HARRIET: A match!

YOUNG BELLAIR: And no match! How do you like this indifference now?

HARRIET: You expect I should take it ill, I see!

YOUNG BELLAIR: 'Tis not unnatural for you women to be a little angry. You miss a conquest, though you would slight the poor man were he in your power.

HARRIET: There are some, it may be, have an eye like Bart'lomew,[1] big enough for the whole fair, but I am not of the number, and you may keep your ginger-bread. 'Twill be more acceptable to the lady whose dear image it wears, sir.

YOUNG BELLAIR: I must confess, madam, you came a day after the fair.

HARRIET: You own then you are in love?

YOUNG BELLAIR: I do.

HARRIET: The confidence is generous, and in return I could almost find in my heart to let you know my inclinations.

YOUNG BELLAIR: Are you in love?

HARRIET: Yes, with this dear town, to that degree, I can

1. *Bart'lomew*: a celebrated London fair held annually for over seven hundred years, till the early nineteenth century.

scarce indure the country in landscapes and in hangings.[1]

YOUNG BELLAIR: What a dreadful thing 'twould be to be hurried back to Hampshire![2]

HARRIET: Ah, name it not!

YOUNG BELLAIR: As for us, I find we shall agree well enough. Would we could do something to deceive the grave people.

HARRIET: Could we delay their quick proceeding, 'twere well. A reprieve is a good step towards the getting of a pardon.

YOUNG BELLAIR: If we give over the game, we are undone! What think you of playing it on booty?[3]

HARRIET: What do you mean?

YOUNG BELLAIR: Pretend to be in love with one another. 'Twill make some dilatory excuses we may feign pass the better.

HARRIET: Let us do't, if it be but for the dear pleasure of dissembling.

YOUNG BELLAIR: Can you play your part?

HARRIET: I know not what it is to love, but I have made pretty remarks by being now and then where lovers meet. Where did you leave their gravities?

YOUNG BELLAIR: I'th' next room. Your mother was censuring our modern gallant.

Enter OLD BELLAIR *and* LADY WOODVILL.

HARRIET: Peace! Here they come. I will lean against this wall, and look bashfully down upon my fan, while you, like an amorous spark, modishly entertain me.

LADY WOODVILL: Never go about to excuse 'em. Come, come, it was not so when I was a young woman.

OLD BELLAIR: A-dod, they're something disrespectful.

LADY WOODVILL: Quality was then considered, and not railled by every fleering[4] fellow.

1. *Hangings*: tapestries.
2. *Hampshire*: a generic epithet for the country.
3. *Playing . . . booty*: to join with other players to cheat one; to play with the intention of losing.
4. *Fleering*: mocking.

OLD BELLAIR: Youth will have its jest, a-dod it will.

LADY WOODVILL: 'Tis good breeding now to be civil to none but players and Exchange women. They are treated by 'em as much above their condition as others are below theirs.

OLD BELLAIR: Out a pise on 'em! Talk no more, the rogues ha' got an ill habit of preferring beauty no matter where they find it.

LADY WOODVILL: See, your son and my daughter, they have improved their acquaintance since they were within.

OLD BELLAIR: A-dod, methinks they have! Let's keep back and observe.

YOUNG BELLAIR: Now for a look and gestures that may persuade 'em I am saying all the passionate things imaginable –

HARRIET: Your head a little more on one side, ease yourself on your left leg, and play with your right hand.

YOUNG BELLAIR: Thus, is it not?

HARRIET: Now set your right leg firm on the ground, adjust your belt, then look about you.

YOUNG BELLAIR: A little exercising will make me perfect.

HARRIET: Smile and turn to me again very sparkish.

YOUNG BELLAIR: Will you take your turn and be instructed?

HARRIET: With all my heart.

YOUNG BELLAIR: At one motion play your fan, roul your eyes, and then settle a kind look upon me.

HARRIET: So?

YOUNG BELLAIR: Now spread your fan, look down upon it, and tell the sticks with a finger.

HARRIET: Very modish.

YOUNG BELLAIR: Clap your hands up to your bosom, hold down your gown, shrug a little, draw up your breasts and let 'em fall again, gently, with a sigh or two, etc.

HARRIET: By the good instructions you give, I suspect you for one of those malicious observers who watch people's eyes, and from innocent looks make scandalous conclusions.

YOUNG BELLAIR: I know some indeed who out of mere love to mischief are as vigilant as jealousy itself, and will give you an account of every glance that passes at a play and i'th'Circle![1]

HARRIET: 'Twill not be amiss now to seem a little pleasant.

YOUNG BELLAIR: Clap your fan then, in both your hands, snatch it to your mouth, smile, and with a lively motion fling your body a little forwards. So – now spread it; fall back on the sudden, cover your face with it, and break out into a loud laughter – take up! Look grave, and fall a-fanning of yourself – admirably well acted.

HARRIET: I think I am pretty apt at these matters.

OLD BELLAIR: A-dod I like this well.

LADY WOODVILL: This promises something.

OLD BELLAIR: Come, there is love i'th'case a-dod there is, or will be. What say you, young lady?

HARRIET: All in good time sir. You expect we should fall to and love as game-cocks fight, as soon as we are set together. A-dod, y'are unreasonable!

OLD BELLAIR: A-dod sirrah, I like thy wit well.

Enter a servant.

SERVANT: The coach is at the door, madam.

OLD BELLAIR: Go, get you and take the air together.

LADY WOODVILL: Will not you go with us?

OLD BELLAIR: Out a pise! A-dod, I ha' business and cannot. We shall meet at night at my sister Townley's.

YOUNG BELLAIR [*aside*]: He's going to Emilia. I overheard him talk of a collation.

Exeunt.

SCENE TWO

(LADY TOWNLEY'S *house.*)
Enter LADY TOWNLEY, EMILIA, *and* MR MEDLEY.

LADY TOWNLEY: I pity the young lovers we last talked of, though to say truth their conduct has been so indiscreet they deserve to be unfortunate.

MEDLEY: Y'have had an exact account from the great lady i'th'box down to the little orange wench.

1. *Circle*: the 'Tour' or Ring in Hyde Park, a haunt of fashionable society.

EMILIA: Y'are a living libel, a breathing lampoon. I wonder you are not torn in pieces.

MEDLEY: What think you of setting up an office of intelligence for these matters? The project may get money.

LADY TOWNLEY: You would have great dealings with country ladies.

MEDLEY: More than Muddiman[1] has with their husbands.

Enter BELINDA.

LADY TOWNLEY: Belinda, what has been become of you? We have not seen you here of late with your friend Mrs Loveit.

BELINDA: Dear creature, I left her but now so sadly afflicted.

LADY TOWNLEY: With her old distemper, jealousy.

MEDLEY: Dorimant has played her some new prank.

BELINDA: Well, that Dorimant is certainly the worst man breathing.

EMILIA: I once thought so.

BELINDA: And do you not think so still?

EMILIA: No indeed.

BELINDA: Oh Jesu!

EMILIA: The town does him a great deal of injury, and I will never believe what it says of a man I do not know again, for his sake.

BELINDA: You make me wonder.

LADY TOWNLEY: He's a very well-bred man.

BELINDA: But strangely ill-natured.

EMILIA: Then he's a very witty man.

BELINDA: But a man of principles.

MEDLEY: Your man of principles is a very fine thing indeed.

BELINDA: To be preferred to men of parts by women who have regard to their reputation and quiet. Well, were I minded to play the fool, he should be the last man I'd think of.

MEDLEY: He has been the first in many ladies' favours, though you are so severe, madam.

LADY TOWNLEY: What he may be for a lover I know not, but he's a very pleasant acquaintance I am sure.

1. *Muddiman*: Henry Muddiman (1629–92) compiled occasional news-letters which were widely read by the country gentry.

BELINDA: Had you seen him use Mrs Loveit as I have done, you would never indure him more.

EMILIA: What, he has quarrelled with her again?

BELINDA: Upon the slightest occasion. He's jealous of Sir Fopling.

LADY TOWNLEY: She never saw him in her life but yesterday, and that was here.

EMILIA: On my conscience, he's the only man in town that's her aversion. How horribly out of humour she was all the while he talked to her!

BELINDA: And somebody has wickedly told him –

EMILIA: Here he comes.

Enter DORIMANT.

MEDLEY: Dorimant! You are luckily come to justify yourself. Here's a lady –

BELINDA: Has a word or two to say to you from a disconsolate person.

DORIMANT: You tender[1] your reputation too much I know, madam, to whisper with me before this good company.

BELINDA: To serve Mrs Loveit, I'll make a bold venture.

DORIMANT: Here's Medley, the very spirit of scandal.

BELINDA: No matter.

EMILIA: 'Tis something you are unwilling to hear, Mr Dorimant.

LADY TOWNLEY: Tell him, Belinda, whether he will or no.

BELINDA [*aloud*]: Mrs Loveit!

DORIMANT: Softly, these are laughers, you do not know 'em.

BELINDA [*to* DORIMANT, *apart*]: In a word, y'ave made me hate you, which I thought you never could have done.

DORIMANT: In obeying your commands.

BELINDA: 'Twas a cruel part you played. How could you act it?

DORIMANT: Nothing is cruel to a man who could kill himself to please you. Remember five a clock tomorrow morning.

BELINDA: I tremble when you name it.

DORIMANT: Be sure you come.

1. *Tender*: regard tenderly.

BELINDA: I sha' not.

DORIMANT: Swear you will.

BELINDA: I dare not.

DORIMANT: Swear I say.

BELINDA: By my life, by all the happiness I hope for –

DORIMANT: You will.

BELINDA: I will.

DORIMANT: Kind.

BELINDA: I am glad I've sworn, I vow I think I should ha' failed you else!

DORIMANT: Surprisingly kind! In what temper did you leave Loveit?

BELINDA: Her raving was prettily over, and she began to be in a brave way of defying you and all your works. Where have you been since you went from thence?

DORIMANT: I looked in at the play.

BELINDA: I have promised and must return to her agen.

DORIMANT: Persuade her to walk in the Mall this evening.

BELINDA: She hates the place and will not come.

DORIMANT: Do all you can to prevail with her.

BELINDA: For what purpose?

DORIMANT: Sir Fopling will be here anon; I'll prepare him to set upon her there before me.

BELINDA: You persecute her too much, but I'll do all you'll ha' me.

DORIMANT [aloud]: Tell her plainly, 'tis grown so dull a business I can drudge on no longer.

EMILIA: There are afflictions in love, Mr Dorimant.

DORIMANT: You women make 'em, who are commonly as unreasonable in that as you are at play; without the advantage be on your side, a man can never quietly give over when he's weary.

MEDLEY: If you would play without being obliged to complaisance, Dorimant, you should play in public places.

DORIMANT: Ordinaries[1] were a very good thing for that, but gentlemen do not of late frequent 'em. The deep play is now in private houses.

BELINDA *offering to steal away.*

1. *Ordinaries*: taverns.

LADY TOWNLEY: Belinda, are you leaving us so soon?

BELINDA: I am to go to the Park with Mrs Loveit, madam. [*Exit* BELINDA.]

LADY TOWNLEY: This confidence will go nigh to spoil this young creature.

MEDLEY: 'Twill do her good, madam. Young men who are brought up under practising lawyers prove the abler counsel when they are come to be called to the bar themselves.

DORIMANT: The town has been very favourable to you this afternoon, my Lady Townley. You use to have an embarras of chairs and coaches at your door, an uproar of footmen in your hall, and a noise of fools above here.

LADY TOWNLEY: Indeed, my house is the general rendevouze, and next to the playhouse is the common refuge of all the young idle people.

EMILIA: Company is a very good thing, madam, but I wonder you do not love it a little more chosen.

LADY TOWNLEY: 'Tis good to have an universal taste. We should love wit, but, for variety, be able to divert ourselves with the extravagancies of those who want it.

MEDLEY: Fools will make you laugh.

EMILIA: For once or twice, but the repetition of their folly after a visit or two grows tedious and unsufferable.

LADY TOWNLEY: You are a little too delicate, Emilia.
        Enter a PAGE.

PAGE: Sir Fopling Flutter, madam, desires to know if you are to be seen.

LADY TOWNLEY: Here's the freshest fool in town, and one who has not cloyed you yet. Page!

PAGE: Madam?

LADY TOWNLEY: Desire him to walk up.
        Exit PAGE.

DORIMANT: Do not you fall on him, Medley, and snub him. Soothe him up in his extravagance, he will shew the better.

MEDLEY: You know I have a natural indulgence for fools, and need not this caution. Sir!
        Enter SIR FOPLING FLUTTER, *with his* PAGE *after him*.

SIR FOPLING: Page! Wait without. [*To* LADY TOWNLEY]

Madam, I kiss your hand. I see yesterday was nothing of chance; the bellès assemblès form themselves here every day. [*To* EMILIA] Lady, your servant. Dorimant, let me embrace thee; without lying, I have not met with any of my acquaintance who retain so much of Paris as thou dost. The very air thou hadst when the Marquise mistook thee i'th'Tuileries, and cried Hey Chevalier, and then begged thy pardon.

DORIMANT: I would fain wear in fashion as long as I can, sir, 'tis a thing to be valued in men as well as baubles.

SIR FOPLING: Thou art a man of wit, and understands the town. Prithee let thee and I be intimate; there is no living without making some good man the confidant of our pleasures.

DORIMANT: 'Tis true, but there is no man so improper for such a business as I am.

SIR FOPLING: Prithee, why hast thou so modest an opinion of thyself?

DORIMANT: Why first, I could never keep a secret in my life, and then, there is no charm so infallibly makes me fall in love with a woman as my knowing a friend loves her. I deal honestly with you.

SIR FOPLING: Thy humour's very gallant or let me perish. I knew a French count so like thee.

LADY TOWNLEY: Wit I perceive has more power over you than beauty, Sir Fopling, else you would not have let this lady stand so long neglected.

SIR FOPLING [*to* EMILIA]: A thousand pardons, madam. Some civilities due of course upon the meeting a long absent friend. The eclat of so much beauty, I confess, ought to have charmed me sooner.

EMILIA: The brillian[1] of so much good language, sir, has much more power than the little beauty I can boast.

SIR FOPLING: I never saw anything prettier than this high work on your point d'espaigne –

EMILIA: 'Tis not so rich as point de Venice . . .

SIR FOPLING: Not altogether, but looks cooler, and is more proper for the season. Dorimant, is not that Medley?

1. *Brillian*: Fr. *brilliant*.

DORIMANT: The same, sir.

SIR FOPLING: Forgive me, sir, in this embarras of civilities I could not come to have you in my arms sooner. You understand an equipage[1] the best of any man in town, I hear.

MEDLEY: By my own you would not guess it.

SIR FOPLING: There are critics who do not write, sir.

MEDLEY: Our peevish poets will scarce allow it.

SIR FOPLING: Damn 'em, they'll allow no man wit who does not play the fool like themselves and show it. Have you taken notice of the gallesh[2] I brought over?

MEDLEY: Oh yes, 't has quite another air than th'English makes.

SIR FOPLING: 'Tis as easily known from an English tumbril as an Inns of Court man is from one of us.

DORIMANT: Truly there is a bell-air in galleshes as well as men.

MEDLEY: But there are few so delicate to observe it.

SIR FOPLING: The world is generally very grossier here indeed.

LADY TOWNLEY: He's very fine.

EMILIA: Extreme proper.

SIR FOPLING: A slight suit I made to appear in at my first arrival, not worthy your consideration, ladies.

DORIMANT: The pantaloon is very well mounted.

SIR FOPLING: The tassels are new and pretty.

MEDLEY: I never saw a coat better cut.

SIR FOPLING: It makes me show long-waisted, and I think slender.

DORIMANT: That's th'shape our ladies dote on.

MEDLEY: Your breech though is a handful too high in my eye, Sir Fopling.

SIR FOPLING: Peace, Medley, I have wished it lower a thousand times, but a pox on't, 'twill not be.

LADY TOWNLEY: His gloves are well fringed, large and graceful.

SIR FOPLING: I was always eminent for being bien ganté.

1. *Equipage*: articles for personal ornament. Also retinue.
2. *Gallesh*: low-wheeled vehicle – Fr. *calèche*.

EMILIA: He wears nothing but what are originals of the most famous hands in Paris.

SIR FOPLING: You are in the right, madam.

LADY TOWNLEY: The suit.

SIR FOPLING: Barroy.

EMILIA: The garniture.

SIR FOPLING: Le Gras –

MEDLEY: The shoes.

SIR FOPLING: Piccard.

DORIMANT: The periwig.

SIR FOPLING: Chedreux.[1]

LADY TOWNLEY and EMILIA: The gloves.

SIR FOPLING: Orangerie. You know the smell, ladies. Dorimant, I could find in my heart for an amusement to have a gallantry with some of our English ladies.

DORIMANT: 'Tis a thing no less necessary to confirm the reputation of your wit than a duel will be to satisfy the town of your courage.

SIR FOPLING: Here was a woman yesterday –

DORIMANT: Mistress Loveit.

SIR FOPLING: You have named her!

DORIMANT: You cannot pitch on a better for your purpose.

SIR FOPLING: Prithee, what is she?

DORIMANT: A person of quality, and one who has a rest[2] of reputation enough to make the conquest considerable. Besides, I hear she likes you too!

SIR FOPLING: Methoughts she seemed, though, very reserved and uneasy all the time I entertained her.

DORIMANT: Grimace and affectation; you will see her i'th' Mall tonight.

SIR FOPLING: Prithee, let thee and I take the air together.

DORIMANT: I am engaged to Medley, but I'll meet you at Saint James', and give you some information upon the which you may regulate your proceedings.

SIR FOPLING: All the world will be in the Park tonight. Ladies, 'twere pity to keep so much beauty longer within

1. *Chedreux*: a fashionable wig-maker; also a wig invented by him.
2. *Rest*: residue, surplus.

doors, and rob the Ring[1] of all those charms that should adorn it. – Hey, page.

Enter PAGE, *and goes out again.*

See that all my people be ready. Dorimant, a revoir.

MEDLEY: A fine-mettled coxcomb.

DORIMANT: Brisk[2] and insipid.

MEDLEY: Pert and dull.

EMILIA: However you despise him, gentlemen, I'll lay my life he passes for a wit with many.

DORIMANT: That may very well be. Nature has her cheats, stums[3] a brain and puts sophisticate dullness often on the tasteless multitude for true wit and good humour. Medley, come.

MEDLEY: I must go a little way, I will meet you i'the Mall.

DORIMANT [*to the women*]: I'll walk through the garden thither, we shall meet anon and bow.

LADY TOWNLEY: Not tonight; we are engaged about a business the knowledge of which may make you laugh hereafter.

MEDLEY: Your servant, ladies.

DORIMANT: A revoir, as Sir Fopling says.

Exit MEDLEY *and* DORIMANT.

LADY TOWNLEY: The old man will be here immediately.

EMILIA: Let's expect[4] him i'th'garden.

LADY TOWNLEY: Go, you are a rogue.

EMILIA: I can't abide you.

Exeunt.

SCENE THREE

The Mall.
Enter HARRIET, YOUNG BELLAIR, *she pulling him.*

HARRIET: Come along.

YOUNG BELLAIR: And leave your mother?

---

1. *Ring*: see note p. 83.
2. *Brisk*: the word was used in an unfavourable sense.
3. *Stums*: to stum = re-ferment wine by adding stum or must; hence, to produce false sparkle or wit.   4. *Expect*: wait for.

HARRIET: Busy will be sent with a hue and cry after us; but that's no matter.

YOUNG BELLAIR: 'Twill look strangely in me.

HARRIET: She'll believe it a freak of mine, and never blame your manners.

YOUNG BELLAIR: What reverend acquaintance is that she has met?

HARRIET: A fellow beauty of the last king's time, though by the ruins you would hardly guess it.

Exeunt.
Enter DORIMANT *and crosses the stage.*
Enter YOUNG BELLAIR *and* HARRIET.

YOUNG BELLAIR: By this time your mother is in a fine taking.[1]

HARRIET: If your friend Mr Dorimant were but here now, that she might find me talking with him.

YOUNG BELLAIR: She does not know him, but dreads him, I hear, of all mankind.

HARRIET: She concludes if he does but speak to a woman she's undone, is on her knees every day to pray Heaven defend me from him.

YOUNG BELLAIR: You do not apprehend him so much as she does?

HARRIET: I never saw anything in him that was frightful.

YOUNG BELLAIR: On the contrary, have you not observed something extreme delightful in his wit and person?

HARRIET: He's agreeable and pleasant I must own, but he does so much affect being so, he displeases me.

YOUNG BELLAIR: Lord, madam, all he does and says is so easy and so natural.

HARRIET: Some men's verses seem so to the unskilful, but labour i'the one and affectation in the other to the judicious plainly appear.

YOUNG BELLAIR: I never heard him accused of affectation before.

Enter DORIMANT *and stares upon her.*

HARRIET: It passes on the easy town, who are favourably pleased to call it humour.

1. *Taking*: agitation.

Exit YOUNG BELLAIR *and* HARRIET.

DORIMANT: 'Tis she! It must be she, that lovely hair, that easy shape, those wanton eyes, and all those melting charms about her mouth, which Medley spoke of. I'll follow the lottery and put in for a prize with my friend Bellair.

Exit DORIMANT *repeating*:

> *In love the victors from the vanquished fly;*
> *They fly that wound, and they pursue that die.*[1]

Enter YOUNG BELLAIR *and* HARRIET *and after them* DORIMANT *standing at a distance.*

YOUNG BELLAIR: Most people prefer High Park[2] to this place.

HARRIET: It has the better reputation I confess; but I abominate the dull diversions there, the formal bows, the affected smiles, the silly by-words, and amorous tweers[3] in passing. Here one meets with a little conversation now and then.

YOUNG BELLAIR: These conversations have been fatal to some of your sex, madam.

HARRIET: It may be so. Because some who want temper have been undone by gaming, must others who have it wholly deny themselves the pleasure of play?

DORIMANT [*coming up gently, and bowing to her*]: Trust me, it were unreasonable, madam.

HARRIET: Lord! Who's this? [*She starts and looks grave.*]

YOUNG BELLAIR: Dorimant.

DORIMANT: Is this the woman your father would have you marry?

YOUNG BELLAIR: It is.

DORIMANT: Her name?

YOUNG BELLAIR: Harriet.

DORIMANT: I am not mistaken. She's handsome.

YOUNG BELLAIR: Talk to her, her wit is better than her face. We were wishing for you but now.

DORIMANT [*to* HARRIET]: Overcast with seriousness o'the

---

1. *In love . . . die*: closing couplet of Waller's *To a Friend, of the Different Success of their Loves.*

2. *High Park*: Hyde Park.

3. *Tweers*: sly glances.

sudden! A thousand smiles were shining in that face but now; I never saw so quick a change of weather.

HARRIET [*aside*]: I feel as great a change within; but he shall never know it.

DORIMANT: You were talking of play, madam. Pray, what may be your stint?[1]

HARRIET: A little harmless discourse in public walks, or at most, an appointment in a box barefaced at the playhouse. You are for masks and private meetings where women engage for all they are worth, I hear.

DORIMANT: I have been used to deep play, but I can make one at small game, when I like my gamester well.

HARRIET: And be so unconcerned you'll ha' no pleasure in't.

DORIMANT: Where there is a considerable sum to be won, the hope of drawing people in makes every trifle considerable.

HARRIET: The sordidness of men's natures, I know, makes 'em willing to flatter and comply with the rich, though they are sure never to be the better for 'em.

DORIMANT: 'Tis in their power to do us good, and we despair not but at some time or other they may be willing.

HARRIET: To men who have fared in this town like you, 'twould be a great mortification to live on hope. Could you keep a Lent for a mistress?

DORIMANT: In expectation of a happy Easter, and though time be very precious, think forty days well lost to gain your favour.

HARRIET: Mr Bellair, let us walk, 'tis time to leave him. Men grow dull when they begin to be particular.

DORIMANT: Y'are mistaken; flattery will not ensue, though I know y'are greedy of the praises of the whole Mall.

HARRIET: You do me wrong.

DORIMANT: I do not; as I followed you, I observed how you were pleased when the fops cried *She's handsome, very handsome, by God she is*, and whispered aloud your name. The thousand several forms you put your face into then, to make yourself more agreeable! How wantonly you

1. *Stint*: limit.

played with your head, flung back your locks, and looked
smilingly over your shoulder at 'em!

HARRIET: I do not go begging the men's as you do the
ladies' good liking, with a sly softness in your looks and a
gentle slowness in your bows as you pass by 'em – as thus,
sir [*acts him*]. Is not this like you?

Enter LADY WOODVILL *and* BUSY.

YOUNG BELLAIR: Your mother, madam. [*Pulls* HARRIET.
She composes herself.]

LADY WOODVILL: Ah, my dear child Harriet!

BUSY: Now is she so pleased with finding her agen she cannot
chide her.

LADY WOODVILL: Come away!

DORIMANT: 'Tis now but high Mall, madam, the most entertaining time of all the evening.

HARRIET: I would fain see that Dorimant, mother, you so
cry out of for a monster. He's in the Mall I hear.

LADY WOODVILL: Come away then! The plague is here and
you should dread the infection.

YOUNG BELLAIR: You may be misinformed of the gentleman.

LADY WOODVILL: Oh no! I hope you do not know him. He
is the prince of all the devils in the town, delights in nothing but in rapes and riots.

DORIMANT: If you did but hear him speak, madam!

LADY WOODVILL: Oh! He has a tongue they say would tempt
the angels to a second fall.

Enter SIR FOPLING, *with his Equipage, six Footmen, and a
Page.*

SIR FOPLING: Hey, Champaine,[1] Norman, La Rose, La
Fleur, La Tour, La Verdure. Dorimant –

LADY WOODVILL: Here, here he is among this rout, he names
him. Come away Harriet, come away.

Exit LADY WOODVILL, HARRIET, BUSY *and* YOUNG
BELLAIR.

DORIMANT: This fool's coming has spoiled all. She's gone,
but she has left a pleasing image of herself behind, that
wanders in my soul – it must not settle there.

SIR FOPLING: What reverie is this! Speak man.

1. *Champaine, etc.*: the names of Sir Fopling's footmen.

DORIMANT:
>   *Snatched from myself how far behind*
>   *Already I behold the shore!*[1]

Enter MEDLEY.

MEDLEY: Dorimant, a discovery! I met with Bellair.

DORIMANT: You can tell me no news sir, I know all.

MEDLEY: How do you like the daughter?

DORIMANT: You never came so near truth in your life as you did in her description.

MEDLEY: What think you of the mother?

DORIMANT: Whatever I think of her, she thinks very well of me I find.

MEDLEY: Did she know you?

DORIMANT: She did not; whether she does now or no I know not. Here was a pleasant scene towards, when in came Sir Fopling, mustering up his equipage, and at the latter end named me, and frighted her away.

MEDLEY: Loveit and Belinda are not far off, I saw 'em alight at St James'.

DORIMANT: Sir Fopling hark you, a word or two [*whispers*]. Look you do not want assurance.

SIR FOPLING: I never do on these occasions.

DORIMANT: Walk on, we must not be seen together; make your advantage of what I have told you, the next turn you will meet the lady.

SIR FOPLING: Hey – follow me all.

Exit SIR FOPLING *and his Equipage.*

DORIMANT: Medley, you shall see good sport anon between Loveit and this Fopling.

MEDLEY: I thought there was something toward by that whisper.

DORIMANT: You know a worthy principle of hers?

MEDLEY: Not to be so much as civil to a man who speaks to her in the presence of him she professes to love.

DORIMANT: I have encouraged Fopling to talk to her to-night.

MEDLEY: Now you are here she will go nigh to beat him.

1. *Snatched from . . . the shore*: third and fourth lines of Waller's *Of Loving at First Sight.*

DORIMANT: In the humour she's in, her love will make her do some very extravagant thing, doubtless.

MEDLEY: What was Belinda's business with you at my Lady Townley's?

DORIMANT: To get me to meet Loveit here in order to an eclercisement. I made some difficulty of it, and have prepared this rencounter to make good my jealousy.

MEDLEY: Here they come!

Enter LOVEIT, BELINDA *and* PERT.

DORIMANT: I'll meet her and provoke her with a deal of dumb civility in passing by, then turn short and be behind her when Sir Fopling sets upon her –

> *See how unregarded now*
> *That piece of Beauty passes –* [1]

Exit DORIMANT *and* MEDLEY.

BELINDA: How wonderfully respectfully he bowed!

PERT: He's always over-mannerly when he has done a mischief.

BELINDA: Methoughts indeed at the same time he had a strange despising countenance.

PERT: The unlucky look he thinks becomes him.

BELINDA: I was afraid you would have spoke to him, my dear.

MRS LOVEIT: I would have died first. He shall no more find me the loving fool he has done.

BELINDA: You love him still!

MRS LOVEIT: No.

PERT: I wish you did not.

MRS LOVEIT: I do not, and I will have you think so. What made you hale me to this odious place, Belinda?

BELINDA: I hate to be hulched up [2] in a coach; walking is much better.

MRS LOVEIT: Would we could meet Sir Fopling now.

BELINDA: Lord! Would you not avoid him?

MRS LOVEIT: I would make him all the advances that may be.

BELINDA: That would confirm Dorimant's suspicion, my dear.

1. *See how ... Beauty passes*: the opening lines of Suckling's Sonnet I with the first word ('Dost') left out.   2. *Hulched up*: bent double.

MRS LOVEIT: He is not jealous, but I will make him so, and be revenged a way he little thinks on.

BELINDA [*aside*]: If she should make him jealous, that may make him fond of her again. I must dissuade her from it. Lord! My dear, this will certainly make him hate you.

MRS LOVEIT: 'Twill make him uneasy though he does not care for me; I know the effects of jealousy on men of his proud temper.

BELINDA: 'Tis a fantastic remedy, its operations are dangerous and uncertain.

MRS LOVEIT: 'Tis the strongest cordial we can give to dying love. It often brings it back when there's no sign of life remaining. But I design not so much the reviving his as my revenge.

    Enter SIR FOPLING *and his Equipage.*

SIR FOPLING: Hey! Bid the coachman send home four of his horses and bring the coach to Whitehall. I'll walk over the Park. – Madam, the honour of kissing your fair hands is a happiness I missed this afternoon at my Lady Townley's.

MRS LOVEIT: You were very obliging, Sir Fopling, the last time I saw you there.

SIR FOPLING: The preference was due to your wit and beauty. Madam, your servant. There never was so sweet an evening.

BELINDA: 'T has drawn all the rabble of the town hither.

SIR FOPLING: 'Tis pity there's not an order made that none but the beau monde should walk here.

MRS LOVEIT: 'Twould add much to the beauty of the place. See what a sort of nasty fellows are coming.

    Enter three[1] *ill-fashioned fellows, singing:*
        'Tis not for kisses alone, etc.

MRS LOVEIT: Fo! Their periwigs are scented with tobacco so strong –

SIR FOPLING: It overcomes our pulvilio.[2] – Methinks I smell the coffee-house they come from.

FIRST MAN: Dorimant's convenient, Madam Loveit.

1. *Three*: Q mentions four. I have followed Verity in reducing the number (see Dramatis Personae).
2. *Pulvilio*: scented powder.

SECOND MAN: I like the oily[1] buttock with her.

THIRD MAN: What spruce prig is that?

FIRST MAN: A caravan lately come from Paris.

SECOND MAN: Peace, they smoke.[2]

All of them coughing.

Exit singing:

      There's something else to be done, etc.

Enter DORIMANT *and* MEDLEY.

DORIMANT: They're engaged –

MEDLEY: She entertains him as if she liked him.

DORIMANT: Let us go forward – seem earnest in discourse and shew ourselves. Then you shall see how she'll use him.

BELINDA: Yonder's Dorimant, my dear.

MRS LOVEIT: I see him, he comes insulting; but I will disappoint him in his expectation. [*Aside to* SIR FOPLING] I like this pretty nice humour of yours, Sir Fopling. – With what a loathing eye he looked upon those fellows!

SIR FOPLING: I sat near one of 'em at a play today and was almost poisoned with a pair of cordivant[3] gloves he wears.

MRS LOVEIT: Oh! Filthy cordivant, how I hate the smell! [*Laughs in a loud affected way.*]

SIR FOPLING: Did you observe, madam, how their cravats hung loose an inch from their neck, and what a frightful air it gave 'em?

MRS LOVEIT: Oh, I took particular notice of one that is always spruced up with a deal of dirty sky-coloured ribbon.

BELINDA: That's one of the walking flageolets who haunt the Mall o'nights.

MRS LOVEIT: Oh! I remember him! H' has a hollow tooth enough to spoil the sweetness of an evening.

SIR FOPLING: I have seen the tallest walk the streets with a dainty pair of boxes,[4] neatly buckled on.

MRS LOVEIT: And a little footboy at his heels pocket-high, with a flat-cap, a dirty face –

    1. *Oily*: greasy, fat.
    2. *Smoke*: suspect (that they are being talked of).
    3. *Cordivant*: Cordovan leather. Cordwain.
    4. *Boxes*: overshoes (?).

SIR FOPLING: And a snotty nose.

MRS LOVEIT: O odious! There's many of my own sex with that Holborn equipage trig[1] to Grey's-Inn Walks, and now and then travail hither on a Sunday.

MEDLEY: She takes no notice of you.

DORIMANT: Damn her! I am jealous of a counter-plot.

MRS LOVEIT: Your liveries are the finest, Sir Fopling. – Oh that page! That page is the prettiliest dressed. – They are all Frenchmen?

SIR FOPLING: There's one damned English blockhead among 'em; you may know him by his meine.[2]

MRS LOVEIT: Oh! That's he, that's he. What do you call him?

SIR FOPLING: Hey – I know not what to call him –

MRS LOVEIT: What's your name?

FOOTMAN: John Trott, madam!

SIR FOPLING: O unsufferable! Trott, Trott, Trott! There's nothing so barbarous as the names of our English servants. What countryman are you sirrah?

FOOTMAN: Hampshire, sir.

SIR FOPLING: Then Hampshire be your name. Hey, Hampshire!

MRS LOVEIT: O that sound, that sound becomes the mouth of a man of quality!

MEDLEY: Dorimant, you look a little bashful on the matter!

DORIMANT: She dissembles better than I thought she could have done.

MEDLEY: You have tempted her with too luscious a bait. She bites at the coxcomb.

DORIMANT: She cannot fall from loving me to that!

MEDLEY: You begin to be jealous in earnest.

DORIMANT: Of one I do not love.

MEDLEY: You did love her.

DORIMANT: The fit has long been over.

MEDLEY: But I have known men fall into dangerous relapses when they have found a woman inclining to another.

DORIMANT [to himself]: He guesses the secret of my heart! I

1. *Trig*: walk smartly.
2. *Meine*: meinie (?), retinue, crew; or perhaps a misprint for 'mien'.

am concerned, but dare not show it, lest Belinda should mistrust all I have done to gain her.

BELINDA [*aside*]: I have watched his look, and find no alteration there. Did he love her, some signs of jealousy would have appeared.

DORIMANT: I hope this happy evening, madam, has reconciled you to the scandalous Mall. We shall have you now hankering here agen . . .

MRS LOVEIT: Sir Fopling, will you walk?

SIR FOPLING: I am all obedience, madam.

MRS LOVEIT: Come along then, and let's agree to be malicious on all the ill-fashioned things we meet.

SIR FOPLING: We'll make a critique on the whole Mall, madam.

MRS LOVEIT: Belinda, you shall engage –

BELINDA: To the reserve of our friends, my dear.

MRS LOVEIT: No! No exceptions!

SIR FOPLING: We'll sacrifice all to our diversion.

MRS LOVEIT: All, all.

SIR FOPLING: All.

BELINDA: All? Then let it be.

   Exit SIR FOPLING, LOVEIT, BELINDA, *and* PERT, *laughing*.

MEDLEY: Would you had brought some more of your friends, Dorimant, to have been witnesses of Sir Fopling's disgrace and your triumph.

DORIMANT: 'Twere unreasonable to desire you not to laugh at me; but pray do not expose me to the town this day or two.

MEDLEY: By that time you hope to have regained your credit?

DORIMANT: I know she hates Fopling, and only makes use of him in hope to work me on agen; had it not been for some powerful considerations which will be removed tomorrow morning, I had made her pluck off this mask, and shew the passion that lies panting under.

   Enter a FOOTMAN.

MEDLEY: Here comes a man from Bellair, with news of your last adventure.

DORIMANT: I am glad he sent him. I long to know the consequence of our parting.

FOOTMAN: Sir, my master desires you to come to my Lady Townley's presently, and bring Mr Medley with you. My Lady Woodvill and her daughter are there.

MEDLEY: Then all's well, Dorimant.

FOOTMAN: They have sent for the fiddles and mean to dance. He bid me tell you, sir, the old lady does not know you, and would have you own yourself to be Mr Courtage. They are all prepared to receive you by that name.

DORIMANT: That foppish admirer of quality, who flatters the very meat at honourable tables, and never offers love to a woman below a lady-grandmother!

MEDLEY: You know the character you are to act, I see!

DORIMANT: This is Harriet's contrivance – wild, witty, lovesome, beautiful and young.[1] – Come along Medley.

MEDLEY: This new woman would well supply the loss of Loveit.

DORIMANT: That business must not end so. Before tomorrow sun is set, I will revenge and clear it.

      And you and Loveit to her cost shall find
      I fathom all the depths of womankind.

Exeunt.

1. *Wild . . . young*: adaptation of l. 13 of Waller's *Of the Danger His Majesty Escaped in the Road at St Andrews.*

Act Four

(LADY WOODVILL's *lodging.*)
The scene opens with the fiddles playing a country dance.
Enter DORIMANT, LADY WOODVILL, YOUNG BELLAIR,
and MRS HARRIET, OLD BELLAIR, *and* EMILIA, MR
MEDLEY *and* LADY TOWNLEY, *as having just ended the dance.*

OLD BELLAIR: So, so, so! A smart bout, a very smart bout a-dod!

LADY TOWNLEY: How do you like Emilia's dancing, brother?

OLD BELLAIR: Not at all! Not at all!

LADY TOWNLEY: You speak not what you think, I am sure.

OLD BELLAIR: No matter for that, go, bid her dance no more, it don't become her, it don't become her, tell her I say so. [*Aside*] A-dod I love her.

DORIMANT [*to* LADY WOODVILL]: All people mingle nowadays, madam. And in public places, women of quality have the least respect showed 'em.

LADY WOODVILL: I protest you say the truth, Mr Courtage.

DORIMANT: Forms and ceremonies, the only things that uphold quality and greatness, are now shamefully laid aside and neglected.

LADY WOODVILL: Well, this is not the women's age, let 'em think what they will. Lewdness is the business now, love was the business in my time.

DORIMANT: The women indeed are little beholding to the young men of this age; they're generally only dull admirers of themselves, and make their court to nothing but their periwigs and their cravats, and would be more concerned for the disordering of 'em, tho' on a good occasion, than a young maid would be for the tumbling of her head or handkercher.

LADY WOODVILL: I protest you hit 'em.

DORIMANT: They are very assiduous to show themselves at court well-dressed to the women of quality, but their business is with the stale mistresses of the town, who are prepared to receive their lazy addresses by industrious old lovers who have cast 'em off and made 'em easy.

HARRIET: He fits my mother's humour so well, a little more and she'll dance a kissing dance with him anon.

MEDLEY: Dutifully observed, madam.

DORIMANT: They pretend to be great critics in beauty; by their talk you would think they liked no face, and yet can dote on an ill one, if it belong to a laundress or a tailor's daughter. They cry a woman's past her prime at twenty, decayed at four and twenty, old and unsufferable at thirty.

LADY WOODVILL: Unsufferable at thirty! That they are in the wrong, Mr Courtage. At five and thirty, there are living proofs enough to convince 'em.

DORIMANT: Ay madam! There's Mrs Setlooks, Mrs Droplip, and my Lady Lowd! Shew me among all our opening buds a face that promises so much beauty as the remains of theirs.

LADY WOODVILL: The depraved appetite of this vicious age tastes nothing but green fruit, and loaths it when 'tis kindly[1] ripened.

DORIMANT: Else so many deserving women, madam, would not be so untimely neglected.

LADY WOODVILL: I protest, Mr Courtage, a dozen such good men as you would be enough to atone for that wicked Dorimant, and all the under debauchees of the town.

HARRIET, EMILIA, YOUNG BELLAIR, MEDLEY, LADY TOWNLEY, *break out into a laughter.*

What's the matter there?

MEDLEY: A pleasant mistake, madam, that a lady has made, occasions a little laughter.

OLD BELLAIR: Come, come, you keep 'em idle! They are impatient till the fiddles play again.

DORIMANT: You are not weary, madam?

LADY WOODVILL: One dance more! I cannot refuse you, Mr Courtage.

They dance. After the dance, OLD BELLAIR, *singing and dancing up to* EMILIA.

EMILIA: You are very active, sir.

1. *Kindly*: by due process of nature (kind).

OLD BELLAIR: A-dod sirrah, when I was a young fellow I could ha' capered up to my woman's gorget.[1]

DORIMANT: You are willing to[2] rest yourself, madam.

LADY TOWNLEY: We'll walk into my chamber and sit down.

MEDLEY: Leave us Mr Courtage; he's a dancer, and the young ladies are not weary yet.

LADY WOODVILL: We'll send him out again.

HARRIET: If you do not quickly, I know where to send for Mr Dorimant.

LADY WOODVILL: This girl's head, Mr Courtage, is ever running on that wild fellow.

DORIMANT: 'Tis well you have got her a good husband madam; that will settle it.

Exit LADY TOWNLEY, LADY WOODVILL *and* DORIMANT.

OLD BELLAIR [*to* EMILIA]: A-dod sweetheart, be advised, and do not throw thyself away on a young idle fellow.

EMILIA: I have no such intention, sir.

OLD BELLAIR: Have a little patience! Thou shalt have the man I spake of. A-dod he loves thee, and will make a good husband, but no words –

EMILIA: But sir –

OLD BELLAIR: No answer – out a pise! Peace, and think on't.
    Enter DORIMANT.

DORIMANT: Your company is desired within, sir.

OLD BELLAIR: I go, I go, good Mr Courtage. – Fare you well! [*To* EMILIA] Go, I'll see you no more.

EMILIA: What have I done sir?

OLD BELLAIR: You are ugly, you are ugly! Is she not, Mr Courtage?

EMILIA: Better words or I sha'nt abide you.

OLD BELLAIR: Out a pise – a-dod, what does she say? Hit her a pat for me there. [*Exit* OLD BELLAIR.]

MEDLEY: You have charms for the whole family.

DORIMANT: You'll spoil all with some unseasonable jest, Medley.

MEDLEY: You see I confine my tongue, and am content to be a bare spectator, much contrary to my nature.

---

1. *Gorget*: wimple or neck ornament.
2. *Willing to*: wanting to.

EMILIA: Methinks, Mr Dorimant, my Lady Woodvill is (not) a little fond of you.

DORIMANT: Would her daughter were.

MEDLEY: It may be you may find her so. Try her; you have an opportunity.

DORIMANT: And I will not lose it. Bellair, here's a lady has something to say to you.

YOUNG BELLAIR: I wait upon her. Mr Medley, we have both business with you.

DORIMANT: Get you all together then. [*To* HARRIET] That demure curtsy is not amiss in jest, but do not think in earnest it becomes you.

HARRIET: Affectation is catching, I find; from your grave bow I got it.

DORIMANT: Where had you all that scorn and coldness in your look?

HARRIET: From nature sir; pardon my want of art. I have not learnt those softnesses and languishings which now in faces are so much in fashion.

DORIMANT: You need 'em not; you have a sweetness of your own, if you would but calm your frowns and let it settle.

HARRIET: My eyes are wild and wand'ring like my passions, and cannot yet be tied to rules of charming.

DORIMANT: Women indeed have commonly a method of managing those messengers of love. Now they will look as if they would kill, and anon they will look as if they were dying. They point and rebate their glances the better to invite us.

HARRIET: I like this variety well enough, but hate the set face that always looks as it would say, Come love me – a woman who at plays makes the deux yeux[1] to a whole audience and at home cannot forbear 'em to her monkey!

DORIMANT: Put on a gentle smile and let me see how well it will become you.

HARRIET: I am sorry my face does not please you as it is, but I shall not be complaisant and change it.

DORIMANT: Though you are obstinate, I know 'tis capable of improvement, and shall do you justice, madam, if I chance

1. *Deux yeux*: doux yeux.

to be at court, when the critics of the Circle pass their judgement; for thither you must come.

HARRIET: And expect to be taken in pieces, have all my features examined, every motion censured, and on the whole be condemned to be but pretty, or a beauty of the lowest rate? What think you?

DORIMANT: The women, nay, the very lovers who belong to the drawing-room will maliciously allow you more than that; they always grant what is apparent, that they may the better be believed when they name concealed faults they cannot easily be disproved in.

HARRIET: Beauty runs as great a risk exposed at court as wit does on the stage, where the ugly and the foolish all are free to censure.

DORIMANT [*aside*]: I love her, and dare not let her know it. I fear sh'as an ascendant o'er me and may revenge the wrongs I have done her sex. [*To her*] Think of making a party, madam; love will engage.

HARRIET: You make me start! I did not think to have heard of love from you.

DORIMANT: I never knew what 'twas to have a settled ague yet, but now and then have had irregular fits.

HARRIET: Take heed, sickness after long health is commonly more violent and dangerous.

DORIMANT [*aside*]: I have took the infection from her, and feel the disease now spreading in me. [*To her*] Is the name of love so frightful that you dare not stand it?

HARRIET: 'Twill do little execution out of your mouth on me, I am sure.

DORIMANT: It has been fatal –

HARRIET: To some easy women, but we are not all born to one destiny. I was informed you use to laugh at love, and not make it.

DORIMANT: The time has been, but now I must speak –

HARRIET: If it be on that idle subject, I will put on my serious look, turn my head carelessly from you, drop my lip, let my eyelids fall, and hang half o'er my eyes – thus – while you buzz a speech of an hour long in my ear, and I answer never a word. Why do you not begin?

DORIMANT: That the company may take notice how passionately I make advances of love, and how disdainfully you receive 'em.

HARRIET: When your love's grown strong enough to make you bear being laughed at, I'll give you leave to trouble me with it. Till when, pray forbear, sir.

Enter SIR FOPLING *and others in masks.*

DORIMANT: What's here, masquerades?

HARRIET: I thought that foppery had been left off, and people might have been in private with a fiddle.

DORIMANT: 'Tis endeavoured to be kept on foot still by some who find themselves the more acceptable the less they are known.

YOUNG BELLAIR: This must be Sir Fopling.

MEDLEY: That extraordinary habit shews it.

YOUNG BELLAIR: What are the rest?

MEDLEY: A company of French rascals whom he picked up in Paris and has brought over to be his dancing equipage on these occasions. Make him own himself; a fool is very troublesome when he presumes he is incognito.

SIR FOPLING [*to* HARRIET]: Do you know me?

HARRIET: Ten to one but I guess at you!

SIR FOPLING: Are you women as fond of a vizard[1] as we men are?

HARRIET: I am very fond of a vizard that covers a face I do not like, sir.

YOUNG BELLAIR: Here are no masks you see, sir, but those which came with you. This was intended a private meeting, but because you look like a gentleman, if you will discover yourself and we know you to be such, you shall be welcome.

SIR FOPLING [*pulling off his mask*]: Dear Bellair.

MEDLEY: Sir Fopling! How came you hither?

SIR FOPLING: Faith, as I was coming late from Whitehall, after the king's couchée,[2] one of my people told me he had heard fiddles at my Lady Townley's, and –

DORIMANT: You need not say any more, sir.

1. *Vizard*: with a play on the secondary sense of prostitute.
2. *Couchée*: evening reception.

SIR FOPLING: Dorimant, let me kiss thee.

DORIMANT: Hark you, Sir Fopling – [*Whispers.*]

SIR FOPLING: Enough, enough, Courtage. A pretty kind of young woman that, Medley. I observed her in the Mall more eveliè[1] than our English women commonly are. Prithee, what is she?

MEDLEY: The most noted coquette in town; beware of her.

SIR FOPLING: Let her be what she will, I know how to take my measures. In Paris the mode is to flatter the prudè, laugh at the faux-proudè, make serious love to the demi-proudè, and only rally with the coquetté. Medley, what think you?

MEDLEY: That for all this smattering of the mathematics, you may be out in your judgement at tennis.

SIR FOPLING: What a coque-à-lasne[2] is this? I talk of women and thou answer'st tennis.

MEDLEY: Mistakes will be for want of apprehension.

SIR FOPLING: I am very glad of the acquaintance I have with this family.

MEDLEY: My Lady truly is a good woman.

SIR FOPLING: Ah Dorimant, Courtage I would say, would thou hadst spent the last winter in Paris with me. When thou wert there, La Corneùs and Sallyes[3] were the only habitudes we had; a comedian would have been a boné fortune. No stranger ever passed his time so well as I did some months before I came over. I was well received in a dozen families, where all the women of quality used to visit. I have intrigues to tell thee more pleasant than ever thou read'st in a novel.

HARRIET: Write 'em, sir, and oblige us women. Our language wants such little stories.

SIR FOPLING: Writing, madam's a mechanic part of wit. A gentleman should never go beyond a song or a billet.

HARRIET: Bussie[4] was a gentleman.

---

1. *Eveliè*: Fr. *éveillée* ('awakened').
2. *Coque-à-lasne*: coq-à-l'âne: incoherent chatter.
3. *La Corneùs and Sallyes*: possibly Mesdames Cornuel and Selles, minor literary personages in late seventeenth-century France.
4. *Bussie ... Rabutin*: Roger de Rabutin, Comte de Bussy (1618–93),

SIR FOPLING: Who, D'Ambois?

MEDLEY: Was there ever such a brisk blockhead?

HARRIET: Not D'Ambois, sir, but Rabutin, he who writ the *Loves of France*.

SIR FOPLING: That may be, madam. Many gentlemen do things that are below 'em. Damn your authors, Courtage; women are the prettiest things we can fool away our time with.

HARRIET: I hope ye have wearied yourself tonight at court, sir, and will not think of fooling with anybody here.

SIR FOPLING: I cannot complain of my fortune there, madam. Dorimant –

DORIMANT: Again!

SIR FOPLING: Courtage, a pox on't! I have something to tell thee. When I had made my court within, I came out and flung myself upon the mat under the state[1] i'th'outward room, i'th'midst of half a dozen beauties who were withdrawn to jeer among themselves, as they called it.

DORIMANT: Did you know 'em?

SIR FOPLING: Not one of 'em by heav'ns, not I! But they were all your friends.

DORIMANT: How are you sure of that?

SIR FOPLING: Why, we laughed at all the town, spared nobody but yourself; they found me a man for their purpose.

DORIMANT: I know you are malicious to your power.

SIR FOPLING: And faith, I had occasion to shew it, for I never saw more gaping fools at a ball or on a birthday.

DORIMANT: You learned who the women were.

SIR FOPLING: No matter, they frequent the drawing-room.

DORIMANT: And entertain themselves pleasantly at the expense of all the fops who come there.

SIR FOPLING: That's their business. Faith, I sifted 'em and find they have a sort of wit among them. [*Pinches a tallow candle.*] Ah, filthy!

DORIMANT: Look, he has been pinching the tallow candle.

---

wrote the celebrated *Histoire Amoreuse des Gaules*. Characteristically, Sir Fopling gets him mixed up with an earlier Bussy (d'Ambois), the hero of Chapman's tragedy.

1. *State*: canopy.

SIR FOPLING: How can you breathe in a room where there's grease frying? Dorimant, thou art intimate with my Lady. Advise her for her own sake and the good company that comes hither to burn wax lights.

HARRIET: What are these masquerades who stand so obsequiously at a distance?

SIR FOPLING: A set of balladins whom I picked out of the best in France and brought over, with a flutes deux or two, my servants. They shall entertain you.

HARRIET: I had rather see you dance yourself, Sir Fopling.

SIR FOPLING: And I had rather do it – all the company knows it – but madam –

MEDLEY: Come, come, no excuses, Sir Fopling.

SIR FOPLING: By heav'ns, Medley –

MEDLEY: Like a woman I find you must be struggled with before one brings you what you desire.

HARRIET [aside]: Can he dance?

EMILIA: And fence and sing too, if you'll believe him.

DORIMANT: He has no more excellence in his heels than in in his head. He went to Paris a plain bashful English blockhead, and is returned a fine undertaking French fop.

MEDLEY: I cannot prevail.

SIR FOPLING: Do not think it want of complaisance,[1] madam.

HARRIET: You are too well bred to want that, Sir Fopling. I believe it want of power.

SIR FOPLING: By heavens, and so it is. I have sat up so damn'd late and drunk so curs'd hard since I came to this lewd town that I am fit for nothing but low dancing now, a corant,[2] a borée,[3] or a minuet. But St André[4] tells me, if I will but be regular, in one month I shall rise agen. Pox on this debauchery! [Endeavours at a caper.]

EMILIA: I have heard your dancing much commended.

SIR FOPLING: It had the good fortune to please in Paris. I

1. *Complaisance*: desire to please.
2. *Corant*: Fr. *courante*, literally a 'running dance'.
3. *Borée*: Fr. *bourrée*, a dance of the Auvergne.
4. *St André*: a famous French dancing master who often appeared at the English court as well.

was judged to rise within an inch as high as the Basqué[1] in an entry I danced there.

HARRIET: I am mightily taken with this fool. – Let us sit; here's a seat, Sir Fopling.

SIR FOPLING: At your feet, madam; I can be nowhere so much at ease. By your leave, gown.

HARRIET and EMILIA: Ah, you'll spoil it!

SIR FOPLING: No matter, my clothes are my creatures. I make 'em to make my court to you ladies. Hey . . .

Dance

Qu'on comencè – to an English dancer English motions. I was forced to entertain this fellow, one of my set miscarrying – O horrid! Leave your damn'd manner of dancing, and put on the French air; have you not a pattern before you – pretty well! Imitation in time may bring him to something.

After the dance, enter OLD BELLAIR, LADY WOODVILL *and* LADY TOWNLEY.

OLD BELLAIR: Hey a-dod! What have we here, a mumming?

LADY WOODVILL: Where's my daughter? Harriet!

DORIMANT: Here, here, madam. I know not but under the disguises there may be dangerous sparks. I gave the young lady warning.

LADY WOODVILL: Lord, I am so obliged to you, Mr Courtage.

HARRIET: Lord, how you admire this man!

LADY WOODVILL: What have you to except against him?

HARRIET: He's a fop.

LADY WOODVILL: He's not a Dorimant, a wild extravagant fellow of the times.

HARRIET: He's a man made up of forms and commonplaces sucked out of the remaining lees of the last age.

LADY WOODVILL: He's so good a man that were you not engaged . . .

LADY TOWNLEY: You'll have but little night to sleep in.

LADY WOODVILL: Lord! 'Tis perfect day.

DORIMANT [*aside*]: The hour is almost come, I appointed Belinda, and I am not so foppishly in love here to forget; I am flesh and blood yet.

1. *Basqué*: skirt of a coat.

LADY TOWNLEY: I am very sensible, madam.

LADY WOODVILL: Lord, madam!

HARRIET: Look in what a struggle is my poor mother yonder!

YOUNG BELLAIR: She has much ado to bring out the compliment.

DORIMANT: She strains hard for it.

HARRIET: See, see! Her head tottering, her eyes staring, and her under-lip trembling –

DORIMANT: Now, now, she's in the very convulsions of her civility. [*Aside*] 'Sdeath, I shall lose Belinda; I must fright her hence, she'll be an hour in this fit of good manners else. [*To* LADY WOODVILL] Do you not know Sir Fopling, madam?

LADY WOODVILL: I have seen that face – O heaven, 'tis the same we met in the Mall. How came he here?

DORIMANT: A fiddle in this town is a kind of fop-call; no sooner it strikes up, but the house is besieged with an army of masquerades straight.

LADY WOODVILL: Lord, I tremble, Mr Courtage! For certain Dorimant is in the company.

DORIMANT: I cannot confidently say he is not; you had best begone. I will wait upon you. Your daughter is in the hands of Mr Bellair.

LADY WOODVILL: I'll see her before me. Harriet, come away.

YOUNG BELLAIR: Lights! Lights!

LADY TOWNLEY: Light down there.

OLD BELLAIR: A-dod it needs not –

DORIMANT: Call my Lady Woodvill's coach to the door quickly.

OLD BELLAIR: Stay Mr Medley, let the young fellows do that duty; we will drink a glass of wine together, 'tis good after dancing. What mumming spark is that?

MEDLEY: He is not to be comprehended in few words.

SIR FOPLING: Hey, La Tour!

MEDLEY: Whither away, Sir Fopling?

SIR FOPLING: I have business with Courtage –

MEDLEY: He'll but put the ladies into their coach and come up agen.

OLD BELLAIR: In the meantime I'll call for a bottle. [*Exit* OLD BELLAIR.]

    Enter YOUNG BELLAIR.

MEDLEY: Where's Dorimant?

YOUNG BELLAIR: Stol'n home. He has had business waiting for him there all this night, I believe, by an impatience I observed in him.

MEDLEY: Very likely, 'tis but dissembling drunkenness, railing at his friends, and the kind soul will embrace the blessing and forget the tedious expectation.

SIR FOPLING: I must speak with him before I sleep.

YOUNG BELLAIR: Emilia and I are resolved on that business.

MEDLEY: Peace, here's your father.

    Enter OLD BELLAIR, *and Butler with a bottle of wine.*

OLD BELLAIR: The women are all gone to bed. Fill, boy! Mr Medley, begin a health.

MEDLEY [*whispers*]: To Emilia.

OLD BELLAIR: Out a pise! She's a rogue and I'll not pledge you.

MEDLEY: I know you will.

OLD BELLAIR: A-dod, drink it then.

SIR FOPLING: Let us have the new Bachique.[1]

OLD BELLAIR: A-dod, that is a hard word! What does it mean sir?

MEDLEY: A catch or drinking song.

OLD BELLAIR: Let us have it then.

SIR FOPLING: Fill the glasses round, and draw up in a body. Hey, music!

    They sing:

    The pleasures of love and the joys of good wine,

    To perfect our happiness wisely we join.

    We to beauty all day

    Give the soveraign sway,

    And her favourite nymphs devoutly obey.

    At the plays we are constantly making our court

    And when they are ended we follow the sport.

    To the Mall and the Park

    Where we love till 'tis dark;

        1. *Bachique*: chant bacchique, drinking song.

Then sparkling champagne
Puts an end to their reign;
It quickly recovers
Poor languishing lovers,
Makes us frolic and gay, and drowns all our sorrow.
But alas! We relapse again on the morrow.
    Let every man stand
    With his glass in his hand,
And briskly discharge at the word of command.
    Here's a health to all those
    Whom tonight we depose.
Wine and beauty by turns great souls should inspire.
Present all together; and now boys give fire –

OLD BELLAIR: A-dod, a pretty business, and very merry.

SIR FOPLING: Hark you, Medley, let you and I take the fiddles and go waken Dorimant.

MEDLEY: We shall do him a courtesy, if it be as I guess. For after the fatigue of this night, he'll quickly have his bellyful, and be glad of an occasion to cry, take away Handy.

YOUNG BELLAIR: I'll go with you, and there we'll consult about affairs, Medley.

OLD BELLAIR [looks on his watch]: A-dod, 'tis six o'clock.

SIR FOPLING: Let's away then.

OLD BELLAIR: Mr Medley, my sister tells me you are an honest man, and a-dod, I love you. Few words and hearty, that's the way with old Harry, old Harry.

SIR FOPLING: Light your flambeaux, hey!

OLD BELLAIR: What does the man mean?

MEDLEY: 'Tis day, Sir Fopling.

SIR FOPLING: No matter. Our serenade will look the greater.
    Exeunt omnes.

SCENE TWO

DORIMANT's *lodging. A table, a candle, a toilet, etc.*
HANDY *tying up linen.*
Enter DORIMANT *in his gown and* BELINDA.

DORIMANT: Why will you be gone so soon?

BELINDA: Why did you stay out so late?

DORIMANT: Call a chair, Handy. What makes you tremble so?

BELINDA: I have a thousand fears about me. Have I not been seen, think you?

DORIMANT: By nobody but myself and trusty Handy.

BELINDA: Where are all your people?

DORIMANT: I have disperst 'em on sleeveless[1] errands. What does that sigh mean?

BELINDA: Can you be so unkind to ask me? – Well – [*Sighs.*] Were it to do again –

DORIMANT: We should do it, should we not?

BELINDA: I think we should; the wickeder man you to make me love so well. Will you be discreet now?

DORIMANT: I will.

BELINDA: You cannot.

DORIMANT: Never doubt it.

BELINDA: I will not expect it.

DORIMANT: You do me wrong.

BELINDA: You have no more power to keep the secret than I had not to trust you with it.

DORIMANT: By all the joys I have had, and those you keep in store –

BELINDA: You'll do for my sake what you never did before –

DORIMANT: By that truth thou hast spoken, a wife shall sooner betray herself to her husband –

BELINDA: Yet I had rather you should be false in this than in another thing you promised me.

DORIMANT: What's that?

BELINDA: That you would never see Loveit more but in public places, in the Park, at court and plays.

DORIMANT: 'Tis not likely a man should be fond of seeing a damned old play when there is a new one acted.

BELINDA: I dare not trust your promise.

DORIMANT: You may.

BELINDA: This does not satisfy me. You shall swear you never will see her more.

DORIMANT: I will! A thousand oaths – by all –

1. *Sleeveless*: futile.

BELINDA: Hold – you shall not, now I think on't better.

DORIMANT: I will swear –

BELINDA: I shall grow jealous of the oath, and think I owe your truth to that, not to your love.

DORIMANT: Then, by my love, no other oath I'll swear.

Enter HANDY.

HANDY: Here's a chair.

BELINDA: Let me go.

DORIMANT: I cannot.

BELINDA: Too willingly, I fear.

DORIMANT: Too unkindly feared. When will you promise me again?

BELINDA: Not this fortnight.

DORIMANT: You will be better than your word.

BELINDA: I think I shall. Will it not make you love me less?

Fiddles without.

[*Starting.*] Hark! What fiddles are these?

DORIMANT: Look out, Handy.

Exit HANDY *and returns.*

HANDY: Mr Medley, Mr Bellair, and Sir Fopling, they are coming up.

DORIMANT: How got they in?

HANDY: The door was open for the chair.

BELINDA: Lord! Let me fly –

DORIMANT: Here, here, down the back stairs. I'll see you into your chair.

BELINDA: No, no, stay and receive 'em. And be sure you keep your word and never see Loveit more. Let it be a proof of your kindness.

DORIMANT: It shall. – Handy, direct her. Everlasting love go along with thee. [*Kissing her hand.*]

Exit BELINDA *and* HANDY.

Enter YOUNG BELLAIR, MEDLEY, *and* SIR FOPLING.

YOUNG BELLAIR: Not a-bed yet!

MEDLEY: You have had an irregular fit, Dorimant.

DORIMANT: I have.

YOUNG BELLAIR: And is it off already?

DORIMANT: Nature has done her part, gentlemen; when she

falls kindly[1] to work, great cures are effected in little time, you know.

SIR FOPLING: We thought there was a wench in the case by the chair that waited. Prithee make us a confidance.

DORIMANT: Excuse me.

SIR FOPLING: Le sage Dorimant! Was she pretty?

DORIMANT: So pretty she may come to keep her coach and pay parish duties if the good humour of the age continue.

MEDLEY: And be of the number of the ladies kept by public-spirited men for the good of the whole town.

SIR FOPLING: Well said, Medley. [SIR FOPLING *dancing by himself.*]

YOUNG BELLAIR: See Sir Fopling dancing.

DORIMANT: You are practising and have a mind to recover, I see.

SIR FOPLING: Prithee Dorimant, why hast not thou a glass hung up here? A room is the dullest thing without one!

YOUNG BELLAIR: Here is company to entertain you.

SIR FOPLING: But I mean in case of being alone. In a glass a man may entertain himself.

DORIMANT: The shadow of himself indeed.

SIR FOPLING: Correct the errors of his motion and his dress.

MEDLEY: I find, Sir Fopling, in your solitude you remember the saying of the wise man, and study yourself.

SIR FOPLING: 'Tis the best diversion in our retirements. Dorimant, thou art a pretty fellow and wear'st thy clothes well, but I never saw thee have a handsome cravat. Were they made up like mine, they'd give another air to thy face. Prithee, let me send my man to dress thee but one day. By heavens, an Englishman cannot tie a ribbon.

DORIMANT: They are something clumsy-fisted.

SIR FOPLING: I have brought over the prettiest fellow that ever spread a toilet. He served some time under Merille,[2] the greatest genie in the world for a valet d'chambré.

DORIMANT: What, he who formerly belonged to the Duke of Candale?

1. *Kindly*: see note 1, p. 104.
2. *Merille*: valet to the Duc de Candale and the Duc d'Orléans in the last quarter of the seventeenth century.

SIR FOPLING: The same, and got him his immortal reputation.

DORIMANT: Y'have a very fine Brandenburgh[1] on, Sir Fopling.

SIR FOPLING: It serves to wrap me up, after the fatigue of a ball.

MEDLEY: I see you often in it, with your periwig tied up.

SIR FOPLING: We should not always be in a set dress, 'tis more en cavalier to appear now and then in a dissabilleé.

MEDLEY: Pray, how goes your business with Loveit?

SIR FOPLING: You might have answered yourself in the Mall last night. Dorimant, did you not see the advances she made me? I have been endeavouring at a song.

DORIMANT: Already!

SIR FOPLING: 'Tis my coup d'essay in English. I would fain have thy opinion of it.

DORIMANT: Let's see it.

SIR FOPLING: Hey, page, give me my song. – Bellair, here, thou hast a pretty voice, sing it.

YOUNG BELLAIR: Sing it yourself, Sir Fopling.

SIR FOPLING: Excuse me.

YOUNG BELLAIR: You learnt to sing in Paris.

SIR FOPLING: I did, of Lambert,[2] the greatest master in the world; but I have his own fault, a weak voice, and care not to sing out of a ruel.[3]

DORIMANT: A ruel is a pretty cage for a singing fop, indeed.

YOUNG BELLAIR *reads the song:*

> *How charming Phillis is, how fair!*
> *Ah that she were as willing*
> *To ease my wounded heart of care*
> *And make her eyes less killing.*
> *I sigh! I sigh! I languish now,*
> *And love will not let me rest,*
> *I drive about the Park, and bow*
> *Still as I meet my dearest.*

1. *Brandenburgh*: morning gown, from the Prussian city noted for woollen articles.
2. *Lambert*: Michel Lambert (1610–96), master of the King's music.
3. *Ruel*: a bedroom where ladies of fashion in France received visitors

SIR FOPLING: Sing it, sing it man, it goes to a pretty new tune which I am confident was made by Baptist.[1]

MEDLEY: Sing it yourself, Sir Fopling, he does not know the tune.

SIR FOPLING: I'll venture. [SIR FOPLING *sings*.]

DORIMANT: Ay marry! Now 'tis something. I shall not flatter you, Sir Fopling, there is not much thought in't. But 'tis passionate and well turned.

MEDLEY: After the French way.

SIR FOPLING: That I aimed at. Does it not give you a lively image of the thing? Slap, down goes the glass, and thus we are at it.

DORIMANT: It does indeed. I perceive, Sir Fopling, you'll be the very head of the sparks who are lucky in compositions of this nature.

   Enter SIR FOPLING'S FOOTMAN.

SIR FOPLING: La Tour, is the bath ready?

FOOTMAN: Yes, sir.

SIR FOPLING: Adieu donc, mes cheres. [*Exit* SIR FOPLING.]

MEDLEY: When have you your revenge on Loveit, Dorimant?

DORIMANT: I will but change my linen and about it.

MEDLEY: The powerful considerations which hindered have bin removed, then?

DORIMANT: Most luckily, this morning. You must along with me, my reputation lies at stake there.

MEDLEY: I am engaged to Bellair.

DORIMANT: What's your business?

MEDLEY: Ma-tri-mony, an't like you.

DORIMANT: It does not, sir.

YOUNG BELLAIR: It may in time, Dorimant. What think you of Mrs Harriet?

DORIMANT: What does she think of me?

YOUNG BELLAIR: I am confident she loves you.

DORIMANT: How does it appear?

YOUNG BELLAIR: Why, she's never well but when she's talking of you, but then she finds all the faults in you she can.

1. *Baptist*: Jean Baptiste Lully (1633–87), master of court music to Louis XIV, usually considered the founder of French opera.

She laughs at all who commend you, but then she speaks ill
of all who do not.

DORIMANT: Women of her temper betray themselves by their
over-cunning. I had once a growing love with a lady who
would always quarrel with me when I came to see her, and
yet was never quiet if I stayed a day from her.

YOUNG BELLAIR: My father is in love with Emilia.

DORIMANT: That is a good warrant for your proceedings.
Go on and prosper, I must to Loveit. Medley, I am sorry
you cannot be a witness.

MEDLEY: Make her meet Sir Fopling again the same place and
use him ill before me.

DORIMANT: That may be brought about, I think. I'll be at
your aunt's anon and give you joy, Mr Bellair.

YOUNG BELLAIR: You had not best think of Mrs Harriet
too much; without church security there's no taking up
there.

DORIMANT: I may fall into the snare too. But –
        The wise will find a difference in our fate,
        You wed a woman, I a good estate.

Exeunt.

SCENE THREE

(*The Mall.*)
Enter the chair with BELINDA; *the men set it down and open
it.* BELINDA *starting.*

BELINDA [*surprised*]: Lord! Where am I? In the Mall! Whither
have you brought me?

FIRST CHAIRMAN: You gave us no directions, madam.

BELINDA [*aside*]: The fright I was in made me forget it.

FIRST CHAIRMAN: We use to carry a lady from the squire's
hither.

BELINDA [*aside*]: This is Loveit; I am undone if she sees me.
Quickly, carry me away.

FIRST CHAIRMAN: Whither, an't like your honour?

BELINDA: Ask no questions –
        Enter LOVEIT'S FOOTMAN.

FOOTMAN: Have you seen my lady, madam?

BELINDA: I am just come to wait upon her –

FOOTMAN: She will be glad to see you, madam. She sent me to you this morning to desire your company, and I was told you went out by five o'clock.

BELINDA [*aside*]: More and more unlucky!

FOOTMAN: Will you walk in, madam?

BELINDA: I'll discharge my chair and follow, tell your mistress I am here.

　　Exit FOOTMAN.

[*Gives the Chairmen money.*] Take this. And if ever you should be examined, be sure you say, you took me up in the Strand over against the Exchange, as you will answer it to Mr Dorimant.

CHAIRMEN: We will, an't like your honour. [*Exit* CHAIRMEN.]

BELINDA: Now to come off, I must on –

　　　In confidence and lies, some hope is left;
　　　'Twere hard to be found out in the first theft.

　　Exit.

Act Five

SCENE ONE

(MRS LOVEIT'S *house.*)

Enter MISTRESS LOVEIT *and* PERT, *her woman.*

PERT: Well, in my eyes Sir Fopling is no such despicable person.

MRS LOVEIT: You are an excellent judge.

PERT: He's as handsome a man as Mr Dorimant, and as great a gallant.

MRS LOVEIT: Intolerable! Is't not enough I submit to his impertinences, but must I be plagued with yours too?

PERT: Indeed, madam –

MRS LOVEIT: 'Tis false, mercenary malice.

Enter her FOOTMAN.

FOOTMAN: Mrs Belinda, madam –

MRS LOVEIT: What of her?

FOOTMAN: She's below.

MRS LOVEIT: How came she?

FOOTMAN: In a chair; ambling Harry brought her.

MRS LOVEIT: He bring her! His chair stands near Dorimant's door and always brings me from thence. – Run and ask him where he took her up, go. There is no truth in friendship neither. Women, as well as men, all are false, or all are so to me at least.

PERT: You are jealous of her too?

MRS LOVEIT: You had best tell her I am; 'twill become the liberty you take of late. – This fellow's bringing of her, her going out by five o'clock! – I know not what to think.

Enter BELINDA.

Belinda, you are grown an early riser, I hear!

BELINDA: Do you not wonder, my dear, what made me abroad so soon?

MRS LOVEIT: You do not use to be so.

BELINDA: The country gentlewomen I told you of – Lord, they have the oddest diversions! – would never let me rest till I promised to go with them to the markets this morning to eat fruit and buy nosegays.

MRS LOVEIT: Are they so fond of a filthy nosegay?

BELINDA: They complain of the stinks of the town, and are never well but when they have their noses in one.

MRS LOVEIT: There are essences and sweet waters.

BELINDA: Oh, they cry out upon perfumes they are unwholesome; one of 'em was falling into a fit with the smell of these narolii.[1]

MRS LOVEIT: Methinks in complaisance you should have had a nosegay too.

BELINDA: Do you think, my dear, I could be so loathsome to trick myself up with carnations and stock gilly-flowers? I begged their pardon and told them I never wore anything but orange-flowers and tuberose. That which made me willing to go was a strange desire I had to eat some fresh nectarines.

MRS LOVEIT: And had you any?

BELINDA: The best I ever tasted.

MRS LOVEIT: Whence came you now?

BELINDA: From their lodgings, where I crowded out of a coach and took a chair to come and see you, my dear.

MRS LOVEIT: Whither did you send for that chair?

BELINDA: 'Twas going by empty.

MRS LOVEIT: Where do these country gentlewomen lodge, I pray?

BELINDA: In the Strand, over against the Exchange.

PERT: That place is never without a nest of 'em; they are always as one goes by fleering[2] in balconies or staring out of windows.

Enter FOOTMAN.

MRS LOVEIT [*to the* FOOTMAN:] Come hither. [*Whispers.*]

BELINDA [*aside*]: This fellow by her order has been questioning the chairmen! I threatened 'em with the name of Dorimant; if they should have told truth I am lost for ever.

MRS LOVEIT: In the Strand, said you?

FOOTMAN: Yes madam, over against the Exchange. [*Exit* FOOTMAN.]

---

1. *Narolii*: from Latin *nares*, nostrils.   2. *Fleering*: mocking.

MRS LOVEIT: She's innocent and I am much to blame.

BELINDA [*aside*]: I am so frighted, my countenance will betray me.

MRS LOVEIT: Belinda! What makes you look so pale?

BELINDA: Want of my usual rest, and jolting up and down so long in an odious hackney.

   FOOTMAN *returns.*

FOOTMAN: Madam, Mr Dorimant.

MRS LOVEIT: What makes him here?

BELINDA [*aside*]: Then I am betrayed indeed. H' has broke his word, and I love a man that does not care for me.

MRS LOVEIT: Lord, you faint, Belinda!

BELINDA: I think I shall! Such an oppression here on the sudden.

PERT: She has eaten too much fruit, I warrant you.

MRS LOVEIT: Not unlikely!

PERT: 'Tis that lies heavy on her stomach.

MRS LOVEIT: Have her into my chamber, give her some surfeit water and let her lie down a little.

PERT: Come, madam. I was a strange devourer of fruit when I was young, so ravenous!

   Exit BELINDA *and* PERT *leading her off.*

MRS LOVEIT: Oh that my love would be but calm awhile, that I might receive this man with all the scorn and indignation he deserves!

   Enter DORIMANT.

DORIMANT: Now for a touch of Sir Fopling to begin with. – Hey, page! Give positive order that none of my people stir. Let the canaille wait as they should do. – Since noise and nonsense have such powerful charms,

   I that I may successful prove,
   Transform myself to what you love.[1]

MRS LOVEIT: If that would do, you need not change from what you are, you can be vain and loud enough.

DORIMANT: But not with so good a grace as Sir Fopling. Hey, Hampshire – oh, that sound, that sound becomes the mouth of a man of quality.

1. *I that . . . you love*: couplet from Waller's *To the Mutable Fair* (with first word changed from 'And' to 'I').

MRS LOVEIT: Is there a thing so hateful as a senseless mimic?

DORIMANT: He's a great grievance indeed to all who like yourself, madam, love to play the fool in quiet.

MRS LOVEIT: A ridiculous animal, who has more of the ape than the ape has of the man in him.

DORIMANT: I have as mean an opinion of a sheer mimic as yourself, yet were he all ape I should prefer him to the gay, the giddy, brisk-insipid noisy fool you dote on.

MRS LOVEIT: Those noisy fools, however you despise 'em, have good qualities, which weigh more – or ought at least – with us women than all the pernicious wit you have to boast of.

DORIMANT: That I may hereafter have a just value for their merit, pray do me the favour to name 'em.

MRS LOVEIT: You'll despise 'em as the dull effects of ignorance and vanity, yet I care not if I mention some. First, they really admire us, while you at best but flatter us well.

DORIMANT: Take heed, fools can dissemble too –

MRS LOVEIT: They may, but not so artificially as you; there is no fear they should deceive us. Then, they are assiduous, sir, they are ever offering us their service, and always waiting on our will.

DORIMANT: You owe that to their excessive idleness. They know not how to entertain themselves at home, and find so little welcome abroad, they are fain to fly to you who countenance 'em as a refuge against the solitude they would be otherwise condemned to.

MRS LOVEIT: Their conversation too diverts us better.

DORIMANT: Playing with your fan, smelling to your gloves, commending your hair, and taking notice how 'tis cut and shaded after the new way –

MRS LOVEIT: Were it sillier than you can make it, you must allow 'tis pleasanter to laugh at others than to be laughed at ourselves, though never so wittily. Then, though they want skill to flatter us, they flatter themselves so well, they save us the labour. We need not take that care and pains to satisfy 'em of our love which we so often lose on you.

DORIMANT: They commonly indeed believe too well of themselves, and always better of you than you deserve.

MRS LOVEIT: You are in the right, they have an implicit faith in us which keeps 'em from prying narrowly into our secrets, and saves us the vexatious trouble of clearing doubts which your subtle and causeless jealousies every moment raise.

DORIMANT: There is an inbred falsehood in women which inclines 'em still to them whom they may most easily deceive.

MRS LOVEIT: The man who loves above his quality does not suffer more from the insolent impertinence of his mistress than the woman who loves above her understanding does from the arrogant presumptions of her friend.

DORIMANT: You mistake the use of fools; they are designed for properties and not for friends. You have an indifferent stock of reputation left yet. Lose it all like a frank gamester on the square, 'twill then be time enough to turn rook[1] and cheat it up again on a good substantial bubble.[2]

MRS LOVEIT: The old and the ill-favoured are only fit for properties indeed, but young and handsome fools have met with kinder fortunes.

DORIMANT: They have, to the shame of your sex be it spoken. 'Twas this, the thought of this, made me by a timely jealousy endeavour to prevent the good fortune you are providing for Sir Fopling. But against a woman's frailty all our care is vain.

MRS LOVEIT: Had I not with a dear experience bought the knowledge of your falsehood, you might have fooled me yet. This is not the first jealousy you have feigned to make a quarrel with me, and get a week to throw away on some such unknown inconsiderable slut as you have been lately lurking with at plays.

DORIMANT: Women, when they would break off with a man, never want th'address to turn the fault on him.

MRS LOVEIT: You take a pride of late in using of me ill, that the town may know the power you have over me; which now – as unreasonably as yourself – expects that I – do me all the injuries you can – must love you still.

DORIMANT: I am so far from expecting that you should, I begin to think you never did love me.

1. *Rook*: swindler.   2. *Bubble*: swindle, conspiracy.

MRS LOVEIT: Would the memory of it were so wholly worn out in me that I did doubt it too! What made you come to disturb my growing quiet?

DORIMANT: To give you joy of your growing infamy.

MRS LOVEIT: Insupportable! Insulting devil! This from you, the only author of my shame! This from another had been but justice, but from you 'tis a hellish and inhuman outrage. What have I done?

DORIMANT: A thing that puts you below my scorn, and makes my anger as ridiculous as you have made my love.

MRS LOVEIT: I walked last night with Sir Fopling.

DORIMANT: You did, madam, and you talked and laughed aloud ha, ha, ha! – Oh that laugh, that laugh becomes the confidence of a woman of quality.

MRS LOVEIT: You who have more pleasure in the ruin of a woman's reputation than in the indearments of her love, reproach me not with yourself, and I defy you to name the man can lay a blemish on my fame.

DORIMANT: To be seen publicly so transported with the vain follies of that notorious fop, to me is an infamy below[1] the sin of prostitution with another man.

MRS LOVEIT: Rail on, I am satisfied in the justice of what I did; you had provoked me to't.

DORIMANT: What I did was the effect of a passion whose extravagancies you have been willing to forgive.

MRS LOVEIT: And what I did was the effect of a passion you may forgive if you think fit.

DORIMANT: Are you so indifferent grown?

MRS LOVEIT: I am.

DORIMANT: Nay, then 'tis time to part. I'll send you back your letters you have so often asked for; I have two or three of 'em about me.

MRS LOVEIT: Give 'em me.

DORIMANT: You snatch as if you thought I would not. [*Gives her letters.*] There – and may the perjuries in 'em be mine if e'er I see you more. [*Offers to go, she catches him.*]

MRS LOVEIT: Stay!

DORIMANT: I will not.

1. *Below*: i.e., worse than.

MRS LOVEIT: You shall.

DORIMANT: What have you to say?

MRS LOVEIT: I cannot speak it yet.

DORIMANT: Something more in commendation of the fool? Death, I want patience, let me go.

MRS LOVEIT: I cannot. [*Aside*] I can sooner part with the limbs that hold him – I hate that nauseous fool, you know I do.

DORIMANT: Was it the scandal you were fond of then?

MRS LOVEIT: Y'had raised my anger equal to my love, a thing you ne'er could do before, and in revenge I did – I know not what I did. Would you would not think on't any more.

DORIMANT: Should I be willing to forget it, I shall be daily minded of it, 'twill be a commonplace for all the town to laugh at me; and Medley, when he is rhetorically drunk, will ever be declaiming on it in my ears.

MRS LOVEIT: 'Twill be believed a jealous spite. Come, forget it.

DORIMANT: Let me consult my reputation, you are too careless of it. [*Pauses.*] You shall meet Sir Fopling in the Mall again tonight.

MRS LOVEIT: What mean you?

DORIMANT: I have thought on it, and you must. 'Tis necessary to justify my love to the world. You can handle a coxcomb as he deserves when you are not out of humour, madam.

MRS LOVEIT: Public satisfaction for the wrong I have done you! This is some new device to make me more ridiculous!

DORIMANT: Hear me!

MRS LOVEIT: I will not!

DORIMANT: You will be persuaded.

MRS LOVEIT: Never.

DORIMANT: Are you so obstinate?

MRS LOVEIT: Are you so base?

DORIMANT: You will not satisfy my love?

MRS LOVEIT: I would die to satisfy that, but I will not, to save you from a thousand racks, do a shameless thing to please your vanity.

DORIMANT: Farewell, false woman.

MRS LOVEIT: Do! Go!

DORIMANT: You will call me back again.

MRS LOVEIT: Exquisite fiend! I knew you came but to torment me.

Enter BELINDA *and* PERT.

DORIMANT [*surprised*]: Belinda here!

BELINDA [*aside*]: He starts and looks pale! The sight of me
has touched his guilty soul.

PERT: 'Twas but a qualm as I said, a little indigestion; the
surfeit water did it, madam, mixed with a little mirabilis.[1]

DORIMANT: I am confounded, and cannot guess how she
came hither!

MRS LOVEIT: 'Tis your fortune, Belinda, ever to be here,
when I am abused by this prodigy of ill nature.

BELINDA: I am amazed to find him here! How has he the face
to come near you?

DORIMANT [*aside*]: Here is fine work towards! I never was at
such a loss before.

BELINDA: One who makes a public profession of breach of
faith and ingratitude! I loathe the sight of him.

DORIMANT (*aside*): There is no remedy, I must submit to
their tongues now, and some other time bring myself off as
well as I can.

BELINDA: Other men are wicked, but then they have some
sense of shame. He is never well but when he triumphs, nay,
glories to a woman's face in his villainies.

MRS LOVEIT: You are in the right, Belinda, but methinks
your kindness for me makes you concern yourself too much
with him.

BELINDA: It does indeed, my dear. His barbarous carriage[2] to
you yesterday made me hope you ne'er would see him more,
and the very next day to find him here again provokes me
strangely. But because I know you love him I have done.

DORIMANT: You have reproached me handsomely, and I deserve it for coming hither, but –

1. *Mirabilis*: aqua mirabilis, a distillation of cloves, nutmeg, ginger and
spirit of wine.
2. *Carriage*: behaviour.

PERT: You must expect it, sir! All women will hate you for my lady's sake.

DORIMANT: Nay, if she begins too, 'tis time to fly! I shall be scolded to death else. [*Aside to* BELINDA] I am to blame in some circumstances I confess, but as to the main, I am not so guilty as you imagine. – I shall seek a more convenient time to clear myself.

MRS LOVEIT: Do it now! What impediments are here?

DORIMANT: I want time, and you want temper.

MRS LOVEIT: These are weak pretences.

DORIMANT: You were never more mistaken in your life. And so farewell. [DORIMANT *flings off.*]

MRS LOVEIT: Call a footman, Pert, quickly! I will have him dogged.

PERT: I wish you would not, for my quiet and your own.

MRS LOVEIT: I'll find out the infamous cause of all our quarrels, pluck her mask off and expose her bare-faced to the world.

BELINDA [*aside*]: Let me but escape this time, I'll never venture more.

MRS LOVEIT: Belinda, you shall go with me.

BELINDA: I have such a heaviness hangs on me with what I did this morning, I would fain go home and sleep, my dear.

MRS LOVEIT: Death and eternal darkness! I shall never sleep again. Raging fevers seize the world and make mankind as restless all as I am. [*Exit* MRS LOVEIT.]

BELINDA: I knew him false and helped to make him so. Was not her ruin enough to fright me from the danger? It should have been, but love can take no warning. [*Exit* BELINDA.]

SCENE TWO

LADY TOWNLEY's *house.*
Enter MEDLEY, YOUNG BELLAIR, LADY TOWNLEY, EMILIA *and* CHAPLAIN.

MEDLEY: Bear up, Bellair, and do not let us see that repentance in thine, we daily do in married faces.

LADY TOWNLEY: This wedding will strangely surprise my brother when he knows it.

MEDLEY: Your nephew ought to conceal it for a time, madam. Since marriage has lost its good name, prudent men seldom expose their own reputations till 'tis convenient to justify their wives'.

OLD BELLAIR [*without*]: Where are you all there? Out, a-dod, will nobody hear?

LADY TOWNLEY: My brother! Quickly Mr Smirk, into this closet, you must not be seen yet.

(SMIRK) *goes into the closet.*

Enter OLD BELLAIR *and* LADY TOWNLEY'S PAGE.

OLD BELLAIR: Desire Mr Furb[1] to walk into the lower parlour, I will be with him presently. [*To* YOUNG BELLAIR] Where have you been, sir, you could not wait on me today?

YOUNG BELLAIR: About a business.

OLD BELLAIR: Are you so good at business? A-dod I have a business too you shall dispatch out of hand, sir. Send for a parson, sister; my Lady Woodvill and her daughter are coming.

LADY TOWNLEY: What need you huddle up things thus?

OLD BELLAIR: Out a pise, youth is apt to play the fool, and 'tis not good it should be in their power.

LADY TOWNLEY: You need not fear your son.

OLD BELLAIR: H' has been idling this morning, and a-dod I do not like him. [*To* EMILIA] How dost thou do, sweetheart?

EMILIA: You are very severe, sir. Married in such haste!

OLD BELLAIR: Go to, thou'rt a rogue, and I will talk with thee anon. Here's my Lady Woodvill come.

Enter LADY WOODVILL, HARRIET *and* BUSY.

Welcome, madam; Mr Furb's below with the writings.[2]

LADY WOODVILL: Let us down and make an end then.

OLD BELLAIR: Sister, shew the way. [*To* YOUNG BELLAIR, *who is talking to* HARRIET] Harry, your business lies not there yet! Excuse him till we have done, lady, and then

1. *Mr Furb*: presumably Mr Forbes who was sent for in Act Two.
2. *Writings*: legal documents.

a-dod he shall be for thee. Mr Medley, we must trouble you to be a witness.

MEDLEY: I luckily came for that purpose, sir.

Exit OLD BELLAIR, MEDLEY, YOUNG BELLAIR, LADY TOWNLEY *and* LADY WOODVILL.

BUSY: What will you do, madam?

HARRIET: Be carried back and mewed up[1] in the country agen, run away here, anything, rather than be married to a man I do not care for. Dear Emilia, do thou advise me!

EMILIA: Mr Bellair is engaged, you know.

HARRIET: I do; but know not what the fear of losing an estate may fright him to.

EMILIA: In the desperate condition you are in, you should consult with some judicious man. What think you of Mr Dorimant?

HARRIET: I do not think of him at all.

BUSY (*aside*): She thinks of nothing else I am sure.

EMILIA: How fond your mother was of Mr Courtage!

HARRIET: Because I contrived the mistake to make a little mirth, you believe I like the man.

EMILIA: Mr Bellair believes you love him.

HARRIET: Men are seldom in the right when they guess at a woman's mind. Would she whom he loves loved him no better.

BUSY [*aside*]: That's e'en well enough, on all conscience.

EMILIA: Mr Dorimant has a great deal of wit.

HARRIET: And takes a great deal of pains to shew it.

EMILIA: He's extremely well fashioned.

HARRIET: Affected grave, or ridiculously wild and apish.

BUSY: You defend him still against your mother.

HARRIET: I would not were he justly rallied, but I cannot hear anyone undeservedly railed at.

EMILIA: Has your woman learnt the song you were so taken with?

HARRIET: I was fond of a new thing; 'tis dull at second hearing.

EMILIA: Mr Dorimant made it.

1. *Mewed up*: cooped up.

BUSY: She knows it, madam, and has made me sing it at least a dozen times this morning.

HARRIET: Thy tongue is as impertinent as thy fingers.

EMILIA: You have provoked her.

BUSY: 'Tis but singing the song and I shall appease her.

EMILIA: Prithee do.

HARRIET: She has a voice will grate your ears worse than a cat-call, and dresses so ill she's scarce fit to trick up a yeoman's daughter on a holiday.

BUSY *sings:*

Song by Sir C. S.[1]

As Amoret with Phillis sat
One evening on the plain,
And saw the charming Strephon wait
To tell the nymph his pain,

The threatning danger to remove
She whispered in her ear,
Ah Phillis, if you would not love,
This shepherd do not hear.

None ever had so strange an art
His passion to convey
Into a listening virgin's heart
And steal her soul away.

Fly, fly betimes, for fear you give
Occasion for your fate.
In vain said she, in vain I strive,
Alas! 'tis now too late.

Enter DORIMANT.

DORIMANT: *Music so softens and disarms the mind.*

HARRIET: *That not one arrow does resistance find.*[2]

DORIMANT: Let us make use of the lucky minute then.

1. *Sir C. S.*: Sir Car Scroope, who also wrote the prologue to the play, not Sir Charles Sedley, among whose *Works* the song was printed in 1722. It is translated from a French version which appears in *Le Recueil des Pièces Gallantes* by the Comtesse de la Suze (1684 edn., p. 40).

2. *Music so . . . find*: from Waller's *On my Lady Isabella Playing on the Lute* ('an' changed to 'one').

HARRIET [*aside, turning from* DORIMANT]: My love springs with my blood into my face, I dare not look upon him yet.

DORIMANT: What have we here, the picture of celebrated beauty, giving audience in public to a declared lover?

HARRIET: Play the dying fop and make the piece complete, sir.

DORIMANT: What think you if the hint were well improved? The whole mystery of making love pleasantly designed and wrought in a suit of hangings?

HARRIET: 'Twere needless to execute fools in effigy who suffer daily in their own persons.

DORIMANT [*to* EMILIA *aside*]: Mistress bride, for such I know this happy day has made you.

EMILIA: Defer the formal joy you are to give me, and mind your business with her. [*Aloud*] Here are dreadful preparations Mr Dorimant, writings sealing, and a parson sent for –

DORIMANT: To marry this lady –

BUSY: Condemned she is, and what will become of her I know not, without you generously engage in a rescue.

DORIMANT: In this sad condition, madam, I can do no less than offer you my service.

HARRIET: The obligation is not great. You are the common sanctuary for all young women who run from their relations.

DORIMANT: I have always my arms open to receive the distressed. But I will open my heart and receive you, where none yet did ever enter – you have filled it with a secret, might I but let you know it –

HARRIET: Do not speak it, if you would have me believe it; your tongue is so famed for falsehood 'twill do the truth an injury. [*Turns away her head.*]

DORIMANT: Turn not away then, but look on me and guess it.

HARRIET: Did you not tell me there was no credit to be given to faces? That women nowadays have their passions as much at will as they have their complexions, and put on joy and sadness, scorn and kindness, with the same ease they do their paint and patches[1] – are they the only counterfeits?

DORIMANT: You wrong your own, while you suspect my

1. *Patches*: beauty spots.

eyes. – By all the hope I have in you, the inimitable colour in your cheeks is not more free from art than are the sighs I offer.

HARRIET: In men who have been long hardened in sin, we have reason to mistrust the first signs of repentance.

DORIMANT: The prospect of such a heaven will make me persevere, and give you marks that are infallible.

HARRIET: What are those?

DORIMANT: I will renounce all the joys I have in friendship and in wine, sacrifice to you all the interest I have in other women –

HARRIET: Hold – though I wish you devout, I would not have you turn fanatic. Could you neglect these awhile and make a journey into the country?

DORIMANT: To be with you I could live there, and never send one thought to London.

HARRIET: Whate'er you say, I know all beyond High-Park's[1] a desart to you, and that no gallantry can draw you farther.

DORIMANT: That has been the utmost limit of my love, but now my passion knows no bounds, and there's no measure to be taken of what I'll do for you from anything I ever did before.

HARRIET: When I hear you talk thus in Hampshire, I shall begin to think there may be some truth inlarged upon.

DORIMANT: Is this all – will you not promise me –

HARRIET: I hate to promise! What we do then is expected from us, and wants much of the welcome it finds when it surprises.

DORIMANT: May I not hope?

HARRIET: That depends on you, and not on me, and 'tis to no purpose to forbid it. [*Turns to* BUSY.]

BUSY: Faith, madam, now I perceive the gentleman loves you too, e'en let him know your mind and torment yourselves no longer.

HARRIET: Dost think I have no sense of modesty?

BUSY: Think, if you lose this you may never have another opportunity.

1. *High-Park*: Hyde Park.

HARRIET: May he hate me – a curse that frights me when I speak it! – if ever I do a thing against the rules of decency and honour.

DORIMANT [*to* EMILIA]: I am beholding to you for your good intentions, madam.

EMILIA: I thought the concealing of our marriage from her might have done you better service.

DORIMANT: Try her again –

EMILIA: What have you resolved, madam? The time draws near.

HARRIET: To be obstinate and protest against this marriage.
       Enter LADY TOWNLEY *in haste.*

LADY TOWNLEY [*to* EMILIA]: Quickly, quickly, let Mr Smirk out of the closet.

       MR SMIRK *comes out of the closet.*

HARRIET: A parson! Had you laid him in here?

DORIMANT: I knew nothing of him.

HARRIET: Should it appear you did, your opinion of my easiness may cost you dear.
       Enter OLD BELLAIR, YOUNG BELLAIR, MEDLEY, *and* LADY WOODVILL.

OLD BELLAIR: Out a pise! The canonical hour[1] is almost past. Sister, is the man of God come?

LADY TOWNLEY: He waits your leasure.

OLD BELLAIR: By your favour, sir. A-dod, a pretty spruce fellow! What may we call him?

LADY TOWNLEY: Mr Smirk, my Lady Biggot's chaplain.

OLD BELLAIR: A wise woman, a-dod she is. The man will serve for the flesh as well as the spirit. Please you sir, to commission a young couple to go to bed together a-God's name? – Harry.

YOUNG BELLAIR: Here sir –

OLD BELLAIR: Out a pise! Without your mistress in your hand!

SMIRK: Is this the gentleman?

OLD BELLAIR: Yes sir.

SMIRK: Are you not mistaken, sir?

----

1. *Canonical hour*: the hour(s) during which marriages could be solemnized (from eight a.m. until midday).

OLD BELLAIR: A-dod, I think not, sir.

SMIRK: Sure you are, sir.

OLD BELLAIR: You look as if you would forbid the bans, Mr Smirk. I hope you have no pretension to the lady?

SMIRK: Wish him joy, sir! I have done him the good office today already.

OLD BELLAIR: Out a pise, what do I hear?

LADY TOWNLEY: Never storm, brother, the truth is out.

OLD BELLAIR: How say you sir? Is this your wedding day?

YOUNG BELLAIR: It is, sir.

OLD BELLAIR: And a-dod, it shall be mine too. Give me thy hand sweetheart. – [*To* EMILIA] What dost thou mean? Give me thy hand, I say.

[EMILIA *kneels, and* YOUNG BELLAIR.]

LADY TOWNLEY: Come, come, give her your blessing, this is the woman your son loved and is married to.

OLD BELLAIR: Ha! Cheated! Cozened! And by your contrivance, sister!

LADY TOWNLEY: What would you do with her? She's a rogue, and you can't abide her.

MEDLEY: Shall I hit her a pat for you, sir?

OLD BELLAIR: A-dod, you are all rogues, and I never will forgive you.

LADY TOWNLEY: Whither? Whither away?

MEDLEY: Let him go and cool awhile!

LADY WOODVILL [*to* DORIMANT]: Here's a business broke out now, Mr Courtage; I am made a fine fool of.

DORIMANT: You see the old gentleman knew nothing of it.

LADY WOODVILL: I find he did not. I shall have some trick put upon me if I stay in this wicked town any longer. Harriet, dear child, where art thou? I'll into the country straight.

OLD BELLAIR: A-dod madam, you shall hear me first –
   Enter MRS LOVEIT *and* BELINDA.

MRS LOVEIT: Hither my man dogged him –

BELINDA: Yonder he stands, my dear.

MRS LOVEIT: I see him. – [*Aside*] And with him the face that has undone me! Oh that I were but where I might throw out the anguish of my heart! Here it must rage within and break it.

LADY TOWNLEY: Mrs Loveit! Are you afraid to come forward?

MRS LOVEIT: I was amazed to see so much company here in a morning. The occasion sure is extraordinary?

DORIMANT [aside]: Loveit and Belinda! The devil owes me a shame today, and I think never will have done paying it.

MRS LOVEIT: Married! Dear Emilia, how am I transported with the news!

HARRIET [to DORIMANT]: I little thought Emilia was the woman Mr Bellair was in love with. I'll chide her for not trusting me with the secret.

DORIMANT: How do you like Mrs Loveit?

HARRIET: She's a famed mistress of yours, I hear –

DORIMANT: She has been on occasion.

OLD BELLAIR [to LADY WOODVILL]: A-dod madam, I cannot help it.

LADY WOODVILL: You need make no more apologies, sir.

EMILIA [to LOVEIT]: The old gentleman's excusing himself to my Lady Woodvill.

MRS LOVEIT: Ha, ha, ha! I never heard of anything so pleasant.

HARRIET [to DORIMANT]: She's extremely overjoyed at something.

DORIMANT: At nothing; she is one of those hoyting ladies who gaily fling themselves about and force a laugh when their aching hearts are full of discontent and malice.

MRS LOVEIT: O heaven, I was never so near killing myself with laughing! – Mr Dorimant, are you a brideman?

LADY WOODVILL: Mr Dorimant! Is this Mr Dorimant, madam?

MRS LOVEIT: If you doubt it, your daughter can resolve you, I suppose.

LADY WOODVILL: I am cheated too, basely cheated.

OLD BELLAIR: Out a pise, what's here? More knavery yet?

LADY WOODVILL: Harriet! On my blessing come away, I charge you.

HARRIET: Dear mother! Do but stay and hear me.

LADY WOODVILL: I am betrayed and thou art undone, I fear.

HARRIET: Do not fear it – I have not, nor never will do anything against my duty. Believe me, dear mother, do.

DORIMANT [*to* LOVEIT]: I had trusted you with this secret but that I knew the violence of your nature would ruin my fortune as now unluckily it has: I thank you, madam.

MRS LOVEIT: She's an heiress I know, and very rich.

DORIMANT: To satisfy you I must give up my interest wholly to my love; had you been a reasonable woman, I might have secured 'em both, and been happy –

MRS LOVEIT: You might have trusted me with anything of this kind, you know you might. Why did you go under a wrong name?

DORIMANT: The story is too long to tell you now. Be satisfied this is the business; this is the mask has kept me from you.

BELINDA [*aside*]: He's tender of my honour, though he's cruel to my love.

MRS LOVEIT: Was it no idle mistress then?

DORIMANT: Believe me, a wife, to repair the ruins of my estate that needs it.

MRS LOVEIT: The knowledge of this makes my grief hang lighter on my soul; but I shall never more be happy.

DORIMANT: Belinda!

BELINDA: Do not think of clearing yourself with me, it is impossible. Do all men break their words thus?

DORIMANT: Th'extravagant words they speak in love. 'Tis as unreasonable to expect we should perform all we promise then, as do all we threaten when we are angry. When I see you next –

BELINDA: Take no notice of me and I shall not hate you.

DORIMANT: How came you to Mrs Loveit?

BELINDA: By a mistake the chairmen made for want of my giving them directions.

DORIMANT: 'Twas a pleasant one. We must meet agen.

BELINDA: Never.

DORIMANT: Never!

BELINDA: When we do, may I be as infamous as you are false.

LADY TOWNLEY: Men of Mr Dorimant's character always suffer in the general opinion of the world.

MEDLEY: You can make no judgement of a witty man from common fame, considering the prevailing faction, madam.

OLD BELLAIR: A-dod, he's in the right.

MEDLEY: Besides, 'tis a common error among women to believe too well of them they know, and too ill of them they don't.

OLD BELLAIR: A-dod, he observes well.

LADY TOWNLEY: Believe me, madam, you will find Mr Dorimant as civil a gentleman as you thought Mr Courtage.

HARRIET: If you would but know him better –

LADY WOODVILL: You have a mind to know him better! Come away. You shall never see him more.

HARRIET: Dear mother, stay –

LADY WOODVILL: I wo'not be consenting to your ruin.

HARRIET: Were my fortune in your power –

LADY WOODVILL: Your person is.

HARRIET: Could I be disobedient I might take it out of yours and put it into his.

LADY WOODVILL: 'Tis that you would be at! You would marry this Dorimant.

HARRIET: I cannot deny it. I would, and never will marry any other man.

LADY WOODVILL: Is this the duty that you promised?

HARRIET: But I will never marry him against your will.

LADY WOODVILL [aside]: She knows the way to melt my heart. [To HARRIET] Upon yourself light your undoing.

MEDLEY [to OLD BELLAIR]: Come, sir, you have not the heart any longer to refuse your blessing.

OLD BELLAIR: A-dod I ha' not. Rise, and God bless you both. Make much of her Harry, she deserves thy kindness. [To EMILIA] A-dod, sirrah, I did not think it had been in thee.

Enter SIR FOPLING *and his* PAGE.

SIR FOPLING: 'Tis a damn'd windy day! Hey, page, is my periwig right?

PAGE: A little out of order, sir.

SIR FOPLING: Pox o'this apartment, it wants an antechamber to adjust oneself in. [To LOVEIT] Madam, I came from your house and your servants directed me hither.

MRS LOVEIT: I will give order hereafter they shall direct you better.

SIR FOPLING: The great satisfaction I had in the Mall last night has given me much disquiet since.

MRS LOVEIT: 'Tis likely to give me more than I desire.

SIR FOPLING: What the devil makes her so reserved? Am I guilty of an indiscretion, madam?

MRS LOVEIT: You will be of a great one, if you continue your mistake, sir.

SIR FOPLING: Something puts you out of humour.

MRS LOVEIT: The most foolish inconsiderable thing that ever did.

SIR FOPLING: Is it in my power?

MRS LOVEIT: To hang or drown it; do one of 'em and trouble me no more.

SIR FOPLING: So fierè,[1] serviteur, madam. – Medley! Where's Dorimant?

MEDLEY: Methinks the lady has not made you those advances today she did last night, Sir Fopling.

SIR FOPLING: Prithee do not talk of her.

MEDLEY: She would be a bone fortune.

SIR FOPLING: Not to me at present.

MEDLEY: How so?

SIR FOPLING: An intrigue now would be but a temptation to me to throw away that vigour on one which I mean shall shortly make my court to the whole sex in a ballet.

MEDLEY: Wisely considered, Sir Fopling.

SIR FOPLING: No one woman is worth the loss of a cut in a caper.

MEDLEY: Not when 'tis so universally designed.

LADY WOODVILL: Mr Dorimant, everyone has spoke so much in your behalf that I can no longer doubt but I was in the wrong.

MRS LOVEIT: There's nothing but falsehood and impertinence in this world. All men are villains or fools; take example from my misfortunes. Belinda, if thou wouldst be happy, give thyself wholly up to goodness.

1. *Fierè*: haughty (*fière*).

HARRIET [*to* LOVEIT]: Mr Dorimant has been your God almighty long enough, 'tis time to think of another.

MRS LOVEIT: Jeered by her! I will lock myself up in my house, and never see the world again.

HARRIET: A nunnery is the more fashionable place for such a retreat, and has been the fatal consequence of many a belle passion.

MRS LOVEIT: Hold, heart, till I get home! Should I answer 'twould make her triumph greater. [*Is going out.*]

DORIMANT: Your hand, Sir Fopling –

SIR FOPLING: Shall I wait upon you, madam?

MRS LOVEIT: Legion of fools, as many devils take thee! [*Exit* LOVEIT.]

MEDLEY: Dorimant, I pronounce thy reputation clear, and henceforward, when I would know anything of woman, I will consult no other oracle.

SIR FOPLING: Stark mad, by all that's handsome! Dorimant, thou hast engaged me in a pretty business.

DORIMANT: I have not leasure now to talk about it.

OLD BELLAIR: Out a pise, what does this man of mode do here agen?

LADY TOWNLEY: He'll be an excellent entertainment within, brother, and is luckily come to raise the mirth of the company.

LADY WOODVILL: Madam, I take my leave of you.

LADY TOWNLEY: What do you mean, madam?

LADY WOODVILL: To go this afternoon part of my way to Hartley.

OLD BELLAIR: A-dod, you shall stay and dine first! Come, we will all be good friends, and you shall give Mr Dorimant leave to wait upon you and your daughter in the country.

LADY WOODVILL: If his occasions bring him that way, I have now so good an opinion of him, he shall be welcome.

HARRIET: To a great rambling lone house, that looks as it were not inhabited, the family's so small. There you'll find my mother, an old lame aunt, and myself, sir, perched up on chairs at a distance in a large parlour, sitting moping like three or four melancholy birds in a spacious volary[1] – does not this stagger your resolution?

DORIMANT: Not at all, madam. The first time I saw you, you left me with the pangs of love upon me, and this day my soul has quite given up her liberty.

HARRIET: This is more dismal than the country! Emilia, pity me, who am going to that sad place. Methinks I hear the hateful noise of rooks already – kaw, kaw, kaw – there's music in the worst cry in London! My dill and cowcumbers to pickle![2]

OLD BELLAIR: Sister, knowing of this matter, I hope you have provided us some good cheer.

LADY TOWNLEY: I have, brother, and the fiddles too.

OLD BELLAIR: Let 'em strike up then, the young lady shall have a dance before she departs.

Dance.

After the dance:

So now we'll in, and make this an arrant wedding day –
    And if these honest gentlemen rejoice,   [*To the Pit*]
    A-dod, the boy has made a happy choice.

Exeunt omnes.

1. *Volary*: aviary.
2. *Dill and cowcumbers to pickle*: a London street cry (see Addison's Spectator paper, No. 251).

The Epilogue

BY MR DRYDEN

Most modern wits such monstrous fools have shown,
They seemed not of heavens making but their own.
Those nauseous harlequins in farce may pass,
But there goes more to a substantial ass.
Something of man must be exposed to view,
That, gallants, they may more resemble you.
Sir Fopling is a fool so nicely writ,
The ladies would mistake him for a wit.
And when he sings, talks loud, and cocks,[1] would cry,
I[2] vow methinks he's pretty company;
So brisk, so gay, so travelled, so refined,
As he took pains to graff[3] upon his kind.
True fops help nature's work, and go to school,
To file and finish God a'mighty's fool.
Yet none Sir Fopling him, or him can call;
He's knight o'th'shire, and represents ye all.
From each he meets he culls what e'er he can,
Legion's his name, a people in a man.
His bulky folly gathers as it goes,
And, rolling o'er you, like a snowball grows.
His various modes from various fathers follow,
One taught the toss,[4] and one the new French wallow.[5]
His sword-knot this, his cravat this designed,
And this the yard-long snake[6] he twirls behind.
From one the sacred periwig he gained,
Which wind ne'er blew, nor touch of hat profaned.

1. *Cocks*: struts about.
2. *I*: may stand for 'Ay', a common seventeenth-century spelling; in which case 'vow' would be a printer's error for 'now' (Brett Smith's conjecture).
3. *Graff*: graft.
4. *Toss*: of the head.
5. *Wallow*: rolling gait.
6. *Snake*: attachment to wig.

Another's diving bow he did adore,
Which with a shog[1] casts all the hair before:
Till he with full decorum brings it back,
And rises with a water spaniel shake.
As for his songs (the ladies' dear delight)
Those, sure, he took from most of you who write.
Yet every man is safe from what he feared,
For no one fool is hunted from the herd.

1. *Shog*: jerk.

FINIS

Title-page of the first edition, 1675

The Latin reads:

'I hate to see something criticized not for being clumsy and inelegant, but merely because it is modern; I hate to see people demand not merely indulgence for the older writers, but honours and rewards' (Horace, *Epistles*, II, 1, 76–8).

THE

Country-Wife,

A

COMEDY,

Acted at the

THEATRE ROYAL.

Written by Mr. *Wycherley.*

Indignor quicquam reprehendi, non quia crassè
Compositum illepidéve putetur, sed quia nuper:
Nec veniam. Antiquis, sed honorem & præmia posci.
                                        Horat.

LONDON,

Printed for *Thomas Dring*, at the *Harrow*, at the
Corner of *Chancery-Lane* in *Fleet-street.* 1675.

Prologue

Poets, like cudgelled bullies, never do
At first or second blow submit to you;
But will provoke you still, and ne'er have done,
Till you are weary first with laying on.
The late so baffled scribbler of this day,[1]
Though he stands trembling, bids me boldly say,
What we before most plays are used to do,
For poets out of fear first draw on you;
In a fierce prologue the still pit defy,
And ere you speak, like Castril,[2] give the lie;
But though our Bayes's[3] battles oft I've fought,
And with bruised knuckles their dear conquests bought,
Nay, never yet feared odds upon the stage,
In prologue dare not hector with the age,
But would take quarter from your saving hands,
Though Bayes within all yielding countermands,
Says you confed'rate wits no quarter give,
Therefore his play shan't ask your leave to live.
Well, let the vain rash fop, by huffing so,
Think to obtain the better terms of you;
But we, the actors, humbly will submit,
Now, and at any time, to a full pit.
Nay, often we anticipate your rage,
And murder poets for you, on our stage.
We set no guards upon our tiring-room,
But when with flying colours there you come,
We patiently you see, give up to you,
Our poets, virgins, nay our matrons too.

1. *Baffled scribbler*: perhaps a reference to the failure of Wycherley's *The Gentleman Dancing-Master* in 1672.

2. *Castril*: the 'roaring boy' in Johnson's *The Alchemist* (1610).

3. *Bayes's*: poet's. The name given to Dryden in the satirical play *The Rehearsal* (1672).

The Persons

MR HORNER
MR HARCOURT
MR DORILANT
MR PINCHWIFE
MR SPARKISH
SIR JASPER FIDGET
MRS MARGERY PINCHWIFE
MRS ALITHEA
MY LADY FIDGET
MRS DAINTY FIDGET
MRS SQUEAMISH
OLD LADY SQUEAMISH

WAITERS, SERVANTS, AND ATTENDANTS
A BOY
A QUACK
LUCY, ALITHEA'S MAID

THE SCENE: LONDON

Act One

Enter HORNER, *and* QUACK *following him at a distance.*

HORNER [*aside*]: A quack is as fit for a pimp as a midwife for a bawd; they are still but in their way both helpers of nature. – Well, my dear doctor, hast thou done what I desired?

QUACK: I have undone you for ever with the women, and reported you throughout the whole town as bad as an eunuch, with as much trouble as if I had made you one in earnest.

HORNER: But have you told all the midwives you know, the orange-wenches at the playhouses, the city husbands, and old fumbling keepers of this end of the town? For they'll be the readiest to report it.

QUACK: I have told all the chambermaids, waiting women, tire-women, and old women of my acquaintance; nay, and whispered it as a secret to 'em, and to the whisperers of Whitehall; so that you need not doubt 'twill spread, and you will be as odious to the handsome young women as –

HORNER: As the smallpox. Well –

QUACK: And to the married women of this end of the town as –

HORNER: As the great ones, nay, as their own husbands.

QUACK: And to the city dames as aniseed Robin[1] of filthy and contemptible memory; and they will frighten their children with your name, especially their females.

HORNER: And cry, 'Horner's coming to carry you away.' I am only afraid 'twill not be believed. You told 'em 'twas by an English–French disaster,[2] and an English–French chirurgeon, who has given me at once not only a cure but an antidote for the future against that damned malady,

1. *Aniseed Robin*: a hermaphrodite notorious for obscenity who may have sold aniseed water on the streets. Cf. Charles Cotton's poem *On Aniseed Robin the hermaphrodite.*

2. *English–French disaster*: French pox (venereal disease) from an English whore.

and that worse distemper, love, and all other women's evils?

QUACK: Your late journey into France has made it the more credible, and your being here a fortnight before you appeared in public looks as if you apprehended the shame, which I wonder you do not. Well, I have been hired by young gallants to belie 'em t'other way; but you are the first would be thought a man unfit for women.

HORNER: Dear Mr Doctor, let vain rogues be contented only to be thought abler men than they are; generally 'tis all the pleasure they have. But mine lies another way.

QUACK: You take, methinks, a very preposterous way to it, and as ridiculous as if we operators in physic should put forth bills to disparage our medicaments, with hopes to gain customers.

HORNER: Doctor, there are quacks in love as well as physic, who get but the fewer and worse patients for their boasting. A good name is seldom got by giving it oneself, and women no more than honour are compassed by bragging. Come, come, doctor, the wisest lawyer never discovers[1] the merits of his cause till the trial; the wealthiest man conceals his riches, and the cunning gamester his play. Shy husbands and keepers like old rooks[2] are not to be cheated, but by a new unpractised trick; false friendship will pass now no more than false dice upon 'em, no, not in the city.

Enter BOY.

BOY: There are two ladies and a gentleman coming up. (*Exit* BOY.)

HORNER: A pox! Some unbelieving sisters of my former acquaintance, who I am afraid expect their sense should be satisfied of the falsity of the report. No – this formal fool and women!

Enter SIR JASPER FIDGET, LADY FIDGET, *and* MRS DAINTY FIDGET.

QUACK: His wife and sister.

SIR JASPER: My coach breaking just now before your door, sir, I look upon as an occasional[3] reprimand to me, sir, for not kissing your hands, sir, since your coming out of France,

1. *Discovers*: reveals.   2. *Rooks*: swindlers.   3. *Occasional*: timely.

sir; and so my disaster, sir, has been my good fortune, sir; and this is my wife and sister, sir.

HORNER: What then, sir?

SIR JASPER: My lady, and sister, sir. – Wife, this is Master Horner.

LADY FIDGET: Master Horner, husband!

SIR JASPER: My lady, my Lady Fidget, sir.

HORNER: So, sir.

SIR JASPER: Won't you be acquainted with her, sir? [*Aside*] So the report is true, I find by his coldness or aversion to the sex; but I'll play the wag with him. (*Aloud*) Pray salute my wife, my lady, sir.

HORNER: I will kiss no man's wife, sir, for him, sir. I have taken my eternal leave, sir, of the sex already, sir.

SIR JASPER [*aside*]: Hah, hah, hah! I'll plague him yet. – Not know my wife, sir?

HORNER: I do know your wife, sir, she's a woman, sir, and consequently a monster, sir, a greater monster than a husband, sir.

SIR JASPER: A husband! How, sir?

HORNER: So, sir [*makes horns*]; but I make no more cuckolds, sir.

SIR JASPER: Hah, hah, hah! Mercury, Mercury![1]

LADY FIDGET: Pray, Sir Jasper, let us be gone from this rude fellow.

MRS DAINTY FIDGET: Who, by his breeding, would think he had ever been in France?

LADY FIDGET: Foh! he's but too much a French fellow, such as hate women of quality and virtue for their love to their husbands, Sir Jasper; a woman is hated by 'em as much for loving her husband as for loving their money. But pray, let's be gone.

HORNER: You do well, madam, for I have nothing that you came for. I have brought over not so much as a bawdy picture, new postures,[2] nor the second part of the Ecole des Filles,[3] nor –

1. *Mercury*: used to treat venereal disease.
2. *New postures*: indecent illustrations to Aretino's erotic poems.
3. *Ecole des Filles*: a pornographic work.

QUACK [*apart to* HORNER]: Hold, for shame, sir! What d'y mean? You'll ruin yourself for ever with the sex.

SIR JASPER: Hah, hah, hah! He hates women perfectly, I find.

MRS DAINTY FIDGET: What pity 'tis he should.

LADY FIDGET: Ay, he's a base rude fellow for 't; but affectation makes not a woman more odious to them than virtue.

HORNER: Because your virtue is your greatest affectation, madam.

LADY FIDGET: How, you saucy fellow, would you wrong my honour?

HORNER: If I could.

LADY FIDGET: How d'y mean, sir?

SIR JASPER: Hah, hah, hah, no he can't wrong your ladyship's honour, upon my honour; he poor man – hark you in your ear – a mere eunuch.

LADY FIDGET: O filthy French beast, soh, soh! Why do we stay? Let's be gone; I can't indure the sight of him.

SIR JASPER: Stay but till the chairs[1] come; they'll be here presently.

LADY FIDGET: No, no.

SIR JASPER: Nor can I stay longer. 'Tis – let me see, a quarter and a half quarter of a minute past eleven; the Council will be sate, I must away. Business must be preferred always before love and ceremony with the wise, Mr Horner.

HORNER: And the impotent, Sir Jasper.

SIR JASPER: Ay, ay, the impotent, Master Horner, hah, ha, ha!

LADY FIDGET: What, leave us with a filthy man alone in his lodgings?

SIR JASPER: He's an innocent man now, you know. Pray stay, I'll hasten the chairs to you. – Mr Horner, your servant; I should be glad to see you at my house. Pray come and dine with me, and play at cards with my wife after dinner; you are fit for women at that game yet, hah, ha! [*Aside*] 'Tis as much a husband's prudence to provide innocent diversion for a wife as to hinder her unlawful pleasures, and he had better employ her than let her employ herself. – Farewell. [*Exit* SIR JASPER.]

1. *Chairs*: sedan chairs.

HORNER: Your servant, Sir Jasper.

LADY FIDGET: I will not stay with him, foh!

HORNER: Nay, madam, I beseech you stay, if it be but to see I can be as civil to ladies yet as they would desire.

LADY FIDGET: No, no, foh, you cannot be civil to ladies.

MRS DAINTY FIDGET: You as civil as ladies would desire?

LADY FIDGET: No, no, no! foh, foh, foh!

Exeunt LADY FIDGET *and* MRS DAINTY.

QUACK: Now I think I, or you yourself rather, have done your business with the women.

HORNER: Thou art an ass. Don't you see, already upon the report and my carriage,[1] this grave man of business leaves his wife in my lodgings, invites me to his house and wife, who before would not be acquainted with me out of jealousy?

QUACK: Nay, by this means you may be the more acquainted with the husbands, but the less with the wives.

HORNER: Let me alone; if I can but abuse the husbands, I'll soon disabuse the wives. Stay – I'll reckon you up the advantages I am like to have by my stratagem. First, I shall be rid of all my old acquaintances, the most insatiable sorts of duns that invade our lodgings in a morning. And next to the pleasure of making a new mistress is that of being rid of an old one: and of all old debts, love, when it comes to be so, is paid the most unwillingly.

QUACK: Well, you may be so rid of your old acquaintances, but how will you get any new ones?

HORNER: Doctor, thou wilt never make a good chymist,[2] thou art so incredulous and impatient. Ask but all the young fellows of the town if they do not lose more time, like huntsmen, in starting the game than in running it down; one knows not where to find 'em, who will, or will not. Women of quality are so civil you can hardly distinguish love from good breeding, and a man is often mistaken; but now I can be sure she that shews an aversion to me loves the sport, as those women that are gone, whom I warrant to be right.

1. *Carriage*: behaviour.
2. *Chymist*: alchemist, seeking the philosopher's stone which would turn everything into gold.

And then the next thing is your women of honour, as you call 'em, are only chary of their reputations, not their persons, and 'tis scandal they would avoid, not men. Now may I have, by the reputation of an eunuch, the privileges of one; and be seen in a lady's chamber in a morning as early as her husband; kiss virgins before their parents or lovers; and may be in short the passe partout of the town. Now, doctor.

QUACK: Nay, now you shall be the doctor; and your process is so new that we do not know but it may succeed.

HORNER: Not so new neither; probatum est,[1] doctor.

QUACK: Well, I wish you luck and many patients whilst I go to mine.

Exit QUACK.

Enter HARCOURT *and* DORILANT *to* HORNER.

HARCOURT: Come, your appearance at the play yesterday has, I hope, hardened you for the future against the women's contempt and the men's raillery, and now you'll abroad as you were wont?

HORNER: Did I not bear it bravely?

DORILANT: With a most theatrical impudence; nay, more than the orange-wenches shew there, or a drunken vizard-mask,[2] or a great-bellied actress; nay, or the most impudent of creatures, an ill poet; or what is yet more impudent, a second-hand critic.

HORNER: But what say the ladies? Have they no pity?

HARCOURT: What ladies? The vizard-masks, you know, never pity a man when all's gone, though in their service.

DORILANT: And for the women in the boxes, you'd never pity them when 'twas in your power.

HARCOURT: They say 'tis pity but all that deal with common women should be served so.

DORILANT: Nay, I dare swear, they won't admit you to play at cards with them, go to plays with 'em, or do the little duties which other shadows of men are wont to do for 'em.

HORNER: Who do you call shadows of men?

DORILANT: Half-men.

HORNER: What, boys?

---

1. *Probatum est*: it has been tried out.
2. *Vizard-mask*: prostitute.

DORILANT: Ay, your old boys, old *beaux garçons*, who, like superannuated stallions, are suffered to run, feed, and whinny with the mares as long as they live, though they can do nothing else.

HORNER: Well, a pox on love and wenching! Women serve but to keep a man from better company; though I can't enjoy them, I shall you the more. Good fellowship and friendship are lasting, rational and manly pleasures.

HARCOURT: For all that, give me some of those pleasures you call effeminate too; they help to relish one another.

HORNER: They disturb one another.

HARCOURT: No, mistresses are like books; if you pore upon them too much, they doze you, and make you unfit for company, but if used discreetly, you are the fitter for conversation by 'em.

DORILANT: A mistress should be like a little country retreat near the town, not to dwell in constantly, but only for a night and away, to taste the town the better when a man returns.

HORNER: I tell you, 'tis as hard to be a good fellow, a good friend and a lover of women as 'tis to be a good fellow, a good friend and a lover of money. You cannot follow both, then choose your side. Wine gives you liberty, love takes it away.

DORILANT: Gad, he's in the right on't.

HORNER: Wine gives you joy, love grief and tortures, besides the chirurgeon's. Wine makes us witty, love only sots. Wine makes us sleep, love breaks it.

DORILANT: By the world, he has reason, Harcourt.

HORNER: Wine makes –

DORILANT: Ay, wine makes us – makes us princes, love makes us beggars, poor rogues, ygad – and wine –

HORNER: So, there's one converted. No, no, love and wine, oil and vinegar.

HARCOURT: I grant it; love will still be uppermost.

HORNER: Come, for my part I will have only those glorious, manly pleasures of being very drunk and very slovenly.

Enter BOY.

BOY: Mr Sparkish is below, sir.

wit → Spanish

HARCOURT: What, my dear friend? A rogue that is fond of me only, I think, for abusing him.

DORILANT: No, he can no more think the men laugh at him than that women jilt him, his opinion of himself is so good.

HORNER: Well, there's another pleasure by drinking, I thought not of; I shall lose his acquaintance, because he cannot drink; and you know 'tis a very hard thing to be rid of him, for he's one of those nauseous offerers at wit, who, like the worst fiddlers, run themselves into all companies.

HARCOURT: One that, by being in the company of men of sense, would pass for one.

HORNER: And may so to the short-sighted world, as a false jewel amongst true ones is not discerned at a distance. His company is as troublesome to us as a cuckold's when you you have a mind to his wife's.

HARCOURT: No, the rogue will not let us enjoy one another, but ravishes our conversations, though he signifies no more to't than Sir Martin Mar-all's[1] gaping, and aukerd thrumming upon the lute, does to his man's voice and music.

DORILANT: And to pass for a wit in town, shews himself a fool every night to us, that are guilty of the plot.

HORNER: Such wits as he are to a company of reasonable men, like rooks to the gamesters, who only fill a room at the table, but are so far from contributing to the play that they only serve to spoil the fancy of those that do.

DORILANT: Nay, they are used like rooks too, snubbed, checked and abused; yet the rogues will hang on.

HORNER: A pox on 'em, and all that force nature, and would be still what she forbids 'em! Affectation is her greatest monster.

HARCOURT: Most men are the contraries to that they would seem. Your bully you see, is a coward with a long sword; the little humbly fawning physician with his ebony cane is he that destroys men.

DORILANT: The usurer, a poor rogue possessed of mouldy bonds and mortgages; and we they call spendthrifts are only

1. *Sir Martin Mar-all*: in Dryden's comedy of this name (1677) Sir Martin pretends to serenade his mistress with a lute while a servant, hidden behind a screen, sings.

wealthy, who lay out his money upon daily new purchases of pleasure.

HORNER: Ay, your arrantest cheat is your trustee, or executor, your jealous man, the greatest cuckold, your church-man, the greatest atheist, and your noisy pert rogue of a wit, the greatest fop, dullest ass and worst company as you shall see, for here he comes.

Enter SPARKISH *to them.*

SPARKISH: How is't, sparks, how is't? Well, faith, Harry, I must rally thee a little, ha, ha, ha! upon the report in town of thee, ha, ha, ha! I can't hold i' faith; shall I speak?

HORNER: Yes, but you'll be so bitter then.

SPARKISH: Honest Dick and Frank here shall answer for me, I will not be extreme bitter, by the universe.

HARCOURT: We will be bound in ten thousand pound bond, he shall not be bitter at all.

DORILANT: Nor sharp, nor sweet.

HORNER: What, not downright insipid?

SPARKISH: Nay then, since you are so brisk and provoke me, take what follows. You must know, I was discoursing and rallying with some ladies yesterday, and they happened to talk of the fine new signs in town.

HORNER: Very fine ladies I believe.

SPARKISH: Said I, 'I know where the best new sign is.' 'Where?' says one of the ladies. 'In Covent Garden,' I replied. Said another, 'In what street?' 'In Russel Street,' answered I. 'Lord,' says another, 'I'm sure there was ne'er a fine new sign there yesterday.' 'Yes, but there was,' said I again, 'and it came out of France, and has been there a fortnight.'

DORILANT: A pox! I can hear no more, prithee.

HORNER: No, hear him out; let him tune his crowd[1] a while.

HARCOURT: The worst music, the greatest preparation.

SPARKISH: Nay, faith, I'll make you laugh. 'It cannot be,' says a third lady. 'Yes, yes,' quoth I again. Says a fourth lady –

HORNER: Look to't, we'll have no more ladies.

SPARKISH: No? Then mark, mark, now. Said I to the fourth,

1. *Crowd*: fiddle.

'Did you never see Mr Horner? He lodges in Russel Street, and he's a sign of a man, you know, since he came out of France.' Heh, hah, he!

HORNER: But the divel take me if thine be the sign of a jest.

SPARKISH: With that they all fell a-laughing till they bepissed themselves! What, but it does not move you, methinks? Well, I see one had as good go to law without a witness, as break a jest without a laughter on one's side. Come, come, sparks, but where do we dine? I have left at Whitehall an earl to dine with you.

DORILANT: Why, I thought thou hadst loved a man with a title better than a suit with a French trimming to't.

HARCOURT: Go to him again.

SPARKISH: No, sir, a wit to me is the greatest title in the world.

HORNER: But go dine with your earl, sir, he may be exceptious. We are your friends, and will not take it ill to be left, I do assure you.

HARCOURT: Nay, faith, he shall go to him.

SPARKISH: Nay, pray, gentlemen.

DORILANT: We'll thrust you out, if you wo'not. What, disappoint anybody for us?

SPARKISH: Nay, dear gentlemen, hear me.

HORNER: No, no, sir, by no means; pray go, sir.

SPARKISH: Why, dear rogues —

They all thrust him out of the room.

DORILANT: No, no.

ALL: Ha, ha, ha!

SPARKISH *returns.*

SPARKISH: But, sparks, pray hear me. What, d'ye think I'll eat then with gay shallow fops and silent coxcombs? I think wit as necessary at dinner as a glass of good wine, and that's the reason I never have any stomach when I eat alone. Come, but where do we dine?

HORNER: Ev'n where you will.

SPARKISH: At Chateline's?

DORILANT: Yes, if you will.

SPARKISH: Or at the Cock?

DORILANT: Yes, if you please.

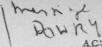 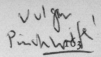

SPARKISH: Or at the Dog and Partridge?

HORNER: Ay, if you have mind to't, for we shall dine at neither.

SPARKISH: Pshaw! With your fooling we shall lose the new play; and I would no more miss seeing a new play the first day than I would miss sitting in the wits' row. Therefore I'll go fetch my mistress and away. [*Exit* SPARKISH.]

> *Manent* HORNER, HARCOURT, DORILANT. *Enter to them* MR PINCHWIFE.

HORNER: Who have we here? Pinchwife?

PINCHWIFE: Gentlemen, your humble servant.

HORNER: Well, Jack, by thy long absence from the town, the grumness of thy countenance, and the slovenliness of thy habit, I should give thee joy, should I not, of marriage?

PINCHWIFE [*aside*]: Death, does he know I'm married too? I thought to have concealed it from him at least. – My long stay in the country will excuse my dress, and I have a suit of law, that brings me up to town, that puts me out of humour; besides, I must give Sparkish tomorrow five thousand pound to lie with my sister.

HORNER: Nay, you country gentlemen, rather than not purchase, will buy anything; and he is a cracked title, if we may quibble. Well, but am I to give thee joy? I heard thou wert married.

PINCHWIFE: What then?

HORNER: Why, the next thing that is to be heard is, thou'rt a cuckold.

PINCHWIFE [*aside*]: Insupportable name!

HORNER: But I did not expect marriage from such a whore-master as you, one that knew the town so much, and women so well.

PINCHWIFE: Why, I have married no London wife.

HORNER: Pshaw, that's all one; that grave circumspection in marrying a country wife is like refusing a deceitful pampered Smithfield jade,[1] to go and be cheated by a friend in the country.

PINCHWIFE [*aside*]: A pox on him and his simile! – At least

1. *Smithfield jade*: poor horse smartened up to fool gullible buyers; also a whore.

we are a little surer of the breed there, know what her keeping has been, whether foyled [1] or unsound.

HORNER: Come, come, I have known a clap gotten in Wales; and there are cousins, justices, clarks, and chaplains in the country, I won't say coach-men. But she's handsome and young?

PINCHWIFE [aside]: I'll answer as I should do. – No, no, she has no beauty, but her youth; no attraction, but her modesty; wholesome, homely, and huswifely, that's all.

DORILANT: He talks as like a grazier as he looks.

PINCHWIFE: She's too aukerd, ill-favoured, and silly to bring to town.

HARCOURT: Then methinks you should bring her, to be taught breeding.

PINCHWIFE: To be taught? No, sir, I thank you, good wives and private soldiers should be ignorant. [Aside] [2] I'll keep her from your instructions, I warrant you.

HARCOURT: The rogue is as jealous as if his wife were not ignorant.

HORNER: Why, if she be ill-favoured, there will be less danger here for you than by leaving her in the country; we have such variety of dainties that we are seldom hungry.

DORILANT: But they have always coarse, constant, swinging stomachs in the country.

HARCOURT: Foul feeders indeed.

DORILANT: And your hospitality is great there.

HARCOURT: Open house, every man's welcome.

PINCHWIFE: So, so, gentlemen.

HORNER: But prithee, why wouldst thou marry her? If she be ugly, ill-bred and silly, she must be rich then.

PINCHWIFE: As rich as if she brought me twenty thousand pound out of this town; for she'll be as sure not to spend her moderate portion as a London baggage would be to spend hers, let it be what it would; so 'tis all one. Then, because she's ugly, she's the likelier to be my own; and being ill-bred, she'll hate conversation; and since silly and innocent, will

1. *Foyled*: defective.
2. S.D. *Aside*: this is given to Harcourt's next line in all quartos, mistakenly I think.

marriage

not know the difference betwixt a man of one and twenty
and one of forty.

HORNER: Nine – to my knowledge. But if she be silly, she'll
expect as much from a man of forty-nine as from him of one
and twenty. But methinks wit is more necessary than beauty,
and I think no young woman ugly that has it, and no handsome woman agreeable without it.

PINCHWIFE: 'Tis my maxim, he's a fool that marries, but
he's a greater that does not marry a fool. What is wit in a
wife good for, but to make a man a cuckold?

HORNER: Yes, to keep it from his knowledge.

PINCHWIFE: A fool cannot contrive to make her husband a
cuckold.

HORNER: No, but she'll club with a man that can; and what
is worse, if she cannot make her husband a cuckold, she'll
make him jealous, and pass for one, and then 'tis all one.

PINCHWIFE: Well, well, I'll take care for one, my wife shall
make me no cuckold, though she had your help, Mr Horner;
I understand the town, sir.

DORILANT [aside]: His help!

HARCOURT [aside]: He's come newly to town it seems, and
has not heard how things are with him.

HORNER: But tell me, has marriage cured thee of whoring,
which it seldom does?

HARCOURT: 'Tis more than age can do.

HORNER: No, the word is, I'll marry and live honest;[1] but a
marriage vow is like a penitent gamester's oath, and ent'ring
into bonds and penalties to stint himself to such a particular
small sum at play for the future, which makes him but the
more eager, and not being able to hold out, loses his money
again, and his forfeit to boot.

DORILANT: Ay, ay, a gamester will be a gamester, whilst his
money lasts; and a whoremaster whilst his vigour.

HARCOURT: Nay, I have known 'em, when they are broke
and can lose no more, keep a-fumbling with the box[2] in
their hands to fool with only, and hinder other gamesters.

DORILANT: That had wherewithal to make lusty stakes.

1. *Honest*: chaste.
2. *Box*: dice box.

PINCHWIFE: Well, gentlemen, you may laugh at me, but you shall never lie with my wife; I know the town.

HORNER: But prithee, was not the way you were in better? Is not keeping better than marriage?

PINCHWIFE: A pox on't, the jades would jilt me. I could never keep a whore to myself.

HORNER: So then you only married to keep a whore to yourself? Well, but let me tell you, women, as you say, are like soldiers, made constant and loyal by good pay, rather than by oaths and covenants. Therefore I'd advise my friends to keep rather than marry, since too I find by your example it does not serve one's turn, for I saw you yesterday in the eighteen-penny place[1] with a pretty country wench.

PINCHWIFE [aside]: How the divel did he see my wife then? I sate there that she might not be seen. But she shall never go to a play again.

HORNER: What, dost thou blush at nine and forty, for having been seen with a wench?

DORILANT: No, faith, I warrant 'twas his wife, which he seated there out of sight, for he's a cunning rogue, and understands the town.

HORNER: He blushes! Then 'twas his wife, for men are now more ashamed to be seen with them in public than with a wench.

PINCHWIFE [aside]: Hell and damnation! I'm undone, since Horner has seen her, and they know 'twas she.

HORNER: But prithee, was it thy wife? She was exceedingly pretty; I was in love with her at that distance.

PINCHWIFE: You are like never to be nearer to her. Your servant, gentlemen. [Offers to go.]

HORNER: Nay, prithee, stay.

PINCHWIFE: I cannot, I will not.

HORNER: Come, you shall dine with us.

PINCHWIFE: I have dined already.

HORNER: Come, I know thou hast not. I'll treat thee, dear rogue, thou shalt spend none of thy Hampshire[2] money today.

1. *Eighteen-penny place*: part of theatre occupied by whores.
2. *Hampshire*: commonly used to signify the country.

PINCHWIFE [*aside*]: Treat me! So he uses me already like his cuckold.

HORNER: Nay, you shall not go.

PINCHWIFE: I must, I have business at home. [*Exit* PINCHWIFE.]

HARCOURT: To beat his wife. He's as jealous of her as a Cheapside husband of a Covent Garden wife.[1]

HORNER: Why, it is as hard to find an old whoremaster without jealousy and the gout, as a young one without fear or the pox.

> As gout in age from pox in youth proceeds,
> So wenching past, then jealousy succeeds:
> The worst disease that love and wenching breeds.

1. *Cheapside ... Covent Garden*: city (trading class) husband and fashionable wife.

Act Two

(PINCHWIFE's *house*.)

MRS MARGERY PINCHWIFE *and* ALITHEA: MR PINCHWIFE *peeping behind at the door*.

MRS PINCHWIFE: Pray, sister, where are the best fields and woods to walk in in London?

ALITHEA: A pretty question! Why, sister, Mulberry Garden and St James's Park; and for close walks, the New Exchange.

MRS PINCHWIFE: Pray, sister, tell me why my husband looks so grum here in town, and keeps me up so close, and will not let me go a-walking, nor let me wear my best gown yesterday.

ALITHEA: Oh, he's jealous, sister.

MRS PINCHWIFE: Jealous? What's that?

ALITHEA: He's afraid you should love another man.

MRS PINCHWIFE: How should he be afraid of my loving another man, when he will not let me see any but himself?

ALITHEA: Did he not carry you yesterday to a play?

MRS PINCHWIFE: Ay, but we sate amongst ugly people. He would not let me come near the gentry, who sate under us, so that I could not see 'em. He told me none but naughty women sate there, whom they toused and moused; but I would have ventured for all that.

ALITHEA: But how did you like the play?

MRS PINCHWIFE: Indeed I was a-weary of the play, but I liked hugeously the actors; they are the goodliest properest men, sister!

ALITHEA: Oh, but you must not like the actors, sister.

MRS PINCHWIFE: Ay, how should I help it, sister? Pray, sister, when my husband comes in, will you ask leave for me to go a-walking?

ALITHEA [*aside*]: A-walking! Hah, ha! Lord, a country

gentlewoman's leasure is the drudgery of a foot-post; and
she requires as much airing as her husband's horses.

    Enter MR PINCHWIFE *to them.*

But here comes your husband. I'll ask, though I'm sure he'll
not grant it.

MRS PINCHWIFE: He says he won't let me go abroad, for
fear of catching the pox.

ALITHEA: Fie! The smallpox, you should say.

MRS PINCHWIFE: Oh my dear, dear bud, welcome home!
Why dost thou look so fropish?[1] Who has nangered thee?

PINCHWIFE: You're a fool.

    MRS PINCHWIFE *goes aside and cries.*

ALITHEA: Faith so she is, for crying for no fault, poor tender
creature!

PINCHWIFE: What, you would have her as impudent as
yourself, as errant a jilflirt, a gadder, a magpie, and to say
all, a mere notorious town-woman?

ALITHEA: Brother, you are my only censurer, and the honour
of your family shall sooner suffer in your wife there than in
me, though I take the innocent liberty of the town.

PINCHWIFE: Hark you mistress, do not talk so before my
wife. The innocent liberty of the town!

ALITHEA: Why, pray, who boasts of any intrigue with me?
What lampoon has made my name notorious? What ill
women frequent my lodgings? I keep no company with
any women of scandalous reputations.

PINCHWIFE: No, you keep the men of scandalous reputations
company.

ALITHEA: Where? Would you not have me civil? Answer
'em in a box at the plays, in the drawing-room at Whitehall,
in St James's Park, Mulberry Garden, or –

PINCHWIFE: Hold, hold! Do not teach my wife where the
men are to be found. I believe she's the worse for your town
documents already. I bid you keep her in ignorance as I do.

MRS PINCHWIFE: Indeed, be not angry with her bud, she
will tell me nothing of the town, though I ask her a thousand
times a day.

PINCHWIFE: Then you are very inquisitive to know, I find?

    1. *Fropish*: peevish.

MRS PINCHWIFE: Not I indeed, dear, I hate London. Our place-house in the country is worth a thousand of't. Would I were there again!

PINCHWIFE: So you shall, I warrant. But were you not talking of plays and players when I came in? [*To* ALITHEA] You are her encourager in such discourses.

MRS PINCHWIFE: No indeed, dear, she chid me just now for liking the playermen.

PINCHWIFE [*aside*]: Nay, if she be so innocent as to own to me her liking them, there is no hurt in't. – Come my poor rogue, but thou likest none better than me?

MRS PINCHWIFE: Yes indeed, but I do, the playermen are finer folks.

PINCHWIFE: But you love none better than me?

MRS PINCHWIFE: You are mine own dear bud, and I know you. I hate a stranger.

PINCHWIFE: Ay, my dear, you must love me only, and not be like the naughty town-women, who only hate their husbands, and love every man else, love plays, visits, fine coaches, fine clothes, fiddles, balls, treats, and so lead a wicked town-life.

MRS PINCHWIFE: Nay, if to enjoy all these things be a town-life, London is not so bad a place, dear.

PINCHWIFE: How! If you love me, you must hate London.

ALITHEA (*aside*): The fool has forbid me discovering to her the pleasures of the town, and he is now setting her agog upon them himself.

MRS PINCHWIFE: But, husband, do the town-women love the playermen too?

PINCHWIFE: Yes, I warrant you.

ALITHEA: Ay, I warrant you.[1]

PINCHWIFE: Why, you do not, I hope?

MRS PINCHWIFE: No, no, bud, but why have we no playermen in the country?

PINCHWIFE: Ha! Mrs Minx, ask me no more to go to a play.

MRS PINCHWIFE: Nay, why, love? I did not care for going; but when you forbid me, you make me, as't were, desire it.

ALITHEA [*aside*]: So 'twill be in other things, I warrant.

1. *Alithea*: all editions assign this line to Mrs Pinchwife.

MRS PINCHWIFE: Pray, let me go to a play, dear.

PINCHWIFE: Hold your peace, I wo'not.

MRS PINCHWIFE: Why, love?

PINCHWIFE: Why, I'll tell you.

ALITHEA [aside]: Nay, if he tell her, she'll give him more cause to forbid her that place.

MRS PINCHWIFE: Pray, why, dear?

PINCHWIFE: First, you like the actors, and the gallants may like you.

MRS PINCHWIFE: What, a homely country girl? No bud, nobody will like me.

PINCHWIFE: I tell you yes, they may.

MRS PINCHWIFE: No, no, you jest. I won't believe you, I will go.

PINCHWIFE: I tell you then, that one of the lewdest fellows in town who saw you there, told me he was in love with you.

MRS PINCHWIFE: Indeed! Who, who, pray, who was't?

PINCHWIFE [aside]: I've gone too far, and slipped before I was aware. How overjoyed she is!

MRS PINCHWIFE: Was it any Hampshire gallant, any of our neighbours? I promise you, I am beholding to him.

PINCHWIFE: I promise you, you lie; for he would but ruin you, as he has done hundreds. He has no other love for women but that such as he look upon women, like basilisks,[1] but to destroy 'em.

MRS PINCHWIFE: Ay, but if he loves me why should he ruin me? Answer me to that. Methinks he should not. I would do him no harm.

ALITHEA: Hah, ha, ha!

PINCHWIFE: 'Tis very well; but I'll keep him from doing you any harm, or me either.

Enter SPARKISH *and* HARCOURT.

But here comes company; get you in, get you in.

MRS PINCHWIFE: But pray, husband, is he a pretty gentleman, that loves me?

PINCHWIFE: In baggage, in. [*Thrusts her in: shuts the door.*] (*Aside*) What, all the lewd libertines of the town brought

1. *Basilisks*: creatures whose glances were supposed to kill.

to my lodging by this easy coxcomb! S'death, I'll not
suffer it.

SPARKISH: Here, Harcourt, do you approve my choice?
Dear little rogue, I told you I'd bring you acquainted with
all my friends, the wits, and –

    HARCOURT *salutes her.*

PINCHWIFE: Ay, they shall know her as well as you yourself
will, I warrant you.

SPARKISH: This is one of those, my pretty rogue, that are to
dance at your wedding tomorrow; and him you must bid
welcome ever, to what you and I have.

PINCHWIFE [*aside*]: Monstrous! –

SPARKISH: Harcourt, how dost thou like her, faith? Nay,
dear, do not look down; I should hate to have a wife of
mine out of countenance at anything.

PINCHWIFE: Wonderful!

SPARKISH: Tell me, I say, Harcourt, how dost thou like her?
Thou hast stared upon her enough to resolve me.

HARCOURT: So infinitely well that I could wish I had a
mistress too, that might differ from her in nothing but her
love and engagement to you.

ALITHEA: Sir, Master Sparkish has often told me that his
acquaintance were all wits and railleurs,[1] and now I find it.

SPARKISH: No, by the universe, madam, he does not rally
now; you may believe him. I do assure you, he is the
honestest, worthiest, true-hearted gentleman – a man of
such perfect honour, he would say nothing to a lady he does
not mean.

PINCHWIFE (*aside*): Praising another man to his mistress!

HARCOURT: Sir, you are so beyond expectation obliging
that –

SPARKISH: Nay, egad, I am sure you do admire her extremely, I see't in your eyes. – He does admire you, madam.
– By the world, don't you?

HARCOURT: Yes, above the world, or the most glorious part
of it, her whole sex; and till now I never thought I should
have envied you or any man about to marry, but you have
the best excuse for marriage I ever knew.

    1. *Railleurs*: banterers.

ALITHEA: Nay, now sir, I'm satisfied you are of the society of the wits and railleurs, since you cannot spare your friend, even when he is but too civil to you; but the surest sign is, since you are an enemy to marriage, for that I hear you hate as much as business or bad wine.

HARCOURT: Truly, madam, I never was an enemy to marriage till now, because marriage was never an enemy to me before.

ALITHEA: But why, sir, is marriage an enemy to you now? Because it robs you of your friend here? For you look upon a friend married as one gone into a monastery, that is, dead to the world.

HARCOURT: 'Tis indeed, because you marry him. I see madam, you can guess my meaning. I do confess heartily and openly I wish it were in my power to break the match, by heavens I would.

SPARKISH: Poor Frank!

ALITHEA: Would you be so unkind to me?

HARCOURT: No, no, 'tis not because I would be unkind to you.

SPARKISH: Poor Frank! No, egad, 'tis only his kindness to me.

PINCHWIFE [aside]: Great kindness to you indeed! Insensible fop, let a man make love to his wife to his face!

SPARKISH: Come, dear Frank, for all my wife there that shall be, thou shalt enjoy me sometimes, dear rogue. By my honour, we men of wit condole for our deceased brother in marriage as much as for one dead in earnest. I think that was prettily said of me, ha, Harcourt? But come, Frank, be not melancholy for me.

HARCOURT: No, I assure you I am not melancholy for you.

SPARKISH: Prithee, Frank, dost think my wife that shall be there a fine person?

HARCOURT: I could gaze upon her till I became as blind as you are.

SPARKISH: How, as I am? How?

HARCOURT: Because you are a lover, and true lovers are blind, stock blind.

SPARKISH: True, true. But by the world, she has wit too, as

well as beauty. Go, go with her into a corner, and try if she has wit. Talk to her any thing, she's bashful before me.

HARCOURT: Indeed, if a woman wants wit in a corner, she has it nowhere.

ALITHEA [*aside to* SPARKISH]: Sir, you dispose of me a little before your time.

SPARKISH: Nay, nay, madam, let me have an earnest of your obedience, or – go, go, madam.

HARCOURT *courts* ALITHEA *aside.*

PINCHWIFE: How, sir, if you are not concerned for the honour of a wife, I am for that of a sister. He shall not debauch her. Be a pander to your own wife, bring men to her, let 'em make love before your face, thrust 'em into a corner together, then leave 'em in private! Is this your town wit and conduct?

SPARKISH: Hah, ha, ha! A silly wise rogue would make one laugh more than a stark fool, hah, ha! I shall burst. Nay, you shall not disturb 'em; I'll vex thee, by the world.

Struggles with PINCHWIFE *to keep him from* HARCOURT *and* ALITHEA.

ALITHEA: The writings are drawn, sir, settlements made; 'tis too late, sir, and past all revocation.

HARCOURT: Then so is my death.

ALITHEA: I would not be unjust to him.

HARCOURT: Then why to me so?

ALITHEA: I have no obligation to you.

HARCOURT: My love.

ALITHEA: I had his before.

HARCOURT: You never had it; he wants, you see, jealousy, the only fallible sign of it.

ALITHEA: Love proceeds from esteem; he cannot distrust my virtue. Besides, he loves me, or he would not marry me.

HARCOURT: Marrying you is no more sign of his love than bribing your woman, that he may marry you, is a sign of his generosity. Marriage is rather a sign of interest than love; and he that marries a fortune covets a mistress, not loves her. But if you take marriage for a sign of love, take it from me immediately.

ALITHEA: No, now you have put a scruple in my head; but

in short, sir, to end our dispute, I must marry him, my reputation would suffer in the world else.

HARCOURT: No, if you do marry him, with your pardon, madam, your reputation suffers in the world, and you would be thought in necessity for a cloak.

ALITHEA: Nay, now you are rude, sir. – Mr Sparkish, pray come hither, your friend here is very troublesome, and very loving.

HARCOURT [aside to ALITHEA]: Hold, hold!

PINCHWIFE: D'ye hear that?

SPARKISH: Why, d'ye think I'll seem to be jealous, like a country bumpkin?

PINCHWIFE: No, rather be a cuckold, like a credulous cit.[1]

HARCOURT: Madam, you would not have been so little generous as to have told him.

ALITHEA: Yes, since you could be so little generous as to wrong him.

HARCOURT: Wrong him? No man can do't, he's beneath an injury. A bubble,[2] a coward, a senseless idiot, a wretch so contemptible to all the world but you that –

ALITHEA: Hold, do not rail at him, for since he is like to be my husband, I am resolved to like him. Nay, I think I am obliged to tell him you are not his friend. – Master Sparkish, Master Sparkish.

SPARKISH: What, what? How, dear rogue, has not she wit?

HARCOURT [speaks surlily]: Not so much as I thought, and hoped she had.

ALITHEA: Mr Sparkish, do you bring people to rail at you?

HARCOURT: Madam –

SPARKISH: How! No, but if he does rail at me, 'tis but in jest I warrant; what we wits do for one another, and never take any notice of it.

ALITHEA: He spoke so scurrilously of you, I had no patience to hear him; besides, he has been making love to me.

HARCOURT [aside]: True, damn'd tell-tale woman!

---

1. *Cit*: contemptuous term for citizen.
2. *Bubble*: credulous nincompoop.

SPARKISH: Pshaw, to shew his parts. We wits rail and make love often, but to shew our parts, as we have no affections, so we have no malice, we -

ALITHEA: He said you were a wretch, below an injury.

SPARKISH: Pshaw!

HARCOURT (*aside*): Damned, senseless, impudent, virtuous jade! Well, since she won't let me have her, she'll do as good, she'll make me hate her.

ALITHEA: A common bubble.

SPARKISH: Pshaw!

ALITHEA: A coward.

SPARKISH: Pshaw, pshaw!

ALITHEA: A senseless drivelling idiot.

SPARKISH: How! Did he disparage my parts? Nay, then my honour's concern'd, I can't put up that, sir, by the world. Brother, help me to kill him. [*Aside*] I may draw now, since we have the odds of him. 'Tis a good occasion too, before my mistress – [*Offers to draw.*]

ALITHEA: Hold, hold!

SPARKISH: What, what?

ALITHEA [*aside*]: I must not let 'em kill the gentleman neither, for his kindness to me; I am so far from hating him that I wish my gallant had his person and understanding. Nay, if my honour –

SPARKISH: I'll be thy death.

ALITHEA: Hold, hold! Indeed, to tell the truth, the gentleman said after all that what he spoke was but out of friendship to you.

SPARKISH: How! Say, I am – I am a fool, that is, no wit, out of friendship to me?

ALITHEA: Yes, to try whether I was concerned enough for you, and made love to me only to be satisfied of my virtue, for your sake.

HARCOURT [*aside*]: Kind, however –

SPARKISH: Nay, if it were so, my dear rogue, I ask thee pardon. But why would not you tell me so, faith?

HARCOURT: Because I did not think on't, faith.

SPARKISH: Come, Horner does not come; Harcourt, let's be gone to the new play. – Come, madam.

ALITHEA: I will not go if you intend to leave me alone in the box and run into the pit, as you use to do.

SPARKISH: Pshaw! I'll leave Harcourt with you in the box to entertain you, and that's as good; if I sate in the box, I should be thought no judge, but of trimmings.[1] – Come away Harcourt, lead her down.

Exeunt SPARKISH, HARCOURT, *and* ALITHEA.

PINCHWIFE: Well, go thy ways for the flower of the true town fops, such as spend their estates before they come to 'em and are cuckolds before they're married. But let me go look to my own freehold. – How!

Enter MY LADY FIDGET, MRS DAINTY FIDGET, *and* MRS SQUEAMISH.

LADY FIDGET: Your servant, sir. Where is your lady? We are come to wait upon her to the new play.

PINCHWIFE: New play!

LADY FIDGET: And my husband will wait upon you presently.

PINCHWIFE [*aside*]: Damn your civility. Madam, by no means. I will not see Sir Jasper here till I have waited upon him at home; nor shall my wife see you till she has waited upon your ladyship at your lodgings.

LADY FIDGET: Now we are here, sir –

PINCHWIFE: No, madam.

MRS DAINTY FIDGET: Pray let us see her.

MRS SQUEAMISH: We will not stir till we see her.

PINCHWIFE [*aside*]: A pox on you all. – [*Goes to the door, and returns*.] She has locked the door and is gone abroad.

LADY FIDGET: No, you have locked the door, and she's within.

MRS DAINTY FIDGET: They told us below she was here.

PINCHWIFE (*aside*): Will nothing do? Well it must out then. To tell you the truth, ladies, which I was afraid to let you know before lest it might endanger your lives, my wife has just now the smallpox come out upon her. Do not be frightened; but pray be gone ladies. You shall not stay here in danger of your lives. Pray get you gone ladies.

LADY FIDGET: No, no, we have all had 'em.

1. *Trimmings*: clothes.

MRS SQUEAMISH: Alack, alack!

MRS DAINTY FIDGET: Come, come, we must see how it goes with her. I understand the disease.

LADY FIDGET: Come.

PINCHWIFE [*aside*]: Well, there is no being too hard for women at their own weapon, lying; therefore I'll quit the field.

Exit PINCHWIFE.

MRS SQUEAMISH: Here's an example of jealousy.

LADY FIDGET: Indeed, as the world goes, I wonder there are no more jealous, since wives are so neglected.

MRS DAINTY FIDGET: Pshaw! As the world goes, to what end should they be jealous?

LADY FIDGET: Foh, 'tis a nasty world.

MRS SQUEAMISH: That men of parts, great acquaintance, and quality should take up with, and spend themselves and fortunes in keeping little playhouse creatures, foh!

LADY FIDGET: Nay, that women of understanding, great acquaintance, and good quality should fall a keeping too of little creatures, foh!

MRS SQUEAMISH: Why, 'tis the men of quality's fault; they never visit women of honour and reputation, as they used to do; and have not so much as common civility for ladies of our rank, but use us with the same indifferency and ill breeding as if we were all married to 'em.

LADY FIDGET: She says true. 'Tis an errant shame women of quality should be so slighted. Methinks birth – birth should go for something. I have known men admired, courted, and followed for their titles only.

MRS SQUEAMISH: Ay, one would think men of honour should not love, no more than marry out of their own rank.

MRS DAINTY FIDGET: Fie, fie upon 'em! They are come to think cross breeding for themselves best, as well as for their dogs and horses.

LADY FIDGET: They are dogs and horses for't.

MRS SQUEAMISH: One would think, if not for love, for vanity a little.

MRS DAINTY FIDGET: Nay, they do satisfy their vanity upon

us sometimes, and are kind to us in their report; tell all the world they lie with us.

LADY FIDGET: Damned rascals! That we should be only wronged by 'em; to report a man has had a person, when he has not had a person, is the greatest wrong in the whole world that can be done to a person.

MRS SQUEAMISH: Well, 'tis an arrant shame noble persons should be so wronged and neglected.

LADY FIDGET: But still 'tis an arranter shame for a noble person to neglect her own honour, and defame her own noble person with little inconsiderable fellows. Foh!

MRS DAINTY FIDGET: I suppose the crime against our honour is the same with a man of quality as with another.

LADY FIDGET: How! No, sure, the man of quality is likest one's husband, and therefore the fault should be the less.

MRS DAINTY FIDGET: But then the pleasure should be the less.

LADY FIDGET: Fie, fie, fie, for shame sister! Whither shall we ramble? Be continent in your discourse, or I shall hate you.

MRS DAINTY FIDGET: Besides, an intrigue is so much the more notorious for the man's quality.

MRS SQUEAMISH: 'Tis true, nobody takes notice of a private man, and therefore with him 'tis more secret, and the crime's the less when 'tis not known.

LADY FIDGET: You say true. I'faith, I think you are in the right on't. 'Tis not an injury to a husband till it be an injury to our honours; so that a woman of honour loses no honour with a private person. And to say truth –

MRS DAINTY FIDGET [*apart to* MRS SQUEAMISH]: So the little fellow is grown a private person with her.

LADY FIDGET: But still my dear, dear honour.

Enter SIR JASPER, HORNER, DORILANT.

SIR JASPER: Ay, my dear, dear of honour, thou hast still so much honour in thy mouth –

HORNER [*aside*]: That she has none elsewhere.

LADY FIDGET: Oh, what d'ye mean to bring in these upon us?

MRS DAINTY FIDGET: Foh! These are as bad as wits.

MRS SQUEAMISH: Foh!

LADY FIDGET: Let us leave the room.

SIR JASPER: Stay, stay, 'faith, to tell you the naked truth –

LADY FIDGET: Fie, Sir Jasper! Do not use that word 'naked'.

SIR JASPER: Well, well, in short I have business at Whitehall, and cannot go to the play with you, therefore would have you go –

LADY FIDGET: With those two to a play?

SIR JASPER: No, not with t'other, but with Mr Horner. There can be no more scandal to go with him than with Mr Tattle, or Master Limberham.[1]

LADY FIDGET: With that nasty fellow! No – no!

SIR JASPER: Nay, prithee dear, hear me. [*Whispers to* LADY FIDGET.]

HORNER: Ladies – [HORNER, DORILANT *drawing near* SQUEAMISH, *and* DAINTY.]

MRS DAINTY FIDGET: Stand off.

MRS SQUEAMISH: Do not approach us.

MRS DAINTY FIDGET: You herd with the wits, you are obscenity all over.

MRS SQUEAMISH: And I would as soon look upon a picture of Adam and Eve, without fig leaves, as any of you, if I could help it; therefore keep off, and do not make us sick.

DORILANT: What a divel are these?

HORNER: Why, these are pretenders to honour, as critics to wit, only by censuring others; and as every raw, peevish, out-of-humoured, affected, dull, tea-drinking, arithmetical fop sets up for a wit by railing at men of sense, so these for honour, by railing at the Court, and ladies of as great honour as quality.

SIR JASPER: Come, Mr Horner, I must desire you to go with these ladies to the play, sir.

HORNER: I, sir!

SIR JASPER: Ay, ay, come, sir.

HORNER: I must beg your pardon, sir, and theirs, I will not be seen in women's company in public again for the world.

1. *Mr Tattle, or Master Limberham*: characters in plays of Dryden and Congreve; commonly used before this for ineffectual persons.

SIR JASPER: Ha, ha! Strange aversion!

MRS SQUEAMISH: No, he's for women's company in private.

SIR JASPER: He – poor man – he! Hah, ha, ha!

MRS DAINTY FIDGET: 'Tis a greater shame amongst lewd fellows to be seen in virtuous women's company than for the women to be seen with them.

HORNER: Indeed, madam, the time was I only hated virtuous women, but now I hate the other too. I beg your pardon, ladies.

LADY FIDGET: You are very obliging, sir, because we would not be troubled with you.

SIR JASPER: In sober sadness he shall go.

DORILANT: Nay, if he wo'not, I am ready to wait upon the ladies; and I think I am the fitter man.

SIR JASPER: You, sir? No I thank you for that – Master Horner is a privileged man amongst the virtuous ladies; 'twill be a great while before you are so, heh, he, he! He's my wife's gallant, heh, he, he! No, pray, withdraw, sir, for as I take it, the virtuous ladies have no business with you.

DORILANT: And I am sure he can have none with them. 'Tis strange a man can't come amongst virtuous women now but upon the same terms as men are admitted into the Great Turk's Seraglio. But heavens keep me from being an ombre player with 'em! But where is Pinchwife? [*Exit* DORILANT.]

SIR JASPER: Come, come, man. What, avoid the sweet society of woman-kind? That sweet, soft, gentle, tame, noble creature woman, made for man's companion?

HORNER: So is that soft, gentle, tame, and more noble creature a spaniel, and has all their tricks; can fawn, lie down, suffer beating, and fawn the more; barks at your friends when they come to see you, makes your bed hard, gives you fleas, and the mange sometimes. And all the difference is, the spaniel's the more faithful animal, and fawns but upon one master.

SIR JASPER: Heh, he, he!

MRS SQUEAMISH: Oh, the rude beast!

MRS DAINTY FIDGET: Insolent brute!

LADY FIDGET: Brute! Stinking, mortified, rotten French wether,[1] to dare –

SIR JASPER: Hold, an't please your ladyship. For shame, Master Horner, your mother was a woman. [*Aside*] Now shall I never reconcile 'em. – Hark you, madam, take my advice in your anger. You know you often want one to make up your drolling[2] pack of ombre players; and you may cheat him easily, for he's an ill gamester, and consequently loves play. Besides, you know, you have but two old civil gentlemen (with stinking breaths too) to wait upon you abroad; take in the third into your service. The other are but crazy. And a lady should have a supernumerary gentleman-usher, as a supernumerary coach-horse, lest sometimes you should be forced to stay at home.

LADY FIDGET: But are you sure he loves play, and has money?

SIR JASPER: He loves play as much as you, and has money as much as I.

LADY FIDGET: Then I am contented to make him pay for his scurrillity. Money makes up in a measure all other wants in men. Those whom we cannot make hold for gallants, we make fine.[3]

SIR JASPER [*aside*]: So, so. Now to mollify, to wheedle him. Master Horner, will you never keep civil company? Methinks 'tis time now, since you are only fit for them. Come, come, man, you must e'en fall to visiting our wives, eating at our tables, drinking tea with our virtuous relations after dinner, dealing cards to 'em, reading plays and gazettes to 'em, picking fleas out of their shocks[4] for 'em, collecting receipts, new songs, women, pages, and footmen for 'em.

HORNER: I hope they'll afford me better employment, sir.

SIR JASPER: Heh, he, he! 'Tis fit you know your work before you come into your place. And since you are unprovided of a lady to flatter and a good house to eat at,

1. *French wether*: castrated ram; man made impotent by venereal disease.
2. *Drolling*: comical.
3. *Fine*: pay.
4. *Shocks*: poodles.

pray frequent mine, and call my wife mistress, and she
shall call you gallant, according to the custom.

HORNER: Who, I?

SIR JASPER: Faith, thou shalt for my sake, come, for my sake
only.

HORNER: For your sake –

SIR JASPER: Come, come, (*to ladies*) here's a gamester for
you, let him be a little familiar sometimes. Nay, what if a
little rude? Gamesters may be rude with ladies, you know.

LADY FIDGET: Yes, losing gamesters have a privilege with
women.

HORNER: I always thought the contrary, that the winning
gamester had most privilege with women; for when you
have lost your money to a man, you'll lose anything you
have, all you have, they say, and he may use you as he
pleases.

SIR JASPER: Heh, he, he! Well, win or lose, you shall have
your liberty with her.

LADY FIDGET: As he behaves himself; and for your sake I'll
give him admittance and freedom.

HORNER: All sorts of freedom, madam?

SIR JASPER: Ay, ay, ay, all sorts of freedom thou canst take.
And so go to her, begin thy new employment. Wheedle
her, jest with her, and be better acquainted one with
another.

HORNER [*aside*]: I think I know her already, therefore may
venture with her, my secret for hers.

   HORNER *and* LADY FIDGET *whisper*.

SIR JASPER: Sister cuz, I have provided an innocent playfellow for you there.

MRS DAINTY FIDGET: Who, he?

MRS SQUEAMISH: There's a playfellow indeed.

SIR JASPER: Yes, sure; what, he is good enough to play at
cards, blind-man's buff, or the fool with sometimes.

MRS SQUEAMISH: Foh! We'll have no such playfellows.

MRS DAINTY FIDGET: No, sir, you shan't choose playfellows for us, we thank you.

SIR JASPER: Nay, pray hear me. [*Whispering to them.*]

LADY FIDGET (*aside to* HORNER): But, poor gentleman,

could you be so generous, so truly a man of honour, as for the sakes of us women of honour to cause yourself to be reported no man? No man! And to suffer yourself the greatest shame that could fall upon a man, that none might fall upon us women by your conversation? But indeed, sir, as perfectly, perfectly, the same man as before your going into France, sir? As perfectly, perfectly, sir?

HORNER: As perfectly, perfectly, madam. Nay, I scorn you should take my word; I desire to be tried only, madam.

LADY FIDGET: Well, that's spoken again like a man of honour; all men of honour desire to come to the test. But indeed, generally you men report such things of yourselves, one does not know how or whom to believe; and it is come to that pass, we dare not take your words, no more than your tailor's, without some staid servant of yours be bound with you. But I have so strong a faith in your honour, dear, dear, noble sir, that I'd forfeit mine for yours at any time, dear sir.

HORNER: No, madam, you should not need to forfeit it for me. I have given you security already to save you harmless, my late reputation being so well known in the world, madam.

LADY FIDGET: But if upon any future falling out, or upon a suspicion of my taking the trust out of your hands to employ some other, you yourself should betray your trust, dear sir? I mean, if you'll give me leave to speak obscenely, you might tell, dear sir.

HORNER: If I did, nobody would believe me. The reputation of impotency is as hardly recovered again in the world as that of cowardice, dear madam.

LADY FIDGET: Nay then, as one may say, you may do your worst, dear, dear, sir.

SIR JASPER: Come, is your ladyship reconciled to him yet? Have you agreed on matters? For I must be gone to Whitehall.

LADY FIDGET: Why indeed, Sir Jasper, Master Horner is a thousand thousand times a better man than I thought him. Cosen Squeamish, Sister Dainty, I can name him now. Truly, not long ago you know, I thought his very name obscenity, and I would as soon have lain with him as have named him.

SIR JASPER: Very likely, poor madam.

MRS DAINTY FIDGET: I believe it.

MRS SQUEAMISH: No doubt on't.

SIR JASPER: Well, well. That your ladyship is as virtuous as any she, I know, and him all the town knows – heh, he, he! Therefore now you like him, get you gone to your business together. Go, go, to your business, I say, pleasure, whilst I go to my pleasure, business.

LADY FIDGET: Come then, dear gallant.

HORNER: Come away, my dearest mistress.

SIR JASPER: So, so, why, 'tis as I'd have it. [*Exit* SIR JASPER.]

HORNER: And as I'd have it.

LADY FIDGET: Who for his business from his wife will run,
　　　　　　Takes the best care, to have her business done.

Exeunt omnes.

Act Three

SCENE ONE

(PINCHWIFE's *house*.)
ALITHEA *and* MRS PINCHWIFE.

ALITHEA: Sister, what ails you? You are grown melancholy.

MRS PINCHWIFE: Would it not make anyone melancholy, to see you go every day fluttering about abroad, whilst I must stay at home like a poor, lonely, sullen bird in a cage?

ALITHEA: Ay, sister, but you came young, and just from the nest to your cage, so that I thought you liked it, and could be as cheerful in't as others that took their flight themselves early, and are hopping abroad in the open air.

MRS PINCHWIFE: Nay, I confess I was quiet enough till my husband told me what pure[1] lives the London ladies live abroad, with their dancing, meetings and junketings, and dressed every day in their best gowns; and I warrant you, play at ninepins every day of the week, so they do.

Enter MR PINCHWIFE.

PINCHWIFE: Come, what's here to do? You are putting the town pleasures in her head and setting her a-longing.

ALITHEA: Yes, after nine pins. You suffer none to give her those longings you mean, but yourself.

PINCHWIFE: I tell her of the vanities of the town like a confessor.

ALITHEA: A confessor! Just such a confessor as he that by forbidding a silly oastler to grease the horse's teeth, taught him to do't.

PINCHWIFE: Come Mistress Flippant, good precepts are lost when bad examples are still before us. The liberty you take abroad makes her hanker after it, and out of humour at home. Poor wretch! She desired not to come to London; I would bring her.

ALITHEA: Very well.

1. *Pure*: grand.

PINCHWIFE: She has been this week in town, and never desired, till this afternoon, to go abroad.

ALITHEA: Was she not at a play yesterday?

PINCHWIFE: Yes, but she ne'er asked me. I was myself the cause of her going.

ALITHEA: Then if she ask you again, you are the cause of her asking, and not my example.

PINCHWIFE: Well, tomorrow night I shall be rid of you; and the next day before 'tis light, she and I'll be rid of the town, and my dreadful apprehensions. (*To* MRS PINCHWIFE) Come, be not melancholy, for thou shalt go into the country after tomorrow, dearest.

ALITHEA: Great comfort!

MRS PINCHWIFE: Pish, what d'ye tell me of the country for?

PINCHWIFE: How's this! What, pish at the country?

MRS PINCHWIFE: Let me alone, I am not well.

PINCHWIFE: Oh, if that be all. What ails my dearest?

MRS PINCHWIFE: Truly I don't know. But I have not been well since you told me there was a gallant at the play in love with me.

PINCHWIFE: Ha!

ALITHEA: That's by my example too!

PINCHWIFE: Nay, if you are not well, but are so concerned because a lewd fellow chanced to lie and say he liked you, you'll make me sick too.

MRS PINCHWIFE: Of what sickness?

PINCHWIFE: Oh, of that which is worse than the plague, jealousy.

MRS PINCHWIFE: Pish, you jeer. I'm sure there's no such disease in our receipt-book at home.

PINCHWIFE: No, thou never met'st with it, poor innocent. – [*Aside*] Well, if thou cuckold me, 'twill be my own fault, for cuckolds and bastards are generally makers of their own fortune.

MRS PINCHWIFE: Well, but pray bud, let's go to a play tonight.

PINCHWIFE (*aside*): 'Tis just done, she comes from it. (*To* MRS PINCHWIFE) But why are you so eager to see a play?

MRS PINCHWIFE: Faith dear, not that I care one pin for their talk there. But I like to look upon the playermen, and would see, if I could, the gallant you say loves me. That's all, dear bud.

PINCHWIFE: Is that all, dear bud?

ALITHEA: This proceeds from my example!

MRS PINCHWIFE: But if the play be done, let's go abroad however, dear bud.

PINCHWIFE: Come, have a little patience, and thou shalt go into the country on Friday.

MRS PINCHWIFE: Therefore I would see first some sights, to tell my neighbours of. Nay, I will go abroad, that's once.

ALITHEA: I'm the cause of this desire too.

PINCHWIFE: But now I think on't, who was the cause of Horner's coming to my lodging today? That was you.

ALITHEA: No, you, because you would not let him see your handsome wife out of your lodging.

MRS PINCHWIFE: Why, O Lord! Did the gentleman come hither to see me indeed?

PINCHWIFE: No, no. You are not the cause of that damned question too, Mistress Alithea? [*Aside*] Well, she's in the right of it. He is in love with my wife, and comes after her; 'tis so; but I'll nip his love in the bud, lest he should follow us into the country and break his chariot-wheel near our house, on purpose for an excuse to come to't. But I think I know the town.

MRS PINCHWIFE: Come, pray bud, let's go abroad before 'tis late; for I will go, that's flat and plain.

PINCHWIFE [*aside*]: So! The obstinacy already of a town-wife, and I must, whilst she's here, humour her like one. – Sister, how shall we do, that she may not be seen or known?

ALITHEA: Let her put on her mask.

PINCHWIFE: Pshaw! A mask makes people but the more inquisitive, and is as ridiculous a disguise as a stage-beard; her shape, stature, habit will be known. And if we should meet with Horner, he would be sure to take acquaintance with us, must wish her joy, kiss her, talk to her, leer upon her, and the devil and all. No, I'll not use her to a mask, 'tis dangerous; for masks have made more cuckolds than the best faces that ever were known.

ALITHEA: How will you do then?

MRS PINCHWIFE: Nay, shall we go? The Exchange will be shut, and I have a mind to see that.

PINCHWIFE: So – I have it – I'll dress her up in the suit we are to carry down to her brother, little Sir James; nay, I understand the town tricks. Come, let's go dress her. A mask! No – a woman masked, like a covered dish, gives a man curiosity and appetite, when, it may be, uncovered, 'twould turn his stomach. No, no.

ALITHEA: Indeed, your comparison is something a greasy one. But I had a gentle gallant used to say, a beauty masked, like the sun in eclipse, gathers together more gazers than if it shined out.

Exeunt.

SCENE TWO

The scene changes to the New Exchange. Enter HORNER, HARCOURT, DORILANT.

DORILANT: Engaged to women, and not sup with us?

HORNER: Ay, a pox on 'em all!

HARCOURT: You were much a more reasonable man in the morning, and, had as noble resolutions against 'em as a widower of a week's liberty.

DORILANT: Did I ever think to see you keep company with women in vain?

HORNER: In vain! No – 'tis, since I can't love 'em, to be revenged on 'em.

HARCOURT: Now your sting is gone, you looked in the box, amongst all those women, like a drone in the hive, all upon you; shoved and ill-used by 'em all, and thrust from one side to t'other.

DORILANT: Yet he must be buzzing amongst 'em still, like other old beetle-headed, liquorish drones. Avoid 'em, and hate 'm as they hate you.

HORNER: Because I do hate 'em, and would hate 'em yet

more, I'll frequent 'em. You may see by marriage, nothing makes a man hate a woman more than her constant conversation. In short, I converse with 'em, as you do with rich fools, to laugh at 'em and use 'em ill.

DORILANT: But I would no more sup with women, unless I could lie with 'em, than sup with a rich coxcomb unless I could cheat him.

HORNER: Yes, I had known thee sup with a fool for his drinking. If he could set out your hand that way only, you were satisfied, and if he were a wine-swallowing mouth 'twas enough.

HARCOURT: Yes, a man drinks often with a fool, as he tosses with a marker,[1] only to keep his hand in ure.[2] But do the ladies drink?

HORNER: Yes, sir, and I shall have the pleasure at least of laying 'em flat with a bottle, and bring as much scandal that way upon 'em as formerly t'other.

HARCOURT: Perhaps you may prove as weak a brother amongst 'em that way as t'other.

DORILANT: Foh! Drinking with women is as unnatural as scolding with 'em; but 'tis a pleasure of decayed fornicators, and the basest way of quenching love.

HARCOURT: Nay, 'tis drowning love instead of quenching it. But leave us for civil women too!

DORILANT: Ay, when he can't be the better for 'em. We hardly pardon a man that leaves his friend for a wench, and that's a pretty lawful call.

HORNER: Faith, I would not leave you for 'em, if they would not drink.

DORILANT: Who would disappoint his company at Lewis's for a gossiping?

HARCOURT: Foh! Wine and women, good apart, together as nauseous as sack and sugar. But hark you, sir, before you go, a little of your advice; an old maimed general, when unfit for action, is fittest for counsel. I have other designs upon women than eating and drinking with them. I am in love with Sparkish's mistress, whom he is to marry tomorrow. Now how shall I get her?

1. *Marker*: scorer.   2. *Ure*: practice.

Enter SPARKISH, *looking about.*

HORNER: Why, here comes one will help you to her.

HARCOURT: He! He, I tell you, is my rival, and will hinder my love.

HORNER: No, a foolish rival and a jealous husband assist their rival's designs; for they are sure to make their women hate them, which is the first step to their love for another man.

HARCOURT: But I cannot come near his mistress, but in his company.

HORNER: Still the better for you, for fools are most easily cheated when they themselves are accessories. And he is to be bubbled[1] of his mistress, as of his money, the common mistress, by keeping him company.

SPARKISH: Who is that, that is to be bubbled? Faith let me snack,[2] I han't met with a bubble since Christmas. Gad, I think bubbles are like their brother woodcocks,[3] go out with the cold weather.

HARCOURT [*apart to* HORNER]: A pox! He did not hear all, I hope.

SPARKISH: Come, you bubbling rogues you, where do we sup? Oh, Harcourt, my mistress tells me you have been making fierce love to her all the play long, hah, ha! But I –

HARCOURT: I make love to her?

SPARKISH: Nay, I forgive thee; for I think I know thee, and I know her, but I am sure I know myself.

HARCOURT: Did she tell you so? I see all women are like these of the Exchange, who, to enhance the price of their commodities, report to their fond customers offers which were never made 'em.

HORNER: Ay, women are as apt to tell before the intrigue as men after it, and so shew themselves the vainer sex. But hast thou a mistress, Sparkish? 'Tis as hard for me to believe it as that thou ever hadst a bubble, as you bragged just now.

SPARKISH: Oh, your servant, sir; are you at your raillery sir? But we were some of us beforehand with you today at the play. The wits were something bold with you, sir. Did you not hear us laugh?

1. *Bubbled*: cheated.   2. *Snack*: share.   3. *Woodcocks*: fools.

HARCOURT: Yes, but I thought you had gone to plays to laugh at the poet's wit, not at your own.

SPARKISH: Your servant, sir, no, I thank you. Gad, I go to a play as to a country treat, I carry my own wine to one, and my own wit to t'other, or else I'm sure I should not be merry at either. And the reason why we are so often louder than the players is because we think we speak more wit, and so become the poet's rivals in his audience. For to tell you the truth, we hate the silly rogues. Nay, so much that we find fault even with their bawdy upon the stage, whilst we talk nothing else in the pit as loud.

HORNER: But why shouldst thou hate the silly poets? Thou hast too much wit to be one, and they, like whores, are only hated by each other; and thou dost scorn writing, I'm sure.

SPARKISH: Yes, I'd have you to know, I scorn writing. But women, women, that make men do all foolish things, make 'em write songs too; everybody does it. 'Tis even as common with lovers as playing with fans; and you can no more help rhyming to your Phyllis than drinking to your Phyllis.

HARCOURT: Nay, poetry in love is no more to be avoided than jealousy.

DORILANT: But the poets damned your songs, did they?

SPARKISH: Damn the poets! They turned 'em into burlesque, as they call it. That burlesque is a hocus-pocus-trick they have got, which by the virtue of hictius doctius, topsey turvey they make a wise and witty man in the world a fool upon the stage you know not how. And 'tis therefore I hate 'em too, for I know not but it may be my own case; for they'll put a man into a play for looking a-squint. Their predecessors were contented to make serving-men only their stage fools, but these rogues must have gentlemen, with a pox to 'em, nay, knights. And indeed, you shall hardly see a fool upon the stage but he's a knight; and to tell you the truth, they have kept me these six years from being a knight in earnest, for fear of being knighted in a play, and dubbed a fool.

DORILANT: Blame 'em not; they must follow their copy, the age.

HARCOURT: But why shouldst thou be afraid of being in a

play, who expose yourself every day in the playhouses, and as public places?

HORNER: 'Tis but being on the stage, instead of standing on a bench in the pit.

DORILANT: Don't you give money to painters to draw you like? And are you afraid of your pictures at length in a playhouse, where all your mistresses may see you?

SPARKISH: A pox! Painters don't draw the smallpox or pimples in one's face. Come, damn all your silly authors whatever, all books and booksellers, by the world, and all readers, courteous or uncourteous.

HARCOURT: But who comes here, Sparkish?

Enter MR PINCHWIFE, *and his wife in man's clothes,* ALITHEA, LUCY *her maid.*

SPARKISH: Oh hide me, there's my mistress too. [SPARKISH *hides himself behind* HARCOURT.]

HARCOURT: She sees you.

SPARKISH: But I will not see her. 'Tis time to go to White-hall, and I must not fail the drawing-room.

HARCOURT: Pray, first carry me, and reconcile me to her.

SPARKISH: Another time. Faith, the King will have supped.

HARCOURT: Not with the worse stomach for thy absence. Thou art one of those fools that think their attendance at the King's meals as necessary as his physicians', when you are more troublesome to him than his doctors or his dogs.

SPARKISH: Pshaw! I know my interest, sir. Prithee hide me.

HORNER: Your servant, Pinchwife. – What, he knows us not!

PINCHWIFE [*to his wife aside*]: Come along.

MRS PINCHWIFE: Pray, have you any ballads? Give me sixpenny worth.

CLASP: We have no ballads.

MRS PINCHWIFE: Then give me *Covent Garden Drollery*,[1] and a play or two. – Oh, here's *Tarugo's Wiles*,[2] and *The Slighted Maiden*,[3] I'll have them.

PINCHWIFE [*apart to her*]: No, plays are not for your reading. Come along: will you discover yourself?

1. *Covent Garden Drollery*: an anthology published in 1672.
2. *Tarugo's Wiles*: comedy by Sir Thomas St Serfe (1667).
3. *The Slighted Maid*: comedy by Sir Robert Stapleton (1663).

HORNER: Who is that pretty youth with him, Sparkish?

SPARKISH: I believe his wife's brother, because he's some-thing like her, but I never saw her but once.

HORNER: Extremely handsome; I have seen a face like it too. Let us follow 'em.

Exeunt PINCHWIFE, MRS PINCHWIFE, ALITHEA, LUCY; HORNER, DORILANT *following them.*

HARCOURT: Come, Sparkish, your mistress saw you and will be angry you go not to her. Besides, I would fain be reconciled to her, which none but you can do, dear friend.

SPARKISH: Well, that's a better reason, dear friend. I would not go near her now for her's or my own sake, but I can deny you nothing. For though I have known thee a great while, never go if I do not love thee as well as a new acquaintance.

HARCOURT: I am obliged to you indeed, dear friend. I would be well with her only to be well with thee still. For these ties to wives usually dissolve all ties to friends. I would be contented she should enjoy you a-nights, but I would have have you to myself a-days, as I have had, dear friend.

SPARKISH: And thou shalt enjoy me a-days, dear, dear friend, never stir; and I'll be divorced from her sooner than from thee. Come along.

HARCOURT [*aside*]: So, we are hard put to't when we make our rival our procurer. But neither she nor her brother would let me come near her now. When all's done, a rival is the best cloak to steal to a mistress under, without suspicion; and when we have once got to her as we desire, we throw him off like other cloaks.

Exit SPARKISH, *and* HARCOURT *following him.*

Re-enter MR PINCHWIFE, MRS PINCHWIFE *in man's clothes.*

PINCHWIFE [*to* ALITHEA (*offstage*)]: Sister, if you will not go, we must leave you. – [*Aside*] The fool her gallant and she will muster up all the young saunterers of this place, and they will leave their dear seamstresses to follow us. What a swarm of cuckolds and cuckold-makers are here! Come, let's be gone, Mistress Margery.

MRS PINCHWIFE: Don't you believe that, I han't half my bellyful of sights yet.

PINCHWIFE: Then walk this way.

MRS PINCHWIFE: Lord, what a power of brave signs are here! Stay – the Bull's Head, the Ram's Head, and the Stag's Head, dear –

PINCHWIFE: Nay, if every husband's proper sign here were visible, they would be all alike.

MRS PINCHWIFE: What d'ye mean by that, bud?

PINCHWIFE: 'Tis no matter – no matter, bud.

MRS PINCHWIFE: Pray tell me; nay, I will know.

PINCHWIFE: They would be all bulls', stags', and rams' heads.

Exeunt MR PINCHWIFE, MRS PINCHWIFE.
Re-enter SPARKISH, HARCOURT, ALITHEA, LUCY *at t'other door.*

SPARKISH: Come, dear madam, for my sake you shall be reconciled to him.

ALITHEA: For your sake I hate him.

HARCOURT: That's something too cruel, madam, to hate me for his sake.

SPARKISH: Ay indeed, madam, too, too cruel to me, to hate my friend for my sake.

ALITHEA: I hate him because he is your enemy; and you ought to hate him too, for making love to me, if you love me.

SPARKISH: That's a good one! I hate a man for loving you! If he did love you, 'tis but what he can't help, and 'tis your fault not his, if he admires you. I hate a man for being of my opinion! I'll ne'er do't, by the world.

ALITHEA: Is it for your honour or mine, to suffer a man to make love to me, who am to marry you tomorrow?

SPARKISH: Is it for your honour or mine, to have me jealous? That he makes love to you is a sign you are handsome; and that I am not jealous is a sign you are virtuous. That, I think, is for your honour.

ALITHEA: But 'tis your honour too I am concerned for.

HARCOURT: But why, dearest madam, will you be more concerned for his honour than he is himself? Let his honour alone, for my sake and his. He, he has no honour –

SPARKISH: How's that?

HARCOURT: But what my dear friend can guard himself.

SPARKISH: Oho – that's right again.

HARCOURT: Your care of his honour argues his neglect of it, which is no honour to my dear friend here; therefore once more, let his honour go which way it will, dear madam.

SPARKISH: Ay, ay, were it for my honour to marry a woman whose virtue I suspected, and could not trust her in a friend's hands?

ALITHEA: Are you not afraid to lose me?

HARCOURT: He afraid to lose you, madam! No, no – you may see how the most estimable and most glorious creature in the world is valued by him. Will you not see it?

SPARKISH: Right, honest Frank. I have that noble value for her that I cannot be jealous of her.

ALITHEA: You mistake him, he means you care not for me, nor who has me.

SPARKISH: Lord, madam, I see you are jealous. Will you wrest a poor man's meaning from his words?

ALITHEA: You astonish me, sir, with your want of jealousy.

SPARKISH: And you make me giddy, madam, with your jealousy and fears, and virtue, and honour. Gad, I see virtue makes a woman as troublesome as a little reading or learning.

ALITHEA: Monstrous!

LUCY [behind]: Well, to see what easy husbands these women of quality can meet with; a poor chambermaid can never have such lady-like luck. Besides, he's thrown away upon her; she'll make no use of her fortune, her blessing; none to a gentleman for a pure cuckold, for it requires good breeding to be a cuckold.

ALITHEA: I tell you then plainly, he pursues me to marry me.

SPARKISH: Pshaw!

HARCOURT: Come, madam, you see you strive in vain to make him jealous of me. My dear friend is the kindest creature in the world to me.

SPARKISH: Poor fellow.

HARCOURT: But his kindness only is not enough for me, without your favour. Your good opinion, dear madam, 'tis that must perfect my happiness. Good gentleman, he believes all I say; would you would do so. Jealous of me! I would not wrong him nor you for the world.

SPARKISH: Look you there; hear him, hear him, and do not walk away so.

ALITHEA *walks carelessly, to and fro.*

HARCOURT: I love you, madam, so –

SPARKISH: How's that! Nay, now you begin to go too far indeed.

HARCOURT: So much I confess, I say I love you, that I would not have you miserable, and cast yourself away upon so unworthy and inconsiderable a thing as what you see here. [*Clapping his hand on his breast, points at* SPARKISH.]

SPARKISH: No, faith, I believe thou wouldst not, now his meaning is plain. But I knew before thou wouldst not wrong me nor her.

HARCOURT: No, no, heavens forbid the glory of her sex should fall so low as into the embraces of such a contemptible wretch, the last of mankind – my dear friend here – I injure him. [*Embracing* SPARKISH.]

ALITHEA: Very well.

SPARKISH: No, no, dear friend, I knew it. Madam, you see he will rather wrong himself than me, in giving himself such names.

ALITHEA: Do not you understand him yet?

SPARKISH: Yes, how modestly he speaks of himself, poor fellow.

ALITHEA: Methinks he speaks impudently of yourself, since – before yourself too; insomuch that I can no longer suffer his scurrilous abusiveness to you, no more than his love to me. [*Offers to go.*]

SPARKISH: Nay, nay, madam, pray stay. His love to you! Lord, madam, has he not spoke yet plain enough?

ALITHEA: Yes indeed, I should think so.

SPARKISH: Well then, by the world, a man can't speak civilly to a woman now, but presently she says he makes love to her. Nay, madam, you shall stay, with your pardon, since you have not yet understood him, till he has made an eclaircisment of his love to you, that is, what kind of love it is – [*To* HARCOURT] Answer to thy catechism, friend; do you love my mistress here?

HARCOURT: Yes, I wish she would not doubt it.

SPARKISH: But how do you love her?

HARCOURT: With all my soul.

ALITHEA: I thank him, methinks he speaks plain enough now.

SPARKISH [*to* ALITHEA]: You are out still. – But with what kind of love, Harcourt?

HARCOURT: With the best and truest love in the world.

SPARKISH: Look you there then, that is with no matrimonial love, I'm sure.

ALITHEA: How's that? Do you say matrimonial love is not best?

SPARKISH: Gad, I went too far ere I was aware. But speak for thyself, Harcourt. You said you would not wrong me nor her.

HARCOURT: No, no, madam, e'en take him, for heaven's sake –

SPARKISH: Look you there, madam.

HARCOURT: Who should in all justice be yours, he that loves you most. [*Claps his hand on his breast.*]

ALITHEA: Look you there, Mr Sparkish, who's that?

SPARKISH: Who should it be? Go on Harcourt.

HARCOURT: Who loves you more than women titles, or fortune fools. [*Points at* SPARKISH.]

SPARKISH: Look you there, he means me still, for he points at me.

ALITHEA: Ridiculous!

HARCOURT: Who can only match your faith and constancy in love.

SPARKISH: Ay.

HARCOURT: Who knows, if it be possible, how to value so much beauty and virtue.

SPARKISH: Ay.

HARCOURT: Whose love can no more be equalled in the world than that heavenly form of yours.

SPARKISH: No.

HARCOURT: Who could no more suffer a rival than your

absence, and yet could no more suspect your virtue than his own constancy in his love to you.

SPARKISH: No.

HARCOURT: Who in fine loves you better than his eyes, that first made him love you.

SPARKISH: Ay – nay, madam, faith you shan't go till –

ALITHEA: Have a care, lest you make me stay too long.

SPARKISH: But till he has saluted you, that I may be assured you are friends, after his honest advice and declaration. Come, pray, madam, be friends with him.

Enter MASTER PINCHWIFE, MRS PINCHWIFE.

ALITHEA: You must pardon me, sir, that I am not yet so obedient to you.

PINCHWIFE: What, invite your wife to kiss men? Monstrous! Are you not ashamed? I will never forgive you.

SPARKISH: Are you not ashamed that I should have more confidence in the chastity of your family than you have? You must not teach me; I am a man of honour, sir, though I am frank and free. I am frank, sir –

PINCHWIFE: Very frank,[1] sir, to share your wife with your friends.

SPARKISH: He is an humble, menial[2] friend, such as reconciles the differences of the marriage bed. You know man and wife do not always agree. I design him for that use, therefore would have him well with my wife.

PINCHWIFE: A menial friend! You will get a great many menial friends by shewing your wife as you do.

SPARKISH: What then? It may be I have a pleasure in't, as I have to shew fine clothes at a playhouse the first day, and count money before poor rogues.

PINCHWIFE: He that shews his wife or money will be in danger of having them borrowed sometimes.

SPARKISH: I love to be envied, and would not marry a wife that I alone could love. Loving alone is as dull as eating alone. Is it not a frank age? And I am a frank person. And to tell you the truth, it may be I love to have rivals in a wife, they make her seem to a man still but as a kept mistress.

1. *Frank*: open, generous.
2. *Menial*: domestic.

And so good night, for I must to Whitehall. Madam, I hope you are now reconciled to my friend; and so I wish you a good night, madam, and sleep if you can, for tomorrow you know I must visit you early with a canonical gentleman. Good night, dear Harcourt. [*Exit* SPARKISH.]

HARCOURT: Madam, I hope you will not refuse my visit tomorrow, if it should be earlier, with a canonical gentleman, than Mr Sparkish's.

PINCHWIFE [*coming between* ALITHEA *and* HARCOURT]: This gentlewoman is yet under my care, therefore you must yet forbear your freedom with her, sir.

HARCOURT: Must, sir?

PINCHWIFE: Yes, sir, she is my sister.

HARCOURT: 'Tis well she is, sir, for I must be her servant, sir. – Madam –

PINCHWIFE: Come away, sister, we had been gone, if it had not been for you, and so avoided these lewd rakehells, who seem to haunt us.

Enter HORNER, DORILANT *to them.*

HORNER: How now, Pinchwife?

PINCHWIFE: Your servant.

HORNER: What! I see a little time in the country makes a man turn wild and unsociable, and only fit to converse with his horses, dogs, and his herds.

PINCHWIFE: I have business, sir and must mind it; your business is pleasure, therefore you and I must go different ways.

HORNER: Well, you may go on, but this pretty young gentleman – [*Takes hold of* MRS PINCHWIFE.]

HARCOURT: The lady –

DORILANT: And the maid –

HORNER: Shall stay with us, for I suppose their business is the same with ours, pleasure.

PINCHWIFE [*aside*]: 'Sdeath, he knows her, she carries it so sillily! Yet if he does not, I should be more silly to discover it first.

ALITHEA: Pray, let us go, sir.

PINCHWIFE: Come, come –

HORNER [*to* MRS PINCHWIFE]: Had you not rather stay

with us? Prithee, Pinchwife, who is this pretty young gentleman?

PINCHWIFE: One to whom I'm a guardian. [*Aside*] I wish I could keep her out of your hands –

HORNER: Who is he? I never saw anything so pretty in all my life.

PINCHWIFE: Pshaw! Do not look upon him so much, he's a poor bashful youth; you'll put him out of countenance. Come away, brother. [*Offers to take her away.*]

HORNER: Oh, your brother!

PINCHWIFE: Yes, my wife's brother. – Come, come, she'll stay supper for us.

HORNER: I thought so, for he is very like her I saw you at the play with, whom I told you I was in love with.

MRS PINCHWIFE [*aside*]: O Jeminy! Is this he that was in love with me? I am glad on't I vow, for he's a curious fine gentleman, and I love him already too. [*To* MR PINCHWIFE] Is this he, bud?

PINCHWIFE [*to his wife*]: Come away, come away.

HORNER: Why, what haste are you in? Why won't you let me talk with him?

PINCHWIFE: Because you'll debauch him; he's yet young and innocent, and I would not have him debauched for any thing in the world. [*Aside*] How she gazes on him! The divel!

HORNER: Harcourt, Dorilant, look you here, this is the likeness of that dowdy he told us of, his wife. Did you ever see a lovelier creature? The rogue has reason to be jealous of his wife, since she is like him, for she would make all that see her in love with her.

HARCOURT: And as I remember now, she is as like him here as can be.

DORILANT: She is indeed very pretty, if she be like him.

HORNER: Very pretty? A very pretty commendation! She is a glorious creature, beautiful beyond all things I ever beheld.

PINCHWIFE: So, so.

HARCOURT: More beautiful than a poet's first mistress of imagination.

HORNER: Or another man's last mistress of flesh and blood.

MRS PINCHWIFE: Nay, now you jeer, sir. Pray don't jeer me.

PINCHWIFE: Come, come. [*Aside*] By heavens, she'll discover herself.

HORNER: I speak of your sister, sir.

PINCHWIFE: Ay, but saying she was handsome, if like him, made him blush. [*Aside*] I am upon a wrack!

HORNER: Methinks he is so handsome he should not be a man.

PINCHWIFE (*aside*): Oh there, 'tis out, he has discovered her! I am not able to suffer any longer. [*To his wife*] Come, come away, I say.

HORNER: Nay, by your leave, sir, he shall not go yet. – [*To them*] Harcourt, Dorilant, let us torment this jealous rogue a little.

HARCOURT
DORILANT } How?

HORNER: I'll shew you.

PINCHWIFE: Come, pray let him go, I cannot stay fooling any longer. I tell you his sister stays supper for us.

HORNER: Does she? Come then we'll all go sup with her and thee.

PINCHWIFE: No, now I think on't, having stayed so long for us, I warrant she's gone to bed. – [*Aside*] I wish she and I were well out of their hands. – Come, I must rise early tomorrow, come.

HORNER: Well then, if she be gone to bed, I wish her and you a good night. But pray, young gentleman, present my humble service to her.

MRS PINCHWIFE: Thank you heartily, sir.

PINCHWIFE [*aside*]: S'death, she will discover herself yet in spite of me. – He is something more civil to you for your kindness to his sister than I am, it seems.

HORNER: Tell her, dear sweet little gentleman for all your brother there, that you have revived the love I had for her at first sight in the playhouse.

MRS PINCHWIFE: But did you love her indeed, and indeed?

PINCHWIFE [*aside*]: So, so. – Away, I say.

HORNER: Nay, stay. Yes indeed, and indeed, pray do you tell her so, and give her this kiss from me. [*Kisses her.*]

PINCHWIFE [*aside*]: O heavens! What do I suffer! Now 'tis too plain he knows her, and yet –

HORNER: And this, and this – [*Kisses her again.*]

MRS PINCHWIFE: What do you kiss me for? I am no woman.

PINCHWIFE [*aside*]: So – there, 'tis out. Come, I cannot, nor will stay any longer.

HORNER: Nay, they shall send your lady a kiss too. Here Harcourt, Dorilant, will you not? [*They kiss her.*]

PINCHWIFE [*aside*]: How do I suffer this? Was I not accusing another just now for this rascally patience, in permitting his wife to be kissed before his face? Ten thousand ulcers gnaw away their lips! – Come, come.

HORNER: Good night, dear little gentleman. Madam, good night. Farewell Pinchwife. [*Apart to* HARCOURT *and* DORILANT] Did not I tell you I would raise his jealous gall?

Exeunt HORNER, HARCOURT, *and* DORILANT.

PINCHWIFE: So, they are gone at last. Stay, let me see first if the coach be at this door. [*Exit.*]

HORNER, HARCOURT, DORILANT *return.*

HORNER: What, not gone yet? Will you be sure to do as I desired you, sweet sir?

MRS PINCHWIFE: Sweet sir, but what will you give me then?

HORNER: Anything; come away into the next walk.

Exit HORNER, *haling away* MRS PINCHWIFE.

ALITHEA: Hold, hold! What d'ye do?

LUCY: Stay, stay, hold –

HARCOURT: Hold, madam, hold! Let him present him, he'll come presently. Nay, I will never let you go till you answer my question.

LUCY: For God's sake, sir, I must follow 'em.

DORILANT: No, I have something to present you with too, you shan't follow them.

ALITHEA, LUCY, *struggling with* HARCOURT *and* DORILANT.

PINCHWIFE *returns.*

PINCHWIFE: Where? – how? – what's become of – gone! – whither?

LUCY: He's only gone with the gentleman, who will give him something, an't please your worship.

PINCHWIFE: Something! – give him something, with a pox! Where are they?

ALITHEA: In the next walk only, brother.

PINCHWIFE: Only, only! Where, where?

   Exit PINCHWIFE, *and returns presently, then goes out again.*

HARCOURT: What's the matter with him? Why so much concerned? But dearest madam –

ALITHEA: Pray let me go, sir, I have said and suffered enough already.

HARCOURT: Then you will not look upon, nor pity my sufferings?

ALITHEA: To look upon 'em when I cannot help 'em, were cruelty, not pity; therefore I will never see you more.

HARCOURT: Let me then, madam, have my privilege of a banished lover, complaining or railing, and giving you but a farewell reason why, if you cannot condescend to marry me, you should not take that wretch my rival.

ALITHEA: He only, not you, since my honour is engaged so far to him, can give me a reason why I should not marry him; but if he be true, and what I think him to me, I must be so to him. Your servant, sir.

HARCOURT: Have women only constancy when 'tis a vice, and like fortune only true to fools?

DORILANT [*to* LUCY, *who struggles to get from him*]: Thou shalt not stir, thou robust creature. You see I can deal with you, therefore you should stay the rather, and be kind.

   Enter PINCHWIFE.

PINCHWIFE: Gone, gone, not to be found! Quite gone! Ten thousand plagues go with 'em! Which way went they?

ALITHEA: But into t'other walk, brother.

LUCY: Their business will be done presently, sure, an't please your worship; it can't be long in doing, I'm sure on't.

ALITHEA: Are they not there?

PINCHWIFE: No, you know where they are, you infamous wretch, eternal shame of your family, which you do not dishonour enough yourself, you think, but you must help her to do it too, thou legion of bawds!

ALITHEA: Good brother –

PINCHWIFE: Damned, damned sister!

ALITHEA: Look you here, she's coming.

Enter MRS PINCHWIFE *in man's clothes, running with her hat under her arm, full of oranges and dried fruit,* HORNER *following.*

MRS PINCHWIFE: O dear bud, look you here what I have got, see!

PINCHWIFE [*aside, rubbing his forehead*]: And what I have got here, too, which you can't see.[1]

MRS PINCHWIFE: The fine gentleman has given me better things yet.

PINCHWIFE: Has he so? [*Aside*] Out of breath and coloured! I must hold yet.

HORNER: I have only given your little brother an orange, sir.

PINCHWIFE [*to* HORNER]: Thank you, sir. [*Aside*] You have only squeezed my orange, I suppose, and given it me again; yet I must have a city patience. [*To his wife*] Come, come away.

MRS PINCHWIFE: Stay till I have put up my fine things, bud.

Enter SIR JASPER FIDGET.

SIR JASPER: O Master Horner, come, come, the ladies stay for you. Your mistress, my wife, wonders you make not more haste to her.

HORNER: I have stayed this half hour for you here, and 'tis your fault I am not now with your wife.

SIR JASPER: But pray, don't let her know so much. The truth on't is, I was advancing a certain project to his Majesty, about – I'll tell you.

HORNER: No, let's go, and hear it at your house. – Good night, sweet little gentleman. One kiss more; you'll remember me now, I hope. [*Kisses her.*]

DORILANT: What, Sir Jasper, will you separate friends? He promised to sup with us; and if you take him to your house, you'll be in danger of our company too.

SIR JASPER: Alas, gentleman, my house is not fit for you.

1. *And what . . . can't see*: a reference to the cuckold's horns.

There are none but civil women there, which are not for your turn. He, you know, can bear with the society of civil women now, ha, ha, ha! Besides, he's one of my family – he's – heh, heh, heh!

DORILANT: What is he?

SIR JASPER: Faith, my eunuch, since you'll have it, heh, he, he!

Exit SIR JASPER FIDGET *and* HORNER.

DORILANT: I rather wish thou wert his, or my cuckold. Harcourt, what a good cuckold is lost there for want of a man to make him one! Thee and I cannot have Horner's privilege, who can make use of it.

HARCOURT: Ay, to poor Horner 'tis like coming to an estate at three-score, when a man can't be the better for 't.

PINCHWIFE: Come.

MRS PINCHWIFE: Presently, bud.

DORILANT: Come, let us go too. [*To* ALITHEA] Madam, your servant. [*To* LUCY] Good night, strapper.

HARCOURT: Madam, though you will not let me have a good day or night, I wish you one; but dare not name the other half of my wish.

ALITHEA: Good night, sir, for ever.

MRS PINCHWIFE: I don't know where to put this here, dear bud, you shall eat it. Nay, you shall have part of the fine gentleman's good things, or treat as you call it, when we come home.

PINCHWIFE: Indeed I deserve it, since I furnished the best part of it. [*Strikes away the orange.*]

> The gallant treats, presents, and gives the ball;
> But 'tis the absent cuckold pays for all.

Exeunt.

Act Four

SCENE ONE

In PINCHWIFE'S *house in the morning.*
LUCY, ALITHEA *dressed in new clothes.*

LUCY: Well madam, now have I dressed you, and set you out with so many ornaments, and spent upon you ounces of essence and pulvilio;[1] and all this for no other purpose but as people adorn and perfume a corpse for a stinking second-hand grave; such or as bad I think Master Sparkish's bed.

ALITHEA: Hold your peace!

LUCY: Nay, madam, I will ask you the reason why you would banish poor Master Harcourt for ever from your sight. How could you be so hard-hearted?

ALITHEA: 'Twas because I was not hard-hearted.

LUCY: No, no. 'Twas stark love and kindness, I warrant.

ALITHEA: It was so. I would see him no more because I love him.

LUCY: Hey-day, a very pretty reason!

ALITHEA: You do not understand me.

LUCY: I wish you may yourself.

ALITHEA: I was engaged to marry, you see, another man, whom my justice will not suffer me to deceive or injure.

LUCY: Can there be a greater cheat or wrong done to a man than to give him your person without your heart? I should make a conscience of it.

ALITHEA: I'll retrieve it for him after I am married a-while.

LUCY: The woman that marries to love better will be as much mistaken as the wencher that marries to live better. No, madam, marrying to increase love is like gaming to become rich; alas, you only lose what little stock you had before.

ALITHEA: I find by your rhetoric you have been bribed to betray me.

LUCY: Only by his merit, that has bribed your heart, you see, against your word and rigid honour. But what a divel is

1. *Pulvilio*: perfumed powder.

this honour? 'Tis sure a disease in the head, like the megrim,[1] or falling sickness,[2] that always hurries people away to do themselves mischief. Men lose their lives by it; women what's dearer to 'em, their love, the life of life.

ALITHEA: Come, pray talk you no more of honour, nor Master Harcourt. I wish the other would come to secure my fidelity to him, and his right in me.

LUCY: You will marry him then?

ALITHEA: Certainly. I have given him already my word, and will my hand too, to make it good, when he comes.

LUCY: Well, I wish I may never stick pin more if he be not an arrant natural[3] to t'other fine gentleman.

ALITHEA: I own he wants the wit of Harcourt, which I will dispense withal, for another want he has, which is want of jealousy, which men of wit seldom want.

LUCY: Lord, madam, what should you do with a fool to your husband? You intend to be honest, don't you? Then that husbandly virtue, credulity, is thrown away upon you.

ALITHEA: He only that could suspect my virtue should have cause to do it; 'tis Sparkish's confidence in my truth that obliges me to be so faithful to him.

LUCY: You are not sure his opinion may last.

ALITHEA: I am satisfied 'tis impossible for him to be jealous after the proofs I have had of him. Jealousy in a husband – heaven defend me from it! It begets a thousand plagues to a poor woman, the loss of her honour, her quiet, and her –

LUCY: And her pleasure.

ALITHEA: What d'ye mean, impertinent?

LUCY: Liberty is a great pleasure, madam.

ALITHEA: I say loss of her honour, her quiet, nay, her life sometimes; and what's as bad almost, the loss of this town. That is, she is sent into the country, which is the last ill usage of a husband to a wife, I think.

LUCY [aside]: Oh, does the wind lie there? – Then of necessity, madam, you think a man must carry his wife into the country, if he be wise. The country is as terrible, I find, to our

1. *Megrim*: migraine.
2. *Falling sickness*: epilepsy.
3. *Natural*: born fool.

young English ladies as a monastery to those abroad. And on my virginity, I think they would rather marry a London gaoler than a High Sheriff of a county, since neither can stir from his employment. Formerly women of wit married fools for a great estate, a fine seat, or the like; but now 'tis for a pretty seat only in Lincoln's Inn fields, St James's fields, or the Pall Mall.[1]

Enter to them SPARKISH, *and* HARCOURT *dressed like a Parson.*

SPARKISH: Madam, your humble servant, a happy day to you, and to us all.

HARCOURT: Amen.

ALITHEA: Who have we here?

SPARKISH: My chaplain, faith. O madam, poor Harcourt remembers his humble service to you; and in obedience to your last commands, refrains coming into your sight.

ALITHEA: Is not that he?

SPARKISH: No, fie, no; but to shew that he ne'er intended to hinder our match, has sent his brother here to join our hands. When I get me a wife, I must get her a chaplain, according to the custom; this is his brother, and my chaplain.

ALITHEA: His brother?

LUCY [*aside*]: And your chaplain, to preach in your pulpit then.

ALITHEA: His brother!

SPARKISH: Nay, I knew you would not believe it. – I told you, sir, she would take you for your brother Frank.

ALITHEA: Believe it!

LUCY [*aside*]: His brother! Hah, ha, he! He has a trick left still, it seems.

SPARKISH: Come, my dearest, pray let us go to church before the canonical hour[2] is past.

ALITHEA: For shame, you are abused still.

SPARKISH: By the world, 'tis strange now you are so incredulous.

ALITHEA: 'Tis strange you are so credulous.

1. *Lincoln's Inn fields*, etc.: fashionable London walks.
2. *Canonical hour*: see note, p. 137.

SPARKISH: Dearest of my life, hear me. I tell you this is Ned Harcourt of Cambridge, by the world; you see he has a sneaking college look. 'Tis true he's something like his brother Frank, and they differ from each other no more than in their age, for they were twins.

LUCY: Hah, ha, he!

ALITHEA: Your servant, sir, I cannot be so deceived, though you are. But come, let's hear, how do you know what you affirm so confidently?

SPARKISH: Why, I'll tell you all. Frank Harcourt coming to me this morning, to wish me joy and present his service to you, I asked him if he could help me to a parson; whereupon he told me he had a brother in town who was in orders, and he went straight away and sent him you see there to me.

ALITHEA: Yes, Frank goes and puts on a black-coat, then tells you he is Ned. That's all you have for't.

SPARKISH: Pshaw, pshaw! I tell you by the same token the midwife put her garter about Frank's neck to know 'em asunder, they were so like.

ALITHEA: Frank tells you this too.

SPARKISH: Ay, and Ned there too; nay, they are both in a story.

ALITHEA: So, so. Very foolish!

SPARKISH. Lord if you won't believe one, you had best try him by your chambermaid there, for chambermaids must needs know chaplains from other men, they are so used to 'em.

LUCY: Let's see. Nay, I'll be sworn he has the canonical smirk, and the filthy, clammy palm of a chaplain.

ALITHEA: Well, most reverend doctor, pray let us make an end of this fooling.

HARCOURT: With all my soul, divine, heavenly creature, when you please.

ALITHEA: He speaks like a chaplain indeed.

SPARKISH: Why, was there not 'soul', 'divine', 'heavenly', in what he said?

ALITHEA: Once more, most impertinent black-coat, cease your persecution, and let us have a conclusion of this ridiculous love.

HARCOURT [*aside*]: I had forgot. I must suit my style to my coat, or I wear it in vain.

ALITHEA: I have no more patience left. Let us make once an end of this troublesome love, I say.

HARCOURT: So be it, seraphic lady, when your honour shall think it meet and convenient so to do.

SPARKISH: Gad, I'm sure none but a chaplain could speak so, I think.

ALITHEA: Let me tell you, sir, this dull trick will not serve your turn; though you delay our marriage, you shall not hinder it.

HARCOURT: Far be it from me, munificent patroness, to delay your marriage. I desire nothing more than to marry you presently, which I might do, if you yourself would; for my noble, good-natured and thrice-generous patron here would not hinder it.

SPARKISH: No, poor man, not I, faith.

HARCOURT: And now, madam, let me tell you plainly, nobody else shall marry you. By heavens, I'll die first, for I'm sure I should die after it.

LUCY (*aside*): How his love has made him forget his function, as I have seen it in real parsons.

ALITHEA: That was spoken like a chaplain too. – Now you understand him, I hope.

SPARKISH: Poor man, he takes it heinously to be refused. I can't blame him, 'tis putting an indignity upon him not to be suffered. But you'll pardon me madam, it shan't be; he shall marry us. Come away, pray, madam.

LUCY: Hah, ha, he! More ado! 'Tis late.

ALITHEA: Invincible stupidity! I tell you he would marry me as your rival, not as your chaplain.

SPARKISH [*pulling her away*]: Come, come, madam.

LUCY: I pray madam, do not refuse this reverend divine the honour and satisfaction of marrying you; for I dare say he has set his heart upon't, good doctor.

ALITHEA (*to* HARCOURT): What can you hope or design by this?

HARCOURT (*aside*): I could answer her, a reprieve for a day only often revokes a hasty doom. At worst, if she will not take mercy on me and let me marry her, I have at least the lover's second pleasure, hind'ring my rival's enjoyment, though but for a time.

SPARKISH: Come, madam, 'tis e'en twelve a clock, and my mother charged me never to be married out of the canonical hours. Come, come, Lord, here's such a deal of modesty, I warrant, the first day.

LUCY: Yes, an't please your worship, married women shew all their modesty the first day, because married men shew all their love the first day.

Exeunt SPARKISH, ALITHEA, HARCOURT, *and* LUCY.

SCENE TWO

The scene changes to a bedchamber, where appear PINCHWIFE, MRS PINCHWIFE.

PINCHWIFE: Come, tell me, I say.

MRS PINCHWIFE: Lord, han't I told it an hundred times over?

PINCHWIFE [*aside*]: I would try if, in the repetition of the ungrateful tale, I could find her altering it in the least circumstance, for if her story be false, she is so too. – Come, how was't, baggage?

MRS PINCHWIFE: Lord, what pleasure you take to hear it, sure!

PINCHWIFE: No, you take more in telling it I find. But speak, how was't?

MRS PINCHWIFE: He carried me up into the house next to the Exchange.

PINCHWIFE: So; and you two were only in the room?

MRS PINCHWIFE: Yes, for he sent away a youth that was there for some dried fruit and China oranges.

PINCHWIFE: Did he so? Damn him for it – and for –

MRS PINCHWIFE: But presently came up the gentlewoman of the house.

PINCHWIFE: Oh, 'twas well she did. But what did he do whilst the fruit came?

MRS PINCHWIFE: He kissed me an hundred times, and told me he fancied he kissed my fine sister, meaning me you

know, whom he said he loved with all his soul, and bid me
be sure to tell her so, and to desire her to be at her window
by eleven of the clock this morning, and he would walk
under it at that time.

PINCHWIFE [*aside*]: And he was as good as his word, very
punctual, a pox reward him for't.

MRS PINCHWIFE: Well, and he said if you were not within,
he would come up to her, meaning me you know, bud,
still.

PINCHWIFE: So. [*Aside*] He knew her certainly, but for this
confession, I am obliged to her simplicity. – But what, you
stood very still when he kissed you?

MRS PINCHWIFE: Yes, I warrant you; would you have had
me discovered myself?

PINCHWIFE: But you told me he did some beastliness to you,
as you called it. What was't?

MRS PINCHWIFE: Why, he put –

PINCHWIFE: What?

MRS PINCHWIFE: Why he put the tip of his tongue between
my lips, and so musled[1] me. And I said I'd bite it.

PINCHWIFE: An eternal canker seize it, for a dog!

MRS PINCHWIFE: Nay, you need not be so angry with him
neither, for to say truth, he has the sweetest breath I ever
knew.

PINCHWIFE: The devil! – You were satisfied with it then,
and would do it again?

MRS PINCHWIFE: Not unless he should force me.

PINCHWIFE: Force you, changeling! I tell you no woman
can be forced.

MRS PINCHWIFE: Yes, but she may sure, by such a one as he,
for he's a proper, goodly strong man. 'Tis hard, let me tell
you, to resist him.

PINCHWIFE (*aside*): So, 'tis plain she loves him, yet she has
not love enough to make her conceal it from me; but the
sight of him will increase her aversion for me, and love for
him, and that love instruct her how to deceive me, and
satisfy him, all idiot as she is. Love! 'Twas he gave women
first their craft, their art of deluding. Out of nature's hands

1. *Musled*: (mousled) handled roughly.

they came plain, open, silly and fit for slaves, as she and Heaven intended 'em; but damned love – well, I must strangle that little monster whilst I can deal with him. (*To her*) Go, fetch pen, ink and paper out of the next room.

MRS PINCHWIFE: Yes bud. [*Exit* MRS PINCHWIFE.]

PINCHWIFE [*aside*]: Why should women have more invention in love than men? It can only be because they have more desires, more soliciting passions, more lust, and more of the devil.

   MRS PINCHWIFE *returns*.

Come, minx, sit down and write.

MRS PINCHWIFE: Ay, dear bud, but I can't do't very well.

PINCHWIFE: I wish you could not at all.

MRS PINCHWIFE: But what should I write for?

PINCHWIFE: I'll have you write a letter to your lover.

MRS PINCHWIFE: O Lord, to the fine gentleman, a letter!

PINCHWIFE: Yes, to the fine gentleman.

MRS PINCHWIFE: Lord, you do but jeer; sure you jest.

PINCHWIFE: I am not so merry. Come, write as I bid you.

MRS PINCHWIFE: What, do you think I am a fool?

PINCHWIFE [*aside*]: She's afraid I would not dictate any love to him, therefore she's unwilling. – But you had best begin.

MRS PINCHWIFE: Indeed, and indeed, but I won't, so I won't.

PINCHWIFE: Why?

MRS PINCHWIFE: Because he's in town; you may send for him if you will.

PINCHWIFE: Very well, you would have him brought to you. Is it come to this? I say take the pen and write, or you'll provoke me.

MRS PINCHWIFE: Lord, what d'ye make a fool of me for? Don't I know that letters are never writ but from the country to London, and from London into the country? Now he's in town, and I am in town too; therefore I can't write to him, you know.

PINCHWIFE [*aside*]: So; I am glad it is no worse, she is innocent enough, yet – Yes, you may, when your husband bids you, write letters to people that are in town.

MRS PINCHWIFE: Oh, may I so? Then I'm satisfied.

PINCHWIFE: Come, begin. [*Dictates*] 'Sir' –

MRS PINCHWIFE: Shan't I say, 'Dear Sir'? – You know one says always something more than bare 'Sir'.

PINCHWIFE: Write as I bid you, or I will write whore with this penknife in your face.

MRS PINCHWIFE: Nay, good bud. [*She writes*] 'Sir' –

PINCHWIFE: 'Though I suffered last night your nauseous, loathed kisses and embraces.' – Write.

MRS PINCHWIFE: Nay, why should I say so? You know I told you he had a sweet breath.

PINCHWIFE: Write!

MRS PINCHWIFE: Let me but put out 'loathed'.

PINCHWIFE: Write, I say!

MRS PINCHWIFE: Well then. [*Writes.*]

PINCHWIFE: Let's see what have you writ. [*Takes the paper, and reads.*] 'Though I suffered last night your kisses and embraces'. – Thou impudent creature, where is 'nauseous' and 'loathed'?

MRS PINCHWIFE: I can't abide to write such filthy words.

PINCHWIFE: Once more, write as I'd have you and question it not, or I will spoil thy writing with this. [*Holds up the penknife.*] I will stab out those eyes that cause my mischief.

MRS PINCHWIFE: O Lord, I will!

PINCHWIFE: So – so. – Let's see now! [*Reads*] 'Though I suffered last night your nauseous, loathed kisses and embraces' – go on – 'yet I would not have you presume that you shall ever repeat them.' – So.

She writes.

MRS PINCHWIFE: I have writ it.

PINCHWIFE: On then. – 'I then concealed myself from your knowledge to avoid your insolencies' –

She writes.

MRS PINCHWIFE: So –

PINCHWIFE: 'The same reason, now I am out of your hands' –

She writes.

MRS PINCHWIFE: So –

PINCHWIFE: 'Makes me own to you my unfortunate, though innocent frolick, of being in man's clothes.'

She writes.

MRS PINCHWIFE: So –

PINCHWIFE: 'That you may for ever more cease to pursue her, who hates and detests you' –

She writes on.

MRS PINCHWIFE: So – h – [*Sighs.*]

PINCHWIFE: What, do you sigh? – 'detests you – as much as she loves her husband and her honour'.

MRS PINCHWIFE: I vow, husband, he'll ne'er believe I should write such a letter.

PINCHWIFE: What, he'd expect a kinder from you? Come now, your name only.

MRS PINCHWIFE: What, shan't I say 'Your most faithful, humble servant till death'?

PINCHWIFE: No, tormenting fiend! [*Aside*] Her style, I find, would be very soft. – Come, wrap it up now, whilst I go fetch wax and a candle; and write on the back side, 'For Mr Horner'.

Exit PINCHWIFE.

MRS PINCHWIFE: 'For Mr Horner'. – So, I am glad he has told me his name. Dear Mr Horner! But why should I send thee such a letter that will vex thee, and make thee angry with me? – Well, I will not send it. – Ay, but then my husband will kill me, for I see plainly he won't let me love Mr Horner – but what care I for my husband? – I won't, so I won't, send poor Mr Horner such a letter – but then my husband – But oh – what if I writ at bottom my husband made me write it? – Ay, but then my husband would see't. – Can one have no shift? Ah, a London woman would have had a hundred presently. Stay – what if I should write a letter, and wrap it up like this, and write on't too? Ay, but then my husband would see't. – I don't know what to do. – But yet y'vads, I'll try, so I will – for I will not send this letter to poor Mr Horner, come what will on't. [*She writes, and repeats what she hath writ.*]

'Dear, sweet Mr Horner' – so – 'my husband would have me send you a base, rude, unmannerly letter – but I won't' – so – 'and would have me forbid you loving me – but I won't' – so – 'and would have me say to you I hate you,

poor Mr Horner – but I won't tell a lie for him' – there –
'for I'm sure if you and I were in the country at cards together', – so – 'I could not help treading on your toe under
the table' – so – 'or rubbing knees with you, and staring in
your face till you saw me' – very well – 'and then looking
down, and blushing for an hour together' – so – 'but I must
make haste before my husband come; and now he has
taught me to write letters, you shall have longer ones from
me, who am

> Dear, dear, poor dear Mr Horner, your most
> humble friend, and servant to command
> 'till death, Margery Pinchwife.'

Stay, I must give him a hint at bottom – so – now wrap it
up just like t'other – so – now write 'For Mr Horner'. –
But oh now what shall I do with it? For here comes my
husband.

Enter PINCHWIFE.

PINCHWIFE [*aside*]: I have been detained by a sparkish coxcomb who pretended a visit to me; but I fear 'twas to my
wife. – What, have you done?

MRS PINCHWIFE: Ay, ay bud, just now.

PINCHWIFE: Let's see. What d'ye tremble for? What, you
would not have it go?

MRS PINCHWIFE: Here. [*Aside*] No, I must not give him
that; so I had been served if I had given him this.

PINCHWIFE [*he opens, and reads the first letter*]: Come, where's
the wax and seal?

MRS PINCHWIFE [*aside*]: Lord, what shall I do now? Nay
then I have it. – Pray let me see't. Lord you think me
so arrant a fool I cannot seal a letter; I will do't, so I
will.

*Snatches the letter from him, changes it for the other, seals it,
and delivers it to him.*

PINCHWIFE: Nay, I believe you will learn that, and other
things too, which I would not have you.

MRS PINCHWIFE: So, han't I done it curiously?[1] [*Aside*] I
think I have; there's my letter going to Mr Horner; since
he'll needs have me send letters to folks.

1. *Curiously*: elegantly.

PINCHWIFE: 'Tis very well, but I warrant you would not have it go now?

MRS PINCHWIFE: Yes indeed, but I would, bud – now.

PINCHWIFE: Well, you are a good girl then. Come, let me lock you up in your chamber till I come back; and be sure you come not within three strides of the window when I am gone, for I have a spy in the street.

Exit MRS PINCHWIFE.

PINCHWIFE *locks the door.*

At least, 'tis fit she think so. If we do not cheat women, they'll cheat us; and fraud may be justly used with secret enemies, of which a wife is the most dangerous; and he that has a handsome one to keep, and a frontier town, must provide against treachery rather than open force. Now I have secured all within, I'll deal with the foe without with false intelligence. [*Holds up the letter. Exit* PINCHWIFE.]

SCENE THREE

The scene changes to HORNER'S *lodging.*

QUACK *and* HORNER.

QUACK: Well sir, how fadges[1] the new design? Have you not the luck of all your brother projectors,[2] to deceive only yourself at last?

HORNER: No, good domine doctor, I deceive you it seems, and others too; for the grave matrons and old rigid husbands think me as unfit for love as they are; but their wives, sisters and daughters know, some of 'em, better things already.

QUACK: Already!

HORNER: Already, I say. Last night I was drunk with half a dozen of your civil persons, as you call 'em, and people of honour, and so was made free of their society and dressing-rooms for ever hereafter; and am already come to the privileges of sleeping upon their pallets, warming smocks, tying shoes and garters and the like, doctor – already, already doctor.

QUACK: You have made use of your time, sir.

1. *Fadges*: prospers.   2. *Projectors*: speculators.

HORNER: I tell thee, I am now no more interruption to 'em, when they sing or talk bawdy, than a little squab[1] French page, who speaks no English.

QUACK: But do civil persons and women of honour drink and sing bawdy songs?

HORNER: Oh, amongst friends, amongst friends. For your bigots in honour are just like those in religion; they fear the eye of the world more than the eye of Heaven, and think there is no virtue but railing at vice, and no sin but giving scandal. They rail at a poor little kept player, and keep themselves some young, modest, pulpit comedian[2] to be privy to their sins in their closets, not to tell 'em of them in their chapels.

QUACK: Nay, the truth on't is, priests amongst the women now have quite got the better of us lay confessors, physicians.

HORNER: And they are rather their patients, but –

Enter MY LADY FIDGET, *looking about her.*

Now we talk of women of honour, here comes one. Step behind the screen there, and but observe if I have not particular privileges with the women of reputation already, doctor, already.

(QUACK *hides behind screen.*)

LADY FIDGET: Well, Horner, am not I a woman of honour? You see, I'm as good as my word.

HORNER: And you shall see madam, I'll not be behindhand with you in honour; and I'll be as good as my word too, if you please but to withdraw into the next room.

LADY FIDGET: But first, my dear sir, you must promise to have a care of my dear honour.

HORNER: If you talk a word more of your honour, you'll make me incapable to wrong it. To talk of honour in the mysteries of love is like talking of Heaven or the Deity in an operation of witchcraft, just when you are employing the devil; it makes the charm impotent.

LADY FIDGET: Nay, fie, let us not be smooty.[3] But you talk of mysteries and bewitching to me; I don't understand you.

1. *Squab*: chubby.   2. *Pulpit comedian*: priest.
3. *Smooty*: smutty.

HORNER: I tell you madam, the word 'money' in a mistress's mouth at such a nick of time is not a more disheart'ning sound to a younger brother[1] than that of honour to an eager lover like myself.

LADY FIDGET: But you can't blame a lady of my reputation to be chary.

HORNER: Chary! I have been chary of it already, by the report I have caused of myself.

LADY FIDGET: Ay, but if you should ever let other women know that dear secret, it would come out. Nay, you must have a great care of your conduct; for my acquaintance are so censorious – oh 'tis a wicked, censorious world, Mr Horner! – I say, are so censorious and detracting that perhaps they'll talk to the prejudice of my honour, though you should not let them know the dear secret.

HORNER: Nay, madam, rather than they shall prejudice your honour, I'll prejudice theirs; and to serve you, I'll lie with 'em all, make the secret their own, and then they'll keep it. I am a Machiavel in love, madam.

LADY FIDGET: Oh no sir, not that way!

HORNER: Nay, the devil take me if censorious women are to be silenced any other way.

LADY FIDGET: A secret is better kept, I hope, by a single person than a multitude; therefore pray do not trust anybody else with it, dear, dear Mr Horner. [*Embracing him.*]

Enter SIR JASPER FIDGET.

SIR JASPER: How now!

LADY FIDGET [*aside*]: O my husband – prevented – and what's almost as bad, found with my arms about another man – that will appear too much – what shall I say? – Sir Jasper come hither. I am trying if Mr Horner were ticklish, and he's as ticklish as can be. I love to torment the confounded toad; let you and I tickle him.

SIR JASPER: No, your ladyship will tickle him better without me, I suppose. But is this your buying china? I thought you had been at the china house.

HORNER [*aside*]: China house, that's my cue, I must take it. – A pox! Can't you keep your impertinent wives at home?

1. *Younger brother*: who did not usually inherit anything.

Some men are troubled with the husbands, but I with the wives. But I'd have you to know, since I cannot be your journeyman by night, I will not be your drudge by day, to squire your wife about and be your man of straw, or scarecrow, only to pies and jays¹ that would be nibbling at your forbidden fruit. I shall be shortly the hackney² gentleman-usher of the town.

SIR JASPER [*aside*]: Heh, heh, he! Poor fellow, he's in the right on't, faith. To squire women about for other folks is as ungrateful³ an employment as to tell money for other folks. – Heh, he, he! Ben't angry, Horner.

LADY FIDGET: No, 'tis I have more reason to be angry, who am left by you, to go abroad indecently alone; or, what is more indecent, to pin myself upon such ill-bred people of your acquaintance as this is.

SIR JASPER: Nay, prithee, what has he done?

LADY FIDGET: Nay, he has done nothing.

SIR JASPER: But what d'ye take ill, if he has done nothing?

LADY FIDGET: Hah, hah, hah! Faith, I can't but laugh however. Why d'ye think the unmannerly toad would not⁴ come down to me to the coach? I was fain to come up to fetch him, or go without him, which I was resolved not to do; for he knows china very well, and has himself very good, but will not let me see it lest I should beg some. But I will find it out, and have what I came for yet.

Exit LADY FIDGET, *and locks the door, followed by* HORNER *to the door.*

HORNER [*apart to* LADY FIDGET]: Lock the door, madam. (*Aloud*) So, she has got into my chamber, and locked me out. Oh, the impertinency of woman-kind! Well, Sir Jasper, plain dealing is a jewel; if ever you suffer your wife to trouble me again here, she shall carry you home a pair of horns, by my Lord Mayor she shall; though I cannot furnish you myself, you are sure, yet I'll find a way.

SIR JASPER [*aside*]: Hah, ha, he! At my first coming in, and finding her arms about him, tickling him it seems, I was

---

1. *Pies and jays*: fops.   2. *Hackney*: hired.
3. *Ungrateful*: thankless.   4. *Would not*: Q5 *would* (1695).

half jealous, but now I see my folly. – Heh he, he! Poor Horner.

HORNER: Nay, though you laugh now, 'twill be my turn ere long. Oh women, more impertinent, more cunning, and more mischievous than their monkeys, and to me almost as ugly! Now is she throwing my things about, and rifling all I have, but I'll get into her the back way, and so rifle her for it –

SIR JASPER: Hah, ha, ha! Poor angry Horner.

HORNER: Stay here a little, I'll ferret her out to you presently, I warrant.

Exit HORNER *at t'other door.*

SIR JASPER [SIR JASPER *calls through the door to his wife, she answers from within*]: Wife! My Lady Fidget! Wife! He is coming into you the back way.

LADY FIDGET: Let him come, and welcome, which way he will.

SIR JASPER: He'll catch you, and use you roughly, and be too strong for you.

LADY FIDGET: Don't you trouble yourself, let him if he can.

QUACK [*behind*]: This indeed, I could not have believed from him, nor any but my own eyes.

Enter MRS SQUEAMISH.

MRS SQUEAMISH: Where's this woman-hater, this toad, this ugly, greasy, dirty sloven?

SIR JASPER [*aside*]: So, the women all will have him ugly. Methinks he is a comely person, but his wants make his form contemptible to 'em. And 'tis e'en as my wife said yesterday, talking of him, that a proper handsome eunuch was as ridiculous a thing as a gigantic coward.

MRS SQUEAMISH: Sir Jasper, your servant. Where is the odious beast?

SIR JASPER: He's within in his chamber, with my wife. She's playing the wag with him.

MRS SQUEAMISH: Is she so? And he's a clownish beast, he'll give her no quarter, he'll play the wag with her again, let me tell you. Come, let's go help her. – What, the door's locked?

SIR JASPER: Ay, my wife locked it –

MRS SQUEAMISH: Did she so? Let us break it open then.

SIR JASPER: No, no, he'll do her no hurt.

MRS SQUEAMISH: No. – [*Aside*] But is there no other way to get into 'em? Whither goes this? I will disturb 'em.

Exit MRS SQUEAMISH *at another door.*

Enter OLD LADY SQUEAMISH.

OLD LADY SQUEAMISH: Where is this harlotry, this impudent baggage, this rambling tomrigg?[1] O Sir Jasper, I'm glad to see you here. Did you not see my vild[2] grandchild come in hither just now?

SIR JASPER: Yes.

OLD LADY SQUEAMISH: Ay, but where is she then? Where is she? Lord, Sir Jasper, I have e'en rattled myself to pieces in pursuit of her. But can you tell what she makes here? They say below, no woman lodges here.

SIR JASPER: No.

OLD LADY SQUEAMISH: No! What does she here then? Say, if it be not a woman's lodging, what makes she here? But are you sure no woman lodges here?

SIR JASPER: No, nor no man neither. This is Mr Horner's lodging.

OLD LADY SQUEAMISH: Is it so? Are you sure?

SIR JASPER: Yes, yes.

OLD LADY SQUEAMISH: So; then there's no hurt in't, I hope. But where is he?

SIR JASPER: He's in the next room with my wife.

OLD LADY SQUEAMISH: Nay, if you trust him with your wife, I may with my Biddy. They say he's a merry harmless man now, e'en as harmless a man as ever came out of Italy with a good voice,[3] and as pretty harmless company for a lady, as a snake without his teeth.

SIR JASPER: Ay, ay, poor man.

Enter MRS SQUEAMISH.

MRS SQUEAMISH: I can't find 'em. – Oh, are you here grandmother? I followed, you must know, My Lady Fidget hither; 'tis the prettiest lodging, and I have been staring on the prettiest pictures.

1. *Tomrigg*: tomboy.   2. *Vild*: vile.

3. *With a good voice*: i.e., a castrato.

Enter LADY FIDGET *with a piece of china in her hand, and* HORNER *following.*

LADY FIDGET: And I have been toiling and moiling[1] for the prettiest piece of china, my dear.

HORNER: Nay, she has been too hard for me, do what I could.

MRS SQUEAMISH: O Lord, I'll have some china too, good Mr Horner. Don't think to give other people china, and me none. Come in with me too.

HORNER: Upon my honour, I have none left now.

MRS SQUEAMISH: Nay, nay, I have known you deny your china before now, but you shan't put me off so. Come –

HORNER: This lady had the last there.

LADY FIDGET: Yes indeed, madam, to my certain knowledge he has no more left.

MRS SQUEAMISH: Oh, but it may be he may have some you could not find.

LADY FIDGET: What? D'ye think if he had had any left, I would not have had it too? For we women of quality never think we have china enough.

HORNER: Do not take it ill, I cannot make china for you all, but I will have a roll-wagon[2] for you too another time.

MRS SQUEAMISH: Thank you, dear toad.

LADY FIDGET [*to* HORNER, *aside*]: What do you mean by that promise?

HORNER [*apart to* LADY FIDGET]: Alas, she has an innocent, literal understanding.

OLD LADY SQUEAMISH: Poor Mr Horner, he has enough to do to please you all, I see.

HORNER: Ay, madam, you see how they use me.

OLD LADY SQUEAMISH: Poor gentleman, I pity you.

HORNER: I thank you madam, I could never find pity, but from such reverend ladies as you are; the young ones will never spare a man.

MRS SQUEAMISH: Come come, beast, and go dine with us, for we shall want a man at hombre after dinner.

HORNER: That's all their use of me madam, you see.

1. *Toiling and moiling*: working hard.
2. *Roll-wagon*: vehicle for carrying goods.

MRS SQUEAMISH: Come sloven, I'll lead you to be sure of you. [*Pulls him by the cravat.*]

OLD LADY SQUEAMISH: Alas, poor man, how she tugs him! Kiss, kiss her, that's the way to make such nice[1] women quiet.

HORNER: No madam, that remedy is worse than the torment. They know I dare suffer anything rather than do it.

OLD LADY SQUEAMISH: Prithee kiss her, and I'll give you her picture in little that you admired so last night; prithee do.

HORNER: Well, nothing but that could bribe me; I love a woman only in effigy, and good painting as much as I hate them. I'll do't, for I could adore the devil well painted. [*Kisses* MRS SQUEAMISH.]

MRS SQUEAMISH: Foh, you filthy toad! Nay, now I've done jesting.

OLD LADY SQUEAMISH: Ha, ha, ha! I told you so.

MRS SQUEAMISH: Foh! A kiss of his –

SIR JASPER: Has no more hurt in't than one of my spaniel's.

MRS SQUEAMISH: Nor no more good neither.

QUACK [*behind*]: I will now believe anything he tells me.

Enter MR PINCHWIFE.

LADY FIDGET: O Lord, here's a man! Sir Jasper, my mask, my mask! I would not be seen here for the world.

SIR JASPER: What, not when I am with you?

LADY FIDGET: No, no, my honour – let's be gone.

MRS SQUEAMISH: Oh, grandmother, let us be gone, make haste, make haste, I know not how he may censure us.

LADY FIDGET: Be found in the lodging of anything like a man! Away!

Exeunt SIR JASPER, LADY FIDGET, OLD LADY SQUEAMISH, MRS SQUEAMISH.

QUACK [*behind*]: What's here? Another cuckold? He looks like one, and none else, sure, have any business with him.

HORNER: Well, what brings my dear friend hither?

PINCHWIFE: Your impertinency.

HORNER: My impertinency? Why, you gentlemen that have

1. *Nice*: fussy.

got handsome wives think you have a privilege of saying anything to your friends, and are as brutish as if you were our creditors.

PINCHWIFE: No sir, I'll ne'er trust you any way.

HORNER: But why not dear Jack? Why diffide in[1] me thou know'st so well?

PINCHWIFE: Because I do know you so well.

HORNER: Han't I been always thy friend, honest Jack? Always ready to serve thee, in love, or battle, before thou wert married, and am so still?

PINCHWIFE: I believe so; you would be my second now, indeed.

HORNER: Well then, dear Jack, why so unkind, so grum, so strange to me? Come, prithee kiss me, dear rogue. Gad, I was always I say, and am still as much thy servant as –

PINCHWIFE: As I am yours, sir. What, you would send a kiss to my wife, is that it?

HORNER: So, there 'tis – a man can't shew his friendship to a married man, but presently he talks of his wife to you. Prithee, let thy wife alone, and let thee and I be all one, as we were wont. What, thou art as shy of my kindness as a Lumbard Street alderman[2] of a courtier's civility at Locket's.[3]

PINCHWIFE: But you are overkind to me, as kind as if I were your cuckold already. Yet I must confess you ought to be kind and civil to me, since I am so kind, so civil to you as to bring you this. Look you there, sir. [*Delivers him a letter.*]

HORNER: What is't?

PINCHWIFE: Only a love letter sir.

HORNER: From whom? – how! This is from your wife! – hum – and – hum – [*Reads.*]

PINCHWIFE: Even from my wife sir. Am I not wondrous kind and civil to you now too? [*Aside*] But you'll not think her so.

HORNER [*aside*]: Ha! Is this a trick of his or hers?

1. *Diffide in*: mistrust.
2. *Lumbard Street*: address of many goldsmiths, who would be wealthy and therefore suspicious of politeness from impecunious aristocrats.
3. *Locket's*: fashionable restaurant.

PINCHWIFE: The gentleman's surprised I find. What, you expected a kinder letter?

HORNER: No faith, not I, how could I?

PINCHWIFE: Yes yes, I'm sure you did. A man so well made as you are must needs be disappointed if the women declare not their passion at first sight or opportunity.

HORNER: But what should this mean? Stay, the postscript. [*Reads aside*] 'Be sure you love me whatsoever my husband says to the contrary, and let him not see this, lest he should come home and pinch me, or kill my squirrel.' [*Aside*] It seems he knows not what the letter contains.

PINCHWIFE: Come, ne'er wonder at it so much.

HORNER: Faith, I can't help it.

PINCHWIFE: Now I think I have deserved your infinite friendship and kindness, and have shewed myself sufficiently an obliging kind friend and husband. Am I not so, to bring a letter from my wife to her gallant?

HORNER: Ay, the devil take me, art thou, the most obliging, kind friend and husband in the world. Ha, ha!

PINCHWIFE: Well, you may be merry sir, but in short I must tell you, sir, my honour will suffer no jesting.

HORNER: What dost thou mean?

PINCHWIFE: Does the letter want a comment? Then know sir, though I have been so civil a husband as to bring you a letter from my wife, to let you kiss and court her to my face, I will not be a cuckold sir, I will not.

HORNER: Thou art mad with jealousy. I never saw thy wife in my life but at the play yesterday, and I know not if it were she or no. I court her, kiss her!

PINCHWIFE: I will not be a cuckold, I say. There will be danger in making me a cuckold.

HORNER: Why, wert thou not well cured of thy last clap?

PINCHWIFE: I wear a sword.

HORNER: It should be taken from thee, lest thou shouldst do thyself a mischief with it. Thou art mad, man.

PINCHWIFE: As mad as I am, and as merry as you are, I must have more reason from you ere we part. I say again, though you kissed and courted last night my wife in man's clothes, as she confesses in her letter –

HORNER [*aside*]: Ha!

PINCHWIFE: Both she and I say you must not design it again, for you have mistaken your woman, as you have done your man.

HORNER [*aside*]: Oh – I understand something now. – Was that thy wife? Why wouldst thou not tell me 'twas she? Faith, my freedom with her was your fault, not mine.

PINCHWIFE [*aside*]: Faith, so 'twas.

HORNER: Fie! I'd never do't to a woman before her husband's face, sure.

PINCHWIFE: But I had rather you should do't to my wife before my face than behind my back, and that you shall never do.

HORNER: No – you will hinder me.

PINCHWIFE: If I would not hinder you, you see by her letter she would.

HORNER: Well, I must e'en acquiesce then, and be contented with what she writes.

PINCHWIFE: I'll assure you 'twas voluntarily writ. I had no hand in't, you may believe me.

HORNER: I do believe thee, faith.

PINCHWIFE: And believe her too, for she's an innocent creature, has no dissembling in her. And so fare you well, sir.

HORNER: Pray, however, present my humble service to her, and tell her I will obey her letter to a tittle, and fulfil her desires be what they will, or with what difficulty soever I do't, and you shall be no more jealous of me, I warrant her, and you.

PINCHWIFE: Well then, fare you well, and play with any man's honour but mine, kiss any man's wife but mine, and welcome. [*Exit* MR PINCHWIFE.]

HORNER: Ha, ha, ha! Doctor.

QUACK [*coming out*]: It seems he has not heard the report of you, or does not believe it.

HORNER: Ha, ha! Now, doctor, what think you?

QUACK: Pray let's see the letter [*reads the letter*] – hum – 'for – dear – love you' –

HORNER: I wonder how she could contrive it? What say'st thou to't? 'Tis an original.

QUACK: So are your cuckolds too, originals, for they are like no other common cuckolds; and I will henceforth believe it not impossible for you to cuckold the Grand Signior[1] amidst his guards of eunuchs, that I say.

HORNER: And I say for the letter, 'tis the first love letter that ever was without flames, darts, fates, destinies, lying and dissembling in't.

Enter SPARKISH *pulling in* MR PINCHWIFE.

SPARKISH: Come back, you are a pretty brother-in-law, neither go to church, nor to dinner with your sister bride!

PINCHWIFE: My sister denies her marriage, and you see is gone away from you dissatisfied.

SPARKISH: Pshaw! Upon a foolish scruple that our parson was not in lawful orders, and did not say all the Common Prayer; but 'tis her modesty only, I believe. But let women be never so modest the first day, they'll be sure to come to themselves by night, and I shall have enough of her then. In the meantime, Harry Horner, you must dine with me. I keep my wedding at my aunt's in the Piazza.[2]

HORNER: Thy wedding! What stale maid has lived to despair of a husband, or what young one of a gallant?

SPARKISH: Oh, your servant, sir – this gentleman's sister then – no stale maid.

HORNER: I'm sorry for't.

PINCHWIFE [*aside*]: How comes he so concerned for her?

SPARKISH: You sorry for't? Why, do you know any ill by her?

HORNER: No, I know none but by thee. 'Tis for her sake, not yours, and another man's sake that might have hoped, I thought.

SPARKISH: Another man, another man? What is his name?

HORNER: Nay, since 'tis past he shall be nameless. [*Aside*] Poor Harcourt, I am sorry thou hast missed her.

PINCHWIFE [*aside*]: He seems to be much troubled at the match –

SPARKISH: Prithee tell me – nay, you shan't go, brother.

---

1. *Grand Signior*: Turkish sultan.
2. *Piazza*: arcade near Covent Garden.

PINCHWIFE: I must of necessity, but I'll come to you to dinner. [*Exit* PINCHWIFE.]

SPARKISH: But Harry, what, have I a rival in my wife already? But with all my heart, for he may be of use to me hereafter. For though my hunger is now my sauce, and I can fall on heartily without, but the time will come when a rival will be as good sauce for a married man to a wife as an orange to veal.

HORNER: O thou damned rogue! Thou hast set my teeth on edge with thy orange.

SPARKISH: Then let's to dinner – there, I was with you again. Come.

HORNER: But who dines with thee?

SPARKISH: My friends and relations. My brother Pinchwife you see, of your acquaintance.

HORNER: And his wife?

SPARKISH: No gad, he'll ne'er let her come amongst us good fellows. Your stingy country coxcomb keeps his wife from his friends as he does his little firkin of ale for his own drinking, and a gentleman can't get a smack on't; but his servants, when his back is turned, broach it at their pleasures, and dust it away. Ha, ha, ha! Gad, I am witty, I think, considering I was married today, by the world. But come –

HORNER: No, I will not dine with you, unless you can fetch her too.

SPARKISH: Pshaw! What pleasure canst thou have with women now, Harry?

HORNER: My eyes are not gone; I love a good prospect yet, and will not dine with you unless she does too. Go fetch her therefore, but do not tell her husband 'tis for my sake.

SPARKISH: Well, I'll go try what I can do. In the meantime come away, to my aunt's lodging, 'tis in the way to Pinchwife's.

HORNER (*whispers to* QUACK): The poor woman has called for aid, and stretched forth her hand, doctor; I cannot but help her over the pale out of the briars.

Exeunt SPARKISH, HORNER, QUACK.

SCENE FOUR

The scene changes to PINCHWIFE's *house.*
MRS PINCHWIFE *alone, leaning on her elbow. A table, pen, ink, and paper.*

MRS PINCHWIFE: Well, 'tis e'en so; I have got the London disease they call love. I am sick of my husband, and for my gallant. I have heard this distemper called a fever but methinks 'tis liker an ague, for when I think of my husband I tremble and am in a cold sweat and have inclinations to vomit; but when I think of my gallant, dear Mr Horner, my hot fit comes and I am all in a fever, indeed, and as in other fevers my own chamber is tedious to me, and I would fain be removed to his, and then methinks I should be well. Ah, poor Mr Horner! Well, I cannot, will not stay here, therefore I'll make an end of my letter to him, which shall be a finer letter than my last, because I have studied it like anything; O sick, sick! [*Takes the pen and writes.*]

Enter MR PINCHWIFE *who seeing her writing steals softly behind her, and looking over her shoulder, snatches the paper from her.*

PINCHWIFE: What, writing more letters?
MRS PINCHWIFE: O lord bud, why d'ye fright me so? [*She offers to run out: he stops her and reads.*]
PINCHWIFE: How's this! Nay, you shall not stir, madam. 'Dear, dear, dear, Mr Horner' – very well – I have taught you to write letters to good purpose – but let's see't.

'First, I am to beg your pardon for my boldness in writing to you, which I'd have you to know I would not have done, had not you said first you loved me so extremely, which if you do, you will never suffer me to lie in the arms of another man, whom I loathe, nauseate, and detest.' – Now you can write these filthy words. But what follows? – 'Therefore I hope you will speedily find some way to free me from this unfortunate match, which was never, I assure you, of my choice, but I'm afraid 'tis already too far gone. However, if you love me, as I do you, you will try what you can do, but you must help me away before tomorrow, or else, alas, I

shall be for ever out of your reach, for I can defer no longer
our' – 'our' – [*the letter concludes*] what is to follow 'our'? –
Speak, what? Our journey into the country, I suppose? –
Oh woman, damned woman, and love, damned love, their
old tempter! For this is one of his miracles; in a moment he
can make those blind that could see, and those see that were
blind, those dumb that could speak, and those prattle who
were dumb before. Nay, what is more than all, make these
dow[1]-baked, senseless, indocile animals, women, too hard
for us, their politic lords and rulers, in a moment. But make
an end of your letter, and then I'll make an end of you thus,
and all my plagues together. [*Draws his sword.*]

MRS PINCHWIFE: O Lord, O Lord, you are such a passionate
man, bud!

    Enter SPARKISH.

SPARKISH: How now, what's here to do?

PINCHWIFE: This fool here now!

SPARKISH: What, drawn upon your wife? You should never
do that but at night in the dark when you can't hurt her.
This is my sister-in-law is it not? [*Pulls aside her handker-chief.*] Ay, faith, e'en our country Margery, one may know
her. Come, she and you must go dine with me; dinner's
ready, come. But where's my wife? Is she not come home
yet? Where is she?

PINCHWIFE: Making you a cuckold; 'tis that they all do, as
soon as they can.

SPARKISH: What, the wedding day? No, a wife that designs
to make a cully[2] of her husband will be sure to let him win
the first stake of love, by the world. But come, they stay
dinner for us. Come, I'll lead down our Margery.

MRS PINCHWIFE: No – sir, go, we'll follow you.

SPARKISH: I will not wag[3] without you.

PINCHWIFE [*aside*]: This coxcomb is a sensible torment to me
amidst the greatest in the world.

SPARKISH: Come, come, Madam Margery.

PINCHWIFE: No, I'll lead her my way. What, would you

    1. *Dow*: dough.
    2. *Cully*: fool.
    3. *Wag*: stir.

treat your friends with mine, for want of your own wife?
[*Leads her to t'other door, and locks her in and returns.*] [*Aside*] I
am contented my rage should take breath.

SPARKISH: I told Horner this.

PINCHWIFE: Come now.

SPARKISH: Lord how shy you are of your wife! But let me
tell you, brother, we men of wit have amongst us a saying
that cuckolding, like the smallpox, comes with a fear; and
you may keep your wife as much as you will out of danger of
infection, but if her constitution incline her to't, she'll have
it sooner or later, by the world, say they.

PINCHWIFE [*aside*]: What a thing is a cuckold, that every fool
can make him ridiculous! Well sir — but let me advise you,
now you are come to be concerned, because you suspect the
danger, not to neglect the means to prevent it, especially
when the greatest share of the malady will light upon your
own head, for —

How s'e'er the kind wife's belly comes to swell.
The husband breeds for her, and first is ill.

Act Five

MR PINCHWIFE's *house.*
Enter MR PINCHWIFE *and* MRS PINCHWIFE. *A table and candle.*

PINCHWIFE: Come, take the pen and make an end of the letter, just as you intended. If you are false in a tittle, I shall soon perceive it, and punish you with this as you deserve. [*Lays his hand on his sword.*] Write what was to follow – let's see – 'You must make haste and help me away before to-morrow, or else I shall be for ever out of your reach, for I can defer no longer our' – What follows 'our'? –

MRS PINCHWIFE: Must all out then, bud? [MRS PINCH-WIFE *takes the pen and writes.*] Look you there then.

PINCHWIFE: Let's see – 'For I can defer no longer our – wedding – Your slighted *Alithea.*' What's the meaning of this? My sister's name to't? Speak, unriddle!

MRS PINCHWIFE: Yes indeed, bud.

PINCHWIFE: But why her name to't? Speak – speak, I say!

MRS PINCHWIFE: Ay, but you'll tell her then again; if you would not tell her again –

PINCHWIFE: I will not – I am stunned, my head turns round. Speak!

MRS PINCHWIFE: Won't you tell her indeed, and indeed?

PINCHWIFE: No. Speak, I say!

MRS PINCHWIFE: She'll be angry with me, but I had rather she should be angry with me than you, bud; and to tell you the truth, 'twas she made me write the letter, and taught me what I should write.

PINCHWIFE (*aside*): Ha! I thought the style was somewhat better than her own. – But how could she come to you to teach you, since I had locked you up alone?

MRS PINCHWIFE: O – through the keyhold, bud.

PINCHBECK: But why should she make you write a letter for her to him, since she can write herself?

MRS PINCHWIFE: Why, she said because – for I was unwilling to do it.

PINCHWIFE: Because what – because?

MRS PINCHWIFE: Because, lest Mr Horner should be cruel, and refuse her, or vain afterwards, and shew the letter, she might disown it, the hand not being hers.

PINCHWIFE [*aside*]: How's this? Ha! Then I think I shall come to myself again. This changeling could not invent this lie, but if she could, why should she? She might think I should soon discover it – stay – now I think on't too, Horner said he was sorry she had married Sparkish, and her disowning her marriage to me makes me think she has evaded it for Horner's sake. Yet why should she take this course? But men in love are fools, women may well be so. – But hark you madam, your sister went out in the morning, and I have not seen her within since.

MRS PINCHWIFE: Alackaday, she has been crying all day above, it seems, in a corner.

PINCHWIFE: Where is she? Let me speak with her.

MRS PINCHWIFE [*aside*]: O Lord, then he'll discover all. – Pray hold, bud; what, d'ye mean to discover me? She'll know I have told you then. Pray bud, let me talk with her first.

PINCHWIFE: I must speak with her to know whether Horner ever made her any promise, and whether she be married to Sparkish or no.

MRS PINCHWIFE: Pray dear bud don't, till I have spoken with her and told her that I have told you all, for she'll kill me else.

PINCHWIFE: Go then, and bid her come out to me.

MRS PINCHWIFE: Yes, yes, bud.

PINCHWIFE: Let me see –

MRS PINCHWIFE (*aside*): I'll go, but she is not within to come to him. I have just got time to know of Lucy her maid, who first set me on work, what lie I shall tell next, for I am e'en at my wits end. [*Exit* MRS PINCHWIFE.]

PINCHWIFE: Well, I resolve it; Horner shall have her. I'd rather give him my sister than lend him my wife, and such an alliance will prevent his pretensions to my wife, sure.

I'll make him of kin to her, and then he won't care for
her.

    MRS PINCHWIFE *returns*.

MRS PINCHWIFE: O Lord, bud, I told you what anger you
would make me with my sister.

PINCHWIFE: Won't she come hither?

MRS PINCHWIFE: No, no, alackaday, she's ashamed to look
you in the face, and she says if you go in to her, she'll run
away downstairs, and shamefully go herself to Mr Horner,
who has promised her marriage, she says, and she will
have no other, so she won't.

PINCHWIFE: Did he so – promise her marriage? – Then she
shall have no other. Go tell her so, and if she will come and
discourse with me a little concerning the means, I will
about it immediately. Go.

    Exit MRS PINCHWIFE.

His estate is equal to Sparkish's, and his extraction as much
better than his as his parts are; but my chief reason is, I'd
rather be of kin to him by the name of brother-in-law than
that of cuckold.

    Enter MRS PINCHWIFE.

Well, what says she now?

MRS PINCHWIFE: Why, she says she would only have you
lead her to Horner's lodging – with whom she first will discourse the matter before she talk with you, which yet she
cannot do; for alack, poor creature, she says she can't so
much as look you in the face. Therefore she'll come to you
in a mask, and you must excuse her if she make you no
answer to any question of yours, till you have brought her
to Mr Horner; and if you will not chide her, nor question
her, she'll come out to you immediately.

PINCHWIFE: Let her come; I will not speak a word to her,
nor require a word from her.

MRS PINCHWIFE: Oh, I forgot; besides, she says she cannot
look you in the face though through a mask, therefore
would desire you to put out the candle. [*Exit* MRS PINCH-
WIFE.]

PINCHWIFE: I agree to all; let her make haste. There, 'tis out.
[*Puts out the candle.*] My case is something better. I'd rather

fight with Horner for not lying with my sister than for lying with my wife, and of the two I had rather find my sister too forward than my wife. I expected no other from her free education, as she calls it, and her passion for the town. Well – wife and sister are names which make us expect love and duty, pleasure and comfort, but we find 'em plagues and torments, and are equally, though differently, troublesome to their keeper; for we have as much ado to get people to lie with our sisters as to keep 'em from lying with our wives.

Enter MRS PINCHWIFE *masked, and in hoods and scarves, and a nightgown and petticoat of* ALITHEA's, *in the dark.*

What, are you come sister? Let us go then – but first let me lock up my wife. Mrs Margery, where are you?

MRS PINCHWIFE: Here, bud.

PINCHWIFE: Come hither, that I may lock you up. [*Locks the door.*] Get you in. Come sister, where are you now?

MRS PINCHWIFE *gives him her hand, but when he lets her go, she steals softly on t'other side of him, and is led away by him for his sister* ALITHEA.

SCENE TWO

The scene changes to HORNER's *lodging.*

QUACK, HORNER.

QUACK: What, all alone? Not so much as one of your cuckolds here, nor one of their wives! They use to take their turns with you, as if they were to watch you.

HORNER: Yes, it often happens that a cuckold is but his wife's spy, and is more upon family duty when he is with her gallant abroad hindering his pleasure than when he is at home with her playing the gallant. But the hardest duty a married women imposes upon a lover is keeping her husband company always.

QUACK: And his fondness wearies you almost as soon as hers.

HORNER: A pox! Keeping a cuckold company after you have had his wife is as tiresome as the company of a country squire to a witty fellow of the town when he has got all his money.

QUACK: And as at first a man makes a friend of the husband to get the wife, so at last you are fain to fall out with the wife to be rid of the husband.

HORNER: Ay, most cuckold-makers are true courtiers; when once a poor man has cracked his credit for 'em, they can't abide to come near him.

QUACK: But at first, to draw him in, are so sweet, so kind, so dear, just as you are to Pinchwife. But what becomes of that intrigue with his wife?

HORNER: A pox! He's as surly as an alderman that has been bit, and since he's so coy, his wife's kindness is in vain, for she's a silly innocent.

QUACK: Did she not send you a letter by him?

HORNER: Yes, but that's a riddle I have not yet solved. Allow the poor creature to be willing, she is silly too, and he keeps her up so close –

QUACK: Yes, so close that he makes her but the more willing, and adds but revenge to her love, which two when met seldom fail of satisfying each other one way or other.

HORNER: What! Here's the man we are talking of, I think.
    Enter MR PINCHWIFE, *leading in his wife masked, muffled, and in her sister's gown.*

HORNER: Pshaw!

QUACK: Bringing his wife to you is the next thing to bringing a love letter from her.

HORNER: What means this?

PINCHWIFE: The last time, you know, sir, I brought you a love letter; now, you see, a mistress. I think you'll say I am a civil man to you.

HORNER: Ay, the devil take me, will I say thou art the civillest man I ever met with, and I have known some. I fancy I understand thee now better than I did the letter; but hark thee, in thy ear –

PINCHWIFE: What?

HORNER: Nothing but the usual question man: is she sound, on thy word?

PINCHWIFE: What, you take her for a wench, and me for a pimp?

HORNER: Pshaw! Wench and pimp, paw[1] words. I know thou art an honest fellow, and hast a great acquaintance among the ladies, and perhaps hast made love for me rather than let me make love to thy wife.

PINCHWIFE: Come sir, in short, I am for no fooling.

HORNER: Nor I neither. Therefore, prithee, let's see her face presently.[2] Make her show, man; art thou sure I don't know her?

PINCHWIFE: I am sure you do know her.

HORNER: A pox! Why dost thou bring her to me then?

PINCHWIFE: Because she's a relation of mine –

HORNER: Is she, faith, man? Then thou art still more civil and obliging, dear rogue.

PINCHWIFE: – who desired me to bring her to you.

HORNER: Then she is obliging, dear rogue.

PINCHWIFE: You'll make her welcome for my sake, I hope.

HORNER: I hope she is handsome enough to make herself welcome. Prithee let her unmask.

PINCHWIFE: Do you speak to her; she would never be ruled by me.

HORNER: Madam – [MRS PINCHWIFE *whispers to* HORNER.] She says she must speak with me in private. Withdraw, prithee.

PINCHWIFE [*aside*]: She's unwilling, it seems, I should know all her undecent conduct in this business. – Well then, I'll leave you together, and hope when I am gone you'll agree; if not, you and I shan't agree, sir.

HORNER: What means the fool? If she and I agree 'tis no matter what you and I do. [*Whispers to* MRS PINCHWIFE, *who makes signs with her hand for him* (PINCHWIFE) *to be gone.*]

PINCHWIFE: In the meantime I'll fetch a parson, and find out Sparkish and disabuse him. – You would have me fetch a parson, would you not? Well then – now I think I am rid of her, and shall have no more trouble with her. Our sisters and daughters, like usurers' money, are safest when put

1. *Paw*: improper.
2. *Presently*: at once.

out; but our wifes, like their writings, never safe but in our closets under lock and key. [*Exit* MR PINCHWIFE.]

 Enter BOY.

BOY: Sir Jasper Fidget, sir, is coming up.

HORNER: Here's the trouble of a cuckold, now we are talking of. A pox on him! Has he not enough to do to hinder his wife's sport, but he must other women's too? – Step in here, madam.

 Exit MRS PINCHWIFE.

 Enter SIR JASPER.

SIR JASPER: My best and dearest friend.

HORNER (*aside to* QUACK): The old style, doctor. – Well, be short, for I am busy. What would your impertinent wife have now?

SIR JASPER: Well guessed, i'faith, for I do come from her.

HORNER: To invite me to supper? Tell her I can't come; go.

SIR JASPER: Nay, now you are out, faith; for my lady and the whole knot of the virtuous gang, as they call themselves, are resolved upon a frolic of coming to you tonight in a masquerade, and are all dressed already.

HORNER: I shan't be at home.

SIR JASPER: Lord, how churlish he is to women! – Nay, prithee don't disappoint 'em. They'll think 'tis my fault; prithee don't. I'll send in the banquet and the fiddles, but make no noise on't, for the poor virtuous rogues would not have it known for the world that they go a-masquerading, and they would come to no man's ball but yours.

HORNER: Well, well. – Get you gone, and tell 'em if they come, 'twill be at the peril of their honour and yours.

SIR JASPER: Heh, he, he! – we'll trust you for that. Farewell. [*Exit* SIR JASPER.]

HORNER: Doctor, anon you too shall be my guest,
   But now I'm going to a private feast.

SCENE THREE

The scene changes to the Piazza of Covent Garden.
SPARKISH, PINCHWIFE.

SPARKISH [*with the letter*[1] *in his hand*]: But who would have thought a woman could have been false to me? By the world, I could not have thought it.

PINCHWIFE: You were for giving and taking liberty; she has taken it only, sir, now you find in that letter. You are a frank person, and so is she, you see there.

SPARKISH: Nay, if this be her hand – for I never saw it.

PINCHWIFE: 'Tis no matter whether that be her hand or no, I am sure this hand at her desire led her to Mr Horner, with whom I left her just now, to go fetch a parson to 'em at their desire too, to deprive you of her for ever, for it seems yours was but a mock marriage.

SPARKISH: Indeed, she would needs have it that 'twas Harcourt himself in a parson's habit that married us, but I'm sure he told me 'twas his brother Ned.

PINCHWIFE: Oh, there 'tis out and you were deceived, not she, for you are such a frank person – but I must be gone. You'll find her at Mr Horner's; go and believe your eyes.
[*Exit* MR PINCHWIFE.]

SPARKISH: Nay, I'll to her, and call her as many crocodiles, sirens, harpies, and other heathenish names as a poet would do a mistress who had refused to hear his suit, nay more, his verses on her. – But stay, is not that she following a torch at t'other end of the Piazza? And from Horner's certainly – 'tis so.
Enter ALITHEA *following a torch, and* LUCY *behind.*
You are well met, madam, though you don't think so. What, you have made a short visit to Mr Horner? But I suppose you'll return to him presently; by that time the parson can be with him.

ALITHEA: Mr Horner and the parson, sir?

SPARKISH: Come, madam, no more dissembling, no more jilting, for I am no more a frank person.

1. *Letter*: i.e., the letter written to Horner by Mrs Pinchwife.

ALITHEA: How's this?

LUCY [*aside*]: So, 'twill work, I see.

SPARKISH: Could you find out no easy country fool to abuse? None but me, a gentleman of wit and pleasure about the town? But it was your pride to be too hard for a man of parts, unworthy false woman! False as a friend that lends a man money to lose, false as dice, who undo those that trust all they have to 'em.

LUCY [*aside*]: He has been a great bubble by his similes, as they say.

ALITHEA: You have been too merry, sir, at your wedding dinner, sure.

SPARKISH: What, d'ye mock me too?

ALITHEA: Or you have been deluded.

SPARKISH: By you.

ALITHEA: Let me understand you.

SPARKISH: Have you the confidence – I should call it something else, since you know your guilt – to stand my just reproaches? You did not write an impudent letter to Mr Horner, who I find now has clubbed with you in deluding me with his aversion for women, that I might not, forsooth, suspect him for my rival?

LUCY [*aside*]: D'ye think the gentleman can be jealous now, madam?

ALITHEA: I write a letter to Mr Horner!

SPARKISH: Nay, madam, do not deny it. Your brother shewed it me just now, and told me likewise he left you at Horner's lodging to fetch a parson to marry you to him. And I wish you joy madam, joy, joy, and to him too, much joy, and to myself more joy for not marrying you.

ALITHEA [*aside*]: So, I find my brother would break off the match, and I can consent to't, since I see this gentleman can be made jealous. – O Lucy, by his rude usage and jealousy he makes me almost afraid I am married to him. Art thou sure 'twas Harcourt himself and no parson that married us?

SPARKISH: No, madam, I thank you. I suppose that was a contrivance too of Mr Horner's and yours, to make Harcourt play the parson. But I would as little as you have him one now, no, not for the world. For shall I tell you another truth? I never had any passion for you till now, for now I hate you. 'Tis true I might have married your portion, as other men of parts of the town do sometimes; and so your servant. And to shew my unconcernedness, I'll come to your wedding, and resign you with as much joy as I would a stale wench to a new cully, nay with as much joy as I would after the first night, if I had been married to you. There's for you, and so your servant, servant. [*Exit* SPARKISH.]

ALITHEA: How was I deceived in a man!

LUCY: You'll believe then a fool may be made jealous now? For that easiness in him that suffers him to be led by a wife will likewise permit him to be persuaded against her by others.

ALITHEA: But marry Mr Horner! My brother does not intend it, sure; if I thought he did, I would take thy advice, and Mr Harcourt for my husband. And now I wish that if there be any over-wise woman of the town, who, like me, would marry a fool for fortune, liberty, or title, first that her husband may love play, and be a cully to all the town but her, and suffer none but fortune to be mistress of his purse. Then, if for liberty, that he may send her into the country under the conduct of some housewifely mother-in-law. And if for title, may the world give 'em none but that of cuckold.

LUCY: And for her greater curse, madam, may he not deserve it.

ALITHEA: Away, impertinent! – Is not this my old Lady Lanterlu's?[1]

LUCY: Yes, madam. [*Aside*] And here I hope we shall find Mr Harcourt.

Exeunt ALITHEA, LUCY.

1. *Lady Lanterlu's*: allusion to a popular card game, lanterloo (loo).

SCENE FOUR

The scene changes again to HORNER's *lodging.*

HORNER, LADY FIDGET, MRS DAINTY FIDGET, MRS
SQUEAMISH. *A table, banquet, and bottles.*

HORNER [*aside*]: A pox! They are come too soon – before I
have sent back my new mistress. All I have now to do is to
lock her in, that they may not see her.

LADY FIDGET: That we may be sure of our welcome, we
have brought our entertainment with us, and are resolved
to treat thee, dear toad.

MRS DAINTY FIDGET: And that we may be merry to purpose,
have left Sir Jasper and my old Lady Squeamish quarrelling
at home at baggammon.

MRS SQUEAMISH: Therefore let us make use of our time
lest they should chance to interrupt us.

LADY FIDGET: Let us sit then.

HORNER: First, that you may be private, let me lock this
door, and that, and I'll wait upon you presently.

LADY FIDGET: No sir, shut 'em only and your lips for ever,
for we must trust you as much as our women.

HORNER: You know all vanity's killed in me, I have no occasion for talking.

LADY FIDGET: Now, ladies, supposing we had drank each of
us our two bottles, let us speak the truth of our hearts.

MRS DAINTY FIDGET and MRS SQUEAMISH: Agreed.

LADY FIDGET: By this brimmer, for truth is no where else to
be found. [*Aside to* HORNER] Not in thy heart, false man.

HORNER [*aside to* LADY FIDGET]: You have found me a true
man, I'm sure.

LADY FIDGET [*aside to* HORNER]: Not every way. – But let us
sit and be merry.

LADY FIDGET *sings*.

I

Why should our damned tyrants oblige us to live
On the pittance of pleasure which they only give?
  We must not rejoice,
  With wine and with noise,

In vain we must wake in a dull bed alone,
Whilst to our warm rival, the bottle, they're gone.
   Then lay aside charms,
   And take up these arms.*   [*The glasses.]

2

'Tis wine only gives 'em their courage and wit;
Because we live sober, to men we submit.
   If for beauties you'd pass,
   Take a lick of the glass,
'Twill mend your complexions, and when they are gone,
The best red we have is the red of the grape.
   Then sisters, lay't on.
   And damn a good shape.

MRS DAINTY FIDGET: Dear brimmer! Well, in token of our openness and plain dealing, let us throw our masks over our heads.

HORNER: So, 'twill come to the glasses anon.

MRS SQUEAMISH: Lovely brimmer! Let me enjoy him first.

LADY FIDGET: No, I never part with a gallant till I've tried him. Dear brimmer, that makest our husbands short-sighted.

MRS DAINTY FIDGET: And our bashful gallants bold.

MRS SQUEAMISH: And for want of a gallant, the butler lovely in our eyes. – Drink, eunuch.

LADY FIDGET: Drink, thou representative of a husband. Damn a husband!

MRS DAINTY FIDGET: And, as it were a husband, an old keeper.

MRS SQUEAMISH: And an old grandmother.

HORNER: And an English bawd, and a French chirurgeon.

LADY FIDGET: Ay, we have all reason to curse 'em.

HORNER: For my sake, ladies?

LADY FIDGET: No, for our own, for the first spoils all young gallants' industry.

MRS DAINTY FIDGET: And the other's art makes 'em bold only with common women.

MRS SQUEAMISH: And rather run the hazard of the vile distemper amongst them than of a denial amongst us.

MRS DAINTY FIDGET: The filthy toads choose mistresses now as they do stuffs, for having been fancied and worn by others.

MRS SQUEAMISH: For being common and cheap.

LADY FIDGET: Whilst women of quality, like the richest stuffs, lie untumbled and unasked for.

HORNER: Ay, neat, and cheap, and new, often they think best.

MRS DAINTY FIDGET: No sir, the beasts will be known by a mistress longer than by a suit.

MRS SQUEAMISH: And 'tis not for cheapness neither.

LADY FIDGET: No, for the vain fops will take up druggets[1] and embroider 'em. But I wonder at the depraved appetites of witty men; they use to be out of the common road, and hate imitation. Pray tell me, beast, when you were a man, why you rather chose to club with a multitude in a common house for an entertainment than to be the only guest at a good table.

HORNER: Why, faith, ceremony and expectation are unsufferable to those that are sharp bent. People always eat with the best stomach at an ordinary, where every man is snatching for the best bit.

LADY FIDGET: Though he get a cut over the fingers. But I have heard people eat most heartily of another man's meat, that is, what they do not pay for.

HORNER: When they are sure of their welcome and freedom, for ceremony in love and eating is as ridiculous as in fighting; falling on briskly is all should be done in those occasions.

LADY FIDGET: Well, then, let me tell you, sir, there is nowhere more freedom than in our houses, and we take freedom from a young person as a sign of good breeding, and a person may be as free as he pleases with us, as frolic, as gamesome, as wild as he will.

HORNER: Ha'n't I heard you all declaim against wild men?

LADY FIDGET: Yes, but for all that, we think wildness in a man as desirable a quality as in a duck or rabbit; a tame man, foh!

1. *druggets*: wool or silk garments.

HORNER: I know not, but your reputations frightened me as much as your faces invited me.

LADY FIDGET: Our reputation! Lord, why should you not think that we women make use of our reputation, as you men of yours, only to deceive the world with less suspicion? Our virtue is like the statesman's religion, the quaker's word, the gamester's oath, and the great man's honour, but to cheat those that trust us.

MRS SQUEAMISH: And that demureness, coyness, and modesty that you see in our faces in the boxes at plays is as much a sign of a kind woman as a vizard-mask[1] in the pit.

MRS DAINTY FIDGET: For, I assure you, women are least masked when they have the velvet vizard on.

LADY FIDGET: You would have found us modest women in our denials only.

MRS SQUEAMISH: Our bashfulness is only the reflection of the men's.

MRS DAINTY FIDGET: We blush when they are shame-faced.

HORNER: I beg your pardon, ladies, I was deceived in you devilishly. But why that mighty pretence to honour?

LADY FIDGET: We have told you. But sometimes 'twas for the same reason you men pretend business often, to avoid ill company, to enjoy the better and more privately those you love.

HORNER: But why would you ne'er give a friend a wink then?

LADY FIDGET: Faith, your reputation frightened us as much as ours did you. You were so notoriously lewd.

HORNER: And you so seemingly honest.

LADY FIDGET: Was that all that deterred you?

HORNER: And so expensive – you allow freedom you say –

LADY FIDGET: Ay, ay.

HORNER: That I was afraid of losing my little money, as well as my little time, both which my other pleasures required.

LADY FIDGET: Money, foh! You talk like a little fellow now. Do such as we expect money?

HORNER: I beg your pardon, madam, I must confess I have heard that great ladies, like great merchants, set but the

1. *Vizard-mask*: whore's emblem.

higher prices upon what they have, because they are not in necessity of taking the first offer.

MRS DAINTY FIDGET: Such as we make sale of our hearts?

MRS SQUEAMISH: We bribed for our love? Foh!

HORNER: With your pardon, ladies, I know, like great men in offices, you seem to exact flattery and attendance only from your followers; but you have receivers[1] about you, and such fees to pay, a man is afraid to pass your grants.[2] Besides, we must let you win at cards, or we lose your hearts; and if you make an assignation, 'tis at a goldsmith's, jeweller's, or china house, where, for your honour you deposit to him, he must pawn his to the punctual cit, and so paying for what you take up, pays for what he takes up.[3]

MRS DAINTY FIDGET: Would you not have us assured of our gallants' love?

MRS SQUEAMISH: For love is better known by liberality than by jealousy.

LADY FIDGET: For one may be dissembled, the other not. – [*Aside*] But my jealousy can be no longer dissembled, and they are telling-ripe. – Come, here's to our gallants in waiting, whom we must name, and I'll begin. This is my false rogue. [*Claps him on the back.*]

MRS SQUEAMISH: How!

HORNER (*aside*): So all will out now.

MRS SQUEAMISH [*aside to* HORNER]: Did you not tell me 'twas for my sake only you reported yourself no man?

MRS DAINTY FIDGET [*aside to* HORNER]: O wretch! Did you not swear to me 'twas for my love and honour you passed for that thing you do?

HORNER: So, so.

LADY FIDGET: Come, speak, ladies; this is my false villain.

MRS SQUEAMISH: And mine too.

MRS DAINTY FIDGET: And mine.

HORNER: Well then, you are all three my false rogues too, and there's an end on't.

1. *Receivers*: servants to be bribed.
2. *Pass your grants*: accept your favours.
3. *For your honour ... takes up*: in paying for what you obtain, the gallant pawns his 'honour' for yours.

LADY FIDGET: Well then, there's no remedy. Sister sharers, let us not fall out, but have a care of our honour. Though we get no presents, no jewels of him, we are savers of our honour, the jewel of most value and use, which shines yet to the world unsuspected, though it be counterfeit.

HORNER: Nay, and is e'en as good as if it were true, provided the world think so; for honour, like beauty now, only depends on the opinion of others.

LADY FIDGET: Well, Harry Common, I hope you can be true to three. Swear – but 'tis no purpose to require your oath, for you are as often forsworn as you swear to new women.

HORNER: Come, faith, madam, let us e'en pardon one another, for all the difference I find betwixt we men and you women, we forswear ourselves at the beginning of an amour, you as long as it lasts.

Enter SIR JASPER FIDGET *and* OLD LADY SQUEAMISH.

SIR JASPER: Oh, my Lady Fidget, was this your cunning, to come to Mr Horner without me? But you have been nowhere else, I hope?

LADY FIDGET: No, Sir Jasper.

OLD LADY SQUEAMISH: And you came straight hither, Biddy?

MRS SQUEAMISH: Yes indeed, Lady Grandmother.

SIR JASPER: 'Tis well, 'tis well. I knew when once they were throughly acquainted with poor Horner, they'd ne'er be from him. You may let her masquerade it with my wife and Horner, and I warrant her reputation safe.

Enter BOY.

BOY: O sir, here's the gentleman come whom you bid me not suffer to come up without giving you notice, with a lady too, and other gentlemen.

HORNER: Do you all go in there, whilst I send 'em away, and boy, do you desire 'em to stay below till I come, which shall be immediately.

Exeunt SIR JASPER, LADY SQUEAMISH, LADY FIDGET, MRS DAINTY FIDGET, MRS SQUEAMISH.

BOY: Yes sir. [*Exit.*]

Exit HORNER *at t'other door, and returns with* MRS PINCH-WIFE.

HORNER: You would not take my advice to be gone home before your husband came back; he'll now discover all Yet pray, my dearest, be persuaded to go home and leave the rest to my management. I'll let you down the back way

MRS PINCHWIFE: I don't know the way home, so I don't.

HORNER: My man shall wait upon you.

MRS PINCHWIFE: No, don't you believe that I'll go at all What, are you weary of me already?

HORNER: No, my life, 'tis that I may love you long. 'Tis to secure my love, and your reputation with your husband He'll never receive you again else.

MRS PINCHWIFE: What care I? D'ye think to frighten me with that? I don't intend to go to him again. You shall be my husband now.

HORNER: I cannot be your husband, dearest, since you are married to him.

MRS PINCHWIFE: Oh, would you make me believe that? Don't I see, every day at London here, women leave their first husbands and go and live with other men as their wives? Pish, pshaw! You'd make me angry, but that I love you so mainly.[1]

HORNER: So, they are coming up. – In again, in, I hear 'em [*Exit* MRS PINCHWIFE]. Well, a silly mistress is like a weak place, soon got, soon lost; a man has scarce time for plunder. She betrays her husband first to her gallant, and then her gallant to her husband.

Enter PINCHWIFE, ALITHEA, HARCOURT, SPARKISH, LUCY, *and a parson.*

PINCHWIFE: Come, madam, 'tis not the sudden change of your dress, the confidence of your asseverations, and your false witness there, shall persuade me I did not bring you hither, just now. Here's my witness, who cannot deny it, since you must be confronted. – Mr Horner, did not I bring this lady to you just now?

HORNER [*aside*]: Now must I wrong one woman for another's sake, but that's no new thing with me; for in these cases I am still on the criminal's side, against the innocent.

ALITHEA: Pray, speak, sir.

1. *Mainly*: greatly.

HORNER [*aside*]: It must be so – I must be impudent, and try my luck; impudence uses to be too hard for truth.

PINCHWIFE: What, you are studying an evasion or excuse for her. Speak, sir.

HORNER: No, faith, I am something backward only to speak in women's affairs or disputes.

PINCHWIFE: She bids you speak.

ALITHEA: Ay, pray sir, do. Pray satisfy him.

HORNER: Then, truly, you did bring that lady to me just now.

PINCHWIFE: Oho!

ALITHEA: How, sir!

HARCOURT: How, Horner!

ALITHEA: What mean you, sir? I always took you for a man of honour.

HORNER [*aside*]: Ay, so much a man of honour that I must save my mistress, I thank you, come what will on't.

SPARKISH: So, if I had had her, she'd have made me believe the moon had been made of a Christmas pie.

LUCY [*aside*]: Now could I speak, if I durst, and 'solve the riddle, who am the author of it.

ALITHEA: O unfortunate woman! (*To* HARCOURT) A combination against my honour which most concerns me now because you share in my disgrace, sir, and it is your censure which I must now suffer that troubles me, not theirs.

HARCOURT: Madam, then have no trouble, you shall now see 'tis possible for me to love too, without being jealous. I will not only believe your innocence myself, but make all the world believe it. [*Apart to* HORNER] Horner, I must now be concerned for this lady's honour.

HORNER: And I must be concerned for a lady's honour too.

HARCOURT: This lady has her honour, and I will protect it.

HORNER: My lady has not her honour, but has given it me to keep, and I will preserve it.

HARCOURT: I understand you not.

HORNER: I would not have you.

MRS PINCHWIFE [*peeping in behind*]: What's the matter with 'em all?

PINCHWIFE: Come, come, Mr Horner, no more disputing. Here's the parson, I brought him not in vain.

HORNER: No sir, I'll employ him, if this lady please.

PINCHWIFE: How, what d'ye mean?

SPARKISH: Ay, what does he mean?

HORNER: Why, I have resigned your sister to him. He has my consent.

PINCHWIFE: But he has not mine, sir. A woman's injured honour, no more than a man's, can be repaired or satisfied by any but him that first wronged it; and you shall marry her presently, or – [*Lays his hand on his sword.*]

    Enter to them MISTRESS PINCHWIFE.

MRS PINCHWIFE: O Lord, they'll kill poor Mr Horner! Besides, he shan't marry her whilst I stand by and look on. I'll not lose my second husband so.

PINCHWIFE: What do I see?

ALITHEA: My sister in my clothes!

SPARKISH: Ha!

MRS PINCHWIFE [*to* MR PINCHWIFE]: Nay, pray now don't quarrel about finding work for the parson; he shall marry me to Mr Horner, for now, I believe, you have enough of me.

HORNER: Damned, damned loving changeling!

MRS PINCHWIFE: Pray, sister, pardon me for telling so many lies of you.

HARCOURT: I suppose the riddle is plain now.

LUCY: No, that must be my work. Good sir, hear me. [*Kneels to* MR PINCHWIFE, *who stands doggedly, with his hat over his eyes.*]

PINCHWIFE: I will never hear woman again, but make 'em all silent, thus – [*Offers to draw upon his wife.*]

HORNER: No, that must not be.

PINCHWIFE: You then shall go first, 'tis all one to me. [*Offers to draw on* HORNER; *stopped by* HARCOURT.]

HARCOURT: Hold!

    Enter SIR JASPER FIDGET, LADY FIDGET, LADY SQUEAMISH, MRS DAINTY FIDGET, MRS SQUEAMISH.

SIR JASPER: What's the matter, what's the matter? Pray what's the matter, sir? I beseech you, communicate, sir.

PINCHWIFE: Why, my wife has communicated, sir, as your wife may have done too, sir, if she knows him, sir.

SIR JASPER: Pshaw! With him? Ha, ha, he!

PINCHWIFE: D'ye mock me, sir? A cuckold is a kind of a wild beast. Have a care, sir.

SIR JASPER: No sure, you mock me, sir – he cuckold you! It can't be, ha, ha, he! Why, I'll tell you, sir. [*Offers to whisper.*]

PINCHWIFE: I tell you again, he has whored my wife, and yours too, if he knows her, and all the women he comes near. 'Tis not his dissembling, his hypocrisy, can wheedle me.

SIR JASPER: How! Does he dissemble? Is he a hypocrite? Nay then – how – wife – sister, is he an hypocrite?

OLD LADY SQUEAMISH: An hypocrite! A dissembler! Speak, young harlotry, speak, how?

SIR JASPER: Nay then – Oh, my head too! – O thou libidinous lady!

OLD LADY SQUEAMISH: O thou harloting harlotry! Hast thou done't then?

SIR JASPER: Speak, good Horner, art thou a dissembler, a rogue? Hast thou –

HORNER: Soh!

LUCY [*apart to* HORNER]: I'll fetch you off, and her too, if she will but hold her tongue.

HORNER [*apart to* LUCY]: Canst thou? I'll give thee –

LUCY (*to* MR PINCHWIFE): Pray, have but patience to hear me, sir, who am the unfortunate cause of all this confusion. Your wife is innocent, I only culpable; for I put her upon telling you all these lies concerning my mistress, in order to the breaking off the match between Mr Sparkish and her, to make way for Mr Harcourt.

SPARKISH: Did you so, eternal rotten-tooth? Then it seems my mistress was not false to me, I was only deceived by you. Brother that should have been, now, man of conduct, who is a frank person now? To bring your wife to her lover – ha!

LUCY: I assure you, sir, she came not to Mr Horner out of love, for she loves him no more –

MRS PINCHWIFE: Hold, I told lies for you, but you shall tell none for me, for I do love Mr Horner with all my soul, and nobody shall say me nay. Pray don't you go to make poor Mr Horner believe to the contrary, 'tis spitefully done of you, I'm sure.

HORNER [*aside to* MRS PINCHWIFE]: Peace, dear idiot!

MRS PINCHWIFE: Nay, I will not peace.

PINCHWIFE: Not till I make you.

Enter DORILANT, QUACK.

DORILANT: Horner, your servant. I am the doctor's guest, he must excuse our intrusion.

QUACK: But what's the matter, gentlemen? For heaven's sake, what's the matter?

HORNER: Oh, 'tis well you are come. 'Tis a censorious world we live in. You may have brought me a reprieve, or else I had died for a crime I never committed, and these innocent ladies had suffered with me; therefore pray satisfy these worthy, honourable, jealous gentlemen – that – [*whispers*]

QUACK: Oh, I understand you; is that all? – Sir Jasper, by heavens and upon the word of a physician, [*whispers to* SIR JASPER] sir, –

SIR JASPER: Nay, I do believe you truly. – Pardon me, my virtuous lady, and dear of honour.

OLD LADY SQUEAMISH: What, then all's right again?

SIR JASPER: Ay, ay, and now let us satisfy him too. [*They whisper with* MR PINCHWIFE.]

PINCHWIFE: An eunuch! Pray, no fooling with me.

QUACK: I'll bring half the chirurgeons in town to swear it.

PINCHWIFE: They! They'll swear a man that bled to death through his wounds died of an apoplexy.

QUACK: Pray hear me, sir – why all the town has heard the report of him.

PINCHWIFE: But does all the town believe it?

QUACK: Pray inquire a little, and first, of all these.

PINCHWIFE: I'm sure when I left the town he was the lewdest fellow in't.

QUACK: I tell you, sir, he has been in France since. Pray ask but these ladies and gentlemen, your friend Mr Dorilant. Gentlemen and ladies, ha'n't you all heard the late sad report of poor Mr Horner?

ALL THE LADIES: Ay, ay, ay.

DORILANT: Why, thou jealous fool, dost thou doubt it? He's an arrant French capon.[1]

MRS PINCHWIFE: 'Tis false, sir, you shall not disparage poor Mr Horner, for to my certain knowledge –

LUCY: Oh hold!

MRS SQUEAMISH [*aside to* LUCY]: Stop her mouth –

OLD LADY SQUEAMISH [*to* PINCHWIFE]: Upon my honour sir, 'tis as true –

MRS DAINTY FIDGET: D'ye think we would have been seen in his company?

MRS SQUEAMISH: Trust our unspotted reputations with him?

OLD LADY SQUEAMISH [*aside to* HORNER]: This you get, and we too, by trusting your secret to a fool –

HORNER: Peace, madam. – [*Aside to* QUACK] Well, doctor, is not this a good design that carries a man on unsuspected, and brings him off safe.

PINCHWIFE [*aside*]: Well, if this were true, but my wife –
  DORILANT *whispers with* MRS PINCHWIFE.

ALITHEA: Come, brother, your wife is yet innocent, you see. But have a care of too strong an imagination, lest like an over-concerned timorous gamester, by fancying an unlucky cast, it should come. Women and fortune are truest still to those that trust 'em.

LUCY: And any wild thing grows but the more fierce and hungry for being kept up, and more dangerous to the keeper.

ALITHEA: There's doctrine for all husbands, Mr Harcourt.

HARCOURT: I edify, madam, so much, that I am impatient till I am one.

DORILANT: And I edify so much by example I will never be one.

SPARKISH: And because I will not disparage my parts, I'll ne'er be one.

HORNER: And I, alas, can't be one.

PINCHWIFE: But I must be one – against my will, to a country wife, with a country murrain[2] to me.

MRS PINCHWIFE [*aside*]: And I must be a country wife still

---

1. *French capon*: i.e., impotent.
2. *Murrain*: disease of cattle.

too I find, for I can't, like a city one, be rid of my musty husband and do what I list.

HORNER: Now sir, I must pronounce your wife innocent, though I blush whilst I do it, and I am the only man by her now exposed to shame, which I will straight drown in wine, as you shall your suspicion; and the ladies' troubles we'll divert with a ballet.[1] Doctor, where are your maskers?

LUCY: Indeed she's innocent, sir, I am her witness; and her end of coming out was but to see her sister's wedding, and what she has said to your face of her love to Mr Horner was but the usual innocent revenge on a husband's jealousy. Was it not, madam? Speak –

MRS PINCHWIFE [*aside to* LUCY *and* HORNER]: Since you'll have me tell more lies – yes indeed, bud.

PINCHWIFE: For my own sake fain I would all believe.
            Cuckolds, like lovers, should themselves
               deceive.
But [*sighs*] –
            His honour is least safe (too late I find)
            Who trusts it with a foolish wife or friend.
  A dance of cuckolds.

HORNER: Vain fops but court, and dress, and keep a pother,
            To pass for women's men with one another;
            But he who aims by women to be prized,
            First by the men, you see, must be despised.

1. *Ballet*: merry dance.

FINIS

Epilogue

Now you the vigorous, who daily here
O'er vizard-mask, in public domineer,
And what you'd do to her if in place where;
Nay, have the confidence to cry, 'Come out!'
Yet when she says, 'Lead on', you are not stout,
But to your well-dressed brother straight turn round
And cry, 'Pox on her, Ned, she can't be found!'
Then slink away, a fresh one to ingage,
With so much seeming heat and loving rage,
You'd frighten listening actress on the stage;
Till she at last has seen you huffing come,
And talk of keeping in the living-room,
Yet cannot be provoked to lead her home.
Next, you Falstaffs of fifty, who beset
Your buckram maidenheads, which your friends get;
And whilst to them, you of achievements boast,
They share the booty, and laugh at your cost.
In fine, you essenc't[1] boys, both old and young,
Who would be thought so eager, brisk, and strong,
Yet do the ladies, not their husbands, wrong;
Whose purses for your manhood make excuse,
And keep your Flanders mares[2] for shew, not use;
Encouraged by our woman's man today,
A Horner's part may vainly think to play,
And may intrigues so bashfully disown
That they may doubted be by few or none;
May kiss the cards at picquet, hombre, loo,
And so be thought to kiss the lady too.
But gallants, have a care, faith, what you do.
The world, which to no man his due will give,
You by experience know you can deceive,
And men may still believe you vigorous,
But then, we women – there's no coz'ning us.

1. *Essenc't*: perfumed.   2. *Flanders mares*: mistresses.

FINIS

Title-page of the first edition, 1695

The Latin reads:

'Bereft of land and patrimony, the fool is ready to be mad by rule and regulation' (Horace, *Sermonium*, II, 3, 184 and 271).

LOVE for LOVE:

A

COMEDY.

Acted at the

THEATRE in *Little Lincolns-Inn Fields*,

B Y

His Majesty's Servants.

Written by Mr. *CONGREVE.*

Nudus agris, nudus nummis paternis,
Insanire parat certa ratione modoque. Hor.

LONDON:

Printed for *Jacob Tonson*, at the *Judge's-Head*, near the
Inner-Temple-Gate in *Fleetstreet*. 1695.

A Prologue for

The opening of the new playhouse,
proposed to be spoken by Mrs Bracegirdle
in man's clothes

Sent from an unknown hand

Custom, which everywhere bears mighty sway,
Brings me to act the orator today:
But women, you will say, are ill at speeches;
'Tis true, and therefore I appear in breeches:
Not for example to you city-wives;
That by prescription's settled for your lives.
Was it for gain the husband first consented?
Oh, yes, their gains are mightily augmented: Making
And yet, methinks, it must have cost some strife: horns with
A passive husband, and an active wife!   her hands
'Tis awkward, very awkward, by my life.   over her
But to my speech: assemblies of all nations   head.
Still are supposed to open with orations:
Mine shall begin, to shew our obligations.
To you, our benefactors, lowly bowing,
Whose favours have prevented our undoing;
A long Egyptian bondage we endured,
Till freedom, by your justice we procured:
Our taskmasters[1] were grown such very Jews,
We must at length have played in wooden shoes,
Had not your bounty taught us to refuse.
Freedom's of English growth, I think alone;
What for lost English freedom can atone?
A free-born player loathes to be compelled;
Our rulers tyrannized, and we rebelled.
Freedom! the wise man's wish, the poor man's wealth;
Which you, and I, and most of us enjoy by stealth;
The soul of pleasure, and the sweet of life,
The woman's charter, widow, maid or wife,

1. *Taskmasters*: patentees of Drury Lane.

This thcy'd havc cancelled, and thence grew the strife.
But you, perhaps, would have me here confess
How we obtained the favour – can't you guess?
Why then I'll tell you (for I hate a lie),
By brib'ry, arrant brib'ry, let me die:
I was their agent, but by Jove I swear
No honourable member had a share
Tho' young and able members bid me fair:
I chose a wiser way to make you willing,
Which has not cost the house a single shilling.
Now you suspect at least I went a-billing.
You see I'm young, and to that air of youth,
Some will add beauty, and a little truth;
These pow'rful charms, improved by pow'rful arts,
Prevailed to captivate your op'ning hearts.
Thus furnished, I preferred my poor petition,
And bribed ye to commiserate our condition:
I laughed, and sighed, and sung, and leered upon ye
With roguish loving looks, and that way won ye:
The young men kissed me, and the old I kissed,
And luringly I led them as I list.
The ladies in mere pity took our parts,
Pity's the darling passion of their hearts.
Thus bribing, or thus bribed, fear no disgraces;
For thus you may take bribes, and keep your places.

Prologue

Spoken at the opening of the New House

BY MR BETTERTON[1]

The husbandman in vain renews his toil
To cultivate each year a hungry soil;
And fondly hopes for rich and generous fruit,
When what should feed the tree devours the root.
Th'unladen boughs he sees, bode certain dearth,
Unless transplanted to more kindly earth.
So the poor husbands of the stage, who found
Their labours lost upon the ungrateful ground,
This last and only remedy have proved;
And hope new fruit from ancient stocks removed.
Well may they hope, when you so kindly aid,
And plant a soil which you so rich have made.
As Nature gave the world to man's first age,
So from your bounty we receive this stage;
The freedom man was born to, you've restored,
And to our world such plenty you afford,
It seems like Eden, fruitful of its own accord.
But since in Paradise frail flesh gave way,
And when but two were made, both went astray;
Forbear your wonder and the fault forgive,
If in our larger family we grieve
One falling Adam, and one tempted Eve.[2]
We who remain would gratefully repay
What our endeavours can, and bring this day,
The first-fruit offering of a virgin play.

---

1. Betterton, together with some of the finest actors and actresses from the Drury Lane Theatre, opened an independent theatre in Lincoln's Inn Fields in 1695. *Love for Love* was the first play performed at the new theatre.

2. *Adam . . . Eve*: Joseph Williams and Susanna Montfort, two performers who had gone back to Drury Lane.

We hope there's something that may please each taste,
And tho' of homely fare we make the feast,
Yet you will find variety at least.
There's humour, which for cheerful friends we got,
And for the thinking party there's a plot.
We've something too, to gratify ill nature
(If there be any here), and that is satire.
Tho' satire scarce dares grin, 'tis grown so mild;
Or only shews its teeth, as if it smiled.
As asses thistles, poets mumble wit,
And dare not bite, for fear of being bit.
They hold their pens, as swords are held by fools,
And are afraid to use their own edge-tools.
Since The Plain Dealer's scenes of Manly rage,[1]
Not one has dared to lash this crying age.
This time the poet owns the bold essay,
Yet hopes there's no ill-manners in his play:
And he declares by me, he has designed
Affront to none, but frankly speaks his mind.
And should the ensuing scenes not chance to hit,
He offers but this one excuse, 'twas writ
Before your late encouragement of wit.

1. *Plain Dealer's*: Wycherley's *The Plain-Dealer* was first produced in 1671. The hero's name is Manly.

Dramatis Personae

SIR SAMPSON LEGEND, *father to Valentine and Ben*

VALENTINE, *fallen under his father's displeasure by his expensive way of living, in love with Angelica*

SCANDAL, *his friend, a free speaker*

TATTLE, *a half-witted beau, vain of his amours, yet valuing himself for secrecy*

BEN, *Sir Sampson's younger son, half home-bred and half sea-bred, designed to marry Miss Prue*

FORESIGHT, *an illiterate old fellow, peevish and positive, superstitious, and pretending to understand astrology, palmistry, physiognomy, omens, dreams, etc., uncle to Angelica*

JEREMY, *servant to Valentine*

TRAPLAND, *a scrivener*

BUCKRAM, *a lawyer*

ANGELICA, *niece to Foresight, of a considerable fortune in her own hands*

MRS FORESIGHT, *second wife to Foresight*

MRS FRAIL, *sister to Mrs Foresight, a woman of the town*

MISS PRUE, *daughter to Foresight by a former wife, a silly, awkward country girl*

NURSE *to Miss (Prue)*

JENNY, *maid to Angelica*

A Steward, Officers, Sailors, and several Servants

THE SCENE: LONDON

Act One

VALENTINE *in his chamber reading.* JEREMY *waiting.*
Several books upon the table.

VALENTINE: Jeremy.

JEREMY: Sir.

VALENTINE: Here, take away; I'll walk a turn, and digest
what I have read.

JEREMY [*aside, and taking away the books*]: You'll grow devilish
fat upon this paper diet.

VALENTINE: And d'ye hear, go you to breakfast. – There's a
page doubled down in Epictetus that is a feast for an
emperor.

JEREMY: Was Epictetus a real cook, or did he only write
receipts?[1]

VALENTINE: Read, read, sirrah, and refine your appetite.
Learn to live upon instruction; feast your mind, and
mortify your flesh; read, and take your nourishment in at
your eyes; shut up your mouth and chew the cud of understanding. So Epictetus advises.

JEREMY: O Lord! I have heard much of him when I waited
upon a gentleman at Cambridge. Pray what was that
Epictetus?

VALENTINE: A very rich man – not worth a groat.

JEREMY: Humph, and so he has made a very fine feast where
there is nothing to be eaten.

VALENTINE: Yes.

JEREMY: Sir, you're a gentleman, and probably understand
this fine feeding. But if you please, I had rather be at board
wages. Does your Epictetus, or your Seneca here, or any of
these poor rich rogues, teach you how to pay your debts
without money? Will they shut up the mouths of your
creditors? Will Plato be bail for you? Or Diogenes, because
he understands confinement, and lived in a tub, go to

1. *Receipts*: recipes.

prison for you? 'Slife sir, what do you mean, to mew your self up here with three or four musty books in commendation of starving and poverty?

VALENTINE: Why, sirrah, I have no money, you know it; and therefore resolve to rail at all that have. And in that I but follow the examples of the wisest and wittiest men in all ages; these poets and philosophers whom you naturally hate, for just such another reason; because they abound in sense, and you are a fool.

JEREMY: Ay, sir, I am a fool, I know it. And yet, heav'n help me, I'm poor enough to be a wit. But I was always a fool, when I told you what your expenses would bring you to: your coaches and your liveries, your treats and your balls; your being in love with a lady that did not care a farthing for you in your prosperity, and keeping company with wits, that cared for nothing but your prosperity, and now when you are poor, hate you as much as they do one another.

VALENTINE: Well, and now I am poor, I have an opportunity to be revenged on 'em all. I'll pursue Angelica with more love than ever, and appear more notoriously her admirer in this restraint than when I openly rivalled the rich fops that made court to her. So shall my poverty be a mortification to her pride, and perhaps make her compassionate[1] that love which has principally reduced me to this lowness of fortune. And for the wits, I'm sure I'm in a condition to be even with them.

JEREMY: Nay, your condition is pretty even with theirs, that's the truth on't.

VALENTINE: I'll take some of their trade out of their hands.

JEREMY: Now Heav'n of mercy continue the tax upon paper! You don't mean to write!

VALENTINE: Yes, I do; I'll write a play.

JEREMY: Hem! Sir, if you please to give me a small certificate of three lines – only to certify those whom it may concern that the bearer hereof, Jeremy Fetch by name, has for the space of sev'n years truly and faithfully served Valentine Legend Esq, and that he is not now turned away for any

1. *Compassionate*: take pity on.

misdemeanour, but does voluntarily dismiss his master from any future authority over him –

VALENTINE: No, sirrah, you shall live with me still.

JEREMY: Sir, it's impossible – I may die with you, starve with you, or be damned with your works; but to live even three days, the life of a play,[1] I no more expect it than to be canonized for a muse after my decease.

VALENTINE: You are witty, you rogue. I shall want your help. I'll have you learn to make couplets to tag the ends of acts. D'ye hear, get the maids to crambo[2] in an evening, and learn the knack of rhyming. You may arrive at the height of a song sent by an unknown hand, or a chocolate-house lampoon.

JEREMY: But sir, is this the way to recover your father's favour? Why, Sir Sampson will be irreconcilable. If your younger brother should come from sea, he'd never look upon you again. You're undone, sir, you're ruined; you won't have a friend left in the world if you turn poet. Ah, pox confound that Will's coffee-house,[3] it has ruined more young men than the Royal Oak Lottery.[4] Nothing thrives that belongs to't. The man of the house would have been an alderman by this time with half the trade, if he had set up in the city. For my part, I never sit at the door that I don't get double the stomach that I do at a horse-race. The air upon Banstead-Downs[5] is nothing to it for a whetter. Yet I never see it but the spirit of famine appears to me; sometimes like a decayed porter, worn out with pimping and carrying *billet-doux* and songs, not like other porters for hire, but for the jest's sake; now like a thin chairman, melted down to half his proportion with carrying a poet upon tick to visit some great fortune, and his fare to be paid him like the wages of sin, either at the day of marriage, or the day of death.

1. *Three days, the life of a play*: even a bad play usually had a three-day run, the third night being the author's benefit.

2. *Crambo*: capping verses.

3. *Will's coffee-house*: Dryden's literary den. Named after its owner, Will Urwin.

4. *Royal Oak Lottery*: a yearly lottery for the benefit of the Royal Fishing Company.   5. *Banstead-Downs*: Epsom Downs.

VALENTINE: Very well, sir. Can you proceed?

JEREMY: Sometimes like a bilked bookseller, with a meagre terrified countenance, that looks as if he had written for himself, or were resolved to turn author and bring the rest of his brethren into the same condition; and lastly, in the form of a worn-out punk, with verses in her hand, which her vanity had preferred to settlements, without a whole tatter to her tail, but as ragged as one of the muses, or as if she were carrying her linen to the paper-mill, to be converted into folio books of warning to all young maids not to prefer poetry to good sense, or lying in the arms of a needy wit before the embraces of a wealthy fool.

Enter SCANDAL.

SCANDAL: What, Jeremy holding forth?

VALENTINE: The rogue has, with all the wit he could muster up, been declaiming against wit.

SCANDAL: Ay? Why then I'm afraid Jeremy has wit, for wherever it is, it's always contriving its own ruin.

JEREMY: Why so I have been telling my master, sir. Mr Scandal, for Heaven's sake, sir, try if you can dissuade him from turning poet.

SCANDAL: Poet! He shall turn soldier first, and rather depend upon the outside of his head than the lining. Why, what the devil! Has not your poverty made you enemies enough? Must you needs shew your wit to get more?

JEREMY: Ay, more indeed. For who cares for anybody that has more wit than himself?

SCANDAL: Jeremy speaks like an oracle. Don't you see how worthless great men and dull rich rogues avoid a witty man of small fortune? Why, he looks like a writ of inquiry into their titles and estates, and seems commissioned by Heav'n to seize the better half.

VALENTINE: Therefore I would rail in my writings, and be revenged.

SCANDAL: Rail? At whom? The whole world? Impotent and vain! Who would die a martyr to sense in a country where the religion is folly? You may stand at bay for a while, but when the full cry is against you, you won't have fair play for your life. If you can't be fairly run down by the hounds, you will be treacherously shot by the huntsmen. – No, turn pimp, flatterer, quack, lawyer, parson, be chaplain to an atheist, or stallion to an old woman, anything but poet. A modern poet is worse, more servile, timorous and fawning than any I have named: without[1] you could retrieve the ancient honours of the name, recall the stage of Athens, and be allowed the force of open honest satire.

VALENTINE: You are as inveterate against our poets as if your character had been lately exposed upon the stage. Nay, I am not violently bent upon the trade. – [*One knocks.*] Jeremy, see who's there.

Exit JEREMY.

But tell me what you would have me do. What do the world say of me, and of my forced confinement?

SCANDAL: The world behaves itself as it used to do on such occasions; some pity you and condemn your father: others excuse him, and blame you. Only the ladies are merciful and wish you well, since love and pleasurable expense have been your greatest faults.

Enter JEREMY.

VALENTINE: How now?

JEREMY: Nothing new, sir. I have dispatched some half a dozen duns[2] with as much dexterity as a hungry judge does causes at dinner-time.

VALENTINE: What answer have you given 'em?

SCANDAL: Patience, I suppose, the old receipt.

JEREMY: No, faith, sir. I have put 'em off so long with patience and forbearance and other fair words that I was forced now to tell 'em in plain downright English –

VALENTINE: What?

JEREMY: That they should be paid.

VALENTINE: When?

JEREMY: Tomorrow.

VALENTINE: And how the devil do you mean to keep your word?

JEREMY: Keep it? Not at all; it has been so very much stretched that I reckon it will break of course by tomorrow,

---

1. *Without*: unless.
2. *Duns*: debt-collectors.

and nobody be surprised at the matter. – [*Knocking*] Again! Sir, if you don't like my negotiation, will you be pleased to answer these yourself?

VALENTINE: See who they are.

Exit JEREMY.

By this, Scandal, you may see what it is to be great; Secretaries of State, presidents of the council, and generals of an army lead just such a life as I do: have just such crowds of visitants in a morning, all soliciting of past promises, which are but a civiller sort of duns, that lay claim to voluntary debts.

SCANDAL: And you, like a true great man, having engaged their attendance and promised more than ever you intend to perform, are more perplexed to find evasions than you would be to invent the honest means of keeping your word and gratifying your creditors.

VALENTINE: Scandal, learn to spare your friends, and do not provoke your enemies; this liberty of your tongue will one day bring a confinement on your body, my friend.

Re-enter JEREMY.

JEREMY: O sir, there's Trapland the scrivener, with two suspicious fellows like lawful pads,[1] that would knock a man down with pocket-tipstaves,[2] and there's your father's steward, and the nurse with one of your children from Twitnam.[3]

VALENTINE: Pox on her, could she find no other time to fling my sins in my face? Here, give her this [*gives money*], and bid her trouble me no more. A thoughtless two-handed whore,[4] she knows my condition well enough, and might have overlaid the child a fortnight ago if she had had any forecast[5] in her.

SCANDAL: What, is it bouncing Margery and my godson?

JEREMY: Yes, sir.

SCANDAL: My blessing to the boy, with this token [*gives*

1. *Pads*: footpads, highwaymen.
2. *Pocket-tipstaves*: bailiff's official emblem.
3. *Twitnam*: Twickenham.
4. *Two-handed whore*: well-built (also perhaps importunate).
5. *Forecast*: foresight.

money] of my love. And d'ye hear, bid Margery put more flocks in her bed, shift twice a week, and not work so hard, that she may not smell so vigorously. I shall take the air shortly.

VALENTINE: Scandal, don't spoil my boy's milk. [*To* JEREMY] Bid Trapland come in.

 Exit JEREMY.

If I can give that Cerberus a sop, I shall be at rest for one day.

 Enter TRAPLAND *and* JEREMY.

O Mr Trapland! My old friend! Welcome! Jeremy, a chair, quickly. A bottle of sack and a toast – fly! – a chair first.

TRAPLAND: A good morning to you Mr Valentine, and to you Mr Scandal.

SCANDAL: The morning's a very good morning, if you don't spoil it.

VALENTINE: Come, sit you down, you know his way.

TRAPLAND [*sits*]: There is a debt, Mr Valentine, of £1,500, of pretty long standing –

VALENTINE: I cannot talk about business with a thirsty palate. [*To* JEREMY] Sirrah, the sack.

TRAPLAND: And I desire to know what course you have taken for the payment.

VALENTINE: Faith and troth, I am heartily glad to see you. My service to you. Fill, fill, to honest Mr Trapland, fuller.

TRAPLAND: Hold, sweetheart. This is not to our business. My service to you, Mr Scandal – [*drinks*] – I have forborne as long –

VALENTINE: T'other glass, and then we'll talk. Fill, Jeremy.

TRAPLAND: No more, in truth. I have forborne, I say –

VALENTINE: Sirrah, fill when I bid you. And how does your handsome daughter? Come, a good husband to her. [*Drinks.*]

TRAPLAND: Thank you; I have been out of this money –

VALENTINE: Drink first. Scandal, why do you not drink? [*They drink.*]

TRAPLAND: And in short, I can be put off no longer.

VALENTINE: I was much obliged to you for your supply. It did me signal service in my necessity. But you delight in doing good. – Scandal, drink to me, my friend Trapland's health. An honester man lives not, nor one more ready to serve his friend in distress, tho' I say it to his face. Come, fill each man his glass.

SCANDAL: What! I know Trapland has been a whoremaster, and loves a wench still. You never knew a whoremaster that was not an honest fellow.

TRAPLAND: Fie, Mr Scandal, you never knew –

SCANDAL: What don't I know? I know the buxom black widow in the Poultry[1] – £800 a year jointure, and £20,000 in money. Ahah! Old Trap!

VALENTINE: Say you so, i'faith. Come, we'll remember the widow. I know whereabouts you are. Come, to the widow –

TRAPLAND: No more indeed.

VALENTINE: What, the widow's health! Give it him – off with it. [*They drink.*] A lovely girl, i'faith; black sparkling eyes, soft pouting ruby lips! Better sealing there than a bond for a million, hah?

TRAPLAND: No, no, there's no such thing. We'd better mind our business. You're a wag.

VALENTINE: No faith, we'll mind the widow's business, fill again. Pretty round heaving breasts, a Barbary[2] shape, and a jut with her bum, would stir an anchoret.[3] And the prettiest foot! Oh, if a man could but fasten his eyes to her feet as they steal in and out and play at Bo-peep under her petticoats, ah, Mr Trapland?

TRAPLAND: Verily, give me a glass – you're a wag – and here's to the widow. [*Drinks.*]

SCANDAL [*to* VALENTINE]: He begins to chuckle. Ply him close, or he'll relapse into a dun.

Enter OFFICER.

OFFICER: By your leave, gentlemen. Mr Trapland, if we must do our office, tell us. We have half a dozen gentlemen to arrest in Pall Mall and Covent-Garden, and if we don't make haste the chair-men will be abroad and block up the chocolate-houses, and then our labour's lost.

1. *Poultry*: between Cheapside and Cornhill.
2. *Barbary*: elegant, like a Barbary mare.
3. *Anchoret*: anchorite, hermit.

TRAPLAND: Udso, that's true. Mr Valentine, I love mirth, but business must be done. Are you ready to –

JEREMY: Sir, your father's steward says he comes to make proposals concerning your debts.

VALENTINE: Bid him come in. Mr Trapland, send away your officer. You shall have an answer presently.

TRAPLAND: Mr Snap, stay within call.

    Exit OFFICER.

    Enter STEWARD *and whispers to* VALENTINE.

SCANDAL: Here's a dog now, a traitor in his wine. [*To* TRAPLAND] Sirrah, refund the sack: Jeremy, fetch him some warm water, or I'll rip up his stomach, and go the shortest way to his conscience.

TRAPLAND: Mr Scandal, you are uncivil. I did not value your sack, but you cannot expect it again, when I have drunk it.

SCANDAL: And how do you expect to have your money again, when a gentleman has spent it?

VALENTINE [*to* STEWARD]: You need say no more, I understand the conditions. They are very hard, but my necessity is very pressing. I agree to 'em. Take Mr Trapland with you, and let him draw the writing. – Mr Trapland, you know this man. He shall satisfy you.

TRAPLAND: Sincerely, I am loth to be thus pressing, but my necessity –

VALENTINE: No apology, good Mr Scrivener, you shall be paid.

TRAPLAND: I hope you forgive me. My business requires –

    Exeunt STEWARD, TRAPLAND *and* JEREMY.

SCANDAL: He begs pardon like a hangman at an execution.

VALENTINE: But I have got a reprieve.

SCANDAL: I am surprised. What, does your father relent?

VALENTINE: No; he has sent me the hardest conditions in the world. You have heard of a booby brother of mine that was sent to sea three years ago? This brother, my father hears, is landed; whereupon he very affectionately sends me word, if I will make a deed of conveyance of my right to his estate after his death to my younger brother, he will immediately furnish me with four thousand pound to pay my debts and make my fortune. This was once proposed before, and I refused it; but the present impatience of my creditors for their money, and my own impatience of confinement and absence from Angelica, force me to consent.

SCANDAL: A very desperate demonstration of your love to Angelica; and I think she has never given you any assurance of hers.

VALENTINE: You know her temper; she never gave me any great reason either for hope or despair.

SCANDAL: Women of her airy temper, as they seldom think before they act, so they rarely give us any light to guess at what they mean. But you have little reason to believe that a woman of this age, who has had an indifference for you in your prosperity, will fall in love with your ill fortune; besides, Angelica has a great fortune of her own, and great fortunes either expect another great fortune, or a fool.

Enter JEREMY.

JEREMY: More misfortunes, sir.

VALENTINE: What, another dun?

JEREMY: No sir, but Mr Tattle is come to wait upon you.

VALENTINE: Well, I can't help it. You must bring him up; he knows I don't go abroad.

Exit JEREMY.

SCANDAL: Pox on him, I'll be gone.

VALENTINE: No, prithee stay. Tattle and you should never be asunder; you are light and shadow, and shew one another. He is perfectly thy reverse both in humour and understanding, and as you set up for defamation, he is a mender of reputations.

SCANDAL: A mender of reputations! Ay, just as he is a keeper of secrets, another virtue that he sets up for in the same manner. For the rogue will speak aloud in the posture of a whisper, and deny a woman's name while he gives you the marks of her person. He will forswear receiving a letter from her, and at the same time shew you her hand upon the superscription. And yet perhaps he has counterfeited the hand too, and sworn to a truth. But he hopes not to be believed and refuses the reputation of a lady's favour, as a Doctor says 'No' to a bishopric, only that it may be granted him. In short, he is a public professor of secrecy, and makes proclamation that he holds private intelligence. – He's here.

Enter TATTLE.

TATTLE: Valentine, good morrow, Scandal I am yours – that is, when you speak well of me.

SCANDAL: That is, when I am yours; for while I am my own, or anybody's else, that will never happen.

TATTLE: How inhumane!

VALENTINE: Why, Tattle, you need not be much concerned at anything that he says, for to converse with Scandal is to play at Losing Loadum;[1] you must lose a good name to him before you can win it for yourself.

TATTLE: But how barbarous that is, and how unfortunate for him, that the world shall think the better of any person for his calumniation! I thank heaven it has always been a part of my character to handle the reputation of others very tenderly.

SCANDAL: Ay, such rotten reputations as you have to deal with are to be handled tenderly indeed.

TATTLE: Nay, but why rotten? Why should you say rotten, when you know not the persons of whom you speak? How cruel that is!

SCANDAL: Not know 'em? Why, thou never hadst to do with anybody that did not stink to all the town.

TATTLE: Ha, ha, ha; nay, now you make a jest of it indeed. For there is nothing more known than that nobody knows anything of that nature of me. As I hope to be saved, Valentine, I never exposed a woman since I knew what woman was.

VALENTINE: And yet you have conversed with several.

TATTLE: To be free with you, I have. I don't care if I own that. Nay more, I'm going to say a bold word now, I never could meddle with a woman that had to do with anybody else.

SCANDAL: How!

VALENTINE: Nay faith, I'm apt to believe him. Except her husband, Tattle.

1. *Losing Loadum*: a card game in which the object was to gain no tricks.

TATTLE: Oh that –

SCANDAL: What think you of that noble commoner, Mrs Drab?

TATTLE: Pooh, I know Madam Drab has made her brags in three or four places, that I said this and that, and writ to her, and did I know not what. But, upon my reputation, she did me wrong. Well, well, that was malice. But I know the bottom of it. She was bribed to that by one that we all know – a man too. Only to bring me into disgrace with a certain woman of quality –

SCANDAL: Whom we all know.

TATTLE: No matter for that. Yes, yes, everybody knows. No doubt on't, everybody knows my secrets. But I soon satisfied the lady of my innocence. For I told her: Madam, says I, there are some persons who make it their business to tell stories, and say this and that of one and t'other, and everything in the world, and, says I, if your Grace –

SCANDAL: Grace!

TATTLE: O Lord, what have I said? My unlucky tongue!

VALENTINE: Ha, ha, ha!

SCANDAL: Why, Tattle, thou hast more impudence than one can in reason expect. I shall have an esteem for thee. Well, and – ha, ha, ha – well, go on, and what did you say to her Grace?

VALENTINE: I confess this is something extraordinary.

TATTLE: Not a word as I hope to be saved; an errant lapsus linguae.[1] – Come, let's talk of something else.

VALENTINE: Well, but how did you acquit yourself?

TATTLE: Pooh, pooh, nothing at all, I only rallied with you. A woman of ord'nary rank was a little jealous of me, and I told her something or other – faith, I know not what. – Come, let's talk of something else. [Hums a song.]

SCANDAL: Hang him, let him alone, he has a mind we should inquire.

TATTLE: Valentine, I supped last night with your mistress, and her uncle, Old Foresight: I think your father lies at Foresight's.

VALENTINE: Yes.

1. *Lapsus linguae*: slip of the tongue.

TATTLE: Upon my soul, Angelica's a fine woman, and so is Mrs Foresight, and her sister Mrs Frail.

SCANDAL: Yes, Mrs Frail is a very fine woman, we all know her.

TATTLE: Oh, that is not fair.

SCANDAL: What?

TATTLE: To tell.

SCANDAL: To tell what? Why, what do you know of Mrs Frail?

TATTLE: Who, I? Upon honour I don't know whether she be man or woman, but by the smoothness of her chin and roundness of her lips.

SCANDAL: No?

TATTLE: No.

SCANDAL: She says otherwise.

TATTLE: Impossible!

SCANDAL: Yes faith. Ask Valentine else.

TATTLE: Why then, as I hope to be saved, I believe a woman only obliges a man to secrecy that she may have the pleasure of telling herself.

SCANDAL: No doubt on't. Well, but has she done you wrong, or no? You have had her, ha?

TATTLE: Tho' I have more honour than to tell first, I have more manners than to contradict what a lady has declared.

SCANDAL: Well, you own it?

TATTLE: I am strangely surprised! Yes, yes, I can't deny't, if she taxes me with it.

SCANDAL: She'll be here by and by, she sees Valentine every morning.

TATTLE: How?

VALENTINE: She does me the favour – I mean of a visit sometimes. I did not think she had granted more to anybody.

SCANDAL: Nor I, faith. But Tattle does not use to belie a lady; it is contrary to his character. How one may be deceived in a woman, Valentine!

TATTLE: Nay, what do you mean, gentlemen?

SCANDAL: I'm resolved I'll ask her.

TATTLE: O barbarous! Why, did you not tell me –

SCANDAL: No, you told us.

TATTLE: And bid me ask Valentine?

VALENTINE: What did I say? I hope you won't bring me to confess an answer when you never asked me the question.

TATTLE: But, gentlemen, this is the most inhumane proceeding.

VALENTINE: Nay, if you have known Scandal thus long, and cannot avoid such a palpable decoy as this was, the ladies have a fine time whose reputations are in your keeping.

Enter JEREMY.

JEREMY: Sir, Mrs Frail has sent to know if you are stirring.

VALENTINE: Shew her up when she comes.

Exit JEREMY.

TATTLE: I'll be gone.

VALENTINE: You'll meet her.

TATTLE: Have you not a back way?

VALENTINE: If there were, you have more discretion than to give Scandal such an advantage. Why, your running away will prove all that he can tell her.

TATTLE: Scandal, you will not be so ungenerous. – Oh, I shall lose my reputation of secrecy for ever – I shall never be received but upon public days, and my visits will never be admitted beyond a drawing-room. I shall never see a bedchamber again, never be locked in a closet, nor run behind a screen or under a table; never be distinguished among the waiting-women by the name of Trusty Mr Tattle more. You will not be so cruel?

VALENTINE: Scandal, have pity on him, he'll yield to any conditions.

TATTLE: Any, any terms.

SCANDAL: Come then, sacrifice half a dozen women of good reputation to me presently. Come, where are you familiar?[1] And see that they are women of quality too, the first quality.

TATTLE: 'Tis very hard. Won't a baronet's lady pass?

SCANDAL: No, nothing under a Right Honourable.

TATTLE: O inhumane! You don't expect their names?

SCANDAL: No, their titles shall serve.

1. *Where are you familiar?*: Q – 'where are your familiar'.

TATTLE: Alas, that's the same thing. Pray spare me their titles – I'll describe their persons.

SCANDAL: Well, begin then. But take notice, if you are so ill a painter that I cannot know the person by your picture of her, you must be condemned, like other bad painters, to write the name at the bottom.

TATTLE: Well, first then –

Enter MRS FRAIL.

O unfortunate! she's come already; will you have patience till another time – I'll double the number.

SCANDAL: Well, on that condition. Take heed you don't fail me.

MRS FRAIL: Hey-day! I shall get a fine reputation by coming to see fellows in a morning. Scandal, you devil, are you here too? Oh Mr Tattle, everything is safe with you, we know.

SCANDAL: Tattle?

TATTLE: Mum – O madam, you do me too much honour.

VALENTINE: Well Lady Galloper, how does Angelica?

MRS FRAIL: Angelica? Manners!

VALENTINE: What, you will allow an absent lover –

MRS FRAIL: No, I'll allow a lover present with his mistress to be particular. But otherwise I think his passion ought to give place to his manners.

VALENTINE: But what if he have more passion than manners?

MRS FRAIL: Then let him marry and reform.

VALENTINE: Marriage indeed may qualify the fury of his passion, but it very rarely mends a man's manners.

MRS FRAIL: You are the most mistaken in the world. There is no creature perfectly civil but a husband. For in a little time he grows only rude to his wife, and that is the highest good breeding, for it begets his civility to other people. Well, I'll tell you news; but I suppose you hear your brother Benjamin is landed. And my brother Foresight's daughter is come out of the country – I assure you, there's a match talked of by the old people. Well, if he be but as great a sea beast as she is a land monster, we shall have a most amphibious breed. The progeny will be all otters: he has been bred at sea, and she has never been out of the country.

VALENTINE: Pox take 'em, their conjunction bodes no good, I'm sure.

MRS FRAIL: Now you talk of conjunction, my brother Foresight has cast both their nativities, and prognosticates an Admiral and an eminent Justice of the Peace to be the issue-male of their two bodies; 'tis the most superstitious old fool! He would have persuaded me that this was an unlucky day, and would not let me come abroad. But I invented a dream, and sent him to Artimodorus[1] for interpretation, and so stole out to see you. Well, and what will you give me now? Come, I must have something.

VALENTINE: Step into the next room and I'll give you something.

SCANDAL: Ay, we'll all give you something.

MRS FRAIL: Well, what will you all give me?

VALENTINE: Mine's a secret.

MRS FRAIL: I thought you would give me something that would be a trouble to you to keep.

VALENTINE: And Scandal shall give you a good name.

MRS FRAIL: That's more than he has for himself. And what will you give me, Mr Tattle?

TATTLE: I? My soul, madam.

MRS FRAIL: Pooh, no, I thank you. I have enough to do to take care of my own. Well, but I'll come and see you one of these mornings. I hear you have a great many pictures.

TATTLE: I have a pretty good collection at your service, some originals.

SCANDAL: Hang him, he has nothing but the Seasons and the Twelve Caesars, paltry copies, and the Five Senses,[2] as ill represented as they are in himself. And he himself is the only original you will see there.

MRS FRAIL: Ay, but I hear he has a closet of beauties.

---

1. *Artimodorus*: Artemidorus Daldianus of Ephesus, whose *Oneirocritica* was the unchallenged classical authority on the interpretation of dreams.

2. *Seasons . . . Twelve Caesars . . . Five Senses*: cheap popular prints. The Twelve Caesars hang on the walls of the brothel in Hogarth's *Rake's Progress*, III.

SCANDAL: Yes, all that have done him favours, if you will believe him.

MRS FRAIL: Ay, let me see those, Mr Tattle.

TATTLE: Oh, madam, those are sacred to love and contemplation. No man but the painter and myself was ever blest with the sight.

MRS FRAIL: Well, but a woman –

TATTLE: Nor woman, till she consented to have her picture there too, for then she is obliged to keep the secret.

SCANDAL: No, no. Come to me if you would see pictures.

MRS FRAIL: You?

SCANDAL: Yes faith, I can shew you your own picture and most of your acquaintance to the life, and as like as at Knellers.[1]

MRS FRAIL: O lying creature! Valentine, does not he lie? I can't believe a word he says.

VALENTINE: No indeed, he speaks truth now. For as Tattle has pictures of all that have granted him favours, he has the pictures of all that have refused him – if satires, descriptions, characters and lampoons are pictures.

SCANDAL: Yes, mine are most in black and white. And yet there are some set out in their true colours, both men and women. I can shew you Pride, Folly, Affectation, Wantonness, Inconstancy, Covetousness, Dissimulation, Malice, and Ignorance, all in one piece. Then I can shew you Lying, Foppery, Vanity, Cowardice, Bragging, Lechery, Impotence and Ugliness in another piece; and yet one of these is a celebrated beauty, and t'other a profess'd beau. I have paintings too, some pleasant enough.

MRS FRAIL: Come, let's hear 'em.

SCANDAL: Why, I have a beau in a bagnio,[2] cupping[3] for a complexion, and sweating for a shape.

MRS FRAIL: So.

SCANDAL: Then I have a lady burning of brandy in a cellar with a hackney coachman.

MRS FRAIL: O devil! Well, but that story is not true.

1. *Kneller's*: Sir Godfrey Kneller, a celebrated portrait painter of the day.
2. *Bagnio*: Turkish bath.
3. *Cupping*: bleeding.

SCANDAL: I have some hieroglyphics too. I have a lawyer with a hundred hands, two heads and but one face; a divine with two faces and one head; and I have a soldier with his brains in his belly and his heart where his head should be.

MRS FRAIL: And no head?

SCANDAL: No head.

MRS FRAIL: Pooh, this is all invention. Have you ne'er a poet?

SCANDAL: Yes, I have a poet weighing words, and selling praise for praise, and a critic picking his pocket. I have another large piece too, representing a school where there are huge proportioned critics, with long wigs, laced coats, Steinkirk cravats,[1] and terrible faces, with cat-calls[2] in their hands, and horn-books[3] about their necks. I have many more of this kind, very well painted, as you shall see.

MRS FRAIL: Well, I'll come, if it be only to disprove you.

Enter JEREMY.

JEREMY: Sir, here's the steward again from your father.

VALENTINE: I'll come to him. Will you give me leave? I'll wait on you again presently.

MRS FRAIL: No, I'll be gone. Come, who squires me to the Exchange?[4] I must call my sister Foresight there.

SCANDAL: I will. I have a mind to your sister.

MRS FRAIL: Civil!

TATTLE: I will, because I have a tender for your ladyship.

MRS FRAIL: That's somewhat the better reason, to my opinion.

SCANDAL: Well, if Tattle entertains you, I have the better opportunity to engage your sister.

VALENTINE: Tell Angelica I am about making hard conditions to come abroad and be at liberty to see her.

SCANDAL: I'll give an account of you and your proceedings. If indiscretion be a sign of love, you are the most a lover of

1. *Steinkirk cravats*: at the battle of Steenkirk, 3 August 1692, the French officers, being pressed for time, rushed to battle with their neckties undone, thus setting the fashion for the fops of the day.
2. *Cat-calls*: a whistle used for hissing unpopular plays.
3. *Horn-books*: alphabet cards sheathed in translucent horn.
4. *Exchange*: a bazaar on the south side of the Strand.

anybody that I know. You fancy that parting with your estate will help you to your mistress. In my mind he is a thoughtless adventurer,

Who hopes to purchase wealth, by selling land,
Or win a mistress with a losing hand.

Exeunt.

THE END OF THE FIRST ACT

Act Two

A room in FORESIGHT's *house*.
FORESIGHT *and* SERVANT.

FORESIGHT: Hey-day! What, are all the women of my family abroad? Is not my wife come home, nor my sister, nor my daughter?

SERVANT: No, sir.

FORESIGHT: Mercy on us, what can be the meaning of it? Sure the moon is in all her fortitudes.[1] Is my niece Angelica at home?

SERVANT: Yes, sir.

FORESIGHT: I believe you lie, sir.

SERVANT: Sir?

FORESIGHT: I say you lie, sir. It is impossible that anything should be as I would have it; for I was born, sir, when the crab was ascending, and all my affairs go backward.

SERVANT: I can't tell indeed, sir.

FORESIGHT: No, I know you can't, sir. But I can tell, sir, and foretell, sir.

Enter NURSE.

Nurse, where's your young mistress?

NURSE: Wee'st heart,[2] I know not, they're none of 'em come home yet. Poor child, I warrant she's fond o' seeing the town. Marry, pray Heav'n they ha'given her any dinner. Good lack-a-day! Ha, ha, ha! O strange! I'll vow and swear now. Ha, ha, ha! Marry, and did you ever see the like?

FORESIGHT: Why how now, what's the matter?

NURSE: Pray Heav'n send your worship good luck, marry, and amen with all my heart, for you have put on one stocking with the wrong side outward.

---

1. *Fortitudes*: an astrological term denoting any circumstances which heightened a planet's influence.
2. *Wee'st*: superlative of 'wee'. Here used as a term of endearment.

FORESIGHT: Ha, how? Faith and troth I'm glad of it, and so
I have that may be good luck in troth, in troth it may, very
good luck. Nay I have had some omens: I got out of bed
backwards too this morning, without premeditation; pretty
good that too. But then I stumbled coming down stairs, and
met a weasel;[1] bad omens those. Some bad, some good,
our lives are chequer'd. Mirth and sorrow, want and plenty,
night and day, make up our time. – But in troth I am pleas'd
at my stocking, very well pleas'd at my stocking. – Oh,
here's my niece! –

Enter ANGELICA.

Sirrah, go tell Sir Sampson Legend I'll wait on him, if he's
at leisure – 'tis now three a clock, a very good hour for
business; Mercury governs this hour.

Exit SERVANT.

ANGELICA: Is not it a good hour for pleasure too? Uncle,
pray lend me your coach, mine's out of order.

FORESIGHT: What, would you be gadding too? Sure all
females are mad today. It is of evil portent, and bodes
mischief to the master of a family. I remember an old
prophecy written by Messahalah[2] the Arabian, and thus
translated by a Reverend Buckinghamshire Bard.[3]

> *When housewifes all the house forsake,*
> *And leave good man to brew and bake,*
> *Withouten guile, then be it said,*
> *That house doth stand upon its head;*
> *And when the head is set in grond,*
> *Ne marl if it be fruitful fond.*

Fruitful, the head fruitful, that bodes horns; the fruit of the
head is horns. Dear niece, stay at home, for by the head of
the house is meant the husband. The prophecy needs no
explanation.

ANGELICA: Well, but I can neither make you a cuckold, uncle,

1. *Weasel*: a witch's familiar, and therefore unlucky.
2. *Messahalah*: Ma Shā'Allah (Al Misrī), a celebrated ninth-century
Jewish astrologer.
3. *Reverend Buckinghamshire Bard*: John Mason (1646?–94), versifier,
visionary and vicar of Stantonbury, Bucks.

by going abroad, nor secure you from being one by staying
at home.

FORESIGHT: Yes, yes. While there's one woman left, the
prophecy is not in full force.

ANGELICA: But my inclinations are in force. I have a mind
to go abroad, and if you won't lend me your coach, I'll take
a hackney, or a chair, and leave you to erect a scheme, and
find who's in conjunction with your wife. Why don't you
keep her at home, if you're jealous when she's abroad? You
know my aunt is a little retrograde (as you call it) in her
nature. Uncle, I'm afraid you are not lord of the ascendant,
ha, ha, ha.

FORESIGHT: Well, jill-flirt, you are very pert, and always ridi-
culing that celestial science.

ANGELICA: Nay, uncle, don't be angry. If you are, I'll reap
up all your false prophecies, ridiculous dreams, and idle
divinations. I'll swear you are a nuisance to the neighbour-
hood. What a bustle did you keep against the last invisible
eclipse, laying in provision as 'twere for a siege! What a
world of fire and candle, matches and tinderboxes did you
purchase! One would have thought we were ever after to
live underground, or at least making a voyage to Greenland,
to inhabit there all the dark season.

FORESIGHT: Why, you malapert slut –

ANGELICA: Will you lend me your coach, or I'll go on. Nay,
I'll declare how you prophesied popery was coming, only
because the butler had mislaid some of the Apostle spoons,
and thought they were lost. Away went religion and spoon-
meat together. – Indeed, uncle, I'll indite you for a wizard.

FORESIGHT: How, hussy? Was there ever such a provoking
minx?

NURSE: O merciful Father, how she talks!

ANGELICA: Yes, I can make oath of your unlawful midnight
practices; you and the old nurse there.

NURSE: Marry, Heaven defend – I at midnight practices!
O Lord, what's here to do? I in unlawful doings with my
master's worship! Why, did you ever hear the like now?
Sir, did ever I do any thing of your midnight concerns but
warm your bed and tuck you up, and set the candle and

your tobacco box and your urinal by you, and now and then rub the soles of your feet? – O Lord, I!

ANGELICA: Yes, I saw you together, through the key-hole of the closet one night, like Saul and the Witch of Endor, turning the sieve and shears,[1] and pricking your thumbs to write poor innocent servants' names in blood about a little nutmeg grater which she had forgot in the caudle-cup. Nay, I know something worse, if I would speak of it.

FORESIGHT: I defie you, hussy; but I'll remember this, I'll be revenged on you, cockatrice; I'll hamper you. You have your fortune in your own hands, but I'll find a way to make your lover, your prodigal spendthrift gallant, Valentine, pay for all, I will.

ANGELICA: Will you? I care not, but all shall out then. Look to it, nurse. I can bring witness that you have a great un- natural teat under your left arm, and he another, and that you suckle a young devil in the shape of a tabby cat by turns, I can.

NURSE: A teat, a teat, I an unnatural teat![2] O the false slanderous thing; feel, feel here, if I have anything but like another Christian, [crying] or any teats, but two that ha'n't given suck this thirty years.

FORESIGHT: I will have patience, since it is the will of the stars I should be thus tormented. This is the effect of the malicious conjunctions and oppositions in the third house of my nativity. There the curse of kindred was foretold. But I will have my doors locked up. I'll punish you. Not a man shall enter my house.

ANGELICA: Do, uncle, lock 'em up quickly before my aunt come home. You'll have a letter for alimony tomorrow morning. But let me be gone first, and then let no mankind come near the house, but converse with spirits and the celestial signs, the bull, and the ram, and the goat. Bless me! there are a great many horned beasts among the twelve signs, uncle. But cuckolds go to Heav'n.

1. *Turning . . . shears*: a form of divination using a riddle and shears, popular in Scotland.
2. *Teat*: The Devil's Mark or 'little teat' was often referred to by writers on witchcraft and at witchcraft trials.

FORESIGHT: But there's but one virgin among the twelve signs, spitfire, but one virgin.

ANGELICA: Nor there had not been that one, if she had had to do with anything but astrologers, uncle. That makes my aunt go abroad.

FORESIGHT: How, how? Is that the reason? Come, you know something. Tell me, and I'll forgive you. Do, good niece. Come, you shall have my coach and horses, faith and troth you shall. Does my wife complain? Come, I know women tell one another. She is young and sanguine, has a wanton hazel eye, and was born under Gemini, which may incline her to society. She has a mole upon her lip, with a moist palm, and an open liberality on the Mount of Venus.

ANGELICA: Ha, ha, ha!

FORESIGHT: Do you laugh? Well, gentlewoman, I'll – But come, be a good girl, don't perplex your poor uncle, tell me. Won't you speak? Odd, I'll –

Enter SERVANT.

SERVANT: Sir Sampson is coming down to wait upon you.

ANGELICA: Goodbye uncle. Call me a chair. I'll find out my aunt, and tell her she must not come home.

Exit ANGELICA *and* SERVANT.

FORESIGHT: I'm so perplexed and vexed, I am not fit to receive him. I shall scarce recover myself before the hour be past. Go, nurse, tell Sir Sampson I'm ready to wait on him.

NURSE: Yes, sir.

FORESIGHT: Well – Why, if I was born to be a cuckold, there's no more to be said.

Enter SIR SAMPSON LEGEND *with a paper.*

SIR SAMPSON: Nor no more to be done, old boy, that's plain. Here 'tis, I have it in my hand, old Ptolomee.[1] I'll make the ungracious prodigal know who begat him, I will, old Nostrodamus.[2] What, I warrant my son thought nothing

---

1. *Ptolomee*: Ptolomaeus Alexandrinus, the second-century astrologer whose *Almagest* was a standard work for centuries.

2. *Nostrodamus*: Michel de Notredame, astrologer to Catherine de Medici.

belonged to a father but forgiveness and affection. No authority, no correction, no arbitrary power, nothing to be done but for him to offend and me to pardon. I warrant you, if he danced till doomsday, he thought I was to pay the piper. Well, but here it is under black and white, signatum, sigillatum, and deliberatum; that as soon as my son Benjamin is arrived, he is to make over to him his right of inheritance. Where's my daughter that is to be? Hah! Old Merlin, body o' me, I'm so glad I'm revenged on this undutiful rogue.

FORESIGHT: Odso, let me see. Let me see the paper. Ay, faith and troth, here 'tis, if it will but hold. I wish things were done, and the conveyance made. When was this signed, what hour? Odso, you should have consulted me for the time. Well, but we'll make haste.

SIR SAMPSON: Haste, ay, ay, haste enough. My son Ben will be in town tonight. I have ordered my lawyer to draw up writings of settlement and jointure. All shall be done tonight. No matter for the time. Prithee, brother Foresight, leave superstition. Pox o'th'time! There's no time but the time present; there's no more to be said of what's past, and all that is to come will happen. If the sun shine by day, and the stars by night, why, we shall know one another's faces without the help of a candle, and that's all the stars are good for.

FORESIGHT: How, how, Sir Sampson, that all? Give me leave to contradict you, and tell you you are ignorant.

SIR SAMPSON: I tell you I am wise, and sapiens dominabitur astris[1]; there's Latin for you to prove it, and an argument to confound your Ephemeris.[2] Ignorant! I tell you, I have travelled, old Fircu,[3] and know the globe. I have seen the antipodes, where the sun rises at midnight and sets at noonday.

FORESIGHT: But I tell you, I have travelled, and travelled in the celestial spheres, know the signs and the planets, and their houses, can judge of motions direct and retrograde,

1. *Sapiens . . . astris*: the wise (man) is ruled by the stars.
2. *Ephemeris*: astronomical almanac.
3. *Fircu*: name of witch's familiar.

of sextiles, quadrates, trines¹ and oppositions, fiery trigons²
and aquatical trigons, know whether life shall be long or
short, happy or unhappy, whether diseases are curable or
incurable, if journeys shall be prosperous, undertakings
successful, or goods stol'n recovered. I know –

SIR SAMPSON: I know the length of the Emperor of China's
foot, have kissed the Great Mogul's slipper, and rid a hunting upon an elephant with the Cham of Tartary. Body of me,
I have made a cuckold of a king, and the present majesty
of Bantam³ is the issue of these loins.

FORESIGHT: I know when travellers lie or speak truth, when
they don't know it themselves.

SIR SAMPSON: I have known an astrologer made a cuckold
in the twinkling of a star, and seen a conjurer that could
not keep the devil out of his wife's circle.

FORESIGHT [aside]: What, does he twit me with my wife too?
I must be better informed of this. – Do you mean my wife,
Sir Sampson? Tho' you made a cuckold of the King of
Bantam, yet by the body of the sun –

SIR SAMPSON: By the horns of the moon, you would say,
Brother Capricorn.

FORESIGHT: Capricorn in your teeth, thou modern Man-
devil; Ferdinand Mendez Pinto⁴ was but a type of thee,
thou liar of the first magnitude. Take back your paper of
inheritance; send your son to sea again. I'll wed my
daughter to an Egyptian mummy ere she shall incor-
porate with a contemner of sciences, and a defamer of
virtue.

SIR SAMPSON [aside]: Body of me, I have gone too far. I must
not provoke honest Albumazar. [Aloud] An Egyptian
mummy is an illustrious creature, my trusty hieroglyphic,
and may have significations of futurity about him. Odsbud,
I would my son were an Egyptian mummy for thy sake.

---

1. *Sextiles . . . trines*: aspects of heavenly bodies respectively one sixth,
one quarter and one third part of the zodiac distant from each other.

2. *Trigons*: three zodiacal signs of 120° distant from each other.

3. *Bantam*: in Western Java, one of the chief ports of the East Indies.

4. *Ferdinand Mendez Pinto*: a Portuguese traveller whose *Peregrinations*,
recounting incredible Eastern adventures, appeared in 1614.

What, thou art not angry for a jest, my good Haly?[1] I reverence the sun, moon and stars with all my heart. What, I'll make thee a present of a mummy. Now I think on't, body of me, I have a shoulder of an Egyptian King, that I purloined from one of the pyramids, powdered with hieroglyphics. Thou shalt have it sent home to thy house, and make an entertainment for all the philomaths,[2] and students in physic and astrology in and about London.

FORESIGHT: But what do you know of my wife, Sir Sampson?

SIR SAMPSON: Thy wife is a constellation of virtues. She's the moon, and thou art the man in the moon. Nay, she is more illustrious than the moon, for she has her chastity without her inconstancy. 'S'bud, I was but in jest.

Enter JEREMY.

How now, who sent for you? Ha! What would you have?

FORESIGHT: Nay, if you were but in jest. Who's that fellow? I don't like his physiognomy. [JEREMY *whispers to* SIR SAMPSON.]

SIR SAMPSON: My son, sir; what son, sir? My son Benjamin, hoh?

JEREMY: No, sir, Mr Valentine, my master. 'Tis the first time he has been abroad since his confinement, and he comes to pay his duty to you.

SIR SAMPSON: Well, sir.

Enter VALENTINE.

JEREMY: He is here, sir.

VALENTINE: Your blessing, sir.

SIR SAMPSON: You've had it already, sir, I think I sent it you today in a bill of four thousand pound. A great deal of money, brother Foresight.

FORESIGHT: Ay indeed, Sir Sampson, a great deal of money for a young man. I wonder what he can do with it!

SIR SAMPSON: Body o' me, so do I. Hark ye, Valentine, if there is too much, refund the superfluity, do'st hear, boy?

VALENTINE: Superfluity, sir, it will scarce pay my debts.

1. *Albumazar* ... *Haly*: Albumazar and Haly were eighth-century Arab astronomers.
2. *Philomaths*: savants. Often used sarcastically.

I hope you will have more indulgence than to oblige me to those hard conditions which my necessity signed to.

SIR SAMPSON: Sir, how I beseech you, what were you pleased to intimate concerning indulgence?

VALENTINE: Why, sir, that you would not go to the extremity of the conditions, but release me at least from some part –

SIR SAMPSON: Oh, sir, I understand you. That's all, ha?

VALENTINE: Yes, sir, all that I presume to ask. But what you, out of fatherly fondness, will be pleased to add, shall be doubly welcome.

SIR SAMPSON: No doubt of it, sweet sir, but your filial piety and my fatherly fondness would fit like two tallies. Here's a rogue, brother Foresight, makes a bargain under hand and seal in the morning, and would be released from it in the afternoon! Here's a rogue, dog, here's conscience and honesty! This is your wit now, this is the morality of your wits! You are a wit, and have been a beau, and may be a – Why sirrah, is it not here under hand and seal? Can you deny it?

VALENTINE: Sir, I don't deny it.

SIR SAMPSON: Sirrah, you'll be hanged. I shall live to see you go up Holborn Hill.[1] Has he not a rogue's face? Speak, brother, you understand physiognomy. A hanging look to me; of all my boys the most unlike me. A has a damned Tyburn face, without the benefit o'the clergy.

FORESIGHT: Hum. Truly I don't care to discourage a young man. He has a violent death in his face; but I hope no danger of hanging.

VALENTINE: Sir, is this usage for your son? For that old, weather-headed fool, I know how to laugh at him; but you, sir –

SIR SAMPSON: You, sir, and you, sir! Why, who are you, sir?

VALENTINE: Your son, sir.

SIR SAMPSON: That's more than I know, sir, and I believe not.

VALENTINE: Faith, I hope not.

SIR SAMPSON: What, would you have your mother a whore?

1. *Holborn Hill*: between Newgate (prison) and Tyburn (gallows).

Did you ever hear the like! Did you ever hear the like! Body o' me –

VALENTINE: I would have an excuse for your barbarity and unnatural usage.

SIR SAMPSON: Excuse! Impudence! Why sirrah, mayn't I do what I please? Are not you my slave? Did not I beget you? And might not I have chosen whether I would have begot you or no? Ouns, who are you? Whence came you? What brought you into the world? How came you here, sir? Here, to stand here, upon those two legs, and look erect with that audacious face, hah! Answer me that! Did you come a volunteer into the world? Or did I beat up for you with the lawful authority of a parent, and press you to the service?

VALENTINE: I know no more why I came than you do why you called me. But here I am, and if you don't mean to provide for me, I desire you would leave me as you found me.

SIR SAMPSON: With all my heart. Come, uncase, strip, and go naked out of the world as you came into't.

VALENTINE: My clothes are soon put off; but you must also deprive me of reason, thought, passions, inclinations, affections, appetites, senses, and the huge train of attendants that you begot along with me.

SIR SAMPSON: Body o' me, what a many-headed monster have I propagated!

VALENTINE: I am of myself, a plain easy simple creature, and to be kept at small expense, but the retinue that you gave me are craving and invincible. They are so many devils that you have raised, and will have employment.

SIR SAMPSON: Ouns, what had I to do to get children? Can't a private man be born without all these followers? Why, nothing under an emperor should be born with appetites. Why, at this rate a fellow that has but a groat in his pocket may have a stomach capable of a ten shilling ordinary.[1]

JEREMY: Nay, that's as clear as the sun; I'll make oath of it before any justice in Middlesex.

1. *Ordinary*: eating-place.

SIR SAMPSON: Here's a cormorant too. 'S'heart, this fellow was not born with you? I did not beget him, did I?

JEREMY: By the provision that's made for me, you might have begot me too. Nay, and to tell your worship another truth, I believe you did, for I find I was born with those same whoreson appetites, too, that my master speaks of.

SIR SAMPSON: Why, look you there now, I'll maintain it that by the rule of right reason this fellow ought to have been born without a palate. 'S'heart, what should he do with a distinguishing taste? I warrant now he'd rather eat a pheasant than a piece of poor John.[1] And smell, now, why, I warrant he can smell, and loves perfumes above a stink. Why, there's it. And music, don't you love music, scoundrel?

JEREMY: Yes, I have a reasonable good ear, sir, as to jigs and country dances and the like. I don't much matter your Solas or Sonatas, they give me the spleen.

SIR SAMPSON: The spleen! Ha, ha, ha! A pox confound you – Solas and Sonatas? Ouns, whose son are you? How were you engendered, muckworm?

JEREMY: I am by my father, the son of a chairman; my mother sold oysters in winter and cucumbers in summer; and I came upstairs into the world, for I was born in a cellar.

FORESIGHT: By your looks, you should go upstairs out of the world[2] too, friend.

SIR SAMPSON: And if this rogue were anatomized now, and dissected, he has his vessels of digestion and concoction and so forth large enough for the inside of a cardinal, this son of a cucumber. These things are unaccountable and unreasonable. Body of me, why was not I a bear, that my cubs might have lived upon sucking their paws? Nature has been provident only to bears and spiders; the one has its nutriment in his own hands, and t'other spins his habitation out of his entrails.

VALENTINE: Fortune was provident enough to supply all the necessities of my nature, if I had my right of inheritance.

SIR SAMPSON: Again! Ouns han't you four thousand pound?

---

1. *John*: salted dried hake.
2. *Upstairs out of the world*: i.e., up the gallows steps.

If I had it again, I would not give thee a groat. What, wouldst thou have me turn pelican, and feed thee out of my own vitals?[1] 'S'heart, live by your wits. You were always fond of the wits; now let's see if you have wit enough to keep yourself. Your brother will be in town tonight or tomorrow morning, and then look you perform covenants – and so your friend and servant. Come, brother Foresight.

Exeunt SIR SAMPSON *and* FORESIGHT.

JEREMY: I told you what your visit would come to.

VALENTINE: 'Tis as much as I expected. I did not come to see him, I came to Angelica. But since she was gone abroad, it was easily turned another way, and at least looked well on my side. What's here? Mrs Foresight and Mrs Frail? They are earnest – I'll avoid 'em. Come this way, and go and enquire when Angelica will return.

Exeunt.

Enter MRS FORESIGHT *and* MRS FRAIL.

MRS FRAIL: What have you to do to watch me? 'S'life. I'll do what I please.

MRS FORESIGHT: You will?

MRS FRAIL: Yes, marry will I. A great piece of business to go to Covent-Garden Square in a hackney coach and take a turn with one's friend.

MRS FORESIGHT: Nay, two or three turns, I'll take my oath.

MRS FRAIL: Well, what if I took twenty? I'll warrant if you had been there, it had been only innocent recreation. Lord, where's the comfort of this life, if we can't have the happiness of conversing where we like?

MRS FORESIGHT: But can't you converse at home? I own it, I think there's no happiness like conversing with an agreeable man. I don't quarrel at that, nor I don't think but your conversation was very innocent; but the place is public, and to be seen with a man in a hackney coach is scandalous. What if anybody else should have seen you alight as I did? How can anybody be happy while they're in perpetual fear of being seen and censured? Besides, it would not only reflect upon you, sister, but me.

1. *Pelican . . . vitals*: the pelican was believed to feed its young its own blood.

MRS FRAIL: Pooh, here's a clutter. Why should it reflect upon you? I don't doubt but you have thought yourself happy in a hackney coach before now. If I had gone to Knightsbridge, or to Chelsey, or to Spring-Garden, or Barn-Elms[1] with a man alone, something might have been said.

MRS FORESIGHT: Why, was I ever in any of these places? What do you mean, sister?

MRS FRAIL: Was I? What do you mean?

MRS FORESIGHT: You have been at a worse place.

MRS FRAIL: I at a worse place, and with a man!

MRS FORESIGHT: I suppose you would not go alone to the World's End.[2]

MRS FRAIL: The World's End! What, do you mean to banter me?

MRS FORESIGHT: Poor innocent! You don't know that there's a place called the World's End? I'll swear you can keep your countenance purely, you'd make an admirable player.

MRS FRAIL: I'll swear you have a great deal of impudence, and in my mind too much for the stage.

MRS FORESIGHT: Very well, that will appear who has most. You never were at the World's End?

MRS FRAIL: No.

MRS FORESIGHT: You deny it positively to my face?

MRS FRAIL: Your face, what's your face?

MRS FORESIGHT: No matter for that, it's as good a face as yours.

MRS FRAIL: Not by a dozen years' wearing. But I do deny it positively to your face then.

MRS FORESIGHT: I'll allow you now to find fault with my face; for I'll swear your impudence has put me out of countenance. But look you here now, where did you lose this gold bodkin? O sister, sister!

MRS FRAIL: My bodkin!

MRS FORESIGHT: Nay, 'tis yours, look at it.

MRS FRAIL: Well, if you go to that, where did you find this bodkin? O sister, sister! Sister every way!

1. *Knightsbridge . . . Chelsey . . . Spring-Garden . . . Barn-Elms*: all notorious resorts.
2. *World's End*: the name of an inn in Knightsbridge and one in Chelsea.

MRS FORESIGHT [*aside*]: O devil on't, that I could not discover her without betraying myself!

MRS FRAIL: I have heard gentlemen say, sister, that one should take great care when one makes a thrust in fencing, not to lie open oneself.

MRS FORESIGHT: It's very true, sister. Well, since all's out, and as you say, since we are both wounded, let us do that is often done in duels, take care of one another, and grow better friends than before.

MRS FRAIL: With all my heart. Ours are but slight flesh wounds, and if we keep 'em from air, not at all dangerous. Well, give me your hand in token of sisterly secrecy and affection.

MRS FORESIGHT: Here 'tis, with all my heart.

MRS FRAIL: Well, as an earnest of friendship and confidence, I'll acquaint you with a design that I have. To tell truth, and speak openly one to another, I'm afraid the world have observed us more than we have observed one another. You have a rich husband, and are provided for; I am at a loss, and have no great stock either of fortune or reputation, and therefore must look sharply about me. Sir Sampson has a son that is expected tonight, and by the account I have heard of his education can be no conjurer. The estate you know is to be made over to him. Now if I could wheedle him, sister, ha? You understand me?

MRS FORESIGHT: I do, and will help you to the utmost of my power. And I can tell you one thing that falls out luckily enough; my awkard daughter-in-law,[1] who you know is designed for his wife, is grown fond of Mr Tattle. Now if we can improve that, and make her have an aversion for the booby, it may go a great way towards his liking of you. Here they come together; and let us contrive some way or other to leave 'em together.

Enter TATTLE *and* MISS PRUE.

MISS PRUE: Mother, mother, mother, look you here.

MRS FORESIGHT: Fie, fie, Miss, how you bawl! Besides, I have told you, you must not call me mother.

---

1. *Daughter-in-law*: stepdaughter.

MISS PRUE: What must I call you then? Are not you my father's wife?

MRS FORESIGHT: Madam, you must say madam. By my soul, I shall fancy myself old indeed, to have this great girl call me mother. Well, but Miss, what are you so overjoyed at?

MISS PRUE: Look you here, madam then, what Mr Tattle has given me. Look you here, cousin, here's a snuff-box; nay, there's snuff in't. Here, will you have any? Oh, good! How sweet it is! Mr Tattle is all over sweet: his peruke is sweet, and his gloves are sweet, and his handkerchief is sweet, pure sweet, sweeter than roses. Smell him mother, madam, I mean. He gave me this ring for a kiss.

TATTLE: O fie, Miss, you must not kiss and tell.

MISS PRUE: Yes; I may tell my mother. And he says he'll give me something to make me smell so. Oh pray lend me your handkerchief. Smell, cousin; he says, he'll give me something that will make my smocks smell this way. Is not it pure? It's better than lavender mun.[1] I'm resolved I won't let nurse put any more lavender among my smocks. Ha, cousin?

MRS FRAIL: Fie, Miss, amongst your linen, you must say. You must never say smock.

MISS PRUE: Why, it is not bawdy, is it cousin?

TATTLE: Oh, madam, you are too severe upon Miss. You must not find fault with her pretty simplicity, it becomes her strangely. Pretty Miss, don't let 'em persuade you out of your innocency.

MRS FORESIGHT: Oh, demm you, toad. I wish you don't persuade her out of her innocency.

TATTLE: Who, I madam? O Lord, how can your ladyship have such a thought? Sure you don't know me.

MRS FRAIL: Ah devil, sly devil. He's as close, sister, as a confessor. He thinks we don't observe him.

MRS FORESIGHT: A cunning cur. How soon he could find out a fresh harmless creature and left us, sister, presently.

TATTLE: Upon reputation –

MRS FORESIGHT: They're all so, sister, these men. They love to have the spoiling of a young thing, they are as fond of

1. *Mun*: 'man', a meaningless interjection popular at the time.

it as of being first in the fashion or of seeing a new play the first day. I warrant it would break Mr Tattle's heart to think that anybody else should be beforehand with him.

TATTLE: O Lord, I swear I would not for the world.

MRS FRAIL: O hang you, who'll believe you? You'd be hanged before you'd confess. We know you. She's very pretty. Lord, what pure red and white! She looks so wholesome. Ne'er stir, I don't know, but I fancy, if I were a man –

MISS PRUE: How you love to jeer one, cousin.

MRS FORESIGHT: Hark'ee, sister, by my soul the girl is spoiled already. D'ye think she'll ever endure a great lubberly tarpaulin?[1] Gad, I warrant you she won't let him come near her, after Mr Tattle.

MRS FRAIL: O'my soul, I'm afraid not. Eh! filthy creature, that smells all of pitch and tar! [*To* TATTLE] Devil take you, you confounded toad! Why did you see her before she was married?

MRS FORESIGHT: Nay, why did we let him? My husband will hang us. He'll think we brought 'em acquainted.

MRS FRAIL: Come, faith, let us be gone. If my brother Foresight should find us with them, he'd think so sure enough.

MRS FORESIGHT: So he would. But then, leaving 'em together is as bad. And he's such a sly devil, he'll never miss an opportunity.

MRS FRAIL: I don't care; I won't be seen in't.

MRS FORESIGHT: Well, if you should, Mr Tattle, you'll have a world to answer for, remember I wash my hands of it, I'm thoroughly innocent.

Exeunt MRS FORESIGHT *and* MRS FRAIL.

MISS PRUE: What makes 'em go away, Mr Tattle? What do they mean, do you know?

TATTLE: Yes, my dear, I think I can guess. But hang me if I know the reason of it.

MISS PRUE: Come, must not we go too?

TATTLE: No, no, they don't mean that.

MISS PRUE: No! What then? What shall you and I do together?

1. *Tarpaulin*: sailor.

TATTLE: I must make love to you, pretty Miss. Will you let me make love to you?

MISS PRUE: Yes, if you please.

TATTLE [*aside*]: Frank, egad, at least. What a pox does Mrs Foresight mean by this civility? Is it to make a fool of me? Or does she leave us together out of good morality, and do as she would be done by? Gad, I'll understand it so.

MISS PRUE: Well, and how will you make love to me? Come, I long to have you begin. Must I make love too? You must tell me how.

TATTLE: You must let me speak Miss, you must not speak first. I must ask you questions, and you must answer.

MISS PRUE: What, is it like the catechism? Come then, ask me.

TATTLE: De'e you think you can love me?

MISS PRUE: Yes.

TATTLE: Pooh, pox, you must not say yes already. I shan't care a farthing for you then in a twinkling.

MISS PRUE: What must I say then?

TATTLE: Why you must say no, or you believe not, or you can't tell.

MISS PRUE: Why, must I tell a lie then?

TATTLE: Yes, if you would be well-bred. All well-bred persons lie. Besides, you are a woman, you must never speak what you think. Your words must contradict your thoughts, but your actions may contradict your words. So, when I ask you if you can love me, you must say no, but you must love me too. If I tell you you are handsome, you must deny it, and say I flatter you. But you must think yourself more charming than I speak you, and like me, for the beauty which I say you have, as much as if I had it myself. If I ask you to kiss me, you must be angry, but you must not refuse me. If I ask you for more, you must be more angry, but more complying. And as soon as ever I make you say you'll cry out, you must be sure to hold your tongue.

MISS PRUE: O Lord, I swear this is pure. I like it better than our old-fashioned country way of speaking one's mind. And must not you lie too?

TATTLE: Hum – yes. But you must believe I speak truth.

MISS PRUE: O Gemini! Well, I always had a great mind to tell lies, but they frighted me, and said it was a sin.

TATTLE: Well, my pretty creature, will you make me happy by giving me a kiss?

MISS PRUE: No, indeed, I'm angry at you. [*Runs and kisses him.*]

TATTLE: Hold, hold, that's pretty well, but you should not have given it me, but have suffered me to take it.

MISS PRUE: Well, we'll do it again.

TATTLE: With all my heart. Now then, my little angel. [*Kisses her.*]

MISS PRUE: Pish.

TATTLE: That's right. Again, my charmer. [*Kisses again.*]

MISS PRUE: O fie, nay, now I can't abide you.

TATTLE: Admirable! That was as well as if you had been born and bred in Covent-Garden all the days of your life. And won't you shew me, pretty Miss, where your bed-chamber is?

MISS PRUE: No, indeed won't I. But I'll run there, and hide myself from you behind the curtains.

TATTLE: I'll follow you.

MISS PRUE: Ah, but I'll hold the door with both hands and be angry – and you shall push me down before you come in.

TATTLE: No, I'll come in first, and push you down afterwards.

MISS PRUE: Will you? Then I'll be more angry, and more complying.

TATTLE: Then I'll make you cry out.

MISS PRUE: Oh, but you shan't, for I'll hold my tongue.

TATTLE: O my dear apt scholar.

MISS PRUE: Well, now I'll run and make more haste than you. [*Exit* MISS PRUE.]

TATTLE: You shall not fly so fast as I'll pursue. [*Exit after her.*]

THE END OF THE SECOND ACT

Act Three

A room in FORESIGHT'*s house.*
Enter NURSE.

NURSE: Miss, Miss, Miss Prue. Mercy on me, marry and amen. Why, what's become of the child? Why Miss, Miss Foresight. Sure she has not locked herself up in her chamber, and gone to sleep, or to prayers. Miss, Miss! I hear her. Come to your father, child. Open the door. Open the door, Miss. I hear you cry husht. O Lord, who's there? [*Peeps.*] What's here to do? O the Father! a man with her! Why, Miss I say, God's my life, here's fine doings towards. O Lord, we're all undone. O you young harlotry! [*Knocks.*] Ods my life, won't you open the door? I'll come in the back way.
Exit.

TATTLE *and* MISS PRUE *at the door.*

MISS PRUE: O Lord, she's coming – and she'll tell my father. What shall I do now?

TATTLE: Pox take her! If she had stayed two minutes longer, I should have wished for her coming.

MISS PRUE: O dear, what shall I say? Tell me, Mr Tattle, tell me a lie.

TATTLE: There's no occasion for a lie; I could never tell a lie to no purpose. But since we have done nothing, we must say nothing, I think. I hear her. I'll leave you together, and come off as you can. [*Thrusts her in and shuts the door.*]

Enter VALENTINE, SCANDAL, *and* ANGELICA.

ANGELICA: You can't accuse me of inconstancy; I never told you that I loved you.

VALENTINE: But I can accuse you of uncertainty, for not telling me whether you did or no.

ANGELICA: You mistake indifference for uncertainty; I never had concern enough to ask myself the question.

SCANDAL: Nor good nature enough to answer him that did ask you, I'll say that for you, madam.

ANGELICA: What, are you setting up for good nature?

SCANDAL: Only for the affectation of it, as the women do for ill nature.

ANGELICA: Persuade your friend that it is all affectation.

VALENTINE: I shall receive no benefit from the opinion, for I know no effectual difference between continued affectation and reality.

TATTLE [coming up, aside to SCANDAL]: Scandal, are you in private discourse, anything of secrecy?

SCANDAL: Yes, but I dare trust you. We were talking of Angelica's love for Valentine. You won't speak of it?

TATTLE: No, no, not a syllable. I know that's a secret, for it's whispered everywhere.

SCANDAL: Ha, ha ha!

ANGELICA: What is, Mr Tattle? I heard you say something was whispered everywhere.

SCANDAL: Your love of Valentine.

ANGELICA: How!

TATTLE: No, madam, his love for your ladyship. Gad take me, I beg your pardon, for I never heard a word of your ladyship's passion till this instant.

ANGELICA: My passion! And who told you of my passion, pray, sir?

SCANDAL [to TATTLE]: Why, is the devil in you? Did not I tell it you for a secret?

TATTLE: Gadso, but I thought she might have been trusted with her own affairs.

SCANDAL: Is that your discretion? Trust a woman with herself?

TATTLE: You say true. I beg your pardon, I'll bring all off. [To ANGELICA] It was impossible, madam, for me to imagine that a person of your ladyship's wit and gallantry could have so long received the passionate addresses of the accomplished Valentine, and yet remain insensible; therefore you will pardon me, if from a just weight of his merit, with your ladyship's good judgement, I formed the balance of a reciprocal affection.

VALENTINE: O the devil, what damned costive poet has given thee this lesson of fustian to get by rote?

ANGELICA: I dare swear you wrong him, it is his own. And Mr Tattle only judges of the success of others from the effects of his own merit. For certainly Mr Tattle was never denied anything in his life.

TATTLE: O Lord! Yes indeed madam, several times.

ANGELICA: I swear I don't think 'tis possible.

TATTLE: Yes, I vow and swear I have. Lord, madam, I'm the most unfortunate man in the world, and the most cruelly used by the ladies.

ANGELICA: Nay, now you're ungrateful.

TATTLE: No, I hope not. 'Tis as much ingratitude to own some favours as to conceal others.

VALENTINE: There, now it's out.

ANGELICA: I don't understand you now. I thought you had never asked anything but what a lady might modestly grant and you confess.

SCANDAL: So faith, your business is done here. Now you may go brag somewhere else.

TATTLE: Brag! O heavens! Why, did I name anybody?

ANGELICA: No; I suppose that is not in your power; but you would if you could, no doubt on't.

TATTLE: Not in my power, madam! What does your ladyship mean, that I have no woman's reputation in my power?

SCANDAL [aside]: Ouns, why, you won't own it, will you?

TATTLE: Faith, madam, you're in the right. No more I have, as I hope to be saved. I never had it in my power to say anything to a lady's prejudice in my life. For as I was telling you, madam, I have been the most unsuccessful creature living in things of that nature, and never had the good fortune to be trusted once with a lady's secret, not once.

ANGELICA: No?

VALENTINE: Not once, I dare answer for him.

SCANDAL: And I'll answer for him, for I'm sure if he had he would have told me. I find, madam, you don't know Mr Tattle.

TATTLE: No indeed, madam, you don't know me at all, I find. For sure my intimate friends would have known.

ANGELICA: Then it seems you would have told, if you had been trusted.

TATTLE: O pox, Scandal, that was too far put. Never have told particulars, madam. Perhaps I might have talked as of a third person, or have introduced an amour of my own, in conversation, by way of novel, but never have explained particulars.

ANGELICA: But whence comes the reputation of Mr Tattle's secrecy, if he was never trusted?

SCANDAL: Why thence it arises. The thing is proverbially spoken, but may be applied to him. As if we should say in general terms, he only is secret who never was trusted; a satirical proverb upon our sex. There's another upon yours: as she is chaste, who was never asked the question.[1] That's all.

VALENTINE: A couple of very civil proverbs, truly. 'Tis hard to tell whether the lady or Mr Tattle be the more obliged to you. For you found her virtue upon the backwardness of the men, and his secrecy upon the mistrust of the women.

TATTLE: Gad, it's very true, madam, I think we are obliged to acquit ourselves. And for my part – But your ladyship is to speak first.

ANGELICA: Am I? Well, I freely confess I have resisted a great deal of temptation.

TATTLE: And egad, I have given some temptation that has not been resisted.

VALENTINE: Good.

ANGELICA: I cite Valentine here to declare to the court how fruitless he has found his endeavours, and to confess all his solicitations and my denials.

VALENTINE: I am ready to plead not guilty for you, and guilty for myself.

SCANDAL: So, why this is fair. Here's demonstration with a witness.

TATTLE: Well, my witnesses are not present, but I confess I have had favours from persons. But as the favours are numberless, so the persons are nameless.

SCANDAL: Pooh, pox, this proves nothing.

TATTLE: No? I can shew letters, lockets, pictures and rings;

1. *As she is chaste . . . the question*: 'Casta est quam nemo rogavit' – Ovid, *Amorum*, I, viii, 43.

and if there be occasion for witnesses, I can summon the maids at the chocolate houses, all the porters of Pall-Mall and Covent-Garden, the door-keepers at the Playhouse, the drawers at Locket's, Pontack's, the Rummer,[1] Spring-Garden; my own landlady and valet de chambre, all who shall make oath that I receive more letters than the secretary's office, and that I have more vizor-masks to enquire for me than ever went to see the hermaphrodite or the naked prince.[2] And it is notorious that in a country church once, an enquiry being made who I was, it was answered I was the famous Tattle, who had ruined so many women.

VALENTINE: It was there, I suppose, you got the nickname of the Great Turk.

TATTLE: True: I was called Turk Tattle all over the parish. The next Sunday all the old women kept their daughters at home, and the parson had not half his congregation. He would have brought me into the Spiritual Court, but I was revenged upon him, for he had a handsome daughter whom I initiated into the science. But I repented it afterwards, for it was talked of in town. And a lady of quality that shall be nameless, in a raging fit of jealousy, came down in her coach and six horses and exposed herself upon my account. Gad, I was sorry for it with all my heart – you know whom I mean. You know where we raffled[3] –

SCANDAL: Mum, Tattle.

VALENTINE: 'Sdeath, are not you ashamed?

ANGELICA: O barbarous! I never heard so insolent a piece of vanity. Fie, Mr Tattle, I'll swear I could not have believed it. Is this your secrecy?

TATTLE: Gadso, the heat of my story carried me beyond my discretion, as the heat of the lady's passion hurried her beyond her reputation. But I hope you don't know whom I mean; for there were a great many ladies raffled. Pox on't, now could I bite off my tongue.

1. *Locket's, Pontack's, the Rummer*: three famous restaurants in the city.
2. *Hermaphrodite . . . naked prince*: Hermaphrodites were popular side-shows. The naked prince was a tattooed South Sea islander, exhibited in London at the time.
3. *Raffled*: wrangled, quarrelled, joked.

SCANDAL: No, don't; for then you'll tell us no more. Come, I'll recommend a song to you upon the hint of my two proverbs, and I see one in the next room that will sing it. [*Goes to the door.*]

TATTLE: For Heavn's sake, if you do guess, say nothing. Gad, I'm very unfortunate.

    Re-enter SCANDAL, *with one to sing.*

SCANDAL: Pray sing the first song in the last new play.

SONG

1

A nymph and a swain to Apollo once prayed,
The swain had been jilted, the nymph been betrayed.
Their intent was to try if his oracle knew
E'er a nymph that was chaste, or a swain that was true.

2

Apollo was mute, and had like t' have been posed,[1]
But sagely at length he this secret disclosed:
He alone won't betray in whom none will confide,
And the nymph may be chaste that has never been tried.

    Exit SINGER.
    Enter SIR SAMPSON, MRS FRAIL, MISS PRUE *and* SERVANT.

SIR SAMPSON: Is Ben come? Odso, my son Ben come? Odd, I'm glad on't. Where is he? I long to see him. Now, Mrs Frail, you shall see my son Ben. Body o' me, he's the hopes of my family. I ha'n't seen him these three years. I warrant he's grown. Call him in, bid him make haste. I'm ready to cry for joy.

    Exit SERVANT.

MRS FRAIL: Now, Miss, you shall see your husband.

MISS PRUE [*aside to* MRS FRAIL]: Pish, he shall be none of my husband.

MRS FRAIL: Hush. Well he shan't, leave that to me. I'll beckon Mr Tattle to us.

ANGELICA: Won't you stay and see your brother?

        1. *Posed*: baffled.

VALENTINE: We are the twin stars, and cannot shine in one sphere; when he rises I must set. Besides, if I should stay, I don't know but my father in good nature may press one to the immediate signing the deed of conveyance of my estate, and I'll defer it as long as I can. Well, you'll come to a resolution.

ANGELICA: I can't. Resolution must come to me, or I shall never have one.

SCANDAL: Come, Valentine, I'll go with you; I've something in my head to communicate to you.

    Exit VALENTINE *and* SCANDAL.

SIR SAMPSON: What, is my son Valentine gone? What, is he sneaked off, and would not see his brother? There's an un-natural whelp! There's an ill-natured dog! What, were you here too, madam, and could not keep him? Could neither love, nor duty, nor natural affection oblige him? Odsbud, madam, have no more to say to him; he is not worth your consideration. The rogue has not a drachm of generous love about him. All interest, all interest. He's an undone scoundrel, and courts your estate. Body o' me, he does not care a doit[1] for your person.

ANGELICA: I'm pretty even with him, Sir Sampson; for if ever I could have liked anything in him, it should have been his estate too. But since that's gone, the bait's off, and the naked hook appears.

SIR SAMPSON: Odsbud, well spoken! And you are a wiser woman than I thought you were. For most young women nowadays are to be tempted with a naked hook.

ANGELICA: If I marry, Sir Sampson, I'm for a good estate with any man, and for any man with a good estate. Therefore if I were obliged to make a choice, I declare I'd rather have you than your son.

SIR SAMPSON: Faith and troth, you're a wise woman, and I'm glad to hear you say so. I was afraid you were in love with the reprobate. Odd, I was sorry for you with all my heart. Hang him, mungrel! Cast him off, you shall see the rogue shew himself, and make love to some desponding cadua[2]

    1. *Doit*: originally a Dutch coin of low value. Hence 'a jot'.
    2. *Cadua*: an elderly woman seeking courtship.

of fourscore for sustenance. Odd, I love to see a young spendthrift forced to cling to an old woman for support, like ivy round a dead oak, faith I do. I love to see 'em hug and cotton together, like down upon a thistle.

    Enter BEN LEGEND *and* SERVANT.

BEN: Where's father?

SERVANT: There, sir, his back's toward you.

SIR SAMPSON: My son Ben! Bless thee, my dear boy. Body o' me, thou art heartily welcome.

BEN: Thank you, father, and I'm glad to see you.

SIR SAMPSON: Odsbud, and I'm glad to see thee. Kiss me, boy, kiss me again and again, dear Ben. [*Kisses him.*]

BEN: So, so, enough, father. Mess, I'd rather kiss these gentlewomen.

SIR SAMPSON: And so thou shalt. Mrs Angelica, my son Ben.

BEN: Forsooth, an you please. [*Salutes her.*] Nay, mistress, I'm not for dropping anchor here. About ship, i'faith. [*Kisses* MRS FRAIL.] Nay, and you too, my little cock-boat. So! [*Kisses* MISS PRUE.]

TATTLE: Sir, you're welcome ashore.

BEN: Thank you, thank you, friend.

SIR SAMPSON: Thou hast been many a weary league, Ben, since I saw thee.

BEN: Ey, ey, been! Been far enough, an that be all. Well father, and how do all at home? How does brother Dick, and brother Val?

SIR SAMPSON: Dick? Body o' me, Dick has been dead these two years! I writ you word when you were at Legorne.

BEN: Mess, and that's true; marry I had forgot. Dick's dead, as you say. Well, and how? I have a many questions to ask you. Well, you be'nt married again, father, be you?

SIR SAMPSON. No, I intend you shall marry, Ben. I would not marry for thy sake.

BEN: Nay, what does that signify? An you marry again, why then, I'll go to sea again, so there's one for t'other, an that be all. Pray don't let me be your hindrance. E'en marry a God's name an the wind sit that way. As for my part, may-hap I have no mind to marry.

MRS FRAIL: That would be pity, such a handsome young gentleman.

BEN: Handsome! He, he, he! Nay forsooth, an you be for joking, I'll joke with you, for I love my jest, an the ship were sinking, as we sayn at sea. But I'll tell you why I don't much stand towards matrimony. I love to roam about from port to port, and from land to land. I could never abide to be port-bound as we call it. Now a man that is married has as it were, d'ye see, his feet in the bilboes,[1] and mayhap mayn't get 'em out again when he would.

SIR SAMPSON: Ben's a wag.

BEN: A man that is married, d'ye see, is no more like another man than a galley-slave is like one of us free sailors. He is chained to an oar all his life, and mayhap forced to tug a leaky vessel into the bargain.

SIR SAMPSON: A very wag, Ben's a very wag. Only a little rough, he wants a little polishing.

MRS FRAIL: Not at all. I like his humour mightily, it's plain and honest. I should like such a humour in a husband extremely.

BEN: Sayn you so forsooth? Marry and I should like such a handsome gentlewoman for a bed-fellow hugely. How say you, mistress, would you like going to sea? Mess, you're a tight vessel, and well rigged, an you were but as well manned.

MRS FRAIL: I should not doubt that, if you were master of me.

BEN: But I'll tell you one thing, an you come to sea in a high wind, or that, lady, you mayn't carry so much sail o'your head. Top and top-gallant, by the Mess.[2]

MRS FRAIL: No, why so?

BEN: Why an you do, you may run the risk to be overset, and then you'll carry your keels above water, he, he, he!

ANGELICA: I swear, Mr Benjamin is the veriest wag in nature, an absolute sea-wit.

SIR SAMPSON: Nay, Ben has parts, but as I told you before, they want a little polishing. You must not take anything ill, madam.

1. *Bilboes*: ships' irons.
2. *You mayn't ... Mess*: an allusion to the high hairdos of the day.

BEN: No, I hope the gentlewoman is not angry. I mean all in good part, for if I give a jest, I'll take a jest, and so forsooth you may be as free with me.

ANGELICA: I thank you, sir, I am not at all offended. But methinks, Sir Sampson, you should leave him alone with his mistress. Mr Tattle, we must not hinder lovers.

TATTLE [*aside to* MISS PRUE]: Well, Miss, I have your promise.

SIR SAMPSON: Body o' me, madam, you say true. Look you, Ben, this is your mistress. Come, Miss, you must not be shamefaced, we'll leave you together.

MISS PRUE: I can't abide to be left alone. Mayn't my cousin stay with me?

SIR SAMPSON: No, no. Come, let's away.

BEN: Look you, father, mayhap the young woman mayn't take a liking to me.

SIR SAMPSON: I warrant thee, boy. Come, come, we'll be gone. I'll venture that.

Exeunt all but BEN *and* MISS PRUE.

BEN: Come mistress, will you please to sit down? For an you stand a stern a that'n, we shall never grapple together. Come, I'll haul a chair. There, an you please to sit, I'll sit by you.

MISS PRUE: You need not sit so near one. If you have anything to say, I can hear you farther off, I an't deaf.

BEN: Why, that's true as you say, nor I an't dumb; I can be heard as far as another. I'll heave off to please you. [*Sits farther off.*] An we were a league asunder, I'd undertake to hold discourse with you, an 'twere not a main high wind indeed, and full in my teeth. Look you forsooth, I am as it were bound for the land of matrimony. 'Tis a voyage d'ye see that was none of my seeking. I was commanded by father, and if you like of it, mayhap I may steer into your harbour. How say you, mistress? The short of the thing is this, that if you like me, and I like you, we may chance to swing in a hammock together.

MISS PRUE: I don't know what to say to you, nor I don't care to speak with you at all.

BEN: No? I'm sorry for that. But pray, why are you so scornful?

MISS PRUE: As long as one must not speak one's mind, one had better not speak at all, I think, and truly I won't tell a lie for the matter.

BEN: Nay, you say true in that, it's but a folly to lie. For to speak one thing and to think just the contrary way is, as it were, to look one way and to row another. Now for my part d'ye see, I'm for carrying things above board. I'm not for keeping anything under hatches. So that if you ben't as willing as I, say so a God's name, there's no harm done. Mayhap you may be shamefac'd. Some maidens, thof they love a man well enough, yet they don't care to tell'n so to's face. If that's the case, why, silence gives consent.

MISS PRUE: But I'm sure it is not so, for I'll speak sooner than you should believe that. And I'll speak truth, tho' one should always tell a lie to a man. And I don't care, let my father do what he will. I'm too big to be whipped, so I'll tell you plainly, I don't like you, nor love you at all, nor never will, that's more. So, there's your answer for you, and don't trouble me no more, you ugly thing.

BEN: Look you, young woman. You may learn to give good words, however. I spoke you fair, d'ye see, and civil. As for your love or your liking, I don't value it of a rope's end. And mayhap I like you as little as you do me. What I said was in obedience to father. Gad, I fear a whipping no more than you do. But I tell you one thing, if you should give such language at sea, you'd have a cat o' nine tails laid 'cross your shoulders. Flesh, who are you? You heard t'other handsome young woman speak civilly to me, of her own accord. Whatever you think of yourself, Gad I don't think you are any more to compare to her than a can of small beer to a bowl of punch.

MISS PRUE: Well, and there's a handsome gentleman, and a fine gentleman, and a sweet gentleman, that was here that loves me, and I love him; and if he sees you speak to me any more, he'll thrash your jacket for you, he will, you great sea-calf.

BEN: What, do you mean that fair-weather spark that was

here just now? Will he thrash my jacket? Let'n, let'n. But an he comes near me, mayhap I may giv'n a salt eel for's supper for all that. What does father mean to leave me alone as soon as I come home with such a dirty dowdy? Sea-calf! I an't calf enough to lick your chalked face, you cheese-curd you. Marry thee! Ouns! I'll marry a Lapland witch as soon, and live upon selling of contrary winds, and wracked vessels.

MISS PRUE: I won't be called names, nor I won't be abused thus, so I won't. If I were a man – [*cries*] – you durst not talk at this rate. No you durst not, you stinking tar-barrel.

Enter MRS FORESIGHT *and* MRS FRAIL.

MRS FORESIGHT: They have quarrelled just as we could wish.

BEN: Tar-barrel? Let your sweetheart there call me so, if he'll take your part, your Tom Essence,[1] and I'll say something to him. Gad I'll lace his musk-doublet for him! I'll make him stink! He shall smell more like a weasel than a civet cat afore I ha' done with 'en.

MRS FORESIGHT: Bless me, what's the matter, Miss? What, does she cry? Mr Benjamin, what have you done to her?

BEN: Let her cry: the more she cries, the less she'll – she has been gathering foul weather in her mouth, and now it rains out at her eyes.

MRS FORESIGHT: Come, Miss, come along with me, and tell me, poor child.

MRS FRAIL: Lord, what shall we do, there's my brother Foresight, and Sir Sampson coming. Sister, do you take Miss down into the parlour, and I'll carry Mr Benjamin into my chamber, for they must not know that they are fall'n out. Come, sir, will you venture yourself with me? [*Looks kindly on him.*]

BEN: Venture? Mess, and that I will, tho' 'twere to sea in a storm.

Exeunt.

Enter SIR SAMPSON *and* FORESIGHT.

---

1. *Tom Essence*: the eponymous hero of a comedy by Thomas Rawlins (1676).

SIR SAMPSON: I left 'em together here. What, are they gone? Ben's a brisk boy. He has got her into a corner. Father's own son, faith, he'll touzle her, and mouzle her. The rogue's sharp set, coming from sea, if he should not stay for saying grace, old Foresight, but fall to without the help of a parson, ha? Odd, if he should I could not be angry with him. 'Twould be but like me, a chip of the old block. Ha! Thou'rt melancholy, old Prognostication, as melancholy as if thou hadst spilt the salt, or pared thy nails of a Sunday. Come, cheer up, look about thee. Look up, old star-gazer. Now is he poring upon the ground for a crooked pin, or an old horse-nail, with the head towards him.

FORESIGHT: Sir Sampson, we'll have the wedding tomorrow morning.

SIR SAMPSON: With all my heart.

FORESIGHT: At ten a clock, punctually at ten.

SIR SAMPSON: To a minute, to a second. Thou shall set thy watch, and the bridegroom shall observe its motions. They shall be married to a minute, go to bed to a minute, and when the alarm strikes, they shall keep time like the figures of St Dunstan's clock, and consummatum est shall ring all over the parish.

Enter SCANDAL.

SCANDAL: Sir Sampson, sad news.

FORESIGHT: Bless us!

SIR SAMPSON: Why, what's the matter?

SCANDAL: Can't you guess at what ought to afflict you and him, and all of us, more than anything else?

SIR SAMPSON: Body o' me, I don't know any universal grievance but a new tax, and the loss of the Canary Fleet,[1] without popery should be landed in the West, or the French fleet were at anchor at Blackwall.

SCANDAL: No. Undoubtedly Mr Foresight knew all this, and might have prevented it.

FORESIGHT: 'Tis no earthquake!

SCANDAL: No, not yet, nor whirlwind. But we don't know

1. *Canary Fleet*: Lord Russell, First Lord of the Admiralty, was seeking French ships along the coast of Spain in the summer of 1694 to engage them in battle.

what it may come to. But it has had a consequence already that touches us all.

SIR SAMPSON: Why, body o' me, out with't.

SCANDAL: Something has appeared to your son Valentine. He's gone to bed upon't, and very ill. He speaks little, yet says he has a world to say. Asks for his father and the wise Foresight; talks of Raymond Lully, and the ghost of Lilly.[1] He has secrets to impart, I suppose, to you two. I can get nothing out of him but sighs. He desires he may see you in the morning, but would not be disturbed tonight, because he has some business to do in a dream.

SIR SAMPSON: Hoity toity, what have I to do with his dreams or his divination? Body o' me, this is a trick to defer signing the conveyance. I warrant the devil will tell him in a dream that he must not part with his estate. But I'll bring him a parson to tell him that the devil's a liar. Or if that won't do, I'll bring a lawyer that shall out-lie the devil. And so I'll try whether my blackguard or his shall get the better of the day. [*Exit.*]

SCANDAL: Alas, Mr Foresight, I'm afraid all is not right. You are a wise man, and a conscientious man, a searcher into obscurity and futurity, and if you commit an error, it is with a great deal of consideration, and discretion, and caution.

FORESIGHT: Ah, good Mr Scandal –

SCANDAL: Nay, nay, 'tis manifest; I do not flatter you. But Sir Sampson is hasty, very hasty. I'm afraid he is not scrupulous enough, Mr Foresight. He has been wicked, and heaven grant he may mean well in his affair with you. But my mind gives me, these things cannot be wholly insignificant. You are wise, and should not be overreached, methinks you should not –

FORESIGHT: Alas, Mr Scandal – Humanum est errare.

SCANDAL: You say true, man will err, mere man will err; but you are something more. There have been wise men, but they were such as you, men who consulted the stars, and were observers of omens. Solomon was wise, but how?

1. *Raymond Lully ... ghost of Lilly*: Ramon Lull, the medieval philosopher, and William Lilly (d. 1681) were both astrologers.

By his judgement in astrology. So says Pineda[1] in his third book and eighth chapter.

FORESIGHT: You are learned, Mr Scandal.

SCANDAL: A trifler, but a lover of art. And the wise men of the East owed their instruction to a star, which is rightly observed by Gregory the Great in favour of astrology. And Albertus Magnus makes it the most valuable science, because, says he, it teaches us to consider the causation of causes in the causes of things.

FORESIGHT: I protest I honour you, Mr Scandal. I did not think you had been read in these matters. Few young men are inclined –

SCANDAL: I thank my stars that have inclined me. But I fear this marriage and making over this estate, this transferring of a rightful inheritance, will bring judgements upon us. I prophesy it, and I would not have the fate of Cassandra, not to be believed. Valentine is disturbed; what can be the cause of that? And Sir Sampson is hurried on by an unusual violence. I fear he does not act wholly from himself; methinks he does not look as he used to do.

FORESIGHT: He was always of an impetuous nature. But as to this marriage, I have consulted the stars;[2] and all appearances are prosperous.

SCANDAL: Come, come, Mr Foresight, let not the prospect of worldly lucre carry you beyond your judgement, nor against your conscience. You are not satisfied that you act justly.

FORESIGHT: How?

SCANDAL: You are not satisfied, I say. I am loath to discourage you. But it is palpable that you are not satisfied.

FORESIGHT: How does it appear, Mr Scandal? I think I am very well satisfied.

SCANDAL: Either you suffer yourself to deceive yourself, or you do not know yourself.

FORESIGHT: Pray explain yourself.

SCANDAL: Do you sleep well o'nights?

FORESIGHT: Very well.

1. *Pineda*: a Spanish savant (1558–1637).
2. *Stars*: Qq and W 'science'.

SCANDAL: Are you certain? You do not look so.

FORESIGHT: I am in health, I think.

SCANDAL: So was Valentine this morning, and looked just so.

FORESIGHT: How? Am I altered any way? I don't perceive it.

SCANDAL: That may be, but your beard is longer than it was two hours ago.

FORESIGHT: Indeed? Bless me!

    Enter MRS FORESIGHT.

MRS FORESIGHT: Husband, will you go to bed? It's ten a clock. Mr Scandal, your servant.

SCANDAL [*aside*]: Pox on her, she has interrupted my design. But I must work her into the project. [*Aloud*] You keep early hours, madam.

MRS FORESIGHT: Mr Foresight is punctual, we sit up after him.

FORESIGHT: My dear, pray lend me your glass, your little looking-glass.

SCANDAL: Pray lend it him, madam. I'll tell you the reason. [*She gives him the glass*: SCANDAL *and she whisper*.] My passion for you is grown so violent that I am no longer master of my self. I was interrupted in the morning, when you had charity enough to give me your attention, and I had hopes of finding another opportunity of explaining myself to you, but was disappointed all this day, and the uneasiness that has attended me ever since brings me now hither at this unseasonable hour.

MRS FORESIGHT: Was there ever such impudence? To make love to me before my husband's face! I'll swear I'll tell him.

SCANDAL: Do, I'll die a martyr rather than disclaim my passion. But come a little farther this way, and I'll tell you what project I had to get him out of the way, that I might have an opportunity of waiting upon you. [*Whispers.*]

FORESIGHT [*looking in the glass*]: I do not see any revolution here. Methinks I look with a serene and benign aspect – pale, a little pale – but the roses of these cheeks have been gathered many years. Ha! I do not like that suddain flushing. Gone already! Hem, hem, hem! Faintish. My heart is

pretty good, yet it beats; and my pulses? Ha! I have none.
Mercy on me! Hum. Yes, here they are. Gallop, gallop,
gallop, gallop, gallop, gallop. Hey, whither will they hurry
me? Now they're gone again, and now I'm faint again, and
pale again, and hem! and my – hem? – breath, hem! –
grows short. Hem, hem! He, he, hem!

SCANDAL [*aside to* MRS FORESIGHT]: It takes. Pursue it in
the name of love and pleasure.

MRS FORESIGHT: How do you do, Mr Foresight?

FORESIGHT: Hum, not so well as I thought I was. Lend me
your hand.

SCANDAL: Look you there now. Your lady says your sleep
has been unquiet of late.

FORESIGHT: Very likely.

MRS FORESIGHT: Oh, mighty restless, but I was afraid to
tell him so. He has been subject to talking and starting.

SCANDAL: And did not use to be so?

MRS FORESIGHT: Never, never, till within these three nights.
I cannot say that he has once broken my rest since we have
been married.

FORESIGHT: I will go to bed.

SCANDAL: Do so, Mr Foresight, and say your prayers. He
looks better than he did.

MRS FORESIGHT [*calls*]: Nurse, nurse!

FORESIGHT: Do you think so, Mr Scandal?

SCANDAL: Yes, yes, I hope this will be gone by morning,
taking it in time.

FORESIGHT: I hope so.

Enter NURSE.

MRS FORESIGHT: Nurse, your master is not well; put him to
bed.

SCANDAL: I hope you will be able to see Valentine in the
morning. You had best take a little diacodion[1] and cow-
slip water, and lie upon your back. Maybe you may dream.

FORESIGHT: I thank you, Mr Scandal, I will. Nurse, let me
have a watch-light, and lay the *Crumbs of Comfort*[2] by me.

1. *Diacodion*: a narcotic made from poppies.
2. *Crumbs of Comfort*: an early seventeenth-century devotional manual
compiled by Michael Sparks.

NURSE: Yes, sir.

FORESIGHT: And – Hem, hem! I am very faint.

SCANDAL: No, no, you look much better.

FORESIGHT: Do I? And d'ye hear, bring me, let me see, within a quarter of twelve – hem – he, hem! – just upon the turning of the tide, bring me the urinal. And I hope neither the lord of my ascendants nor the moon will be combust,[1] and then I may do well.

SCANDAL: I hope so. Leave that to me; I will erect a scheme; and I hope I shall find both Sol and Venus in the sixth house.

FORESIGHT: I thank you, Mr Scandal. Indeed, that would be a great comfort to me. Hem, hem! Good night. [*Exit*.]

SCANDAL: Good night, good Mr Foresight. And I hope Mars and Venus will be in conjunction while your wife and I are together.

MRS FORESIGHT: Well, and what use do you hope to make of this project? You don't think that you are ever like to succeed in your design upon me?

SCANDAL: Yes, faith, I do. I have a better opinion both of you and myself than to despair.

MRS FORESIGHT: Did you ever hear such a toad? Hark'ee devil, do you think any woman honest?

SCANDAL: Yes, several, very honest. They'll cheat a little at cards sometimes, but that's nothing.

MRS FORESIGHT: Pshaw! but virtuous, I mean?

SCANDAL: Yes, faith, I believe some women are virtuous too; but 'tis as I believe some men are valiant, thro' fear. For why should a man court danger, or a woman shun pleasure?

MRS FORESIGHT: O monstrous! What are conscience and honour?

SCANDAL: Why, honour is a public enemy, and conscience a domestic thief; and he that would secure his pleasure must pay a tribute to one and go halves with the other. As for honour, that you have secured, for you have purchased a perpetual opportunity for pleasure.

1. *Combust*: term applied to planet without influence (within 8½ degrees of the sun).

MRS FORESIGHT: An opportunity for pleasure?

SCANDAL: Ay, your husband, a husband is an opportunity for pleasure. So you have taken care of honour, and 'tis the least I can do to take care of conscience.

MRS FORESIGHT: And so you think we are free for one another?

SCANDAL: Yes faith, I think so. I love to speak my mind.

MRS FORESIGHT: Why then, I'll speak my mind. Now as to this affair between you and me: Here you make love to me. Why, I'll confess it does not displease me. Your person is well enough and your understanding is not amiss.

SCANDAL: I have no great opinion of myself, yet I think I'm neither deformed nor a fool.

MRS FORESIGHT: But you have a villainous character. You are a libertine in speech as well as practice.

SCANDAL: Come, I know what you would say. You think it more dangerous to be seen in conversation with me than to allow some other men the last favour. You mistake; the liberty I take in talking is purely affected for the service of your sex. He that first cries out 'stop thief' is often he that has stolen the treasure. I am a juggler, that act by confederacy; and if you please, we'll put a trick upon the world.

MRS FORESIGHT: Ay, but you are such an universal juggler that I'm afraid you have a great many confederates.

SCANDAL: Faith, I'm sound.

MRS FORESIGHT: O fie, I'll swear you're impudent.

SCANDAL: I'll swear you're handsome.

MRS FORESIGHT: Pish, you'd tell me so, tho' you did not think so.

SCANDAL: And you'd think so, tho' I should not tell you so. And now I think we know one another pretty well.

MRS FORESIGHT: O Lord, who's here?

Enter MRS FRAIL *and* BEN.

BEN: Mess, I love to speak my mind. Father has nothing to do with me. Nay, I can't say that neither, he has something to do with me. But what does that signify? If so be that I ben't minded to be steered by him, 'tis as thof he should drive against wind and tide.

MRS FRAIL: Ay, but my dear, we must keep it secret till the

estate be settled. For, you know, marrying without an estate is like sailing in a ship without ballast.

BEN: He, he, he! Why, that's true. Just so for all the world it
is indeed, as like as two cable ropes.

MRS FRAIL: And tho' I have a good portion, you know one
would not venture all in one bottom.

BEN: Why, that's true again, for mayhap one bottom may
spring a leak. You have hit it indeed, Mess, you've nick'd
the channel.

MRS FRAIL: Well, but if you should forsake me after all,
you'd break my heart.

BEN: Break your heart? I'd rather the *Mary-gold* should break
her cable in a storm, as well as I love her. Flesh, you don't
think I'm false-hearted, like a land-man. A sailor will be
honest, thof mayhap he has never a penny of money in his
pocket. Mayhap I may not have so fair a face as a citizen
or a courtier, but for all that I've as good blood in my veins,
and a heart as sound as a biscuit.

MRS FRAIL: And will you love me always?

BEN: Nay, an I love once, I'll stick like pitch, I'll tell you that.
Come, I'll sing you a song of a sailor.

MRS FRAIL: Hold, there's my sister. I'll call her to hear it.

MRS FORESIGHT: Well, I won't go to bed to my husband
tonight, because I'll retire to my own chamber and think
of what you have said.

SCANDAL: Well, you'll give me leave to wait upon you to
your chamber-door and leave you my last instructions?

MRS FORESIGHT: Hold, here's my sister coming toward us.

MRS FRAIL: If it won't interrupt you, I'll entertain you
with a song.

BEN: The song was made upon one of our ship's crew's wife;
our boatswain made the song. Mayhap you may know her,
sir. Before she was married, she was called buxom Joan
of Deptford.

SCANDAL: I have heard of her.

BEN *sings*:

I

A soldier and a sailor,
A tinker, and a tailor,

Had once a doubtful strife, sir,
To make a maid a wife, sir,
  Whose name was buxom Joan.
For now the time was ended,
When she no more intended,
To lick her lips at men, sir,
And gnaw the sheets in vain, sir,
  And lie o'nights alone.

2

The soldier swore like thunder,
He loved her more than plunder,
And shewed her many a scar, sir,
That he had brought from far, sir,
  With fighting for her sake.
The tailor thought to please her,
With off'ring her his measure.
The tinker, too, with mettle,
Said he could mend her kettle,
  And stop up ev'ry leak.

3

But while these three were prating,
The sailor slily waiting,
Thought if it came about, sir,
That they should all fall out, sir:
  He then might play his part.
And just e'en as he meant, sir,
To loggerheads they went, sir,
And then he let fly at her,
A shot 'twixt wind and water,
  That won this fair maid's heart.

BEN: If some of our crew that came to see me are not gone,
you shall see that we sailors can dance sometimes, as well
as other folks. [*Whistles.*] I warrant that brings 'em, an' they
be within hearing.
  Enter SEAMEN.
Oh here they be, and fiddles along with 'em. Come my lads,
let's have a round, and I'll make one.

Dance.

We're merry folk, we sailors, we han't much to care for. Thus we live at sea; eat biscuit, and drink flip,[1] put on a clean shirt once a quarter, come home and lie with our landladies once a year, get rid of a little money, and then put off with the next fair wind. How d'ye like us?

MRS FRAIL: Oh, you are the happiest, merriest men alive.

MRS FORESIGHT: We're beholding to Mr Benjamin for this entertainment. I believe it's late.

BEN: Why, forsooth, an you think so, you had best go to bed. For my part, I mean to toss a can and remember my sweetheart afore I turn in. Mayhap I may dream of her.

MRS FORESIGHT: Mr Scandal, you had best go to bed and dream too.

SCANDAL: Why, faith, I have a good lively imagination, and can dream as much to the purpose as another, if I set about it. But dreaming is the poor retreat of a lazy, hopeless, and imperfect lover. 'Tis the last glimpse of love to worn-out sinners, and the faint dawning of a bliss to wishing girls and growing boys.

> There's nought but willing, waking love that can
> Make blest the ripened maid, and finished man.

Exeunt.

1. *Flip*: a sweetened mixture of beer and spirit.

THE END OF THE THIRD ACT

Act Four

VALENTINE's *lodging*.
Enter SCANDAL *and* JEREMY.

SCANDAL: Well, is your master ready? Does he look madly and talk madly?

JEREMY: Yes, sir, you need make no great doubt of that. He that was so near turning poet yesterday morning can't be much to seek in playing the madman today.

SCANDAL: Would he have Angelica acquainted with the reason of his design?

JEREMY: No sir, not yet. He has a mind to try whether his playing the madman won't make her play the fool and fall in love with him, or at least own that she has loved him all this while, and concealed it.

SCANDAL: I saw her take coach just now with her maid, and think I heard her bid the coachman drive hither.

JEREMY: Like enough, sir, for I told her maid this morning my master was run stark mad only for love of her mistress. I hear a coach stop; if it should be she, sir, I believe he would not see her till he hears how she takes it.

SCANDAL: Well, I'll try her. 'Tis she, here she comes.

Enter ANGELICA *with* JENNY.

ANGELICA: Mr Scandal, I suppose you don't think it a novelty to see a woman visit a man at his own lodgings in a morning?

SCANDAL: Not upon a kind occasion, madam. But when a lady comes tyrannically to insult a ruined lover, and make manifest the cruel triumphs of her beauty, the barbarity of it something surprises me.

ANGELICA: I don't like raillery from a serious face. Pray tell me what is the matter.

JEREMY: No strange matter, madam; my master's mad, that's all. I suppose your ladyship has thought him so a great while?

ANGELICA: How d'you mean, mad?

JEREMY: Why faith, madam, he's mad for want of his wits, just as he was (poor) for want of money. His head is e'en as light as his pockets, and anybody that has a mind to a bad bargain can't do better than to beg him for his estate.

ANGELICA: If you speak truth, your endeavouring at wit is very unseasonable.

SCANDAL [aside]: She's concerned, and loves him.

ANGELICA: Mr Scandal, you can't think me guilty of so much inhumanity as not to be concerned for a man I must own myself obliged to. Pray tell me truth.

SCANDAL: Faith, madam, I wish telling a lie would mend the matter. But this is no new effect of an unsuccessful passion.

ANGELICA [aside]: I know not what to think – yet I should be vexed to have a trick put upon me. [Aloud] May I not see him?

SCANDAL: I'm afraid the physician is not willing you should see him yet. Jeremy, go in and enquire.

Exit JEREMY.

ANGELICA: Ha! I saw him wink and smile – I fancy 'tis a trick. I'll try. I would disguise to all the world a failing, which I must own to you. I fear my happiness depends upon the recovery of Valentine. Therefore I conjure you as you are his friend, and as you have compassion upon one fearful of affliction, to tell me what I am to hope for. I cannot speak, but you may tell me. Tell me, for you know what I would ask.

SCANDAL [aside]: So, this is pretty plain. [Aloud] Be not too much concerned, madam; I hope his condition is not desperate. An acknowledgement of love from you, perhaps, may work a cure, as the fear of your aversion occasioned his distemper.

ANGELICA [aside]: Say you so? Nay, then I'm convinced, and if I don't play trick for trick, may I never taste the pleasure of revenge. [Aloud] Acknowledgement of love! I find you have mistaken my compassion, and think me guilty of a weakness I am a stranger to. But I have too much sincerity to deceive you, and too much charity to suffer him to be deluded with vain hopes. Good nature and humanity oblige me to be concerned for him, but to love is neither in my power nor inclination, and if he can't be cured without I suck the poison from his wounds, I'm afraid he won't recover his senses till I lose mine.

SCANDAL: Hey, brave woman, i'faith. Won't you see him, then, if he desire it?

ANGELICA: What signify a madman's desires? Besides, 'twould make me uneasy. If I don't see him, perhaps my concern for him may lessen. If I forget him, 'tis no more than he has done by himself; and now the surprise is over, methinks I am not half so sorry for him as I was.

SCANDAL: So, faith, good nature works apace; you were confessing just now an obligation to his love.

ANGELICA: But I have considered that passions are unreasonable and involuntary. If he loves, he can't help it, and if I don't love, I can't help it; no more than he can help his being a man, or I my being a woman; or no more than I can help my want of inclination to stay longer here. Come, Jenny.

Exit ANGELICA *and* JENNY.

SCANDAL: Humh! An admirable composition, faith, this same womankind.

Enter JEREMY.

JEREMY. What, is she gone, sir?

SCANDAL: Gone? Why, she was never here, nor anywhere else, nor I don't know her if I see her, nor you neither.

JEREMY: Good lack! What's the matter now? Are any more of us to be mad! Why, sir, my master longs to see her, and is almost mad in good earnest with the joyful news of her being here.

SCANDAL: We are all under a mistake. Ask no questions, for I can't resolve you; but I'll inform your master. In the meantime, if our project succeed no better with his father than it does with his mistress, he may descend from his exaltation of madness into the road of commonsense and be content only to be made a fool with other reasonable people. I hear Sir Sampson. You know your cue; I'll to your master. [*Exit.*]

Enter SIR SAMPSON LEGEND *with a* LAWYER.

SIR SAMPSON: D'ye see, Mr Buckram, here's the paper signed with his own hand.

BUCKRAM: Good, sir. And the conveyance is ready drawn in this box, if he be ready to sign and seal.

SIR SAMPSON: Ready? Body o' me, he must be ready. His sham sickness shan't excuse him. Oh, here's his scoundrel. Sirrah, where's your master?

JEREMY: Ah, sir, he's quite gone.

SIR SAMPSON: Gone! What, he is not dead?

JEREMY: No, sir, not dead.

SIR SAMPSON: What, is he gone out of town, run away, ha? Has he tricked me? Speak, varlet.

JEREMY: No, no, sir, he's safe enough, sir, an he were but as sound, poor gentleman. He is indeed here, sir, and not here, sir.

SIR SAMPSON: Hey-day, rascal, do you banter me? Sirrah, d'ye banter me? Speak, sirrah, where is he, for I will find him.

JEREMY: Would you could sir, for he has lost himself. Indeed, sir, I have a'most broke my heart about him. I can't refrain tears when I think of him, sir. I'm as melancholy for him as a passing-bell, sir, or a horse in a pound.

SIR SAMPSON: A pox confound your similitudes, sir. Speak to be understood, and tell me in plain terms what the matter is with him, or I'll crack your fool's skull.

JEREMY: Ah, you've hit it, sir. That's the matter with him, sir. His skull's cracked, poor gentleman; he's stark mad, sir.

SIR SAMPSON: Mad!

BUCKRAM: What, is he non compos?

JEREMY: Quite non compos, sir.

BUCKRAM: Why, then all's obliterated, Sir Sampson. If he be non compos mentis, his act and deed will be of no effect, it is not good in law.

SIR SAMPSON. Ouns, I won't believe it. Let me see him, sir. Mad! I'll make him find his senses.

JEREMY: Mr Scandal is with him, sir; I'll knock at the door.

   Goes to the scene,[1] *which opens and discovers* VALENTINE *upon a couch disorderly dressed,* SCANDAL *by him.*

1. *Scene*: inner stage.

SIR SAMPSON: How now, what's here to do?

VALENTINE [*starting*]: Ha! Who's that?

SCANDAL: For Heav'ns sake softly, sir, and gently. Don't provoke him.

VALENTINE: Answer me. Who is that? And that?

SIR SAMPSON: Gads-bobs, does he not know me? Is he mischievous? I'll speak gently. Val, Val, dost thou not know me, boy? Not know thy own father, Val? I am thy own father, and this is honest Brief Buckram, the lawyer.

VALENTINE: It may be so. I did not know you. The world is full. There are people that we do know, and people that we do not know; and yet the sun shines upon all alike. There are fathers that have many children, and there are children that have many fathers. 'Tis strange! But I am truth, and come to give the world the lie.

SIR SAMPSON: Body o' me, I know not what to say to him.

VALENTINE: Why does that lawyer wear black? Does he carry his conscience without-side? Lawyer, what art thou? Dost thou know me?

BUCKRAM: O Lord, what must I say? Yes, sir.

VALENTINE: Thou liest, for I am truth. 'Tis hard, I cannot get a livelihood amongst you. I have been sworn out of Westminster Hall[1] the first day of every term. Let me see – no matter how long – But I'll tell you one thing; it's a question that would puzzle an arithmetician, if you should ask him, whether the Bible saves more souls in Westminster Abbey, or damns more in Westminster Hall. For my part, I am truth, and can't tell; I have very few acquaintance.

SIR SAMPSON: Body o' me, he talks sensibly in his madness. Has he no intervals?

JEREMY: Very short, sir.

BUCKRAM: Sir, I can do you no service while he's in this condition. Here's your paper, sir. He may do me a mischief if I stay. The conveyance is ready, sir, if he recover his senses. [*Exit.*]

SIR SAMPSON: Hold, hold, don't you go yet.

SCANDAL: You'd better let him go, sir, and send for him if

1. *Westminster Hall*: the law-courts at this period.

there be occasion, for I fancy his presence provokes him more.

VALENTINE: Is the lawyer gone? 'Tis well, then we may drink about without going together by the ears.[1] Heigh ho! What a clock is't? My father here? Your blessing, sir.

SIR SAMPSON: He recovers. Bless thee, Val. How dost thou do, boy?

VALENTINE: Thank you, sir, pretty well. I have been a little out of order. Won't you please to sit, sir?

SIR SAMPSON: Ay, boy. Come, thou shalt sit down by me.

VALENTINE: Sir, 'tis my duty to wait.

SIR SAMPSON: No, no; come, come, sit you down, honest Val. How dost thou do? Let me feel thy pulse. Oh, pretty well now, Val. Body o' me, I was sorry to see thee indisposed. But I'm glad thou'rt better, honest Val.

VALENTINE: I thank you, sir.

SCANDAL [aside]: Miracle! the monster grows loving.

SIR SAMPSON: Let me feel thy hand again, Val. It does not shake. I believe thou canst write, Val. Ha, boy? Thou can'st write thy name, Val? [In whisper to JEREMY] Jeremy, step and overtake Mr Buckram, bid him make haste back with the conveyance. Quick, quick!

[Exit JEREMY.]

SCANDAL [aside]: That ever I should suspect such a heathen of any remorse!

SAMPSON: Dost thou know this paper, Val? I know thou'rt honest, and wilt perform articles.

Shews him the paper, but holds it out of his reach.

VALENTINE: Pray let me see it, sir. You hold it so far off that I can't tell whether I know it or no.

SIR SAMPSON: See it, boy? Ay, ay, why thou dost see it. 'Tis thy own hand, Val. Why let me see, I can read it as plain as can be. Look you here [reads]: The condition of this obligation – Look you, as plain as can be, so it begins. And then at the bottom, As witness my hand, Valentine Legend, in great letters. Why, 'tis as plain as the nose in one's face. What, are my eyes better than thine? I believe I can read it farther off yet. Let me see. [Stretches his arm as far as he can.]

1. Going . . . ears: quarrelling.

VALENTINE: Will you please to let me hold it, sir?

SIR SAMPSON: Let thee hold it, say'st thou? Ay, with all my heart. What matter is it who holds it? What need anybody hold it? I'll put it up in my pocket, Val. And then nobody need hold it. [*Puts the paper in his pocket.*] There, Val: it's safe enough, boy. But thou shalt have it as soon as thou hast set thy hand to another paper, little Val.

   Re-enter JEREMY *with* BUCKRAM.

VALENTINE: What, is my bad genius here again? Oh no, 'tis the lawyer with an itching palm, and he's come to be scratched. My nails are not long enough. Let me have a pair of red-hot tongs quickly, quickly, and you shall see me act St Dunstan, and lead the devil by the nose.

BUCKRAM. O Lord, let me be gone; I'll not venture myself with a madman. [*Exit* BUCKRAM.]

VALENTINE: Ha, ha, ha! you need not run so fast, honesty will not overtake you. Ha, ha, ha! The rogue found me out to be in forma pauperis presently.

SIR SAMPSON: Ouns! What a vexation is here! I know not what to do or say, nor which way to go.

VALENTINE: Who's that, that's out of his way? I am truth, and can set him right. Hearkee, friend, the straight road is the worst way you can go. He that follows his nose always will very often be led into a stink. Probatum est. But what are you for? Religion or politics? There's a couple of topics for you, no more like one another than oil and vinegar. And yet those two beaten together by a state-cook[1] make sauce for the whole nation.

SIR SAMPSON: What the devil had I to do, ever to beget sons! Why did I ever marry?

VALENTINE: Because thou wert a monster, old boy. The two greatest monsters in the world are a man and a woman. What's thy opinion?

SIR SAMPSON: Why, my opinion is that those two monsters joined together make yet a greater, that's a man and his wife.

VALENTINE: Aha! Old truepenny, say'st thou so? thou hast nick'd it. But it's wonderful strange, Jeremy!

   1. *State-cook*: politician.

JEREMY: What is, sir?

VALENTINE: That grey hairs should cover a green head –
and I make a fool of my father.

Enter FORESIGHT, MRS FORESIGHT, *and* FRAIL.

VALENTINE: What's here! Erra Pater?[1] or a bearded sybil?
If prophecy comes, truth must give place. [*Exit with*
JEREMY.]

FORESIGHT: What says he? What, did he prophesy? Ha, Sir
Sampson, bless us! How are we?

SIR SAMPSON: Are we? A pox o'your prognostication. Why,
we are fools as we use to be. Ouns, that you could not foresee that the moon would predominate; and my son be mad.
– Where's your oppositions, your trines, and your quadrates? What did your Cardan[2] and your Ptolomee tell you?
Your Messahalah and your Longomontanus,[3] your har-
mony of chiromancy with astrology? Ah! pox on't, that I
that know the world, and men and manners, that don't be-
believe a syllable in the sky and stars, and sun and almanacs,
and trash, should be directed by a dreamer, an omen-hunter,
and defer business in expectation of a lucky hour. When,
body o' me, there never was a lucky hour after the first
opportunity. [*Exit* SIR SAMPSON.]

FORESIGHT: Ah, Sir Sampson, heaven help your head. This
is none of your lucky hour; nemo omnibus horis sapit.[4]
What, is he gone, and in contempt of science? Ill stars and
unconverted ignorance attend him!

SCANDAL: You must excuse his passion, Mr Foresight, for
he has been heartily vexed. His son is non compos mentis,
and thereby incapable of making any conveyance in law, so
that all his measures are disappointed.

FORESIGHT: Ha! say you so?

MRS FRAIL [*aside to* MRS FORESIGHT]: What, has my sea-
lover lost his anchor of hope then?

1. *Erra Pater*: a fabulous astrologer whose name figured on almanac
titles.

2. *Cardan*: Italian physician, mathematician and occultist (1501–76).

3. *Longomontanus*: Christian Langborg (1562–1647), Danish astronomer,
for some time an assistant to Tycho Brahe.

4. *Nemo . . . sapit*: no one is wise at all hours. An abbreviated quotation
from Pliny, *Historia Naturalis*, VII, 41.

MRS FORESIGHT: Oh, sister, what will you do with him?

MRS FRAIL: Do with him? Send him to sea again in the next foul weather. He's used to an inconstant element, and won't be surprised to see the tide turned.

FORESIGHT [*considers*]: Wherein was I mistaken, not to foresee this?

SCANDAL [*aside to* MRS FORESIGHT]: Madam, you and I can tell him something else that he did not foresee, and more particularly relating to his own fortune.

MRS FORESIGHT: What do you mean? I don't understand you.

SCANDAL: Hush, softly. The pleasures of last night, my dear, too considerable to be forgot so soon.

MRS FORESIGHT: Last night! And what would your impudence infer from last night? Last night was like the night before, I think.

SCANDAL: 'S'death, do you make no difference between me and your husband?

MRS FORESIGHT: Not much; he's superstitious, and you are mad, in my opinion.

SCANDAL: You make me mad. You are not serious. Pray recollect yourself.

MRS FORESIGHT: Oh, yes, now I remember. You were very impertinent and impudent, and would have come to bed with me.

SCANDAL: And did not?

MRS FORESIGHT: Did not! With that face can you ask the question?

SCANDAL (*aside*): This I have heard of before, but never believed. I have been told she had that admirable quality of forgetting to a man's face in the morning that she had lain with him all night, and denying favours with more impudence than she could grant 'em. (*Aloud*) Madam, I'm your humble servant, and honour you. You look pretty well, Mr Foresight. How did you rest last night?

FORESIGHT: Truly Mr Scandal, I was so taken up with broken dreams and distracted visions that I remember little.

SCANDAL: 'Twas a very forgetting night. But would you

not talk with Valentine? Perhaps you may understand him. I'm apt to believe there is something mysterious in his discourses, and sometimes rather think him inspired than mad.

FORESIGHT: You speak with singular good judgement, Mr Scandal, truly. I am inclining to your Turkish opinion in this matter, and do reverence a man whom the vulgar think mad. Let us go in to him.

MRS FRAIL: Sister, do you stay with them; I'll find out my lover and give him his discharge, and come to you. O'my conscience, here he comes.

Exeunt FORESIGHT, MRS FORESIGHT *and* SCANDAL.
Enter BEN.

BEN: All mad, I think. Flesh, I believe all the calentures[1] of the sea are come ashore, for my part.

MRS FRAIL: Mr Benjamin in choler?

BEN: No, I'm pleased well enough, now I have found you. Mess, I've had such a hurricane upon your account yonder.

MRS FRAIL. My account? Pray, what's the matter?

BEN: Why, father came and found me squabbling with yon chitty-faced thing, as he would have me marry, so he asked what was the matter. He asked in a surly sort of a way. It seems brother Val is gone mad, and so that put'n into a passion; but what, did I know that, what's that to me? So he asked in a surly sort of manner, and gad, I answered 'n as surlily. What thof he be my father, I an't bound prentice to 'n. So, faith I told 'n in plain terms, if I were minded to marry, I'd marry to please myself, not him. And for the young woman that he provided for me, I thought it more fitting for her to learn her sampler, and make dirt-pies, than to look after a husband. For my part I was none of her man. I had another voyage to make, let him take it as he will.

MRS FRAIL: So then you intend to go to sea again?

BEN: Nay, nay, my mind run upon you, but I would not tell him so much. So he said he'd make my heart ache, and if so be that he could get a woman to his mind, he'd marry himself. Gad, says I, an you play the fool and marry at these years, there's more danger of your head's aching than my

1. *Calentures*: a virulent fever common in tropical seas.

heart. He was woundy angry when I gav'n that wipe. He hadn't a word to say, and so I left'n, and the green girl together. Mayhap the bee may bite, and he'll marry her himself, with all my heart.

MRS FRAIL: And were you this undutiful and graceless wretch to your father?

BEN: Then why was he graceless first? If I am undutiful and graceless, why did he beget me so? I did not get myself.

MRS FRAIL: O Impiety! How have I been mistaken! What an inhumane merciless creature have I set my heart upon? Oh, I am happy to have discovered the shelves and quicksands that lurk beneath that faithless smiling face.

BEN: Hey toss! What's the matter now? Why, you ben't angry, be you?

MRS FRAIL: Oh, see me no more, for thou wert born amongst rocks, suckled by whales, cradled in a tempest, and whistled to by winds; and thou art come forth with fins and scales, and three rows of teeth, a most outrageous fish of prey.

BEN: O Lord, O Lord, she's mad, poor young woman. Love has turned her senses, her brain is quite overset. Well-a-day, how shall I do to set her to rights?

MRS FRAIL: No, no, I am not mad, monster, I am wise enough to find you out. Hadst thou the impudence to aspire at being a husband with that stubborn and disobedient temper? You that know not how to submit to a father, presume to have a sufficient stock of duty to undergo a a wife? I should have been finely fobbed indeed, very finely fobbed.

BEN: Harkee, forsooth. If so be that you are in your right senses, d'ye see, for ought as I perceive I'm like to be finely fobbed, if I have got anger here upon your account, and you are tacked about already. What d'ye mean, after all your fair speeches, and stroking my cheeks, and kissing and hugging, what, would you sheer off so? Would you, and leave me aground?

MRS FRAIL: No, I'll leave you adrift, and go which way you will.

BEN: What, are you false-hearted then?

MRS FRAIL: Only the wind's changed.

BEN: More shame for you! The wind's changed? It's an ill wind blows nobody good. Mayhap I have good riddance on you, if these be your tricks. What d'ye mean all this while, to make a fool of me?

MRS FRAIL: Any fool, but a husband.

BEN: Husband! Gad I would not be your husband if you would have me, now I know your mind, thof you had your weight in gold and jewels, and thof I loved you never so well.

MRS FRAIL: Why, canst thou love, porpoise?

BEN: No matter what I can do, don't call names. I don't love you so well as to bear that, whatever I did. I'm glad you shew yourself, mistress. Let them marry you as don't know you. Gad, I know you too well, by sad experience. I believe he that marries you will go to sea in a hen-pecked frigate – I believe that, young woman – and mayhap may come to an anchor at Cuckold's Point.¹ So there's a dash for you, take it as you will. Mayhap you may holla after me when I won't come too. [*Exit.*]

MRS FRAIL: Ha, ha, ha! No doubt on't. [*Sings.*] My true love is gone to sea. –

Enter MRS FORESIGHT.

O sister, had you come a minute sooner, you would have seen the resolution of a lover. Honest Tar and I are parted; and with the same indifference that we met. O' my life, I am half vexed at the insensibility of a brute that I despised.

MRS FORESIGHT: What then, he bore it most heroically?

MRS FRAIL: Most tyrannically, for you see he has got the start of me, and I, the poor forsaken maid, am left complaining on the shore. But I'll tell you a hint that he has given me. Sir Sampson is enraged, and talks desperately of committing matrimony himself. If he has a mind to throw himself away, he can't do it more effectually than upon me, if we could bring it about.

MRS FORESIGHT: Oh, hang him old fox, he's too cunning; besides, he hates both you and me. But I have a project in my head for you, and I have gone a good way towards it.

---

1. *Cuckold's Point*: a spot on the Thames below Rotherhithe, said to have been marked by a pole set with a gigantic pair of horns.

I have almost made a bargain with Jeremy, Valentine's
man, to sell his master to us.

MRS FRAIL: Sell him, how?

MRS FORESIGHT: Valentine raves upon Angelica, and took
me for her, and Jeremy says will take anybody for her that
he imposes on him. Now I have promised him mountains
if in one of his mad fits he will bring you to him in her
stead, and get you married together, and put to bed together; and after consummation, girl, there's no revoking.
And if he should recover his senses, he'll be glad at least
to make you a good settlement. Here they come, stand
aside a little, and tell me how you like the design.

Enter VALENTINE, SCANDAL, FORESIGHT, *and*
JEREMY.

SCANDAL [*to* JEREMY]: And have you given your master a
hint of their plot upon him?

JEREMY: Yes, sir; he says he'll favour it, and mistake her for
Angelica.

SCANDAL: It may make sport.

FORESIGHT: Mercy on us!

VALENTINE: Husht. Interrupt me not. I'll whisper predic-
tion to thee, and thou shalt prophesy. I am truth, and can
teach thy tongue a new trick. I have told thee what's past;
now I tell what's to come. Dost thou know what will happen tomorrow? Answer me not, for I will tell thee. Tomorrow, knaves will thrive thro' craft, and fools thro' fortune; and honesty will go as it did, frost-nipped in a summer suit. Ask me questions concerning tomorrow.

SCANDAL: Ask him, Mr Foresight.

FORESIGHT: Pray what will be done at court?

VALENTINE: Scandal will tell you. I am truth, I never come
there.

FORESIGHT: In the city?

VALENTINE: Oh, prayers will be said in empty churches at
the usual hours. Yet you will see such zealous faces behind
counters, as if religion were to be sold in every shop. Oh,
things will go methodically in the city, the clocks will strike
twelve at noon, and the horned herd buzz in the Exchange
at two. Wives and husbands will drive distinct trades, and

care and pleasure separately occupy the family. Coffee-houses will be full of smoke and stratagem. And the cropped prentice, that sweeps his master's shop in the morning, may, ten to one, dirty his sheets before night. But there are two things that you will see very strange; which are wanton wives, with their legs at liberty, and tame cuckolds, with chains about their necks. But hold, I must examine you before I go farther, you look suspiciously. Are you a husband?

FORESIGHT: I am married.

VALENTINE: Poor creature! Is your wife of Covent-Garden parish?

FORESIGHT: No. St Martins-in-the-Fields.

VALENTINE: Alas, poor man! His eyes are sunk, and his hands shrivelled, his legs dwindled, and his back bowed. Pray, pray, for a metamorphosis. Change thy shape, and shake off age; get thee Medea's kettle,[1] and be boiled anew, come forth with lab'ring callous hands, a chine of steel, and Atlas shoulders. Let Taliacotus[2] trim the calves of twenty chairmen, and make thee pedestals to stand erect upon, and look matrimony in the face. Ha, ha, ha! That a man should have a stomach to a wedding supper, when the pigeons ought rather to be laid to his feet,[3] ha, ha, ha!

FORESIGHT: His frenzy is very high now, Mr Scandal.

SCANDAL: I believe it is a spring tide.

FORESIGHT: Very likely, truly. You understand these matters, Mr Scandal. I shall be very glad to confer with you about these things which he has uttered. His sayings are very mysterious and hieroglyphical.

VALENTINE: Oh, why would Angelica be absent from my eyes so long?

JEREMY: She's here, sir.

MRS FORESIGHT: Now, sister.

MRS FRAIL: O Lord, what must I say?

SCANDAL: Humour him, madam, by all means.

---

1. *Medea's kettle*: Medea's magic cauldron restored youth to Jason's father (Ovid, *Metamorphoses*, vii, 251 ff.).

2. *Taliacotus*: Gaspare Tagliacozzi (1546–99), celebrated Italian surgeon.

3. *Pigeons . . . feet*: popular treatment for plague.

VALENTINE: Where is she? Oh, I see her. She comes, like riches, health, and liberty at once, to a despairing, starving, and abandoned wretch. Oh, welcome, welcome.

MRS FRAIL: How de'e you, sir? Can I serve you?

VALENTINE: Harkee; I have a secret to tell you. Endymion and the moon shall meet us upon Mount Latmos, and we'll be married in the dead of night. But say not a word. Hymen shall put his torch into a dark lanthorn, that it may be secret; and Juno shall give her peacock poppy-water, that he may fold his ogling tail, and Argus's hundred eyes be shut, ha? Nobody shall know, but Jeremy.

MRS FRAIL: No, no, we'll keep it secret. It shall be done presently.

VALENTINE: The sooner the better. Jeremy, come hither; closer, that none may overhear us. Jeremy, I can tell you news. Angelica is turned nun, and I am turning friar, and yet we'll marry one another in spite of the Pope. Get me a cowl and beads, that I may play my part, for she'll meet me two hours hence in black and white, and a long veil to cover the project, and we won't see one another's faces, till we have done something to be ashamed of; and then we'll blush once for all.

Enter TATTLE *and* ANGELICA.

JEREMY: I'll take care, and –

VALENTINE: Whisper.

ANGELICA: Nay, Mr Tattle, if you make love to me you spoil my design, for I intended to make you my confidant.

TATTLE: But, madam, to throw away your person – such a person! – and such a fortune, on a madman!

ANGELICA: I never loved him till he was mad; but don't tell anybody so.

SCANDAL (*aside*): How's this? Tattle making love to Angelica!

TATTLE: Tell, madam? Alas, you don't know me. I have much ado to tell your ladyship how long I have been in love with you. But encouraged by the impossibility of Valentine's making any more addresses to you, I have ventured to declare the very inmost passion of my heart. Oh madam, look upon us both. There you see the ruins of a poor decayed creature. Here, a complete and lively figure, with youth and health, and all his five senses in perfection, madam, and to all this, the most passionate lover –

ANGELICA: O fie, for shame, hold your tongue. A passionate lover, and five senses in perfection! When you are as mad as Valentine, I'll believe you love me, and the maddest shall take me.

VALENTINE: It is enough. Ha, who's here?

MRS FRAIL [to JEREMY]: O Lord, her coming will spoil all.

JEREMY: No, no, madam, he won't know her; if he should, I can persuade him.

VALENTINE [whispers]: Scandal, who are all these? Foreigners? If they are, I'll tell you what I think. Get away all the company but Angelica, that I may discover my design to her.

SCANDAL (whispers): I will. I have discovered something of Tattle, that is of a piece with Mrs Frail. He courts Angelica. If we could contrive to couple 'em together. – Heark'ee –

MRS FORESIGHT: He won't know you, cousin, he knows nobody.

FORESIGHT: But he knows more than anybody. O niece, he knows things past and to come, and all the profound secrets of time.

TATTLE: Look you, Mr Foresight, it is not my way to make many words of matters, and so I shan't say much, but in short, d'ye see, I will hold you a hundred pound now that I know more secrets than he.

FORESIGHT: How? I cannot read that knowledge in your face, Mr Tattle. Pray, what do you know?

TATTLE: Why, d'ye think I'll tell you, sir? Read it in my face? No sir, 'tis written in my heart. And safer there, sir, than letters writ in juice of lemon, for no fire can fetch it out. I am no blab, sir.

VALENTINE [to SCANDAL]: Acquaint Jeremy with it, he may easily bring it about. They are welcome, and I'll tell 'em so myself. (Aloud) What, do you look strange upon me? Then I must be plain. [Coming up to them.] I am truth, and hate an old acquaintance with a new face.

SCANDAL *goes aside with* JEREMY.

TATTLE: Do you know me, Valentine?

VALENTINE: You? Who are you? No, I hope not.

TATTLE: I am Jack Tattle, your friend.

VALENTINE: My friend, what to do? I am no married man, and thou canst not lie with my wife; I am very poor, and thou canst not borrow money of me. Then what employment have I for a friend?

TATTLE: Hah! A good open speaker, and not to be trusted with a secret.

ANGELICA: Do you know me, Valentine?

VALENTINE: Oh, very well.

ANGELICA: Who am I?

VALENTINE: You're a woman; one to whom heaven gave beauty, when it grafted roses on a briar. You are the reflection of heaven in a pond, and he that leaps at you is sunk. You are all white, a sheet of lovely spotless paper, when you first are born; but you are to be scrawled and blotted by every goose's quill. I know you; for I loved a woman, and loved her so long, that I found out a strange thing: I found out what a woman was good for.

TATTLE: Ay, prithee, what's that?

VALENTINE: Why, to keep a secret.

TATTLE: O Lord!

VALENTINE: O exceeding good to keep a secret. For tho' she should tell, yet she is not to be believed.

TATTLE: Hah! good again, faith.

VALENTINE: I would have music. Sing me the song that I like.

SONG

I

I tell thee, Charmion, could I time retrieve,
    And could again begin to love and live,
To you I should my earliest off'ring give;
    I know my eyes would lead my heart to you,
And I should all my vows and oaths renew,
    But to be plain, I never would be true.

2

For by our weak and weary truth, I find,
Love hates to centre in a point assigned,
But runs with joy the circle of the mind.
  Then never let us chain what should be free,
  But for relief of either sex agree,
  Since women love to change, and so do we.

No more, for I am melancholy. [*Walks musing.*]

JEREMY [*to* SCANDAL]: I'll do't, sir.

SCANDAL: Mr Foresight, we had best leave him. He may grow outrageous, and do mischief.

FORESIGHT: I will be directed by you.

JEREMY [*to* MRS FRAIL]: You'll meet, Madam; I'll take care everything shall be ready.

MRS FRAIL: Thou shalt do what thou wilt, have what thou wilt; in short, I will deny thee nothing.

TATTLE [*to* ANGELICA]: Madam, shall I wait upon you?

ANGELICA: No, I'll stay with him. Mr Scandal will protect me. Aunt, Mr Tattle desires you would give him leave to wait on you.

TATTLE (*aside*): Pox on't, there's no coming off, now she has said that. (*Aloud*) Madam, will you do me the honour?

MRS FORESIGHT: Mr Tattle might have used less ceremony.
  Exeunt FORESIGHT, MRS FORESIGHT, TATTLE, MRS
  FRAIL, JEREMY.

SCANDAL: Jeremy, follow Tattle.

ANGELICA: Mr Scandal, I only stay till my maid comes, and because I had a mind to be rid of Mr Tattle.

SCANDAL: Madam, I am very glad that I overheard a better reason, which you gave to Mr Tattle; for his impertinence forced you to acknowledge a kindness for Valentine, which you denied to all his sufferings and my solicitations. So I'll leave him to make use of the discovery, and your ladyship to the free confession of your inclinations.

ANGELICA: O heavens! You won't leave me alone with a madman?

SCANDAL: No, madam; I only leave a madman to his remedy.
  [*Exit* SCANDAL.]

VALENTINE: Madam, you need not be very much afraid, for I fancy I begin to come to myself.

ANGELICA [*aside*]: Ay, but if I don't fit you, I'll be hanged.

VALENTINE: You see what disguises love makes us put on. Gods have been in counterfeited shapes for the same reason; and the divine part of me, my mind, has worn this mask of madness, and this motley livery only as the slave of love, and menial creature of your beauty.

ANGELICA: Mercy on me, how he talks! Poor Valentine!

VALENTINE: Nay, faith, now let us understand one another, hypocrisy apart. The comedy draws toward an end, and let us think of leaving acting, and be ourselves; and since you have loved me, you must own I have at length deserved you should confess it.

ANGELICA [*sighs*]: I would I had loved you, for Heaven knows I pity you; and could I have foreseen the sad effects, I would have striven. But that's too late. [*Sighs.*]

VALENTINE: What sad effects? What's too late? My seeming madness has deceived my father, and procured me time to think of means to reconcile me to him, and preserve the right of my inheritance to his estate, which otherwise, by articles, I must this morning have resigned. And this I had informed you of today, but you were gone before I knew you had been here.

ANGELICA: How? I thought your love of me had caused this transport in your soul, which it seems you only counterfeited for by mercenary ends and sordid interest.

VALENTINE: Nay, now you do me wrong, for if any interest was considered, it was yours, since I thought I wanted more than love to make me worthy of you.

ANGELICA: Then you thought me mercenary. But how am I deluded by this interval of sense, to reason with a madman?

VALENTINE: Oh, 'tis barbarous to misunderstand me longer.
   Enter JEREMY.

ANGELICA: Oh, here's a reasonable creature; sure he will not have the impudence to persevere. Come, Jeremy, acknowledge your trick, and confess your master's madness counterfeit.

JEREMY: Counterfeit, madam? I'll maintain him to be as

absolutely and substantially mad as any freeholder in
Bethlehem.[1] Nay, he's as mad as any projector,[2] fanatic,
chymist, lover, or poet in Europe.

VALENTINE: Sirrah, you lie. I am not mad.

ANGELICA: Ha, ha, ha! You see, he denies it.

JEREMY: O Lord, madam, did you ever know any madman
mad enough to own it?

VALENTINE: Sot, can't you apprehend?

ANGELICA: Why, he talked very sensibly just now.

JEREMY: Yes, madam, he has intervals: but you see he begins
to look wild again now.

VALENTINE: Why, you thick-skulled rascal, I tell you the
farce is done, and I will be mad no longer. [Beats him.]

ANGELICA: Ha, ha, ha! Is he mad or no, Jeremy?

JEREMY: Partly, I think, for he does not know his mind two
hours. I'm sure I left him just now in a humour to be mad.
And I think I have not found him very quiet at this present.
[One knocks.] Who's there?

VALENTINE: Go see, you sot. [Exit JEREMY.] I'm very glad
that I can move your mirth, tho' not your compassion.

ANGELICA: I did not think you had apprehension enough to be
be exceptious. But madmen shew themselves most by over-
pretending to a sound understanding, as drunken men do
by over-acting sobriety. I was half inclining to believe you,
till I accidentally touched upon your tender part. But now
you have restored me to my former opinion and compassion.

    Enter JEREMY.

JEREMY: Sir, your father has sent to know if you are any
better yet. Will you please to be mad, sir, or how?

VALENTINE: Stupidity! You know the penalty of all I'm
worth must pay for the confession of my senses. I'm mad,
and will be mad to everybody but this lady.

JEREMY: So: just the very backside of truth. But lying is a
figure in speech that interlards the greatest part of my conversation. Madam, your ladyship's woman. [Goes to the
door.]

       1. *Bethlehem*: the lunatic asylum (Bedlam).
       2. *Projector*: speculator.

Enter JENNY.

ANGELICA: Well, have you been there? Come hither.

JENNY [*aside to* ANGELICA]: Yes, madam, Sir Sampson will wait upon you presently.

VALENTINE: You are not leaving me in this uncertainty?

ANGELICA: Would anything but a madman complain of uncertainty? Uncertainty and expectation are the joys of life. Security is an insipid thing, and the overtaking and possessing of a wish discovers the folly of the chase. Never let us know one another better, for the pleasure of a masquerade is done when we come to shew faces. But I'll tell you two things before I leave you. I am not the fool you take me for, and you are mad and don't know it.

Exeunt ANGELICA *and* JENNY.

VALENTINE: From a riddle you can expect nothing but a riddle. There's my instruction and the moral of my lesson.

JEREMY: What, is the lady gone again, sir? I hope you understood one another before she went.

VALENTINE: Understood! She is harder to be understood than a piece of Egyptian antiquity, or an Irish manuscript; you may pore till you spoil your eyes, and not improve your knowledge.

JEREMY: I have heard 'em say, sir, they read hard Hebrew books backwards; maybe you begin to read at the wrong end.

VALENTINE: They say so of a witches' prayer, and dreams and Dutch almanacks[1] are to be understood by contraries. But there's regularity and method in that. She is a medal without a reverse or inscription, for indifference has both sides alike. Yet while she does not seem to hate me, I will pursue her, and know her if it be possible, in spite of the opinion of my satirical friend, Scandal, who says,

> That women are like tricks by slight of hand,
> Which, to admire, we should not understand.

Exeunt.

1. *Dutch almanacks*: gibberish.

THE END OF THE FOURTH ACT

Act Five

A room in FORESIGHT'S *house.*
Enter ANGELICA *and* JENNY.

ANGELICA: Where is Sir Sampson? Did you not tell me he would be here before me?

JENNY: He's at the great glass in the dining-room, madam, setting his cravat and wig.

ANGELICA: How! I'm glad on't. If he has a mind I should like him, it's a sign he likes me; and that's more than half my design.

JENNY: I hear him, madam.

ANGELICA: Leave me, and d'ye hear, if Valentine should come or send, I am not to be spoken with.

Exit JENNY.
Enter SIR SAMPSON.

SIR SAMPSON: I have not been honoured with the commands of a fair lady a great while. Odd, madam, you have revived me; not since I was five and thirty.

ANGELICA: Why, you have no great reason to complain, Sir Sampson, that is not long ago.

SIR SAMPSON: Zooks, but it is, madam, a very great while to a man that admires a fine woman as much as I do.

ANGELICA: You're an absolute courtier, Sir Sampson.

SIR SAMPSON: Not at all, madam. Odsbud, you wrong me; I am not so old neither to be a bare courtier, only a man of words. Odd, I have warm blood about me yet, I can serve a lady any way. Come, come, let me tell you, you women think a man old too soon, faith and troth you do. Come, don't despise fifty; odd, fifty, in a hale constitution, is no such contemptible age.

ANGELICA: Fifty a contemptible age! Not at all, a very fashionable age I think. I assure you I know very considerable beaus that set a good face upon fifty. Fifty! I have seen fifty in a side-box by candle-light out-blossom five and twenty.

SIR SAMPSON: O pox, outsides, outsides, a pise take 'em, mere outsides. Hang your side-box beaus; no, I'm none of those, none of your forced trees that pretend to blossom in the fall, and bud when they should bring forth fruit. I am of a long-lived race, and inherit vigour. None of my family married till fifty, yet they begot sons and daughters till four-score. I am of your patriarchs, I, a branch of one of your antediluvian families, fellows that the flood could not wash away. Well, madam, what are your commands? Has any young rogue affronted you, and shall I cut his throat? Or –

ANGELICA: No, Sir Sampson, I have no quarrel upon my hands. I have more occasion for your conduct than your courage at this time. To tell you the truth, I'm weary of living single, and want a husband.

SIR SAMPSON: Odsbud, and 'tis a pity you should. [*Aside*] Odd, would she would like me, then I should hamper my young rogues. Odd, would she would; faith and troth she's devilish handsome. (*Aloud*) Madam, you deserve a good husband, and 'twere a pity you should be thrown away upon any of these young idle rogues about the town. Odd, there's ne'er a young fellow worth hanging, that is, a very young fellow. Pise on 'em, they never think beforehand of anything; and if they commit matrimony, 'tis as they commit murder, out of a frolic: and are ready to hang themselves, or to be hanged by the law, the next morning. Odso, have a care, madam.

ANGELICA: Therefore I ask your advice, Sir Sampson. I have fortune enough to make any man easy that I can like, if there were such a thing as a young agreeable man, with a reasonable stock of good nature and sense – for I would neither have an absolute wit nor a fool.

SIR SAMPSON: Odd, you are hard to please, madam. To find a young fellow that is neither a wit in his own eye nor a fool in the eye of the world is a very hard task. But, faith and troth, you speak very discreetly; for I hate both a wit and a fool.

ANGELICA: She that marries a fool, Sir Sampson, commits the reputation of her honesty or understanding to the censure of the world. And she that marries a very witty man submits both to the severity and insolent conduct of her husband. I should like a man of wit for a lover, because I would have such an one in my power; but I would no more be his wife than his enemy. For his malice is not a more terrible consequence of his aversion than his jealousy is of his love.

SIR SAMPSON: None of old Foresight's sybils ever uttered such a truth. Odsbud, you have won my heart. I hate a wit. I had a son that was spoiled among 'em; a good hopeful lad, till he learned to be a wit – and might have risen in the state – But a pox on't, his wit run him out of his money, and now his poverty has run him out of his wits.

ANGELICA: Sir Sampson, as your friend I must tell you you are very much abused in that matter. He's no more mad than you are.

SIR SAMPSON: How, madam? Would I could prove it.

ANGELICA: I can tell you how that may be done. But it is a thing that would make me appear to be too much concerned in your affairs.

SIR SAMPSON [aside]: Odsbud, I believe she likes mc. (Aloud) Ah, madam, all my affairs are scarce worthy to be laid at your feet; and I wish, madam, they stood in a better posture, that I might make a more becoming offer to a lady of your incomparable beauty and merit. If I had Peru in one hand, and Mexico in t'other, and the Eastern empire under my feet, it would make me only a more glorious victim to be offered at the shrine of your beauty.

ANGELICA: Bless me, Sir Sampson, what's the matter?

SIR SAMPSON: Odd, madam, I love you. And if you would take my advice in a husband –

ANGELICA: Hold, hold, Sir Sampson. I asked your advice for a husband, and you are giving me your consent. I was indeed thinking to propose something like it in a jest, to satisfy you about Valentine. For if a match were seemingly carried on, between you and me, it would oblige him to throw off his disguise of madness, in apprehension of losing me. For you know he has long pretended a passion for me.

SIR SAMPSON: Gadzooks, a most ingenious contrivance, if we were to go through with it. But why must the match only be seemingly carried on? Odd, let it be a real contract.

ANGELICA: O fie, Sir Sampson, what would the world say?

SIR SAMPSON: Say? They would say you were a wise woman, and I a happy man. Odd, madam, I'll love you as long as I live, and leave you a good jointure when I die.

ANGELICA: Ay, but that is not in your power, Sir Sampson; for when Valentine confesses himself in his senses, he must make over his inheritance to his younger brother.

SIR SAMPSON: Odd, you're cunning, a wary baggage! Faith and troth, I like you the better. But I warrant you, I have a proviso in the obligation in favour of myself. Body o' me I have a trick to turn the settlement upon the issue male of our two bodies begotten. Odsbud, let us find children, and I'll find an estate.

ANGELICA: Will you? Well, do you find the estate, and leave the other to me.

SIR SAMPSON: O rogue! But I'll trust you. And will you consent? Is it a match then?

ANGELICA: Let me consult my lawyer concerning this obligation, and if I find what you propose practicable, I'll give you my answer.

SIR SAMPSON: With all my heart. Come in with me and I'll lend you the bond. You shall consult your lawyer and I'll consult a parson. Odzooks, I'm a young man. Odzooks I'm a young man, and I'll make it appear. Odd, you're devilish handsome. Faith and troth, you're very handsome, and I'm very young, and very lusty. Odsbud, hussy, you know how to choose, and so do I. Odd, I think we are very well met: Give me your hand, odd, let me kiss it. 'Tis as warm and as soft – as what? Odd, as t'other hand. Give me t'other hand, and I'll mumble 'em, and kiss 'em till they melt in my mouth.

ANGELICA: Hold, Sir Sampson, you're profuse of your vigour before your time. You'll spend your estate before you come to it.

SIR SAMPSON: No, no, only give you a rent-roll of my possessions. Ah, baggage! I warrant you for little Sampson. Odd, Sampson's a very good name for an able fellow. Your Sampsons were strong dogs from the beginning.

ANGELICA: Have a care, and don't over-act your part. If you remember, the strongest Sampson of your name pulled an old house over his head at last.

SIR SAMPSON: Say you so, hussy? Come, let's go then. Odd, I long to be pulling down too; come away. Odso, here's somebody coming.

Exeunt.

Enter TATTLE *and* JEREMY.

TATTLE: Is not that she, gone out just now?

JEREMY: Ay, sir, she's just going to the place of appointment. Ah sir, if you are not very faithful and close in this business, you'll certainly be the death of a person that has a most extraordinary passion for your honour's service.

TATTLE: Ay, who's that?

JEREMY: Even my unworthy self, sir. Sir, I have had an appetite to be fed with your commands a great while. And now, sir, my former master having much troubled the fountain of his understanding, it is a very plausible occasion for me to quench my thirst at the spring of your bounty. I thought I could not recommend myself better to you, sir, than by the delivery of a great beauty and fortune into your arms, whom I have heard you sigh for.

TATTLE: I'll make thy fortune; say no more. Thou art a pretty fellow, and canst carry a message to a lady in a pretty soft kind of phrase, and with a good persuading accent.

JEREMY: Sir, I have the seeds of rhetoric and oratory in my head. I have been at Cambridge.

TATTLE: Ay. 'Tis well enough for a servant to be bred at an university, but the education is a little too pedantic for a gentleman. I hope you are secret in your nature, private, close, ha?

JEREMY: O sir, for that sir, 'tis my chief talent. I'm as secret as the head of Nilus.[1]

TATTLE: Ay? Who's he, tho'? A Privy Counsellor?

1. *Head of Nilus*: the source of the Nile had not yet been discovered.

JEREMY [*aside*]: O ignorance! (*Aloud*) A cunning Egyptian, sir, that with his arms would overrun the country, yet nobody could ever find out his headquarters.

TATTLE: Close dog! A good whoremaster, I warrant him. The time draws nigh, Jeremy. Angelica will be veiled like a nun, and I must be hooded like a friar. Ha, Jeremy?

JEREMY: Ay, sir, hooded like a hawk, to seize at first sight upon the quarry. It is the whim of my master's madness to be so dressed. And she is so in love with him, she'll comply with any thing to please him. Poor lady, I'm sure she'll have reason to pray for me, when she finds what a happy exchange she has made, between a madman and so accomplished a gentleman.

TATTLE: Ay, faith, so she will, Jeremy. You're a good friend to her, poor creature. I swear I do it hardly so much in consideration of myself as compassion to her.

JEREMY: 'Tis an act of charity, sir, to save a fine woman with thirty thousand pound from throwing herself away.

TATTLE: So 'tis, faith. I might have saved several others in my time. But i'Gad I could never find in my heart to marry anybody before.

JEREMY: Well, sir, I'll go and tell her my master's coming, and meet you in half a quarter of an hour, with your disguise, at your own lodgings. You must talk a little madly, she won't distinguish the tone of your voice.

TATTLE: No, no, let me alone for a counterfeit. I'll be ready for you.

Enter MISS PRUE.

MISS PRUE: O Mr Tattle, are you here! I'm glad I have found you. I have been looking up and down for you like any thing, till I'm as tired as any thing in the world.

TATTLE [*aside*]: O pox, how shall I get rid of this foolish girl?

MISS PRUE: Oh I have pure news, I can tell you pure news. I must not marry the seaman now – my father says so. Why won't you be my husband? You say you love me, and you won't be my husband. And I know you may be my husband now if you please.

TATTLE: O fie, Miss. Who told you so, child?

MISS PRUE: Why, my father. I told him that you loved me.

TATTLE: O fie, Miss, why did you do so? And who told you so, child?

MISS PRUE: Who? Why, you did, did not you?

TATTLE: O pox, that was yesterday, Miss, that was a great while ago, child. I have been asleep since; slept a whole night, and did not so much as dream of the matter.

MISS PRUE: Pshaw! Oh, but I dreamt that it was so, tho'.

TATTLE: Ay, but your father will tell you that dreams come by contraries, child. O fie! What, we must not love one another now. Pshaw! That would be a foolish thing indeed. Fie, fie, you're a woman now, and must think of a new man every morning, and forget him every night. No, no, to marry is to be a child again, and play with the same rattle always. O fie, marrying is a paw[1] thing.

MISS PRUE: Well, but don't you love me as well as you did last night then?

TATTLE: No, no, child, you would not have me.

MISS PRUE: No? Yes, but I would, tho'.

TATTLE: Pshaw, but I tell you, you would not. You forget you're a woman, and don't know your own mind.

MISS PRUE: But here's my father, and he knows my mind.

Enter FORESIGHT.

FORESIGHT: Oh, Mr Tattle, your servant; you are a close man. But methinks your love to my daughter was a secret I might have been trusted with. Or had you a mind to try if I could discover it by my art, hum, ha? I think there is something in your physiognomy that has a resemblance of her, and the girl is like me.

TATTLE [*aside*]: And so you would infer that you and I are alike. What does the old prig mean? I'll banter him, and laugh at him, and leave him. (*Aloud*) I fancy you have a wrong notion of faces.

FORESIGHT: How? What? A wrong notion? How so?

TATTLE: In the way of art. I have some taking features, not obvious to vulgar eyes, that are indications of a sudden turn of good fortune in the lottery of wives, and promise a great beauty and great fortune reserved alone for me by

1. *Paw*: stupid (perhaps from exclamation 'pah!').

a private intrigue of destiny, kept secret from the piercing eye of perspicuity, from all astrologers, and the stars themselves.

FORESIGHT: How? I will make it appear that what you say is impossible.

TATTLE: Sir, I beg your pardon, I'm in haste.

FORESIGHT: For what?

TATTLE: To be married, sir, married.

FORESIGHT: Ay, but pray take me along with you, sir.

TATTLE: No, sir, 'tis to be done privately. I never make confidants.

FORESIGHT: Well, but my consent I mean. You won't marry my daughter without my consent?

TATTLE: Who, I, sir? I'm an absolute stranger to you and your daughter, sir.

FORESIGHT: Hey-day! What time of the moon is this?

TATTLE: Very true, sir, and desire to continue so. I have no more love for your daughter than I have likeness of you; and I have a secret in my heart which you would be glad to know, and shan't know; and yet you shall know it too, and be sorry for't afterwards. I'd have you to know, sir, that I am as knowing as the stars and as secret as the night. And I'm going to be married just now, yet did not know of it half an hour ago, and the lady stays for me, and does not know of it yet. There's a mystery for you. I know you love to untie difficulties. Or if you can't solve this, stay here a quarter of an hour, and I'll come and explain it to you. [*Exit.*]

MISS PRUE: O father, why will you let him go? Won't you make him be my husband?

FORESIGHT: Mercy on us, what do these lunacies portend? Alas, he's mad, child, stark wild.

MISS PRUE: What, and must not I have e'er a husband then? What, must I go to bed to nurse again, and be a child as long as she's an old woman? Indeed but I won't. For now my mind is set upon a man, I will have a man some way or other. Oh! methinks I'm sick when I think of a man, and if I can't have one, I would go to sleep all my life. For when I'm awake, it makes me wish and long, and I don't know for what. And I'd rather be always a sleeping than sick with thinking.

FORESIGHT: O fearful! I think the girl's influenced too. Hussy, you shall have a rod.

MISS PRUE: A fiddle of a rod, I'll have a husband, and if you won't get me one, I'll get one for myself. I'll marry our Robin the butler; he says he loves me, and he's a handsome man, and shall be my husband. I warrant he'll be my husband and thank me too, for he told me so.

Enter SCANDAL, MRS FORESIGHT, *and* NURSE.

FORESIGHT: Did he so? I'll dispatch him for't presently. Rogue! O nurse, come hither.

NURSE: What is your worship's pleasure?

FORESIGHT: Here, take your young mistress and lock her up presently, till farther orders from me. Not a word, hussy. Do what I bid you, no reply, away! And bid Robin make ready to give an account of his plate and linen, d'ye hear, be gone when I bid you.

Exit NURSE *and* MISS PRUE.

MRS FORESIGHT: What's the matter, husband?

FORESIGHT: 'Tis not convenient to tell you now. Mr Scandal, heav'n keep us all in our senses. I fear there is a contagious frenzy abroad. How does Valentine?

SCANDAL: Oh, I hope he will do well again. I have a message from him to your niece Angelica.

FORESIGHT: I think she has not returned since she went abroad with Sir Sampson.

Enter BEN.

MRS FORESIGHT: Here's Mr Benjamin; he can tell us if his father be come home.

BEN: Who, father? Ay, he's come home with a vengeance.

MRS FORESIGHT: Why, what's the matter?

BEN: Matter! Why, he's mad.

FORESIGHT: Mercy on us, I was afraid of this.

BEN: And there's the handsome young woman, she as they say Brother Val went mad for, she's mad too, I think.

FORESIGHT: O my poor niece, my poor niece, is she gone too? Well, I shall run mad next.

MRS FORESIGHT: Well, but how mad? How d'ye mean?

BEN: Nay, I'll give you leave to guess. I'll undertake to make
a voyage to Antegoa. No, hold, I mayn't say so neither –
but I'll sail as far as Ligorn and back again before you shall
guess at the matter, and do nothing else. Mess, you may
take in all the points of the compass and not hit right.

MRS FORESIGHT: Your experiment will take up a little too
much time.

BEN: Why, then I'll tell you, there's a new wedding upon the
stocks, and they two are a going to be married to rights.

SCANDAL: Who?

BEN: Why father and – the young woman. I can't hit of her
name.

SCANDAL: Angelica?

BEN: Ay, the same.

MRS FORESIGHT: Sir Sampson and Angelica? Impossible!

BEN: That may be, but I'm sure it is as I tell you.

SCANDAL: 'S'death, it's a jest. I can't believe it.

BEN: Look you, friend, it's nothing to me, whether you believe it or no. What I say is true, d'ye see? They are married,
or just going to be married, I know not which.

FORESIGHT: Well, but they are not mad, that is, not lunatic?

BEN: I don't know what you may call madness, but she's mad
for a husband, and he's horn mad, I think, or they'd ne'er
make a match together. Here they come.

Enter SIR SAMPSON, ANGELICA, *with* BUCKRAM.

SIR SAMPSON: Where is this old soothsayer? This uncle of
mine elect? Aha, old Foresight, uncle Foresight, wish me
joy uncle Foresight, double joy, both as uncle and astrologer. Here's a conjunction that was not foretold in all your
Ephemeris. The brightest star in the blue firmament is
'shot from above in a jelly of love',[1] and so forth; and I'm
lord of the ascendant. Odd, you're an old fellow, Foresight –
uncle I mean, a very old fellow, uncle Foresight; and yet
you shall live to dance at my wedding, faith and troth you
shall. Odd, we'll have the music of the spheres for thee, old
Lilly, that we will, and thou shalt lead up a dance in via
Lactea.[2]

1. '*Shot from above . . . love*': a garbled quotation from the Spirit's song
in Dryden's *Tyrannic Love* (1669).   2. *Via Lactea*: the Milky Way.

FORESIGHT: I'm thunder-strook! You are not married to my niece?

SIR SAMPSON: Not absolutely married, uncle, but very near it, within a kiss of the matter, as you see. [*Kisses* ANGELICA.]

ANGELICA: 'Tis very true indeed, uncle. I hope you'll be my father, and give me.

SIR SAMPSON: That he shall, or I'll burn his globes. Body o' me, he shall be thy father, I'll make him thy father, and thou shalt make me a father, and I'll make thee a mother, and we'll beget sons and daughters enough to put the weekly bills out of countenance.

SCANDAL: Death and hell! Where's Valentine? [*Exit.*]

MRS FORESIGHT: This is so surprising –

SIR SAMPSON: How! What does my aunt say? Surprising, aunt? Not at all, for a young couple to make a match in winter? Not at all. It's a plot to undermine cold weather, and destroy that usurper of a bed called a warming-pan.

MRS FORESIGHT: I'm glad to hear you have so much fire in you, Sir Sampson.

BEN: Mess, I fear his fire's little better than tinder. Mayhap it will only serve to light up a match for somebody else. The young woman's a handsome young woman, I can't deny it. But, father, if I might be your pilot in this case, you should not marry her. It's just the same thing as if so be you should sail so far as the Straits without provision.

SIR SAMPSON: Who gave you authority to speak, sirrah? To your element, fish, be mute, fish, and to sea. Rule your helm, sirrah, don't direct me.

BEN: Well, well, take you care of your own helm, or you mayn't keep your own vessel steady.

SIR SAMPSON: Why, you impudent tarpaulin! Sirrah, do you bring your forecastle jests upon your father? But I shall be even with you, I won't give you a groat. Mr Buckram, is the conveyance so worded that nothing can possibly descend to this scoundrel? I would not so much as have him have the prospect of an estate, tho' there were no way to come to it but by the north-east passage.

BUCKRAM: Sir, it is drawn according to your directions; there is not the least cranny of the law unstopped.

BEN: Lawyer, I believe there's many a cranny and leak unstopped in your conscience. If so be that one had a pump to your bosom, I believe we should discover a foul hold. They say a witch will sail in a sieve. But I believe the devil would not venture aboard o'your conscience. And that's for you.

SIR SAMPSON: Hold your tongue, sirrah. How now, who's there?

Enter TATTLE *and* MRS FRAIL.

MRS FRAIL: Oh, sister, the most unlucky accident!

MRS FORESIGHT: What's the matter?

TATTLE: Oh, the two most unfortunate poor creatures in the world we are!

FORESIGHT: Bless us! How so?

MRS FRAIL: Ah Mr Tattle and I, poor Mr Tattle and I are – I can't speak it out.

TATTLE: Nor I. But poor Mrs Frail and I are –

MRS FRAIL: Married.

MRS FORESIGHT: Married! How?

TATTLE: Suddenly – before we knew where we were – that villain Jeremy, by the help of disguises, tricked us into one another.

FORESIGHT: Why, you told me just now you went hence in haste to be married.

ANGELICA: But I believe Mr Tattle meant the favour to me, I thank him.

TATTLE: I did, as I hope to be saved, madam, my intentions were good. But this is the most cruel thing, to marry one does not know how, nor why, nor wherefore. The devil take me if ever I was so much concerned at anything in my life.

ANGELICA: 'Tis very unhappy, if you don't care for one another.

TATTLE: The least in the world. That is for my part, I speak for myself. Gad, I never had the least thought of serious kindness. I never liked anybody less in my life. Poor woman! Gad, I'm sorry for her too, for I have no reason to hate her neither; but I believe I shall lead her a damned sort of a life.

MRS FORESIGHT [*aside to* MRS FRAIL]: He's better than no husband at all, tho' he's a coxcomb.

MRS FRAIL [*to her*]: Ay, ay, it's well it's no worse. (*Aloud*) Nay, for my part I always despised Mr Tattle of all things. Nothing but his being my husband could have made me like him less.

TATTLE: Look you there, I thought as much. Pox on't, I wish we could keep it secret. Why, I don't believe any of this company would speak of it.

MRS FRAIL: But, my dear, that's impossible. The parson and that rogue Jeremy will publish it.

TATTLE: Ay, my dear, so they will, as you say.

ANGELICA: Oh, you'll agree very well in a little time. Custom will make it easy to you.

TATTLE: Easy! Pox on't, I don't believe I shall sleep tonight.

SIR SAMPSON: Sleep, quotha? No, why, you would not sleep o'your wedding night? I'm an older fellow than you and don't mean to sleep.

BEN: Why there's another match now, as thof a couple of privateers were looking for a prize, and should fall foul of one another. I'm sorry for the young man with all my heart. Look you, friend, if I may advise you, when she's going (for that you must expect, I have experience of her), when she's going, let her go. For no matrimony is tough enough to hold her, and if she can't drag her anchor along with her, she'll break her cable, I can tell you that. Who's here, the madman?

Enter VALENTINE *dressed*, SCANDAL *and* JEREMY.

VALENTINE: No here's the fool, and if occasion be, I'll give it under my hand.

SIR SAMPSON: How now?

VALENTINE: Sir, I'm come to acknowledge my errors, and ask your pardon.

SIR SAMPSON: What, have you found your senses at last, then? In good time, sir.

VALENTINE: You were abused, sir, I never was distracted.

FORESIGHT: How? Not mad, Mr Scandal?

SCANDAL: No, really, sir; I'm his witness, it was all counterfeit.

VALENTINE: I thought I had reasons. But it was a poor contrivance, the effect has shewn it such.

SIR SAMPSON: Contrivance! What, to cheat me? To cheat your father? Sirrah, could you hope to prosper?

VALENTINE: Indeed, I thought, sir, when the father endeavoured to undo the son, it was a reasonable return of nature.

SIR SAMPSON: Very good, sir. Mr Buckram, are you ready? Come, sir, will you sign and seal?

VALENTINE: If you please, sir. But first I would ask this lady one question.

SIR SAMPSON: Sir, you must ask my leave first. That lady? No, sir, you shall ask that lady no questions till you have asked her blessing, sir. That lady is to be my wife.

VALENTINE: I have heard as much, sir, but I would have it from her own mouth.

SIR SAMPSON: That's as much as to say, I lie, sir, and you don't believe what I say.

VALENTINE: Pardon me, sir. But I reflect that I very lately counterfeited madness. I don't know but the frolic may go round.

SIR SAMPSON: Come, chuck, satisfy him, answer him. Come, come, Mr Buckram, the pen and ink.

BUCKRAM: Here it is, sir, with the deed, all is ready.

VALENTINE *goes to* ANGELICA.

ANGELICA: 'Tis true, you have a great while pretended love to me; nay, what if you were sincere? Still you must pardon me if I think my own inclinations have a better right to dispose of my person than yours.

SIR SAMPSON: Are you answered now, sir?

VALENTINE: Yes, sir.

SIR SAMPSON: Where's your plot, sir, and your contrivance now, sir? Will you sign, sir? Come will you sign and seal?

VALENTINE: With all my heart, sir.

SCANDAL: 'S'death, you are not mad indeed, to ruin yourself?

VALENTINE: I have been disappointed of my only hope, and he that loses hope may part with any thing. I never valued fortune but as it was subservient to my pleasure, and my only pleasure was to please this lady. I have made many vain attempts, and find at last that nothing but my ruin can effect it, which for that reason I will sign to. Give me the paper.

ANGELICA [*aside*]: Generous Valentine!

BUCKRAM: Here is the deed, sir.

VALENTINE: But where is the bond by which I am obliged to sign this?

BUCKRAM: Sir Sampson, you have it.

ANGELICA: No, I have it. And I'll use it, as I would every thing that is an enemy to Valentine. [*Tears the paper.*]

SIR SAMPSON: How now?

VALENTINE: Ha!

ANGELICA [*to* VALENTINE]: Had I the world to give you, it could not make me worthy of so generous and faithful a passion. Here's my hand, my heart was always yours, and struggled very hard to make this utmost trial of your virtue.

VALENTINE: Between pleasure and amazement I am lost. But on my knees I take the blessing.

SIR SAMPSON: Ouns, what is the meaning of this?

BEN: Mess, here's the wind changed again. Father, you and I may make a voyage together now.

ANGELICA: Well, Sir Sampson, since I have played you a trick, I'll advise you how you may avoid such another. Learn to be a good father, or you'll never get a second wife. I always loved your son, and hated your unforgiving nature. I was resolved to try him to the utmost. I have tried you too, and know you both. You have not more faults than he has virtues, and 'tis hardly more pleasure to me that I can make him and myself happy than that I can punish you.

VALENTINE: If my happiness could receive addition, this kind surprise would make it double.

SIR SAMPSON: Ouns, you're a crocodile.

FORESIGHT: Really, Sir Sampson, this is a sudden eclipse.

SIR SAMPSON: You're an illiterate fool, and I'm another, and the stars are liars, and if I had breath enough, I'd curse them and you, myself and everybody. Ouns! Cullied, bubbled, jilted, woman-bobbed at last – I have not patience. [*Exit* SIR SAMPSON.]

TATTLE: If the gentleman is in this disorder for want of a wife, I can spare him mine. [*To* JEREMY] Oh, are you there, sir? I'm indebted to you for my happiness.

JEREMY: Sir, I ask you ten thousand pardons, 'twas an errant mistake. You see, sir, my master was never mad, or anything like it. Then how could it be otherwise?

VALENTINE: Tattle, I thank you, you would have interposed between me and heaven, but Providence laid Purgatory in your way. You have but justice.

SCANDAL: I hear the fiddles that Sir Sampson provided for his own wedding. Methinks 'tis pity they should not be employed when the match is so much mended. Valentine, tho' it be morning, we may have a dance.

VALENTINE: Anything, my friend, everything that looks like joy and transport.

SCANDAL: Call 'em, Jeremy.

ANGELICA: I have done dissembling now, Valentine, and if that coldness which I have always worn before you should turn to an extreme fondness, you must not suspect it.

VALENTINE: I'll prevent that suspicion, for I intend to dote on at that immoderate rate, that your fondness shall never distinguish itself enough to be taken notice of. If ever you seem to love too much, it must be only when I can't love enough.

ANGELICA: Have a care of large promises; you know you are apt to run more in debt than you are able (to) pay.

VALENTINE: Therefore I yield my body as your prisoner, and make your best on't.

SCANDAL: The music stays for you.

Dance

Well, madam, you have done exemplary justice, in punishing an inhumane father and rewarding a faithful lover. But there is a third good work, which I, in particular, must thank you for. I was an infidel to your sex, and you have converted me. For now I am convinced that all women are not like fortune, blind in bestowing favours, either on those who do not merit, or who do not want 'em.

ANGELICA: 'Tis an unreasonable accusation that you lay upon our sex. You tax us with injustice, only to cover your own want of merit. You would all have the reward of love, but few have the constancy to stay till it becomes your due. Men are generally hypocrites and infidels. They pretend to worship, but have neither zeal nor faith. How few, like Valentine, would persevere even unto martyrdom, and sacrifice their interest to their constancy. In admiring me you misplace the novelty.

> The miracle today is that we find
> A lover true, not that a woman's kind.

Exeunt omnes.

FINIS

Epilogue

Spoken at the opening of the New House

BY MRS BRACEGIRDLE

Sure Providence at first designed this place
To be the player's refuge in distress;[1]
For still in every storm they all run hither,
As to a shed that shields 'em from the weather.
But thinking of this change which last befell us,
It's like what I have heard our poets tell us:
For when behind our scenes their suits are pleading,
To help their love, sometimes they show their reading;
And wanting ready cash to pay for hearts,
They top their learning on us, and their parts.
Once of philosophers they told us stories,
Whom, as I think they called – Py – Pythagories,
I'm sure 'tis some such Latin name they give 'em,
And we, who know no better, must believe 'em.
Now to these men (say they) such souls were given,
That after death, ne'er went to Hell, nor Heaven,
But lived, I know not how, in beasts; and then
When many years were past, in men again.
Methinks, we players resemble such a soul,
That does from bodies, we from houses stroll.
Thus Aristotle's soul, of old that was,
May now be damned to animate an ass;
Or in this very house, for ought we know,
Is doing painful penance in some beau
And this our audience, which did once resort
To shining theatres to see our sport,
Now find us tossed into a tennis-court.

---

1. The site of the Lincoln's Inn Fields theatre had originally been a tennis court. Before Betterton and his party opened there in 1695, it had already been used as a theatre, first by Davenant, and subsequently by the Drury Lane players when their theatre was burnt down in 1672.

These walls but t'other day were filled with noise
Of roaring gamesters, and your damme boys.[1]
Then bounding balls and rackets they encompassed,
And now they're filled with jests, and flights, and bombast!
I vow I don't much like this transmigration,
Strolling from place to place by circulation.
Grant Heaven, we don't return to our first station.
I know not what these think, but for my part
I can't reflect without an aching heart,
How we should end in our original, a cart.[2]
But we can't fear, since you're so good to save us,
That you have only set us up, to leave us.
Thus from the past, we hope for future grace,
I beg it –
And some here know I have a begging face.
Then pray continue this your kind behaviour,
For a clear stage won't do, without your favour.

1. *Damme boys*: swearers, roisterers.
2. *Cart*: Thespis, the first actor, is supposed to have sung ballads from a cart at country fairs. (See Dryden's *Prologue at Oxford*, and Horace *Ars Poetica*, 276.)

MORE ABOUT PENGUINS
AND PELICANS

Penguinews, which appears every month, contains details of all the new books issued by Penguins as they are published. From time to time it is supplemented by the *Penguin Stock List*, which is our complete list of almost 5,000 titles.

A specimen copy of *Penguinews* will be sent to you free on request. Please write to Dept EP, Penguin Books Ltd, Harmondsworth, Middlesex, for your copy.

In the U.S.A.: For a complete list of books available from Penguin in the United States write to Dept CS, Penguin Books, 625 Madison Avenue, New York, New York 10022.

In Canada: For a complete list of books available from Penguin in Canada write to Penguin Books Canada Ltd, 2801 John Street, Markham, Ontario L3R 1B4.

THE PENGUIN ENGLISH LIBRARY

A Selection